SMART TALK
CONTEMPORARY INTERVIEWING AND INTERROGATION

SMART TALK
CONTEMPORARY INTERVIEWING AND INTERROGATION

CUSTOM EDITION

DENISE KINDSCHI GOSSELIN
WESTERN NEW ENGLAND COLLEGE

Cover image courtesy of Brand X Pictures

Taken from:

Terrorism in the Twenty-First Century, Fourth Edition
by Cindy C. Combs
Copyright © 2006, 2003, 2000, 1997 by Pearson Education, Inc.
Published by Prentice Hall
Upper Saddle River, New Jersey 07458

All rights reserved. No part of this book may be reproduced, in any form or by any means, without permission in writing from the publisher.

This special edition published in cooperation with Pearson Custom Publishing.

All trademarks, service marks, registered trademarks, and registered service marks are the property of their respective owners and are used herein for identification purposes only.

Printed in the United States of America

10

ISBN 0-536-55894-9

2008340002

KL

Please visit our web site at *www.pearsoncustom.com*

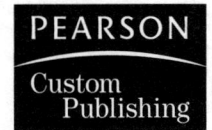

PEARSON CUSTOM PUBLISHING
501 Boylston Street, Suite 900, Boston, MA 02116
A Pearson Education Company

*To my husband, Robert,
with love and gratitude*

Brief Contents

Preface xxiii
Acknowledgments xxv
About the Author xxvii

PART I: LAYING THE GROUNDWORK FOR SUCCESS   1

CHAPTER 1 INTERVIEWING AND INTERROGATION   3
    Key Terms   4
    Chapter Objectives   4
    Introduction   4
    The Nature of Interviewing   5
    The Nature of Interrogation   10
    Purpose of the Interrogation   12
    Personal Qualities of the Interviewer   13
    Communicating   16
    Conclusions   19
    Questions for Review   20
    References   21

CHAPTER 2 THE INTERVIEW PROCESS   23
    Key Terms   24
    Chapter Objectives   24
    Introduction   24
    Phase I: Interview Preparation   25
    Phase II: Establishment of the Psychological Content   30
    Phase III: The Questioning   33
    Conclusions   38
    Questions for Review   39
    References   40

CHAPTER 3 PURPOSEFUL INTERVIEWING AND PROCESSES   41
    Key Terms   42
    Chapter Objectives   42

Introduction 42
Characteristics of Purposeful Interviewing 43
Objectives of Purposeful Interviewing 45
Assessing the Accuracy of a Statement 56
Conclusions 57
Questions for Review 57
References 59

PART II: METHODS AND TECHNIQUES 61

CHAPTER 4 TRADITIONAL, STRUCTURAL, AND INFERENTIAL INTERVIEWING WITH STATEMENT ANALYSIS TECHNIQUES 63

Key Terms 64
Chapter Objectives 64
Introduction 64
Identifying the Sources 65
Guidelines for the Traditional Interviewing Approach 66
What Is Structural Interviewing? 71
Steps for Structural Interviewing 72
Inferential Interviewing 74
Statement Analysis 76
Conducting Statement Analysis 76
Field Statement Analysis 80
Conclusions 81
Questions for Review 82
References 83

CHAPTER 5 FORENSIC HYPNOSIS AND COGNITIVE INTERVIEWING 85

Key Terms 86
Chapter Objectives 86
Introduction 86
What Is Hypnosis? 87
Forensic Hypnosis Interviewing Methods 87
Challenges to Hypnotic Memory Retrieval 91
Hypnosis Evidence in Court 93
What Is Cognitive Interviewing? 94
Cognitive Interviewing Techniques 95
Steps of the Cognitive Interview Method 99
Challenges to Memory Retrieval 101

Conclusions 103
Questions for Review 104
References 105

CHAPTER 6 BEHAVIORAL INTERVIEWING TECHNIQUES 107

Key Terms 108
Chapter Objectives 108
Introduction 108
What Is Behavioral Interviewing? 109
Cultural and Personal Considerations 111
Emotions and Observable Behaviors 112
Eye Movement 116
Sensory Verbal Communication 120
Qualifiers, Hedging, and Manipulators 121
Detecting Deceit 122
Conclusions 124
Questions for Review 124
References 125

PART III: INTERVIEWING SPECIAL POPULATIONS 127

CHAPTER 7 INTERVIEWING CHILDREN 129

Key Terms 130
Chapter Objectives 130
Introduction 130
Child Developmental Stages 131
Field Assessment 133
Initial Considerations for Child Interviews 134
What Is the Forensic Approach to Child Interviewing? 139
Forensic Interviewing Techniques 140
What Is the Cognitive Approach to Interviewing Children? 143
Cognitive Interviewing Technique 143
The Child as Reporter 147
The Child as Victim 148
Bolstering Credibility through Evidence 150
Determining Competency and Reliability 152
Conclusions 153
Questions for Review 153
References 155

CHAPTER 8 INTERVIEWING THE ELDERLY 157

Key Terms   158
Chapter Objectives   158
Introduction   158
Crimes Targeting the Elderly   159
Initial Considerations When Questioning the Older Person   162
Conducting the Interview   165
Empowering the Elderly Victim   167
The Elderly as Witnesses   168
Interdisciplinary Interviewing   172
Crime Perpetrated by the Elderly   173
Conclusions   173
Questions for Review   174
References   175

CHAPTER 9 INTERVIEWING PERSONS WITH DISABILITIES OR MENTAL ILLNESS   177

Key Terms   178
Chapter Objectives   178
Introduction   178
The Americans with Disabilities Act   179
Initial Considerations   181
Identifying When Special Care Is Necessary   183
Field Evaluation   187
Interview Considerations   188
Preparing for the Interview   190
Interrogation Considerations   193
Conclusions   195
Questions for Review   196
References   197

PART IV: INTERROGATION   199

CHAPTER 10 THE INTERROGATION PROCESS AND THE LAW   201

Key Terms   202
Chapter Objectives   202
Introduction   202
Fifth Amendment Considerations   203
The *Miranda* Standard   204
Sixth Amendment Considerations   209

Fourteenth Amendment Considerations   210
Fourth Amendment Considerations   214
Conclusions   218
Questions for Review   219
References   221

CHAPTER 11 CONFESSIONS   223

Key Terms   224
Chapter Objectives   224
Introduction   224
What Is an Interrogation?   225
Since *Miranda*   226
False Confessions   232
What Is Not an Interrogation?   234
Interrogation Tactics   237
Case-Specific Methods of Interrogation   238
Truth and Consequences   244
Conclusions   245
Questions for Review   245
References   246

CHAPTER 12 TECHNIQUES FOR INTERROGATION   249

Key Terms   250
Chapter Objectives   250
Introduction   250
Purpose of the Interrogation   251
Interrogation Approach   252
Confession-Eliciting Models   256
Interrogation Phase I: Preparing   257
Interrogation Phase II: Developing Outcome-Based Tactics   263
Interrogation Phase III: Getting the Confession   269
Conclusions   272
Questions for Review   272
References   274

CHAPTER 13 JUVENILE RIGHTS AND POLICE RESPONSIBILITIES   275

Key Terms   276
Chapter Objectives   276
Introduction   276
What Is a Juvenile?   277

Brief Contents

Juvenile Offending 278
Due Process and the Juvenile 279
Questioning a Juvenile Not in Custody 281
Questioning a Juvenile in Custody 284
Fourth Amendment Considerations 285
Fifth Amendment Considerations 286
The Right to Counsel 286
Juvenile Confession Admissibility 287
Specific Crime Categories 288
Conclusions 292
Questions for Review 292
References 294

Contents

Preface xxiii
Acknowledgments xxv
About the Author xxvii

PART I: LAYING THE GROUNDWORK FOR SUCCESS 1

CHAPTER 1 INTERVIEWING AND INTERROGATION 3
Key Terms 4
Chapter Objectives 4
Introduction 4
The Nature of Interviewing 5
   Victims 6 • Witnesses 7 • Suspects 10
The Nature of Interrogation 10
   Interrogation Controversy 11
Purpose of the Interrogation 12
Personal Qualities of the Interviewer 13
   Willing to Develop Rapport 15 • Knowledgeable 15 • Professional 16
Communicating 16
   Kinesics 17 • Proxemics 18 • Paralanguage 19
Conclusions 19
Questions for Review 20
   Short-Answer Questions 20
   Fill-in Questions 20
   Exercises 20
References 21

CHAPTER 2 THE INTERVIEW PROCESS 23
Key Terms 24
Chapter Objectives 24
Introduction 24
Phase I: Interview Preparation 25
   Case Review 26 • Determine Prior Criminal Record 27 • Viewing the Scene 28 • Misinformation 28

Phase II: Establishment of the Psychological Content 30
- When Should the Questioning Occur? 31 • Where Should the Questioning Occur? 31 • When in the Police Station or an Office 32

Phase III: The Questioning 33
- The Order of Interviews 33 • Types of Questions 34 • Determining an Approach 37

Conclusions 38

Questions for Review 39
- Short-Answer Questions 39
- Fill-in Questions 39
- Exercises 39

References 40

CHAPTER 3 PURPOSEFUL INTERVIEWING AND PROCESSES 41

Key Terms 42

Chapter Objectives 42

Introduction 42

Characteristics of Purposeful Interviewing 43
- Active Listening 43 • Rapport Development 44

Objectives of Purposeful Interviewing 45
- The Nature of the Offense 45 • Was a Crime Committed? 49 • Identifying a Perpetrator 52 • Making an Identification 54 • Field Identification 54 • Lineups 55

Assessing Accuracy of a Statement 56

Conclusions 57

Questions for Review 57
- Short-Answer Questions 57
- Fill-in Questions 58
- Exercises 58

References 59

PART II: METHODS AND TECHNIQUES 61

CHAPTER 4 TRADITIONAL, STRUCTURAL, AND INFERENTIAL INTERVIEWING WITH STATEMENT ANALYSIS TECHNIQUES 63

Key Terms 64

Chapter Objectives 64

Introduction 64

Identifying the Sources 65

Guidelines for the Traditional Interviewing Approach 66

What? 67 • Who? 68 • When? 68 • Where? 69 • Why? 69 • How? 71

What Is Structural Interviewing? 71

Steps for Structural Interviewing 72

Step One: Build Rapport 72 • Step Two: Encourage Participation 72 • Step Three: Review the Statement 73

Inferential Interviewing 74

Statement Coherence 74 • Response Length 74 • Type-Token Ratio 75 • Verbal Hedging 75

Statement Analysis 76

Conducting Statement Analysis 76

Step One: Parts of Speech 76 • Step Two: Extraneous Information 79 • Step Three: Lack of Conviction 80 • Step Four: Balance of the Statement 80

Field Statement Analysis 80

Conclusions 81

Questions for Review 82

Short-Answer Questions 82

Fill-in Questions 82

Exercises 83

References 83

CHAPTER 5 FORENSIC HYPNOSIS AND COGNITIVE INTERVIEWING 85

Key Terms 86

Chapter Objectives 86

Introduction 86

What Is Hypnosis? 87

Forensic Hypnosis Interviewing Methods 87

Guidelines for the Use of Forensic Hypnosis 88 • Preparing for the Hypnotic Session 89 • Induction Phase 89 • Narrative Phase 90 • Closure Phase 91 • Recall Phase 91

Challenges to Hypnotic Memory Retrieval 91

Confabulation 92 • Faking 92 • Memory Hardening and Suggestibility 92

Hypnosis Evidence in Court 93

What Is Cognitive Interviewing? 94

Cognitive Interviewing Techniques 95

Mnemonics 96 • Reconstruction Technique 97 • Reporting-Everything Technique 98 • Changing the Order of Events 98 • Changing the Perspective 98 • Additional Memory-Jogging Techniques 98

Steps of the Cognitive Interview Method 99
  Step One: Meet and Greet 99 • Step Two: Narrative Phases 100 • Step Three: Extensive Recall through Mnemonics 101 • Step Four: Summary and Closure 101
Challenges to Memory Retrieval 101
  Contamination 102 • Emotion 103 • Scripting 103
Conclusions 103
Questions for Review 104
  Short-Answer Questions 104
  Fill-in Questions 104
  Exercises 105
References 105

CHAPTER 6 BEHAVIORAL INTERVIEWING TECHNIQUES 107

Key Terms 108
Chapter Objectives 108
Introduction 108
What Is Behavioral Interviewing? 109
  Kinesics 109 • Neurolinguistic Programming 110
Cultural and Personal Considerations 111
Emotions and Observable Behaviors 112
  Facial Expression 112 • Body Posture 114
Eye Movement 116
  The Visual Right-Handed Person 117 • The Auditory Right-Handed Person 118 • The Kinesthetic Right-Handed Person 119
Sensory Verbal Communication 120
Qualifiers, Hedging, and Manipulators 121
Detecting Deceit 122
Conclusions 124
Questions for Review 124
  Short-Answer Questions 124
  Fill-in Questions 124
  Exercises 125
References 125

PART III: INTERVIEWING SPECIAL POPULATIONS 127

CHAPTER 7 INTERVIEWING CHILDREN 129

Key Terms 130
Chapter Objectives 130
Introduction 130

Child Developmental Stages 131
   Age-Related Limitations on Reporting 132

Field Assessment 133

Initial Considerations for Child Interviews 134
   Step 1: Risk Assessment 134 • Step 2: Models for Evaluating Abuse 135 • Step 3: Preliminary Considerations 136 • Step 4: Remaining Neutral 137

What Is the Forensic Approach to Child Interviewing? 139

Forensic Interviewing Techniques 140
   Phase I: Caretaker Instructions 140 • Phase II: Evaluation 141 • Phase III: Preparing the Child 141 • Phase IV: Establishing Rapport 142 • Phase V: Conducting the Interview 142

What Is the Cognitive Approach to Interviewing Children? 143

Cognitive Interviewing Techniques 143
   Caretaker Instructions 144 • Practice Interview 144 • Establishing Rapport: Cognitive Interview Step 1 144 • Reconstructing and Reporting Everything: Cognitive Interview Step 2 145 • Changing the Order and Perspective: Cognitive Interview Step 3 146

The Child as Reporter 147
   Accuracy 147 • Memory and Fantasy 148

The Child as Victim 148
   Tools for Interviewing Children 149

Bolstering Credibility through Evidence 150

Determining Competency and Reliability 152

Conclusions 153

Questions for Review 153
   Short-Answer Questions 153
   Fill-in Questions 154
   Exercises 154

References 155

CHAPTER 8 INTERVIEWING THE ELDERLY 157

Key Terms 158

Chapter Objectives 158

Introduction 158

Crimes Targeting the Elderly 159
   Domestic Violence 159 • Fiduciary Abuse 161

Initial Considerations When Questioning the Older Person 162
   The Pre-Interview 162 • Case Credibility 165

Conducting the Interview 165
   Step 1: Preparing for the Interview 165 • Step 2: Establishing Rapport 166 • Step 3: Conducting the Interview 166 • Step 4: Ending the Interview 167 • Step 5: Following Up 167

Contents

    Empowering the Elderly Victim   167
    The Elderly as Witnesses   168
        Physical Limitations   169   •   Cognitive Limitations   170
        •   Concerns Due to Dependence   171
    Interdisciplinary Interviewing   172
        Mandatory Elder Abuse Reporting   172
    Crime Perpetrated by the Elderly   173
    Conclusions   173
    Questions for Review   174
        Short-Answer Questions   174
        Fill-in Questions   174
        Exercises   174
    References   175

CHAPTER 9   INTERVIEWING PERSONS WITH DISABILITIES OR MENTAL ILLNESS   177

    Key Terms   178
    Chapter Objectives   178
    Introduction   178
    The Americans with Disabilities Act   179
        Accommodations for Interviewing   180   •   Police Liability under the ADA   180
    Initial Considerations   181
    Identifying When Special Care Is Necessary   183
        Mental Retardation   184   •   Attention Deficit-Hyperactivity Disorder   184
        •   Autism   185   •   Mental Illness   185   •   Personality Disorders   186
    Field Evaluation   187
    Interview Considerations   188
        Legal Issues   189
    Preparing for the Interview   190
        Establishing Rapport   191   •   Conducting the Interview   191
    Interrogation Considerations   193
        Miranda Rights   193   •   False Confessions   194
    Conclusions   195
    Questions for Review   196
        Short-Answer Questions   196
        Fill-in Questions   196
        Exercises   197
    References   197

PART IV: INTERROGATION 199

CHAPTER 10 THE INTERROGATION PROCESS AND THE LAW 201

Key Terms 202
Chapter Objectives 202
Introduction 202
Fifth Amendment Considerations 203
The *Miranda* Standard 204
    When Are the *Miranda* Warnings Required? 205 • When Is a Waiver of *Miranda* Rights Valid? 206 • Right to Counsel under *Miranda* 208
Sixth Amendment Considerations 209
Fourteenth Amendment Considerations 210
    The Exclusionary Rule 210
Fourth Amendment Considerations 214
    Probable Cause 215
Conclusions 218
Questions for Review 219
    Short-Answer Questions 219
    Fill-in Questions 219
    Exercises 220
References 221

CHAPTER 11 CONFESSIONS 223

Key Terms 224
Chapter Objectives 224
Introduction 224
What Is an Interrogation? 225
Since *Miranda* 226
    Who Is Likely to Conduct Interrogations? 227 • Who Is Likely to Waive Rights per *Miranda*? 229 • Why Do People Waive Their Rights? 230 • Why Do Suspects Confess? 231 • Does a Waiver Affect the Case? 231
False Confessions 232
    Improving Interrogations 233
What Is Not an Interrogation? 234
    Subtle Compulsion 235 • Traffic Stop 235 • Sobriety Testing 235 • A Stop and Frisk 236
Interrogation Tactics 237
Case-Specific Methods of Interrogation 238
    Child Pornography Cases 238 • Child Sexual Assault 240 • Hate Crimes 241 • Homicide 242 • Sexual Assault Cases 243

Truth and Consequences 244
Conclusions 245
Questions for Review 245
  Short-Answer Questions 245
  Fill-in Questions 245
  Exercises 246
References 246

CHAPTER 12 TECHNIQUES FOR INTERROGATION 249

Key Terms 250
Chapter Objectives 250
Introduction 250
Purpose of the Interrogation 251
Interrogation Approach 252
  Noncustodial Interrogation Situation 254 • Custodial Interrogation Situation 255
Confession-Eliciting Models 256
Interrogation Phase I: Preparing 257
  Step One: Know the Case 258 • Step Two: Determine the Prior Record 258 • Step Three: View the Scene 259 • Step Four: Establish the Timing 260 • Step Five: Determine Who Will Interrogate 262
Interrogation Phase II: Developing Outcome-Based Tactics 263
  Tactic #1. Appealing to the Suspect's Self-Interest 263
  • Tactic #2. Confronting the Suspect with Evidence of Guilt 264
  • Tactic #3. Undermining the Suspect's Confidence in His or Her Denials 265
  • Tactic #4. Identifying Contradictions in the Suspect's Alibi or Story 265
  • Tactic #5. Asking Specific "Behavioral Analysis" Interview Questions 266
  • Tactic #6. Appealing to the Importance of Cooperating 267
  • Tactic #7. Offering Moral Justifications and Face-Saving Excuses 267
  • Tactic #8. Confronting the Suspect with False Evidence of Guilt 267
  • Tactic #9. Praising or Flattering the Suspect 268
  • Tactic #10. Appealing to the Detective's Expertise and Authority 268
Interrogation Phase III: Getting the Confession 269
  Step One: Make the Claim 269 • Step Two: Lock it in 269
Conclusions 272
Questions for Review 272
  Short-Answer Questions 272
  Fill-in Questions 273
  Exercises 273
References 274

CHAPTER 13 JUVENILE RIGHTS AND POLICE RESPONSIBILITIES 275

Key Terms 276
Chapter Objectives 276
Introduction 276
What Is a Juvenile? 277
   Age of Criminal Responsibility 277
Juvenile Offending 278
   Juvenile Delinquency 279
Due Process and the Juvenile 279
Questioning a Juvenile Not in Custody 281
   Interrogation Methods 282
Questioning a Juvenile in Custody 284
   Temporary Custody and Juveniles 285
Fourth Amendment Considerations 285
Fifth Amendment Considerations 286
The Right to Counsel 286
Juvenile Confession Admissibility 287
Specific Crime Categories 288
   Juvenile Firesetting 288 • Sexual Offending 290
Conclusions 292
Questions for Review 292
   Short-Answer Questions 292
   Fill-in Questions 293
   Exercises 293
References 294

Preface

For 8 years I served the Massachusetts State Police as a trooper assigned to the Detective Unit of the Hampden and Hampshire County District Attorneys' Offices. As a member of the unit my duties included the investigation of major crimes, including homicide, bank robbery, rape, fraud, embezzlement, and larceny, as well as suicides and unattended deaths. I specialized in the investigation of crimes against women and children, particularly children. My additional duties included the rendition of fugitives, protection of state witnesses, and preparation and execution of warrants. During those years I also participated in surveillance, undercover investigations, and narcotics raids. It was my practice in each case in which I was the lead investigator to question every suspected perpetrator, no matter how minor or significant the case appeared.

In all of these duties as well as in police work on the road, I found that communication was the most important ingredient for a successful investigation. A person's professionalism is judged by his or her ability to communicate effectively within the discipline. Proficiency at interviewing and interrogating did not come naturally to me; it was not intuitive. I attended many seminars and training sessions on how to interview and interrogate. The process took years of attention to improving these skills and gaining the knowledge required for proficiency. This training made a positive difference in the quality and quantity of information that I was able to gather from victims, witnesses, and perpetrators. The process was an enjoyable challenge to learning about human behavior. The information in this text is an introduction to the many approaches to both interviewing and interrogating. It contains the information that I found most helpful throughout my career.

When my career changed direction and I moved into academia I discovered that each discipline had its own course in the methods of improving communication skills and thereby enhancing professionalism. Criminal justice was the exception; no colleges in my area offered a course on interviewing and interrogating. Although criminal justice professionals rely on their communication skills for every aspect of the job, there is a lack of educational tools for preparing for this discipline. This void brought about my desire to write this text. I hope that it will provide the basis for good communication skills for students in the criminal justice and related fields.

This book follows the course outline that I developed for my classroom. It was tested and improved over a period of years. It contains a comprehensive introduction to the major interviewing and interrogating methods along with the legal considerations involved in these approaches. Each chapter begins with an introduction that forms the basis for the material to follow. For some of these chapters the introduction contains theoretical background. This is a departure from other texts on interviewing and interrogating, and is not interwoven within the chapter itself. Some students will find it interesting, whereas others will prefer to skip the theory. Its purpose is to satisfy those students and instructors who want to know the theoretical background for the interviewing techniques. One focus of the book is on interviewing special populations—children, the elderly, and persons having a disability or mental illness. There are short-answer questions, fill-in questions, and appropriate exercises to assist the learner in practicing the concepts for each chapter. As an aid for teaching these concepts, a PowerPoint presentation has been prepared for each chapter. The instructor's manual that accompanies this text contains the answers along with suggested additional resources and exercises.

Acknowledgments

There are many people to thank for their contributions to this book. First, I would like to thank Victoria Noble, whose professionalism and caring made the writing of this book possible. My appreciation to the reviewers for their helpful comments on the earlier drafts of these chapters. These include.

Jo Ann Grode
Mid-State Technical College
Wisconsin Rapids, Wi

Bruce Delphia
ECPI Technical College
Richmond, VA

Carol Mathews
Century College
White Bear Lake, MN

Thank you to Philip Koplin for the excellent editing of the text.

I owe a special debt of gratitude to my friend and colleague Dawna Komorosky of California State University at Hayward, whose careful reading and suggestions early on contributed significantly to this text and the Instructors Manual. I thank Patrick J. Faiella of Massasoit Community College, Canton, Massachusetts, who tirelessly read the manuscript and provided insight along with many of the end-of-chapter questions. To my friend and husband, Robert, thank you for your limitless ideas and unwaivering support.

Finally, I also thank my friends, colleagues, and students at Western New England College, who encouraged and supported my efforts.

About The Author

A pioneer in law enforcement, the author was the first uniformed female officer in her hometown, Lunenburg, Massachusetts, and the first female campus police officer at the community college she attended. The Massachusetts Senate honored her in 1978 as the first woman appointed constable for the City of Fitchburg. In 1979 she was named an Outstanding Young Woman of America.

She graduated in the 61st Recruit Training Troop of the Massachusetts State Police in January 1980. During the years that followed she served as a uniformed officer performing route patrol activities, as an instructor at the Massachusetts State Police Academy, and as a detective in major crime investigations. Recognized as a local expert in child abuse investigation, she has spoken on cable television and radio. She appeared on the *America's Most Wanted* television show in connection with a fugitive in a case she was investigating. She has made many presentations at professional meetings with the Department of Social Services, Department of Mental Health, and Office of the District Attorney. She has testified in numerous major crime cases in both criminal and civil hearings.

Like many police officers, her education was fragmented, interrupted over the years by demanding work and family responsibilities. She holds an Associate Degree in Science in Law Enforcement from Mt. Wachusett Community College and Bachelor's and Master's Degrees in Criminal Justice from Westfield State College. At the University of Massachusetts she studied at the doctoral level in the Political Science Department, and she is currently a Ph.D. candidate at Capella University. She was awarded a scholarship to attend the first Child Abuse and Exploitation Investigative Techniques Training Program at the Federal Law Enforcement Training Center. She has additional training in the investigation of homicide, rape, and stalking, as well as in issues related to search and seizure. In 1995 she studied at the International Institute for the Sociology of Law in Onati, Spain.

From 1991 to the present she has lectured at Greenfield Community College, Holyoke Community College, Springfield College, and Westfield State College. She has taught about domestic abuse for the 74th Massachusetts State Police Recruit Training Troop and presented a professional workshop on cognitive interviewing techniques at the Roger Williams Justice Institute.

As a member of the Academy of Criminal Justice Sciences, she has made numerous presentations and served as chair of the publications committee and of the program committee. She is a long-time member of the Northeastern Association of Criminal Justice Sciences, of which she has held the offices of president, vice president, and secretary.

She is a faculty member at the Criminal Justice and Sociology Department at Western New England College. Her publications include *Heavy Hands: An Introduction to the Crimes of Family Violence,* currently in its third edition, and has contributed to the *Encyclopedia of Police Science,* the *Encyclopedia of Juvenile Justice,* and the *Encyclopedia of Domestic Violence,* as well as to other significant texts in the field.

Part I

Laying the Groundwork for Success

Smart Talk is about effective communication; it provides the guidelines for gathering information. Chapter 1 stresses the process of communication and the skills required of an interviewer. This chapter defines interviewing and interrogating. Understanding the differences between them is critical for choosing the appropriate fact-gathering approach. Interviewing requires a flexible process dictated by the nature of the individual being interviewed. Interrogating requires the use of accusatory persuasion. The chapter also addresses the personal qualities needed by an interviewer, in particular knowledge about the people being interviewed, the case being investigated, and the professionalism that is brought to bear in the process. The development of rapport is critical to successful interviewing and is discussed extensively. A brief introduction to various forms of nonverbal communication is also included.

In Chapter 2 the importance of understanding the point of view of the interviewee is recognized and is discussed through social systems theory. A three-phase approach to interviewing is suggested that provides a general framework for the process: preparation, establishment of the psychological content, and the actual questioning. Preparation prior to the interview is as important as the questioning itself. The options for determining when and where the interview should take place are covered. The potential problem of misinformation and its resulting contamination of the interview is outlined. Extensive coverage is given to the types of questions to use in the final phase of interviewing. An important aspect of successful interviewing is knowing which questions illicit the desired responses and which facilitate answers.

Building on the previous chapters, Chapter 3 discusses how to prepare for the questioning. The goals of purposeful interviewing are met by examining the nature of the offense, determining whether a crime was actually committed, and identifying the perpetrator. Some general approaches to determining the nature of the offense and interviewing approaches for victims in specific crime situations are presented. Basic procedures for perpetrator identification are outlined. This chapter also builds on the concept of rapport that was introduced in Chapter 1. The final section introduces the reader to methods of assessing statement accuracy.

CHAPTER 1
Interviewing and Interrogation

Key Terms

Communication process	Rapport
Presumptive prosecution policy	Kinesics
Persuade	Proxemics
Elicit	Paralanguage

Chapter Objectives

After completing this chapter, you should be able to:

- Describe the communication process according to the scheme presented by D. K. Berlo
- Define *interview*
- List the categories of persons that might be interviewed
- Define *interrogation*
- State the purpose of an interview
- Compare and contrast an interview with an interrogation
- State the purpose of an interrogation
- Describe the qualities of a good interviewer
- Explain how rapport affects the quality of the interview or interrogation process
- List numerous forms of nonverbal communication

Introduction

Crimes are solved when someone makes the decision to talk. The talker's level of cooperation is influenced by the communication skills of the interviewer. Enhancing these skills may improve the quality and quantity of credible information made available during an interview or interrogation. The first lesson in communication involves an acknowledgment that the perceptions of both the interviewee and interviewer will influence the dialogue. Communication involves the exchange of thoughts, messages, or information by speech, signals, writing, or behavior. In this chapter, the processes of communication as envisioned by D. K. Berlo are used to illustrate the complexity of communication. Communication is the core of all interviewing or interrogation. Theory may explain or expand the reasoning for the interviewing and interrogation practices. You will find the theoretical concepts in the introduction of each chapter. Think about the theory presented as you read the rest of the chapter.

Berlo's SMCR model describes a **communication process** as an interrelated scheme involving the four most important parts of communication: source, message, channels, and receiver (Berlo, 1960). For an interview to take place between two people, communication must occur back and forth between the person who initiates the interaction (the source) and the one who receives and interprets the meanings (the receiver). The message is made up of content, which is coded (stated) so that it will be

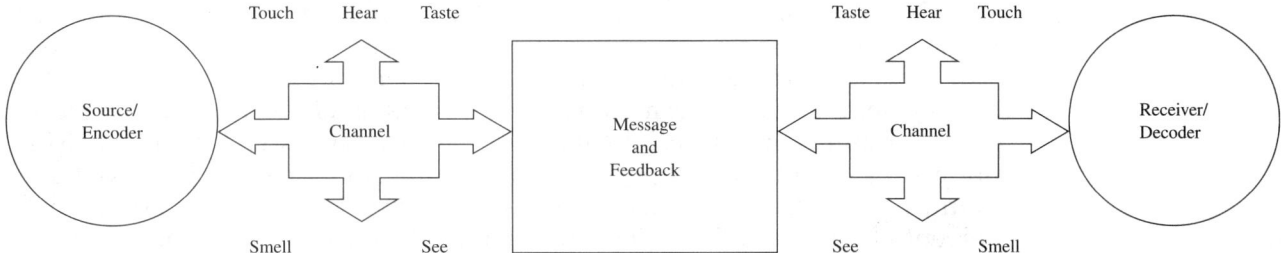

FIGURE 1-1 Berlo's SMCR model.

received in the way that it is intended. The code is a system of agreed-on communication; it could be the English language, Morse code, sign language, images on motion picture film, and so on.

The substance of the communication is given meaning by an interpretation using the five senses through the channels of seeing, hearing, touching, feeling, and tasting. Interest and prejudice affect the reception, rejection, and filtering of the transmission. The process of meaning is affected by the stimulus. A stimulus is anything that a person can receive through one of his or her senses, anything that can produce sensation in the human organism. The stimulus reaches the sense organs and is *decoded* by them. One sets about *interpreting* this stimulus while determining what an appropriate *response* might be.

Berlo stresses the role of relationship between the source and the receiver as an important variable (Wells, Malpass, Lindsay, Fisher, Turtle, & Fulero, 2000). Four factors affect the transmission of the message: communication skills, knowledge level, sociocultural system, and attitudes. The source will make assumptions about the receiver based on these variables; the receiver will do the same regarding the source. The messages back and forth will depend on the opinions formed of the other person according the senses, which determine how the messages are being received. If the source determines that the receiver is "stupid," he or she will phrase questions based on that opinion; the receiver may sense that "he thinks I am stupid" and form the opinion that the source is arrogant!

THE NATURE OF INTERVIEWING

Interviewing is a practice of fact finding that produces information that can lead to conclusions about an event or incident. The core of interviewing is found in the process of communication. The methods of interviewing are as diverse as its many applications. During an interview a person is questioned about his or her knowledge of events that are under investigation. The purpose is to gather information. The person questioned during an interview is assessed by the interviewer for credibility through objective, nonaccusatory conversation. An interview typically is conducted during early stages of an investigation in a variety of environments. On the other hand, an interrogation is an exercise in persuasion. An interview may evolve into an interrogation if the interviewee is perceived as being unwilling to offer the truth.

The interviewing methods and concepts that are described in this text have broad professional applicability. Individuals who use these skills include all government officials tasked with investigations, including, but not limited to, corrections officers, parole officers, police officers, and probation officers. Interviewing proficiency also benefits individuals in civilian employment such as human resources personnel, private investigators, school administrators, social service employees, and social workers. Criminal justice, sociology, and psychology students find ideas for improved communication through the methods used in interviewing. An estimated 80 percent of a police officer's investigative work consists of obtaining information through interviewing (Geffner & Rosenbaum, 2002). Other professions have similarly high needs for the ability to obtain information through interviewing.

Before learning about the methods for interviewing it is important to understand the individuals who may be involved in the process. Keep in mind that these categories are not mutually exclusive, and they sometimes overlap. For example, there are situations in which the assumed victim turns out to be the perpetrator, or in which the witness may also be a victim. Sometimes the suspect is identified as a victim. Further confusing the process is that the reported incident may not constitute a violation. The investigator makes the determination on whether the report does constitute an actionable incident. There are three categories of persons who may be interviewed: victims, witnesses, and suspects.

Victims

A victim is the person who is the object of an incident, crime, or other harm. The victim may be an individual, a public or private corporation, a government, a partnership, or an unincorporated association (Garner, 2004). For investigation purposes, it is important to establish if there is a relationship between the victim and the perpetrator. Knowledge of a relationship will direct questioning and affect the interpretation of information. A victim may be unwilling or unable to provide information for use against the perpetrator if there is a relationship; the victim may be uncooperative if they are intimates. Knowledge of the relationship between the victim and the alleged perpetrator may also shed light on the credibility of the statement should that become an issue.

The amount of cooperation varies from person to person and depends greatly on the type of incident that is being investigated. It may also change during or after the interview; a second interview is not assured. Cooperation is among the many issues of concern. The victim could have substantial injuries that put him or her into a coma or cause death. Investigators must be as thorough as possible when interviewing a victim in order to gain as much information as possible during the first interview.

Another reason for being thorough at the first interviewing opportunity is that in some jurisdictions a presumptive prosecution policy may be in place. A **presumptive prosecution policy** means that prosecution would continue regardless of the victim's participation whenever sufficient evidence exists that a crime was committed (Gosselin, 2005). There are two general approaches taken by the courts: no-drop and evidence-based prosecution policies. Under the no-drop approach the attempts at gathering evidence continue with encouragement for victim

> **BEEN THERE... DONE THAT! 1-1**
>
> The impulse to always believe the victim is strong, but the interviewer must remember that not all allegations are true. A woman reported having been stalked; the investigation was ongoing for 3 years without success. At one point the 21-year-old woman came into the police department with a bruise on her face, which was photographed. She received letters describing sexually descriptive acts that the perpetrator threatened to do to her. She received flowers sent to her office. Despite this evidence of a serious stalking situation, a phone tap, and discrete following by the police, no perpetrator was ever found. Eventually she was sent to me for an interview. When I complimented her on the imaginative letters she had received, she could not hold back a slight smile. At that point she admitted to having written the letters, sent herself the flowers, and, yes, hit herself in the face. The attention from the police had been a very positive thing in her life. It ended and the case was closed.

cooperation. Services such as counseling, housing assistance, and safety planning are among the ways that victim participation is encouraged. No-drop policies exist to remove the responsibility for prosecution from victims and ensure that the state proceeds where there is a compelling public safety interest (Davis, Smith, & Davies, 2001). The evidence-based approach assumes that the victim will not be available and builds a case on physical evidence, medical records, and police testimony. Prosecution without victim participation can only occur when the investigator has taken the time to do a complete investigation and has gathered all verbal and physical evidence at the time of initial access.

In all cases, the victim may fear that the perpetrator will return for retribution; the victim may feel prejudices against or from the person conducting the interview; the victim may feel tired, angry, or in pain at the time of the interview. It is likely that the person will be under immense stress while being interviewed; stress affects memory and recall (Artwohl, 2002). It is worthwhile to put the interviewee at ease through the establishment of rapport. A second interview may be warranted for taking photographs of bruising that may not appear visible at the initial interview. The victim may be a child or an elder with limited cognitive abilities, a person who is developmentally delayed, or someone with something to hide. The victim may be a professor or a student, a prostitute or a member of the clergy. All of these factors will influence the outcome.

Witnesses

A witness is someone who sees, hears, or otherwise observes something relating to the incident under investigation (Garner, 2004). Witnesses may also be called eyewitnesses. Eyewitness reports are notoriously inaccurate, incomplete, and unreliable. However, the eyewitness is still of great value to the interviewer. The witness can provide important information that leads to the perpetrator and ultimately to the offender being held accountable. The witness can also give information that is misleading or inaccurate. Statements must be taken and critically analyzed for their truth, veracity, and relative importance to the case being investigated.

Use of techniques to enhance the recall of witnesses is rapidly gaining credibility. Known as cognitive interviewing, this will be explored in depth later in the text. Kinesics and other behavioral approaches to statements are also frequently employed. The traditional interview technique of fact gathering is still valuable for many cases. A frequent complaint from investigators is that they lack the time to sufficiently interview. Case interviewing can be time consuming, and following up the generated leads and corroborating the information is an essential aspect of investigating.

A witness interview is nonaccusatory by the interviewer and may be conducted in a variety of places. The witness may be the person who is making accusations. At the scene of the crime, as many bystanders as possible should be briefly interviewed. One method of handling a large of number of witnesses at a scene is for an investigator to take names and phone numbers first and then interview as time permits. Witnesses may not want to get involved in the situation, and they have a way of disappearing; learning to access the crowd before that happens can be a challenge.

Witnesses may be reluctant to come forward with information. One reason may be that they simply are unaware that they possess helpful information. Therefore it is often necessary to seek out witnesses. Many other reasons can contribute to the withholding of information, including not wanting to get involved, the fear that the suspect will retaliate against them for having provided information to the police, a general fear of the suspect, and a relationship to the suspect; it also may come from a distrust of the interviewer. Still others with information will think that the incident is none of their business. Although it is generally assumed that the witness will be cooperative, that is not always the case. Gentle persuasion may be employed when necessary to encourage witness cooperation.

Witnesses often struggle to provide accurate detail. Inconsistencies tend to reduce the value of a statement, but do not necessarily mean that it is fabricated. Children in particular may become confused on details of an incident. Receiving similar information from a variety of sources tends to fill in important voids and lend credibility to what is supplied through witness interviews. Perception has a lot to do with differences in reporting. When a manila folder is held up to group of people, numerous colors will be suggested to describe it. In one study of witnesses who were interviewed about a car chase, those who knew that it had crashed reported the speed of the car to be greater than did those who did not know it had crashed (Abrams & Ramsey, 2000).

Anonymous witness reports should always be regarded with suspicion. This is particularly true when the reporter has experienced a personal problem with the accused or is a disgruntled neighbor or when a previous relationship existed. One should approach these complaints with caution and investigate them thoroughly because it is not unheard of that some complaints get filed in an attempt to get someone in trouble. Conversely, when a relationship goes sour, the reporter may feel free to give information that he or she held back while things were going well. Either way, the investigator would be better off to tread slowly and be thorough.

One cannot anticipate the full effect that stress has on those being interviewed. Some research has suggested that witness accounts are more reliable when the person has been under stress (Abrams & Ramsey, 2000), but the opposite effect has also been noted. In highly negative emotional situations, such as witnessing a violent crime, eyewitness accounts may be more susceptible to misinformation (Porter, Spencer, & Birt, 2003). The following basic principles about witness interviewing represent the characteristics of witnesses (Massachusetts Municipal Police Institute, 1981):

1. Witnesses usually see only part of what actually happens and usually recognize only part of what they see.
2. Witnesses usually remember only part of what they observe and usually describe only part of what they remember.
3. Witnesses who are angry, frightened, or emotionally upset usually perceive only a fraction of what they might observe under normal circumstances.
4. Witnesses often see only what they expect or want to see, and as a result they provide a distorted version of what actually happened or an inaccurate physical description of the alleged offender.
5. Witnesses who are involved in violent incidents such as homicides, robberies, rapes, aggravated assaults, and fatal accidents are often unable to immediately provide an adequate description of events or suspects.
6. Witnesses can be affected by a number of possible physical or emotional factors that may influence the validity of their information.
7. Emotional factors can cause a witness to lie, become uncooperative or forgetful, or give prejudicial information.
8. It is not unusual for a number of witnesses describing the same incident to furnish varying accounts of what happened or to provide a variety of descriptions for the alleged offender because every witness see things differently and relates what he or she saw in an individual manner.
9. An interviewer must recognize all these human limitations and individual differences in witness perception and be aware of the personal motives that can be involved in any particular case.

BEEN THERE . . . DONE THAT! 1-2

During an investigation into an allegation of child sexual assault, the mother of the child victim was being interviewed. She gave detailed information on what her daughter had told her. Frequently she cried during the interview. Although her behavior was not unjustified, it was apparent that she had a high stake in the outcome of the case. More than halfway into the interview I discovered that the perpetrator was the woman's father—grandfather to the child victim. The mother confided that he had sexually abused her as a child also, a case that had never been reported. Among other things, she had suffered genital mutilation at the hands of her father. Don't assume that you know who all of the victims are.

> **BEEN THERE... DONE THAT! 1-3**
>
> A frantic call came in to the station by a woman claiming that her child had been kidnapped and that she did not know the man who took the infant. Officers en route to the scene saw a man walking with an infant in his arms and stopped to speak with him. As it turned out, the "kidnapper" was the father of the child, who had the legal right to have custody of her. His story was that his girlfriend—the mother—was an abusive drunk who was hitting the child. Lacking a car, he had left on foot to protect the infant. At the house the woman was found to be intoxicated and combative. She admitted to hitting the child and was arrested for assault. In the police cruiser she kept saying that she could not believe that she had been arrested, she was the mother and, after all, she was a woman; she had even made the call to the police! What was this world coming to?

Suspects

For an initial response to the scene of an offense the responder should remove the suspect immediately if he or she is present. If the suspected perpetrator is not present, interviews with the victim or witness should include attempts to identify the perpetrator. Along with a suspect description the interviewer should ask about locations where the suspect may be found. Any utterances made should be documented, including any alibi. Developing a strategy for a later interrogation begins at this stage.

An interview with a suspect should not take place until the interviewer has examined the facts of the case and spoken with the victim. The interviewer should not jump to conclusions during an initial meeting with a person thought to be the perpetrator. Nor should an interrogation take place until the interviewer is fairly certain that the person is guilty. Approaching the suspect should be similar to the procedure with any witness unless it is a dangerous situation that compromises interviewer safety. This means that the approach is respectful, but not solicitous. A suspect may offer information that clears him or her immediately, so one should be open to that possibility. An interview of a suspect takes on immense importance because it is often the only opportunity for a nonadversarial dialogue. Once an interrogation is started, the ability to freely gather information is over.

THE NATURE OF INTERROGATION

An interrogation is an exercise in persuasion with the goal of eliciting a truthful confession. This working definition is specific to gain a deeper understanding of the nature and purpose for conducting an interrogation. **Persuade** is defined as "To move by argument, entreaty, or expostulation, to a belief or position, or by course of action" (*Merriam-Webster's Collegiate Dictionary*, 2004). **Elicit** means "to draw out or entice forth; to bring to light; to bring out against the will; to deduce by reason or argument; as, to elicit truth by discussion" (*Merriam-Webster Online Dictionary*, 2005).

The interrogation process is a give and take between the suspect and the interrogator, with the majority of the talking done by the interrogator. This back and forth may last as little as 30 minutes or it may take hours. It is structured and purposeful. The extent of cooperation is determined early; therefore the interrogator works within accepted boundaries with the suspect to elicit the information.

The interrogation is different than the interview in many ways. The primary difference between an interview and an interrogation is often in the interviewer's perception. A change from interviewing to interrogation is evidenced by a change from the nonaccusatory approach to one that is accusatory. Often occurring in a controlled environment, an interrogation involves eliciting information from a suspect who is perceived as unwilling to admit his or her role in a crime or it may involve an individual with reason to hide the truth. Statements rather than questions are sometimes asserted by the interrogator. Mere persistence does not make the questioning unfair because there is no requirement that the first answer from a suspect be accepted as truthful (Williamson, 2004).

Concepts about human behavior and communication that are included in this text as interviewing techniques are applicable to interrogation practices also. Many professionals may be in a situation of interviewing suspects, yet relatively few will engage in interrogation. Legal interrogation guidelines limit the actions of law enforcement officials. The reason for this narrowed application is that constitutional requirements generally govern state and federal action. The U.S. Supreme Court has defined interrogation as the questioning initiated by law enforcement officers after a person has been taken into custody or otherwise deprived of his or her freedom of action in any significant way (*Miranda v. Arizona,* 1966). The U.S. Constitution and the Bill of Rights in particular protect citizens from actions of government officials and their agents and not from other citizens. Evidence that is obtained from the interrogation of one citizen by another citizen is not held to the same standard as an interrogation by a government officer. However, the government may not be able to accept evidence from civilians if it was obtained through egregious interrogation methods such as torture or vigilante action.

The law governing interrogation methods is not specified in any one place; criminal interrogations are guided by evolving standards of acceptable practices. Constitutional law, federal and state statutes, and Anglo-American tradition blend together with a current emphasis on the Fifth Amendment right against self-incrimination, the Sixth Amendment guarantee of the right to counsel, and the Fourteenth Amendment guarantee of due process.

Interrogation Controversy

The controversy surrounding interrogation provides sufficient reason for students to study the process, regardless of any direct professional application. Debates over acceptable practices are not new to this generation. Interrogation methods have been controversial at least since the 1600s. Isolated attempts to prohibit torture as an interrogation method are documented in English jurisprudence as early as 1628 (*Bram v. United States,* 1897). Early common law allowed an admission or confession as evidence of guilt regardless of it being the product of force or duress. Rather than conducting an investigation to establish guilt, enforcement officers resorted to torture to extract a confession from the accused during an interrogation.

The courts have alternatively used the unreliability of confessions from torture and the requirement for constitutional protections as reasons for rejecting their use against an individual to prove guilt. Psychologists tell us that some individuals will confess to a crime that they did not commit without exterior pressures and that others are susceptible to falsely confess in an interrogation environment (Kassin, 2005). This provides a dilemma for officials who are tasked with solving crimes. Interrogation information must be consistent with fact or reality, not false or erroneous, real, genuine, reliable, accurate, narrowly particularized, and highly specific.

Although many veteran investigators felt that interrogations would become a lost art after the *Miranda* decision in 1966, the Supreme Court has recognized the need for criminal justice investigators to conduct interrogations. It is in the best interest of society to identify correctly individuals whose acts are illegal. When done properly, the interrogation is still an important tool for an investigator to consider. Some evidence suggests that detectives are successful in obtaining confessions or admissions in 75 percent of the interrogations that are attempted (Leo, 1996).

It is against human nature to implicate oneself in wrongdoing; it is not necessarily in one's best interest. Why would someone confess to having committed an illegal act, knowing that there will be consequences? That individual must be persuaded that it is in their best interest to admit the act. Persuasion can be accomplished through a variety of methods, which will be described in later chapters.

PURPOSE OF THE INTERROGATION

The process of interrogation is meant to encourage the suspect to provide evidence of guilt or involvement in an event. The interrogator seeks a confession or admission regarding participation or knowledge of wrongdoing. A confession is a statement made by a person disclosing his or her guilt of the crime with which he or she is charged, excluding the possibility of a reasonable inference to the contrary (*People v. Anderson,* 1965). A confession is not limited to words, but may also include the demeanor, conduct, and acts of the person charged with a crime. For example, the court has accepted a situation in which the defendant showed the interrogators how he committed the murder of a young girl by acting out the manner in which he stabbed her (*People v. Baldi,* 1974).

In one of the few studies on the practice of interrogation, "success" was considered to have been achieved when any amount of incriminating information was elicited from the suspect (Leo, 1996). Although the goal is to entice a confession, eliciting an admission is considered a successful outcome of the interrogation. An admission is an acknowledgment of guilty conduct that contains only facts from which guilt may or may not

> **BEEN THERE... DONE THAT! 1-4**
>
> Rapport building is a process of developing a willingness to communicate. It can also be thought of as a getting-to-know-you phase. When interviewing a child or an adult, one should show empathy, concern, or interest in order to build rapport. Rapport building can be an important phase for interrogations also. In one case I had just arrested a man who had been restrained by four officers in order to detain him. He was shocked at having been arrested and visibly shaken from the experience. I showed concern and asked if he was all right, making light of the four men having just pounced on him. From the look on his face I detected an immediate reaction of gratitude. Moments later I gave him his rights per *Miranda*, which he waived and agreed to give me a statement. Having sensed his willingness to communicate, I had wasted no time and did the interrogation in the police cruiser on the way to the station. By the time we arrived I had a full confession and a thank-you from the perpetrator.

be inferred (*People v. Anderson*, 1965). The statement of admission may be a word, an act, a conduct, or information that in any other way suggests guilt. Information about the suspect and his or her role or relationship to the crime, the victim, or the place of the offense may be part of the admission. Because the courts do not differentiate among degrees of incrimination, no distinction is drawn between confessions and admissions for purposes of their use as evidence against an individual in court.

PERSONAL QUALITIES OF THE INTERVIEWER

The majority of contacts that occur between an investigator and a citizen are face-to-face and typically one-on-one. The ability to communicate effectively may be the most desirable personal quality of an investigator. Often it is assumed that a person who speaks or writes well comes by it naturally. Those who are reluctant to seek help for improvement may be embarrassed about their lack of skill. Some individuals are oblivious to their deficiencies and may need encouragement from a supervisor in order to improve. Analysis of videotape and audiotape recordings shows that police officers frequently appear inept, nervous, ill at ease, and lacking in confidence (Williamson, 2004). Most good oral and written communication skills are learned. It is therefore necessary to acquire these skills and then practice them for these shortcomings to be addressed.

How things are said may be more important than what is being said. The way that a person communicates dictates the impression that is given about that person to others. It is how the individual's professionalism is judged. Those who sit in judgment are fellow professionals, the public, victims, and the perpetrator. The individual alone determines the impression that is given. People frequently state that an interviewer should above all be friendly. I could not disagree more. If the victim or witness wanted to talk to a friend, he or she would go out for coffee, not for an official interview! More appropriately the interviewer must be approachable, understanding, empathetic, patient, and nonjudgmental. In other words, being neutral and nonoffensive without being distant is a personal quality that will benefit the communication process. Persons who are interviewed may be looking for help or direction; sometimes they are angry and confused. Confidence is therefore a necessary attribute of the interviewer—without arrogance, however. Learning the behaviors needed to be a successful interviewer begins with learning and understanding human nature.

Knowing yourself is the first part of that process. The ability to recognize that each one of us has a perspective that is unique carries with it the acknowledgment that you, the investigator, have prejudices and biases about someone or something. Some people can't stand stupid people or persons who come across as intellectuals. Others dislike certain physical characteristics or appearances. Some individuals are repulsed by those who commit criminal acts generally. The successful interviewer learns to put these biases aside in a conscious choice to be professional. Everyone is entitled to his or her opinions, thoughts, and perspectives, but there is no room during the interview for personal preferences. Learning to look past oneself to the case greatly enhances the value of the police interview. If one has difficulty in putting personal bias aside, a rethinking of job direction may be warranted.

In addition, the individual who conducts frequent interviews should have a genuine curiosity. Curiosity is a term that refers to an emotional pressure to seek information, to explore, and to learn by observation. Wanting to find out everything possible about a case in this context refers to being open-minded about lifestyles and personal choices that may be different than those of the investigator. A positive attitude by the interviewer has a better chance to surface if interest is allowed to overtake bias.

A good interviewer is not necessarily an effective interrogator. Because interrogation is only a small part of the communication process, interview skills are of greater value. However, the skills for interrogation are an extension of the personal qualities needed for an interviewer, so they are addressed at this point. Training, experience, aptitude, and intelligence are prerequisites. The personal qualities for someone making an interrogation include all of the interview skills along with a high degree of confidence. That confidence is achieved internally. The individual must possess self-confidence on his or her ability to face objection and overcome resistance through reason. It is not that different from taking a position on a debating team and arguing for one opinion over another that is being presented. The debate is not a shouting match. It is an intellectual exchange that is based on the position of the interrogator without regard to his or her personal stake in the outcome of the debate. Once a position is taken by the interrogator, it must be backed up with evidence to strengthen that position. In addition, achieving absolute control over personal emotions is paramount for the interrogator. It is natural to feel embarrassment for the suspect when you catch him or her in a lie or to feel pity for the subject because of the circumstance. Emotions can also drive an interrogator to vigorously proceed during an interrogation without regard for the suspect. An interrogation is not an exercise in humiliation, degradation, or torture that is either physical or psychological.

Willing to Develop Rapport

Central to any interview, and in some cases for interrogations, is an exchange called **rapport.** Frequently throughout this book there will be references to rapport; therefore the communication concept behind the process is introduced here. Rapport is the communication that results when two people agree on the means and willingness to communicate (Berlo, 1960). It is established by putting the interviewee at ease through mutual respect or understanding.

The social work interview has long embraced the importance of communication as presented through the theory of David Berlo (Kadushin, 1972). To continue the previous description adopted from Berlo, the nature of the communication involves not only what is said and heard—the message encoded, transmitted, received, processed, and decoded—but also the interpersonal context in which the process takes place. The recent reliance on rapport in policing interviews is demonstrated in *Eyewitness Evidence,* a publication from the National Institute of Justice (U.S. Department of Justice, 1999). If the context of the relationship is positive, then there is a comfortable, trustful, and respectful feeling between the interviewer and person being interviewed. The positive relationship, which is another way to describe rapport, lowers barriers and brings a heightened willingness to participate in the interview. Both interviewer and interviewee are more likely to be receptive to messages being sent after rapport has been established. A good relationship is not necessarily a pleasant one, but it is one that is actively used to further the purpose of the interview (Kadushin, 1972).

The ability to develop rapport with another involves a willingness to use words and behaviors to effectively impart information with openness toward receiving back information from another person. It is earned by the attitude and behavior of the interviewer. Without rapport the statement may lack completeness. At the beginning of any interview of any length or importance, the interviewer must first establish rapport with the person being interviewed. Rapport can be established through verbal or behavioral techniques. The behavior approach to rapport building is discussed later in this chapter. Verbal methods for the development of rapport are covered in Chapter 3.

In painful communication situations of personal concern rapport is what brings a full and frank confession from a subject (Kadushin, 1972). The suspect is unlikely to talk about difficult situations that have hurt, frustrated, or been painful unless the investigator can convince the suspect that he or she is anxious to understand what the experience has meant to him or her.

Knowledgeable

Examination of recorded police interviews indicates that investigators often have only a weak understanding of the legal requirements needed to prove an offense (Williamson, 2004). This deficiency is addressed by the knowledgeable investigator. He or she keeps asking questions and continues to learn from each case that is investigated. The knowledgeable investigator researches the laws pertaining to the offenses that are under investigation prior to conducting major interviews or interrogations. Gathering case facts is done during each investigation, no matter how many times a similar situation was faced or how routine the situation may appear.

The knowledgeable interviewer does not make judgments based on past encounters that were similar or by race, gender, or age. Each situation represents the possibility that an unlikely person is at fault. We now know, for example, that intimate violence occurs between persons of the same sex; that adolescents abuse their parents; and that an older woman is just as likely to perpetrate an offense against an elderly husband as the husband is against his elderly wife. Rape is perpetrated against male and female victims, against persons in a courtship or a marriage relationship, and within same-sex relationships. The knowledgeable officer knows that the answers must be learned from the circumstances and will come only through listening and watching.

Professional

The interviewer must begin without case bias. Because the goal is to obtain information, the situation must allow the witness or victim to freely state his or her views of the situation. A preconceived notion about what the person may say inhibits conversation. Tolerating ambiguity refers to this skill of reacting positively to new, different, and at times unpredictable situations. This will call for patience as well as persistence. Both are firm requirements in particular when dealing with people from other societies and places around the world.

The attitude of the interviewer or interrogator strongly affects the extent of witness cooperation. A necessary ingredient of professionalism the capability to demonstrate respect in whichever way a specific culture requires: respect for age, respect in manner of speech, respect with eye contact, respect with hand or body gestures, respect for personal privacy, and so on.

Being nonjudgmental requires that the investigator learn to withhold judgment until all information is accumulated while also taking into account cultural idiosyncrasies that could color judgment. In addition, one must feel comfortable asking uncomfortable questions. Frequently the details of a statement being given will cause anxiety to the victim or witness. It may necessitate asking personal or probing questions to obtain completeness and accuracy.

COMMUNICATING

Communication is a process that includes sending and receiving both verbal and nonverbal messages. It is estimated that nonverbal communication often conveys a larger share of social information, approximately 65 percent or more, whereas verbal communication plays a less salient role, 35 percent or less (Lanning, 2002). So much information is communicated nonverbally that frequently the verbal aspect is negligible. Body language, facial expressions, gestures, personal spacing, and voice characteristics send messages to the recipient.

These communications can be used to facilitate the building of rapport through matching techniques. Matching is a subtle form of the interviewer mimicking the nonverbal and paralanguage behaviors of the person being interviewed (Sandoval & Adams, 2001). The intent is to match the behavior or voice by making some form of movement in the same manner without attracting conscious attention to it. Nonverbal techniques for interviewing and interrogation are discussed in greater length in Chapter 6.

Kinesics

Kinesics a form of nonverbal communication that includes body language, facial expressions, and gestures (Sandoval & Adams, 2001). How the body expresses itself to others is also referred to as body language. As one of the most effective media, it transmits feelings. The transmission of body language is usually more subconscious than conscious. Observing individuals who are deeply engaged in conversation reveals some similarities between them that they probably aren't consciously aware of. For example, they are probably sitting in a similar fashion, they may make similar types and rhythms of hand gestures, they most likely speak in a similar tonality and tempo, and they probably breathe at a similar rate. Their body language will be aligned somehow. The participants will feel that they understand each other, but they might not be able to put their finger on the reason, except that the other person "makes sense." The practice of an interviewer matching the body language of the interviewee brings that feeling of making sense to the subject. It can facilitate a willingness to provide information during the interview.

Approval, agreement, acceptance, and continuing attention and understanding are indicated by a head nod from the interviewer (Wainwright, 2003). Agreement typically is indicated by the largest nods, whereas feedback on understanding the interviewee is shown by a slight nod. Wainwright (2003) suggested that men tend to use head nods more than women and that it may be useful for women to practice and purposefully use head nods more frequently.

Facial expressions include both conscious and unconscious movement of the nose, lips, eyebrows, tongue, and eyes (Ekman, 2001). In a persuasive communication environment, facial expression, posture, body movement, and eye contact provide about 50 percent of the overall message (Hogan, 2002). For example, lips may move into a grin to show happiness, grimace for fear, or pout to indicate sadness. When the individual has a lot at stake in a situation and lies about it, emotions such as fear and disgust are evidenced through facial expressions (Wright, Boyd, & Tredoux, 2001). Eyebrows frown for anger or concentration and rise for intensity. The most frequent facial expressions, according to Ekman (2001), are the lowering or rising of the eyebrows, often to emphasize speech or show disbelief and skepticism. Wide eyes typically indicate surprise or excitement, and narrowed eyes indicate disagreement or a threat. One of the most reliable facial actions is the narrowing of the lips, which signals anger. An interviewer may facilitate rapport by recognizing and addressing what the face reveals.

Gestures are woven inextricably into our social lives, and that vocabulary of gestures can be informative and entertaining, but also dangerous (Fisher & Geiselman, 1992). Gestures can be menacing (two drivers on a freeway), warm (an open-arm welcome), instructive (a police officer giving road directions), or even sensuous (the liquid movement of a Hawaiian hula dancer), whereas verbal communication transmits words and thoughts. At times understanding the wants and feelings of others is far more important than understanding their words. Crossing of the arms, for example, usually signals a defensive posture indicating that the person has become cautious (Hogan, 2002). When an interviewer attempts to develop rapport, defensive signals need to be overcome for the interview to proceed effectively.

Proxemics. **Proxemics** is the study of our use of space and how differences in that use make us feel more relaxed or more anxious. The term was coined by researcher Edward Hall during the 1950s (Wright & Loftus, 1998). Hall identified four bodily distances—*intimate* (0 to 18 inches), *personal-casual* (1.5 to 4 feet), *social-consultive* (4 to 10 feet), and *public* (10 feet and beyond)—as key points in human spacing behavior. Hall noted that different cultures set distinctive norms for closeness in, for example, speaking, business, and courting, and that standing too close or too far away can lead to misunderstandings. Comfortable communication with someone who is not an intimate should take place outside of the intimate distance, or greater than 18 inches (Hogan, 2002).

Changing the distance between two people can convey a desire for intimacy, declare a lack of interest, or increase/decrease domination. Violation of personal space can nonverbally convey a message; for example, officers are encouraged to use the strategy of sitting close and crowding a suspect during an interrogation to gain the psychological advantage. When our personal bubble of space has been invaded we feel uncomfortable, and tension and fear result. Most people will get up and leave rather than deal with the uncomfortable feeling of someone invading their space. Care should be taken that the interviewer does not violate individual space during the rapport establishment phase. If there are signals that the individual is uncomfortable, the interviewer should back off until he or she notices that the subject is willing to proceed.

According to Hogan (2002), communication spacing differs by gender. Men attempting to influence men should work within a 3- to 6-foot range. Women trying to influence women or men should generally work in the 1.5- to 4-foot range. The most complicated relationship exists when a man attempts to persuade a woman; the successful distance may be between 2 and 8 feet and depends on feedback from the woman.

Where we sit in relation to other people can aid or hinder communication. A comfortable and relaxed arrangement for two people at a table is to sit corner to corner (Hogan, 2002). This allows for maximum eye contact and other nonverbal signals, a good arrangement for cooperative work. In a side-by-side arrangement, body language is difficult to read and physical

FIGURE 1-2 The distance between two people indicates their comfort with each other and their willingness to communicate.

proximity is too close. This position works when both parties need to focus on the task at hand and not on each other. Unintentional conflict can develop between two people who sit across from each other.

Paralanguage

Paralanguage, or the vocal part of speech and its nuances, is communication that goes beyond the specific spoken words and may be the most effective method of establishing rapport (Sandoval & Adams, 2001). Language is only one of the ways that messages are sent; paralanguage includes the person's tone, pitch, and reflection, all of which express emotions. It includes pitch, amplitude, rate, and voice quality of speech. Paralanguage reminds us that people convey their feelings not only in *what* they say, but also in *how* they say it. Active emotions such as anger and fear are typically expressed by a fast rate of speech, loud volume, high pitch, and tone (Hogan, 2002). Passive emotions usually are relayed by a slower rate of speech, lower volume, and lower pitch. In the interview setting, according to Sandoval and Adams (2001), the interviewer should try to match the pace of the witness to allow for enhanced recall and communication.

▲ CONCLUSIONS

This chapter described communication as a process according to the scheme elaborated by Berlo. This model provides a framework for consideration of the interrogation and interviewing methods that will be described throughout this text. The interrogation and the interview were defined in a way so as to compare and contrast the goals and methods employed in these approaches to eliciting information. Although they do not constitute an exhaustive list of the personal qualities required for an interviewer, some qualities were given as a guideline to suggest the sort of person who should engage in the process. The different categories of persons who are to be interviewed and their shifting capabilities were stated. Because the establishment of rapport is such a critical aspect of interviewing, the nonverbal behavioral indicators that may be useful for rapport were covered in detail. The student can look forward to greater details on interviewing and interrogation methods in later chapters.

QUESTIONS FOR REVIEW

Short-Answer Questions

1. How would you define a successful interviewer using the approach described in this chapter?
2. What is Berlo's model of communication?
3. Describe the qualities that make a good interviewer.
4. What are definition and purpose of an interrogation?
5. Define interviewing, and describe how it differs from interrogation.
6. What categories of individuals may be interviewed?
7. What are some of the different types of nonverbal communication discussed in this chapter?

Fill-in Questions

1. _____ is the process of eliciting a confession from a suspect.
2. _____ is the process of gathering information.
3. The three categories of interviewees are _____, _____, and _____.
4. Successful interviewers are _____ and _____ in order to obtain as much pertinent information possible.
5. _____ is the communication that results when two people agree on the means and willingness to communicate.
6. _____ communication often conveys a larger share of social information, approximately 65 percent or more.
7. The study of our use of space and how various differences in that space make us feel more relaxed or more anxious is called _____.
8. The vocal part of speech and its nuances is referred to as _____.

Exercises

1. Kinesics is an approach that has only recently been adapted for criminal justice interviewing. Go online and discover additional ways in which kinesics is used.
2. Test the principles of proxemics. Find someone on campus in the library or at the lunchroom who is sitting alone. Sit at the personal-casual

distance (1.5 to 4 feet) next to this person. Observe what he or she does. Next, sit facing someone else who is alone, without talking to them. Observe what the person does. Was the reaction different when the individual was male or female? Report your findings in a written report to the instructor.

REFERENCES

Abrams, D. E., & Ramsey S. H. (2000). *Children and the law: Doctrine, policy, and practice*. St. Paul, MN: West Group.

Artwohl, A. (2002). Perceptual and memory distortion during officer-involved shootings. *FBI Law Enforcement Bulletin, 158*(10), 18–24.

Berlo, D. K. (1960). *The process of communication*. New York: Holt, Rinehart, and Winston.

Bram v. United States, 168 U.S. 532 (1897).

Davis, R., Smith, B. E., & Davies, H. (2001). No-drop prosecution and domestic violence. *Justice Research and Policy, 3*(2), 1–13.

Ekman, P. (2001). *Telling lies: Clues to deceit in the marketplace, politics, and marriage*. New York: W. W. Norton & Company.

Fisher, R. P., & Geiselman, R. E. (1992). *Memory-enhancing techniques for investigative interviewing: The cognitive interview*. Springfield, IL: Charles C Thomas.

Garner, B. (2004). *Black's law dictionary* (8th ed.). St. Paul, MN: West Publishing Co.

Geffner, R., & Rosenbaum, A. (2002). *Domestic violence offenders: Current interventions, research, and implications for policies and standards*. Binghamton, NY: Haworth Press.

Gosselin, D. K. (2005). *Heavy hands: An introduction to the crimes of family violence* (3rd ed.). Upper Saddle River, NJ: Prentice Hall.

Hogan, K. (2002). *The psychology of persuasion*. Gretna, LA: Pelican Publishing.

Kadushin, A. (1972). *The social work interview*. New York: Columbia University Press.

Kassin, S. M. (2005). True crimes, false confessions. *Scientific American Mind, 16*(2), 24–32.

Lanning, K. (2002). Criminal investigation of sexual victimization of children. In J. Myers, L. Berliner, J. Briere, C. T. Hendrix, C. Jenny, & T. Reid (Eds.), *The APSAC handbook on child maltreatment* (2nd ed., pp. 329–348). Thousand Oaks, CA: Sage Publications.

Leo, R. A. (1996). Inside the interrogation room. *Journal of Criminal Law and Criminology; 86*, 266–303. [Online.] Available: http://www.lexisnexis.com//universe.

Massachusetts Municipal Police Institute. (1981). *Police and procedure: Interviewing witnesses*. Unpublished.

Merriam-Webster Online Dictionary. (2005). [Online.] Available: http://www.m-w.com/.

Merriam-Webster's Collegiate Dictionary (11th ed.). (2004). Springfield, MA: Merriam-Webster.

Miranda v. Arizona, 384 U.S. 436 (1966).

People v. Anderson, 236 Cal. App. 2d 419 (1965).

People v. Baldi, 80 Misc. 2d 118 (1974).

Porter, S., Spencer, L., & Birt, A. (2003). Blinded by emotion: Effect of the emotionality of a scene on susceptibility to false memories. *Canadian Journal of Behavioural Science, 35*(3), 165–175.

Sandoval, V., & Adams, S. (2001). Subtle skills for building rapport using neuro-linguistic programming in the interview room. *FBI Law Enforcement Bulletin, 70*(8), 1–5.

U.S. Department of Justice. (1999). *Eyewitness evidence: A guide for law enforcement* (Report No. NCJ 178240). Washington, DC: U.S. Department of Justice.

Wainwright, G. (2003). *Teach yourself: Body language*. Chicago: McGraw-Hill.

Wells, G. L., Malpass, R. S., Lindsay, R. C. L., Fisher, R. P., Turtle, J. W., & Fulero, S. M. (2000). From the lab to the police station: A successful application of eyewitness research. *American Psychologist, 55*(6), 581.

Williamson, T. (2004). USA and UK responses to miscarriages of justice. In J. R. Adler (Ed.), *Forensic psychology: Concepts, debates and practice* (pp. 39–57). Portland, OR: Willan Publishing.

Wright, D. B., & Loftus, E. F. (1998). How misinformation alters memory. *Journal of Experimental Child Psychology, 71*(1), 155–164.

Wright, D. B., Boyd, C. E., & Tredoux, C. G. (2001). A field of study of own-race bias in South Africa and England. *Psychology, Public Policy, and Law, 7*(1), 119.

CHAPTER 2

The Interview Process

Key Terms

Postmodernism	Clarifying open-ended question
Contamination	Reinforcing behavior
Leading question	Closed-ended question
Initial open-ended question	Confrontational question

Chapter Objectives

After completing this chapter you should be able to:

- Describe the three phases of the interview process
- Change a closed-ended question into the open-ended form
- Explain the difference between open and closed questioning
- Compare and contrast the methods of approaching the interview
- List the ways in which witnesses might make an identification of a suspect
- Describe the characteristics of a social systems approach to interviewing
- Explain the problem of misinformation and contamination
- List ways of minimizing the contamination of witness statements and identification

Introduction

This chapter suggests that the interview process be placed within the context of a social systems approach. This is not a one-two-three method of interviewing. It is a way to conceptualize how interviewing success can be achieved through the approach taken by the interviewer. You should apply the following principles in each and every contact with what ever interviewing method you use.

The social systems approach suggests that interviewing is made up of parts that are intertwined with and dependent on each other and includes the perspectives of everyone involved. What does this mean for the potential interviewer? It means that the interview is a process that does not occur in a vacuum. The successful interviewer takes into account the perspectives of the interviewee in order to maximize the potential of the statement. This includes the viewpoint of the interviewer, the victim(s), the witnesses, and the suspect. To further understand this approach, the theory is broken down into three themes: caring, self-development, and postmodernism (Anderson, Carter, & Lowe, 1999). These three themes refer to the way that the interviewer conducts the interview process.

The first theme, caring, focuses on interviewing with cultural competence. Ours is a culturally diverse society that is bound together by a single system of government. Interviewing within this model requires active listening by the interviewer in order to gather information from ethnic minority persons in a nonthreatening manner (Leigh, 1998). It supports the development and expression throughout the statement from the perspective of ethnic minority members who are being asked to provide information. This means that during an interview the person who relates the event does so from his or her unique point of view. That view is expected to be colored by past experiences as well as physical and cognitive limitations. The model suggests that the individual who conducts the interview should make an attempt to go beyond simply hearing the person. The approach includes the perspective of the interviewee as part of the interview. To apply this model, the interviewer should be sensitive to meaning that goes beyond what is being stated. For example, is the interviewer experiencing hostility from the interviewee? Caring involves taking the time to ask if the subject has had negative experiences in a similar situation. Assure the person that you are there to listen and that you are interested in hearing what he or she has to say.

Self-development is the second theme. Self-development of the interviewer encourages him or her to be constantly vigilant and self-aware during the interview process. When conducting an interview it can be difficult to avoid the pitfalls of having a narrow focus. Time constraints, excessive caseloads, and a desire to bring the investigation to a close are only part of what contributes to this problem. The self-development model suggests the need for openness to redirection and change throughout the entire investigation. It requires a conscious decision to be open and responsive to the individuals who are being interviewed. If one remains flexible during an interview, then objective observations are more readily apparent. Watching for the behavior indicators of deceit should direct the interview process; sensitivity to proximity allows the interviewer to strategically place himself or herself. Cognizance of nonverbal behavior improves the ability of the interviewer to retain control. This means that the interviewer must listen, watch, and be aware of what is going on during the interview. Do not keep asking questions; spend some time listening to what is being said—both verbally and physically.

The third theme in this approach, postmodernism, may affect your interviewing success unless it is understood and embraced. **Postmodernism** emphasizes the role of power that will be inherent in any interview conducted by government officials or police officers. What does this mean to the interviewer? It means that when you conduct an interview the individual does not see you as a person, but as a representative of a powerful organization. Many persons are in awe of this power, some are fearful of it. As the interviewer, you will not be able to change the way an individual views the position that you hold. However, you are responsible for how the individual thinks about you as a member of that powerful organization. Make the effort to be respectful and considerate of the individuals who you interview.

PHASE I: INTERVIEW PREPARATION

Early research on the quality of interviews that had been videotaped found that interviewing skills were generally poor, and interviewers appeared to be inept, nervous, and ill at ease (Williamson, 2004). Studies concluded that police officers overrelied on confession evidence, which meant that victims were frequently not interviewed thoroughly, which resulted in the loss of potentially valuable evidence. Hence the movement for more experienced interviewers began in the early 1990s with a trend toward increased interviewing training for police officers.

One challenge is for the interviewer is to control the events as much as possible, taking the time needed to do a through job while at the same time feeling at ease and comfortable with the process. In a perfect world the following steps would be taken to prepare for an interview: conducting a case review and determining whether there is a prior record. The actual sequence of these steps is not as important as their completeness.

Case Review

The interviewer should not use the case review as a means of determining the outcome. This information should not influence or prejudice the interviewer. The purpose is to gather as much information as possible to compare and contrast when making a determination on the validity of the case and the creditability of the individuals involved. It identifies possible problems with the case and areas that need to be thoroughly explored during an interview. The interviewer must look critically at all case material and determine what part is made up of fact and what statements are investigator conclusions. Disregard the conclusions and scrutinize the facts. Things may not be what they seem!

The dispatcher or other person who takes the emergency call must collect complete and accurate information from the caller. This information becomes the case that will be reviewed by the responding officer(s). Asking open-ended questions followed by closed-ended questions, the 911 or emergency operator avoids suggestive or leading questions. The information is transmitted to the responding officer(s) and is updated when more information becomes available. In addition to informing the caller that the police are on their way, the dispatcher becomes the eyes and ears of the responding officer.

The first responder case review therefore takes place after the initial call for service, typically while an officer is in route to the incident. Just as important as any other case preparation, you need to review the specifics of the case such as the number of people involved, their gender, their approximate ages, and their physical descriptions. Find out if a weapon was displayed or used. Request a records check on both the suspect and the victim for outstanding warrants and prior offenses. Obtain as much information about the incident as possible, including the location of the alleged perpetrator if he or she is no longer at the scene. From this information determine the level of danger or injury of persons at the scene.

When the interview does not involve an emergency response, obtain and read any prior reports that were generated regarding the incident. If another police department or social service agency did a preliminary investigation to determine jurisdiction or whether there was a child in need of services, for example, contact that department for any notes that had been taken. At least speak with the other investigators involved and them to share information about what they did, whom they spoke with, and how and why they came to the conclusion that the case should be handled by another department. This information may be very revealing, but should not influence the interviewer regarding the case or the persons involved.

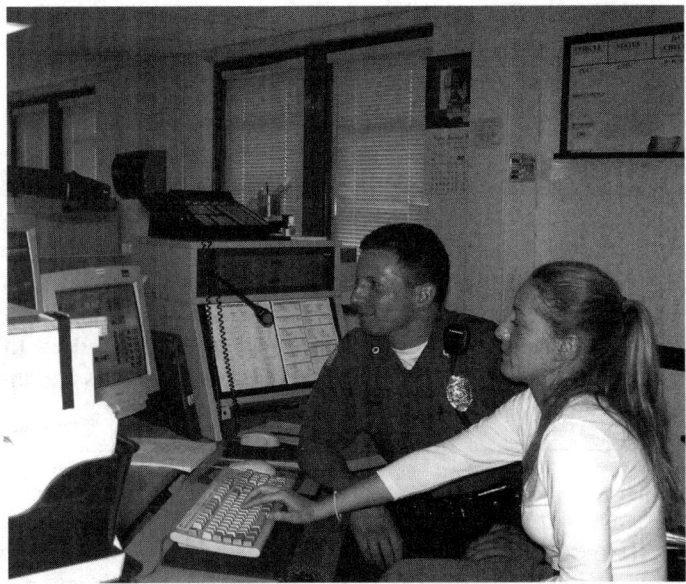

FIGURE 2-1 Conduct a background check on the suspect prior to the interview or interrogation.

Determine if there were other agencies that interviewed relative to the complaint. This would not be unusual if the victim is a child, an older person, or a person with a disability. Investigative powers are vested in specific state agencies for the protection of each of these special populations. Obtain copies of the statements taken. Determine the appropriate avenue to obtain these documents in the event the statements are not readily available or are withheld due to confidentiality. It may be necessary to seek the advice of your local district attorney and request that the documents be made available through court order. The investigator must assume that prior statements would jeopardize the case, particularly if they were taken through a nonforensic approach.

Thoroughly examine the evidence if any has been collected regarding the crime, as well as its status. Determine the relevance that the collected evidence has to the case, the person who collected it, and its initial location at the scene.

Determine Prior Criminal Record

When responding to the scene of a crime where the alleged perpetrator is known, have the dispatcher or desk officer run the name of the alleged offender to determine if a prior record or outstanding warrants exist. In cases of domestic crimes the name of the victim should also be checked for prior offenses. This is done because it is sometimes difficult to determine in cases of domestic violence who is the victim and who is the perpetrator. The existence of a prior record for a similar crime may be helpful in making that difficult decision at the scene.

> **BEEN THERE . . . DONE THAT! 2-1**
>
> A young girl of 10 reported to me that she had been raped by her mother's boyfriend. She described in detail the assault and how it had happened. In addition, she was able to describe the bedroom where it had occurred. The man was arrested and denied the allegations, stating that the girl was trying to break up the adults' relationship. The jury might have believed that, but in her statement I had asked her to describe the things that had been used during the rape and where they might be found. This is information that the girl could not have known. She described where he kept the Vaseline, the rags that were used after the rape, and the place that he hid the magazines he forced her to look at that portrayed child sex. On a search warrant I had confirmed these items and their locations. She was more credible than the adult, and he was convicted.

For interviews scheduled after the initial response the existence of a prior record will expose weaknesses of the individual as possible biases that exist. Use that information to determine the best approach and method of interviewing.

Viewing the Scene

Whenever the investigation involves a major crime, the scene should be viewed and personally documented by the interviewer. In cases where the officer was not dispatched to the scene, review any photographs and sketches that were made by the first responder. It is preferable to return as soon as possible after the incident.

Returning to the scene may also be useful after the interview with the victim. Obtain a court order if the scene is in home rather than a public place; remember that there is no exception to the Fourth Amendment requirement for a search warrant even with a murder scene! Obtain a *Mincey* warrant (*Mincy v. Arizona,* 1978) prior to reentering the scene of a murder. Use this visit to corroborate the statements of the victim with the actual scene. If the victim had never been to the scene prior to the incident or if the victim has no reason to have known the particulars about the scene yet is able to describe it to you, than that scene becomes evidence.

Misinformation

Preparing for an interview includes a conscious effort to reduce witness and victim misinformation. Misinformation refers to internal and external sources of information that produce variation in the answers given by an interviewee. Internal misinformation includes the cognitive and developmental factors of the individual being interviewed (Holliday, 2003) and the relative judgment of that person (Collins, 2004). The relative judgment process is evidenced when the person most like the suspect is selected from a lineup regardless of whether the actual perpetrator is among the group (U.S. Department of Justice, 1999). False eyewitness identification is the largest factor contributing to the conviction of individuals who were later exonerated through DNA testing (Wells & Olson, 2003).

Misinformation from external sources includes any information of an event that is acquired by the interviewee after the event occurred. One of the most common sources of eyewitness error occurs when witnesses' memories become contaminated by information that they acquired since they witnessed the event (Wright & Loftus, 1998). Interviewers using suggestive techniques or questions provide a common source of external change. External influences through suggestive questions from the interviewer are believed to have the strongest impact on victim and witness statements, particularly with vulnerable populations such as children (Finnila, et al., 2003).

When a person's memory of an event is changed due to the introduction of misinformation it is referred to as **contamination.** Contamination can occur at different stages during an investigation. The interviewer has the ability to influence the statements of victims, witnesses, and suspects through the questions that are asked and the way in which they are phrased. Contamination results if the interview process is obstructed or negatively influenced by the interviewer with the result of causing the person being interviewed to provide inaccurate information (Sandoval, 2004). Participants exposed to misinformation who experience contamination later misinform about some aspect of the crime. Cognitive interviewing techniques have been shown to reduce the reporting of internal and external misinformation (Finnila et al., 2003; Holliday, 2003; U.S. Department of Justice, 1999).

The effects of external misinformation can be reduced by decreasing suggestive influences during questioning. Through leading questions, and even the tone or pitch of voice that is used, the interviewer can distort memories. A **leading question** is a question that contains a possible answer. Leading questions or suggestions on what you want to hear are potential contaminants. An example of misinformation would be the following leading question posed by an interviewer: "Please describe the car, it was red wasn't it?" This leading question suggests that a "red" car was already identified and the interviewer is seeking confirmation. The witness that is contaminated by this information may then report that the car was red, thinking that he or she did in fact see a red car. Contamination can occur when lineups are not conducted properly, such as exposing a witness to a person or photo that is later used in a lineup (U.S. Department of Justice, 1999). Contamination to a witness memory can occur when investigators use the same photo in more than one lineup.

The effect of internal misinformation may be reduced through the use of age- and intellect-appropriate language and methods of questioning. Research indicates that older adults are more vulnerable to misinformation than young adults, reporting that they saw something that was actually only suggested to them (Memon, Gabbert, & Hope, 2004). Be particularly careful with persons aged 60 to 80 years when seeking a face identification; in one study, 87 percent of the senior citizens falsely identified a face from a lineup (Memon et al., 2004).

Detecting Contamination. We cannot know when someone else has contaminated a witness prior to our contact. This can impede our search for the truth. In order to minimize the effects of misinformation each person who conducts interviews, either at the scene or later, needs to be

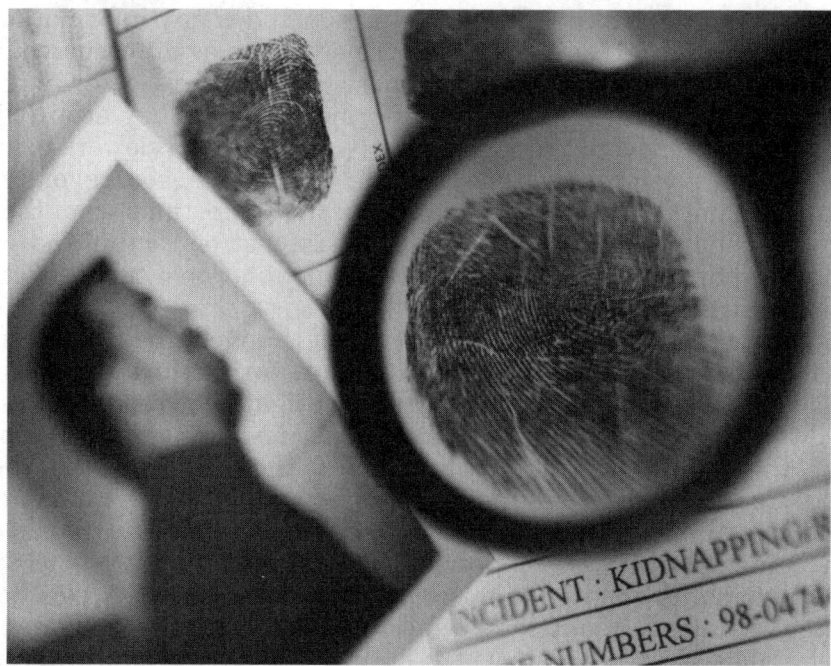

FIGURE 2-2 Avoid misinformation and be vigilant about the possibility of contaminated evidence. To guard against its effects, corroborate all eyewitness information with physical evidence.

aware of the possibility and avoid playing a part in this. Second, investigators must attempt to corroborate all information by interviewing additional subjects and collecting physical evidence.

PHASE II: ESTABLISHMENT OF THE PSYCHOLOGICAL CONTENT

The most common situation is the on-the-scene interview, although criminal justice and social service officials conduct interviews in a variety of settings. The investigator who responds to the scene must seek out and identify those who may have knowledge of the event and whose information may contribute to the investigation. Numerous individuals may have to be questioned to obtain the needed information.

Individuals who are thought to have information about the case are identified and interviewed. The difficulty for an investigator is that a variety of emotions could interfere with the fact-gathering process. Some of the people will be willing to give information but will be nervous or anxious. Others may not be willing to give information because they feel intimidated or threatened by questioning from government officials. Some people may not want to give out information due to bias, fear, or concern for retaliation. Make the person as emotionally comfortable as possible.

Whether the questioning takes place at the scene or elsewhere, all persons being interviewed should be separated from one another. Keeping the individuals apart will minimize the tainting of information due to overhearing another person give details of the offense and prevent individuals from comparing stories prior to being interviewed. Separating the individuals also provides the privacy that is needed to assure that an interested person or perpetrator will not hear the information that is being given.

When Should the Questioning Occur?

The officer should not hesitate to request that witnesses remain at the scene until they have been interviewed. Yet consideration must be given to the physical and emotional needs of the witnesses and the victim. If the person to be interviewed is emotionally upset, take the time to calm that excited person, even if it means a delay of the interview until the witness or victim has regained composure. Avoiding the temptation to rush an interview that is at the scene, the officers should create a favorable atmosphere for the witness to talk freely by selecting a quiet area in which to conduct the interview. Always maintain the privacy of the interviewee to the greatest possible degree. Individuals who are comfortable will likely provide more information. This principle applies to the timing of the interview as well as its setting.

The nature of the offense may dictate the timing of the interviews. When this is not the case, interviewers should retain control over the interviewing timing. Witnesses and victims should be interviewed as soon as possible after the incident under investigation has occurred in order to obtain an identification of the offender. Do this while their memory is still fresh. If the circumstances do not allow for an in-depth interview, such as when the identification is being sought for the perpetrator, do not hesitate to inform that witness that he or she may be contacted for a more thorough interview in the future.

Special populations such as children, older people, and persons with a disability should be interviewed at a time when they are likely to be most alert and responsive to questioning (Baladerian, 1998). Evening or early-morning interviews are not likely to result in quality information from special-population individuals. Prior to scheduling an interview find out from a caretaker when the best interview time for that individual would be.

Where Should the Questioning Occur?

At all times the needs and desires of the person being interviewed are paramount. Questioning must take place in an area that is free of distractions. Note whether someone appears nervous or reluctant to speak with you; the individual may prefer a more private place to talk. The place where the interview occurs is selected for one of the following three reasons:

- Convenience
- A desired effect
- Available resources

Convenience. For short interviews or to gather preliminary information it is often more convenient to interview people at the scene of the crime. The primary benefit to the at-the-scene interview is the freshness of the information. Another benefit is that victim and witness cooperation tends to be highest when the crisis is being resolved and the police officer represents protection. When potential witnesses are not identified at the scene there is the risk that they will not be located at a later date.

The downside of conducting a short interview at the scene is that people may be reluctant to speak freely to the police in the presence of others. Be aware of this reluctance to speak with the officer and offer another meeting place if the witness prefers. Look for an overall nervous appearance, glancing around, or extreme hesitation on the part of the person being questioned. In addition, an individual may be injured or otherwise unable to give a full and accurate accounting at the scene. Respect the needs of your victims and witnesses in order to obtain maximum truthful information.

A Desired Effect. Another factor in determining the place for an interview arises when there is a calculated determination for a desired effect on the interviewee. For intimidation or control, interviewing at the police station may provide the best choice. An office can be preset with the order of chairs and designed for minimizing distractions. Interviewing someone in their home, with consent, provides a false sense of control to the interviewee that can be used to the advantage of the interviewer. Typically an individual has his or her guard down when in a familiar and comfortable location.

Available Resources. Interview special populations where there are resources available to facilitate communication. The Americans with Disabilities Act (U.S. Department of Justice, 2003) requires accommodations be made for interviewing victims with a disability. Special rooms may be designed for interviewing children and the elderly. Videotaping of interviews is most appropriately conducted in areas designed for this purpose. Documenting the interview through audiotaping can free the interviewer to concentrate on the phrasing of questions.

When in the Police Station or an Office

The greatest control over the environment is achieved when the interview takes place in a designated room of the police station or in an office. The location should be quiet and free of distractions, preferably within a 10 foot by 12 foot room (Yeschke, 2003). No phones, beepers, clocks, or other electronic devices should be in the room unless they are specifically used for the interview purpose. There should not be any windows and limited wall hangings, if any.

Yeschke (2003) suggested that the chair of the interviewer should be at a 45-degree angle to the interviewee to avoid presenting a threat at the beginning of the interview. This practical use of proxemics recognizes the tension that is inherent when the position is changed to face-to-face interrogation seating. The moderate location straddles the social space and personal space where the participants are within 4 feet of each other. This distance allows for questioning that respects personal territory without creating undue stress on the interviewee. Another advantage to this placement is the ease with which the interviewer can lean forward purposefully in order to cause anxiety in the persuasive interview approach. If there is a third person in the interviewing room he or she

FIGURE 2-3 Use proxemics in this interview position with the chairs placed at a 45° angle. The interviewer can lean forward or move his or her chair to face the interviewee to change the level of comfort.

will be sitting out of the direct sight of the person being interviewed. If the placement from Figure 2-3 were used, the third person would sit to the left of the table, which is behind the interviewee.

PHASE III: THE QUESTIONING

Plan to conduct an in-depth interview with the victim as soon as he or she is emotionally and physically able to do so. With the passing of time an individual may become confused and statements may lose detail. Avoid asking more than one question at a time, giving the person ample opportunity to provide an answer.

The trained interviewer knows that environmental and personal factors can influence what people hear and see. The lack of sleep, illness, weather, and light conditions are all potential distorters. During an interview attempt to determine if any extreme influences are involved. Consider the location and distance from the event when questioning witnesses. The ability to accurately observe and interpret things is also affected by pain, hunger, and distress. Emotions such as fear, anger, or worry impair perception. On the other hand, special interests may enable a witness to provide details that seem remarkable, such as a young boy who is interested in cars. What people see can be influenced by smells and sounds. Weave into questioning the five senses of smell, taste, and touch in addition to sight and hearing.

Typically an interview should be one-on-one. If two interviewers are in the room one should be the obvious lead and do most of the talking. The second investigator should help by taking notes and assessing the witness's verbal and nonverbal behavior (Sandoval, 2004). When a second interviewer is included it is preferable for that person to stay off to the side and out of the vision of the person being interviewed so as not to cause a distraction. At the end of the questioning the lead can be given to the second interviewer to fill in any gaps that were noted.

The Order of Interviews

The first officer at a scene should attempt to verify the identity of the suspect if he or she is known, as well as his or her location if the suspect is not at the scene. All witnesses should be separated and asked not to discuss the details of the incident with others. The area should be canvassed to identify additional witnesses for questioning.

The type of crime and the availability of personnel to assist with the investigation may dictate the order of the interviews. If there is a victim, he or she should be interviewed by the first responder to obtain an identification of the suspect and the nature of any injuries. The suspect may be interviewed at the scene for determining culpability prior to making an arrest. When no person is placed in danger and an arrest is not mandated it may be helpful to conduct a preliminary interview of the suspect. Generally the witnesses are questioned second.

Types of Questions

No specific information or opinion about the case should be offered prior to the taking of statements. An open-ended question is a question asked in a way that encourages a narrative by giving direction to the interviewee because it does not limit the answer; it is broad and nonspecific. An open-ended question is asked in order to get as much information as possible about the person or the event. Open-ended questions are used initially and as clarifiers throughout the interview whenever narrative statements are expected. Closed-ended questions limit the information that the person might give, augment information already received, and fill a specific need of the interviewer. A good balanced interview contains both question types used purposefully. Avoid using emotional or suggestive words. Do not rapid-fire questions at a person; give the person time to answer completely.

Open-Ended Questions. An open-ended question is one that does not limit or direct the answer; therefore the phrasing of each open-ended question is important. An **initial open-ended question** seeks a full-undirected narrative response. A **clarifying open-ended question** seeks to complete or expand on the information already given. In order to illicit a full response, don't interrupt the account by asking another question. Not interrupting indicates to the interviewee that you are willing to listen to his or her perspective, and that you respect what he or she has have to say. Interrupting the initial narrative gives an impression that what the subject has to say is of little importance. The way in which the question is phrased can increase or decrease the willingness of the person to respond. Good initial open-ended questions include the following:

- Please tell me what happened to you.
- Would you tell me everything that you know about...
- Please tell me everything that you did this past Saturday.

Initial open-ended questions avoid asking something that involves an imaginative answer or conclusion. Examples of bad initial open-ended questions include the following:

- Why did he do that to you?
- So what did you do to get her so angry?
- What was your involvement in the Saturday incident?

Encourage the person to continue their narrative through forced silence and reinforcing behaviors. A **reinforcing behavior** does not indicate approval or disapproval of what is being said. The behavior to encourage narratives can be verbal or nonverbal. Investigators must be aware that both verbal and nonverbal behavior will influence the statement being taken. Care must be taken to appear objective and nonjudgmental at all times. Good reinforcing narrative behaviors include the following:

- Saying "okay" in a matter-of-fact manner.
- Saying, "Please continue."
- Saying, "I'm listening."

Negative reinforcing behaviors during an initial narrative include the following:

- Wincing (in response to a painful recollection of the victim).
- Knitting of the brow or pursing of one's lips (as if angry).
- Saying, "You have to be kidding" (as in disbelief).

The nondirected quality of open-ended questions allows the interviewee to say whatever he or she wants without having preconceived expectations of what the interviewer wants to hear, so the questions are necessarily nonleading. Good questions include the following:

- Describe your assailant, please.
- What did the car look like?
- Tell me what you saw (heard, felt, did, etc.).

Bad open-ended questions that limit the answer and suggest an expected response include the following:

- Why don't you start off by telling me what your husband did to you?
- Describe that red car that was used during the incident.
- Did it hurt when he did that to you?

When the person is being truthful the initial open-ended narrative should contain segments that are relatively equal in importance. These segments include what happened prior to the event, the event itself, and what the person did after the event.

BEEN THERE... DONE THAT! 2-2

During an interview with a rape victim she appeared to be withholding information. Requests for details of the assault were met with obvious resistance. At first I thought she was lying about having been raped. It then became apparent that she was hesitating because the details included things that were extremely difficult for her to talk about. The assailant had done things to her that she did not want to admit had happened. The interview was made easier after I told her why it was necessary for me to know everything, including the things that were embarrassing. She went on to give details, although it was not easy for her to do so. Keep in mind that hesitation may be due to embarrassment or shame.

It may be helpful for the interviewer to encourage a narrative response at some additional point during the questioning or at the end. It can be used to explain events in greater detail, to develop information about subjective feelings, or to wrap things up. Examples of the clarifying open-ended question include the following:

- What did you do?
- What was your first reaction?
- Has anything like this ever happened to you before?
- Is there anything else you think I should know (or that you want to tell me)?

Closed-Ended Questions. A **closed-ended question** requires a yes or no or otherwise brief response. They are the most common type of question and are useful for verifying information, filling in gaps of the interview, and obtaining specific factual information. Examples of good closed-ended questions include the following:

- What time did you go to bed on Saturday?
- Do you know the name of the person who did this to you?
- What is your age?

Care must be taken not to carelessly lead the witness through suggestive closed-ended questions. For example:

- Was the car a blue Ford?
- Did you go to bed at 10 PM on Saturday?
- Did your father do this to you?

Follow-up Questions. When the narrative is complete, asking follow-up questions probes deeper into the issues presented. Follow-up questions can be of either the open or closed type, and seek to elaborate or to clarify what has already been said. Examples of follow-up questions include the following:

- You said that you "had sex"; please tell me what that means and explain in detail what happened.
- Where exactly did he touch you?
- What time had you gone to bed that night?

Direct or Forced-Choice Questions. These closed-ended questions are reserved for when you suspect that the person being interviewed knows more than he or she is telling you. They are asked in a nonaccusatory tone of voice and without emotion. The purpose for using a direct or forced-choice question is to pin someone down for later impeachment.

- After you tripped and dropped the baby, was he still breathing?
- What did you trip on?
- Was your boyfriend angry when the baby would not stop crying that night?

Control Questions. The person who asks the questions is in control of the interview. When you sense that you have lost that control, bring it back with a statement that requires the attention of the person being interviewed. The control question firmly establishes that the interview is not over. Examples of questions used to take back control are as follows:

- I understand that you are upset about this. Please take a deep breath and prepare yourself to answer these questions.
- These questions are difficult, I understand, but I am unable to help you without the details of what happened.
- We are almost finished; there are a few things that I am not clear on that need to be answered before we are done.

Leading Questions. Use leading questions when you want to guide the interviewee through a particular line of reasoning in a persuasive interview. By their nature, leading questions suggest an answer and should be avoided except for intentional use. These tend to distort the memory or perception of the person being questioned, and the responses seldom reflect the thoughts of the interviewee. The following are examples:

- According to your neighbor ...
- As you know ...
- Your wife said ...

Confrontational Questions. A **confrontational question** is a question that is accusatory, typically involving a show of anger or disgust. When confrontational questions are introduced into the interview you can no longer go back to being friendly and helpful. Be sure that it is time to leave the relationship behind before bridging the interview with the interrogation. The decision to nudge toward an interrogation may begin with this manner of questioning. It is typically firm, but not necessarily loud. For example:

- John, I have interviewed your son—he tells me that you were the one who touched him. Can you tell me why you did that to him?
- You are real good, Pete; if I didn't know better I would think these signatures were done by someone else.
- So why did you pick her for your victim?

Determining an Approach

Behavior and personalities can affect your ability to obtain information during an interview. Prior to determining who will conduct the interview, each witness or suspect should be evaluated. Consider the personality who may influence what she or he sees, what might be remembered, and obvious likes or dislikes. Do not attempt the interview if there is obvious distain toward the potential interviewer and another other option is available.

Oblique Approach. This approach is suited for the interview in which the interviewee will tell his or her story without prompting. As an avid listener, ask questions only to clarify points, and avoid asking leading questions.

> ### BEEN THERE . . . DONE THAT! 2-3
>
> Armed with an arrest warrant, my male partner and I picked up a man as he came out of work. He snarled at me in a way that a man under arrest should not be doing, as if he thought he would try to intimidate me. So I took the upper hand and passed him on to my partner. On the way to the station I said two words to the suspect: YOU STINK! It hurt his pride, and he quickly started to explain that he was a working man and had just gotten out without having the chance to shower. Having gotten a reaction, I said it again: YOU STINK! Again he went on that he was not a bad man, just dirty. We arrived at the station and the two men went into the interrogation room. My partner (quite amused at knowing he was the good guy—again) said, "She's a real bitch, ha?" In their common alliance, rapport had been established. The arrestee said he would answer any questions . . . as long as I was not in the room. Mission accomplished—a full confession resulted. Never underestimate the value of a good partner!

Regardless of the setting that is chosen for the interview, at the scene or at a designated place, the voluntariness of the statement is of great importance. If the person is willing to give information AND the person is not in custody, then *Miranda* warnings are not required.

Formal Approach. The formal interview is conducted in a controlled environment such as a police station or detective office. This is best used to manage an individual who appears overly confident or condescending toward the interviewer. As a home court advantage, the formal setting is usually intimidating enough to free the interviewer to think about more important considerations.

Informal Approach. Taking the informal route takes a lot of confidence! It works well for low-key interrogations that are conducted in the home of the perpetrator. It requires the willingness to sit and have conversation and the ability to persuade the person to invite you in. This is nonadversarial, and no custody occurs with this approach. By asking questions and encouraging the suspect to talk, you become a gatherer of incriminating evidence that may be used to apply for an arrest warrant.

▲ CONCLUSIONS

This chapter brought you through the process of interviewing. The three phases represent a progression rather methods for being a successful interviewer. Each phase should be given equal weight toward the goal of obtaining the truth from witnesses and victims. It should be noted that interviewing is not just about talking. Of equal importance is listening. The process involves knowledge and planning. What is said becomes just as important as how and why it is said. Saying the wrong thing can cause contamination, and failure to ask the right questions can leave the interviewer empty handed. The bottom line is that interviewing is a learned skill.

QUESTIONS FOR REVIEW

Short-Answer Questions

1. What is the social systems approach to interviewing and what themes are found in modern social systems theory?
2. Phase I of the interview process entails preparation for the interview. What happens during the case review step and what is its purpose?
3. What information should the first responder collect on arriving at the scene of a crime?
4. What is contamination and when can it occur?
5. When should the interview take place and where should questioning occur?
6. What is the difference between open-ended and closed-ended questions?
7. Briefly explain the other types of questions used in an interview.
8. Preparing for an interview takes a lot of work. There are many variables to consider, and the interview approach is one of them. Briefly describe each approach and when it is most useful.

Fill-in Questions

1. The approach to interviewing used in this chapter focuses on caring, self-development, and _____, which emphasizes the role of power that is inherent in any interview.
2. The focus of Phase I is _____.
3. The purpose of _____ is to gather as much information possible to determine the validity of the case.
4. _____ occurs when witnesses or victims give misinformation either through leading questions, when lineups are not conducted properly, or when memories are distorted.
5. Short interviews done at the scene of the crime are usually done out of _____.
6. When interviewers are seeking a full narrative response they will ask _____ questions.
7. _____ are used to verify information.
8. When _____ are introduced into the interview the interviewer can no longer go back to being friendly or helpful.
9. The best approach toward interviewees who are willing to talk is the _____.
10. _____ is the most desirable physical arrangement between the interviewer and the interviewee.

Exercises

1. Find at least one article in the library containing an interview; in particular, news articles on controversial issues or political candidates often contain interviews. From the written interviews, identify the type of questioning mostly used, open-ended or closed-ended. Evaluate

the article and the quality of responses as well as the type of question that elicited the response. Write a short paper citing the source used and the evaluation.

2. View the PowerPoint presentation with audio interviews from *Eyewitness Evidence: A Trainer's Manual for Law Enforcement*. View only Part 1: Interviewing Procedures—Initial Response to the Crime. During the PowerPoint presentation, closed-ended questions are provided. Convert these to open-ended questions in writing.

REFERENCES

Anderson, R. E., Carter, I., & Lowe, G. R. (1999). *Human behavior in the social environment: A social systems approach* (5th ed.). New York: Aldine De Gruyter.

Baladerian, N. J. (1998). *Interviewing skills to use with abuse victims who have developmental disabilities*. Washington, DC: National Center on Elder Abuse.

Collins, W. (2004). Looks can be deceiving: Safeguards for eyewitness identification. [Online.] Available: http://www.wisbar.org/AM/Template.cfm?Section=Wisconsin_Lawyer&TEMPLATE=/CM/ContentDisplay.cfm&CONTENTID=47654.

Finnila, K., Mahlberg, N., Santtila, P., Sandnabba, K., & Niemi, P. (2003). Validity of a test of children's suggestibility for predicting responses to two interview situations differing in their degree of suggestiveness. *Journal of Experimental Child Psychology, 85*(1), 32–50.

Holliday, R. (2003). Reducing misinformation effects in children with cognitive interviews: Dissociating recollection and familiarity. *Child Development, 74*(3), 728–752.

Leigh, J. (1998). *Communicating for cultural competence*. Prospect Heights, IL: Waveland Press.

Memon, A., Gabbert, F., & Hope, L. (2004). The ageing eyewitness. In J. R. Adler (Ed.), *Forensic psychology: Concepts, debates and practice* (pp. 96–112). Devon, UK: Willan Publishing.

Mincey v. Arizona, 437 U.S. 385 (1978).

Sandoval, V. (2004). Strategies to avoid interview contamination. *Crime & Justice International, 20*(79), 29–37.

U. S. Department of Justice. (1999). *Eyewitness evidence: A guide for law enforcement* (Report No. NCJ 178240). Washington, DC: U.S. Department of Justice.

U.S. Department of Justice. (2003). *Enforcing the ADA: A status report from the Department of Justice* (Report No. 1). Washington, DC: U.S. Department of Justice.

Wells, G., & Olson, E. (2003). Eyewitness testimony. *Annual Review of Psychology, 54*(277), 277–295.

Williamson, T. (2004). USA and UK responses to miscarriages of justice. In J. R. Adler (Ed.), *Forensic psychology: Concepts, debates and practices* (pp. 36–57). Devon, UK: Willan Publishing.

Wright, D. B., & Loftus, E. F. (1998). How misinformation alters memory. *Journal of Experimental Child Psychology, 71*(1), 155–164.

Yeschke, C. (2003). *The art of investigative interviewing* (2nd ed.). Boston: Butterworth-Heinemann.

CHAPTER 3
Purposeful Interviewing and Processes

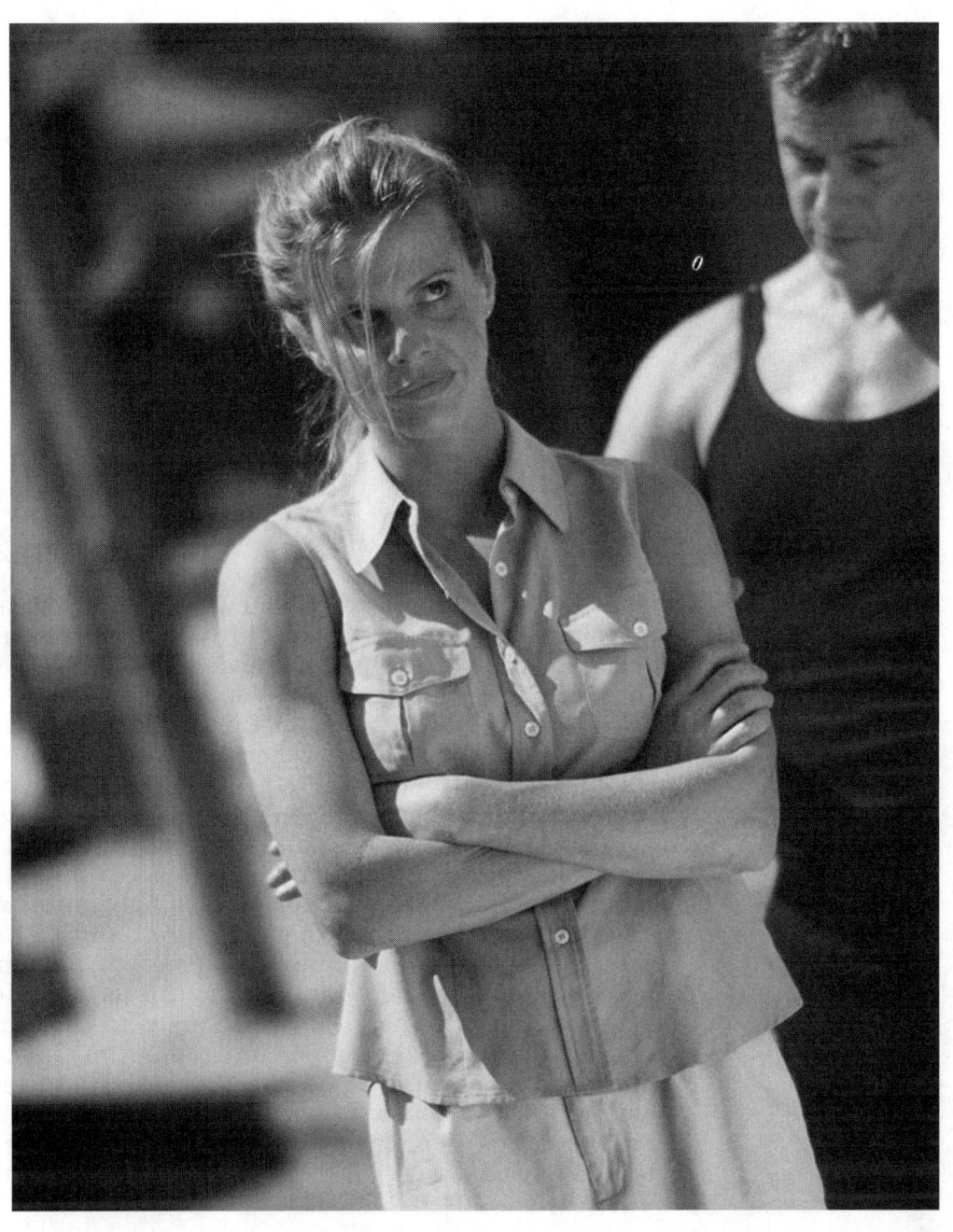

KEY TERMS

Comprehensive questioning	Testamentary evidence
Morphostasis	Incendiary
Purposeful interviewing	Hate crime
Active listening	Primary aggressor

CHAPTER OBJECTIVES

After completing this chapter you should be able to:

- Explain *morphostasis*
- Explain the primary objectives of purposeful *interviewing*
- Define the term *hate crime* along with the suggested interviewing approach
- Compare and contrast the terms *technique* and *method*
- List the ways in which comprehensive questioning is useful for interviewing
- Describe the characteristics of active listening
- Explain the statement analysis approach
- List ways of developing rapport

INTRODUCTION

This section discusses additional aspects of the broad application of social systems theory to the interviewing process. Do not think of social systems theory as an interviewing method. You will not see it woven throughout the chapter because it stands on its own. This is a broad way to think about interviewing, not a method on conducting an interview. Social systems theory has three general characteristics that assist in framing the purposeful interview. First, it involves a comprehensive approach to interviewing. What this means to the potential interviewer is that there is a bigger picture that looms over each statement and personal contact that takes place. Tying together the pieces presents a greater potential for description and integration of seemingly unrelated events into a single situation. An example is the concept of **comprehensive questioning.** Comprehensive questioning means getting as much information as possible. Some people would refer to this as "thinking outside of the box." At a car stop with more than one person in the vehicle, does one of them appear upset? Have that person step out of the car away from earshot and ask, "Are you ok?" At the domestic disturbance, speak with the children in the house. When interrogating a sexual offender, ask, "Who did this to you?" For the astute interviewer, looking at the big picture and tying the pieces together brings thoroughness to the process of gathering information.

The concept of continuation is another aspect of social systems theory. This relates to the belief that human behavior is multifaceted yet somewhat predictable. Continuation is also called morphostasis. **Morphostasis** is the understanding that the continuation of a system or family relationship may take priority due to the fear of the anticipated consequences of change. When a family is in danger of being destroyed or radically changed, the individuals may pool their energies. What this means to the potential interviewer is that family members will most likely pull together and forget past differences when faced with something that threatens them. It is a natural response to a perceived threat from the outside. You as the interviewer should expect that family members will work to protect each other in negative situations. Don't expect family members to be totally candid when supplying information about a crime that may have been committed by one of their own. The concept also applies in domestic violence situations in which the victim is unwilling to break apart the family unit. Saying to a domestic violence victim, "When you going to leave this creep?," is counterproductive. A different approach is to say, "If you are going to stay in this relationship, perhaps you should think of safety planning in the event things get out of hand." The first statement creates an enemy. The second recognizes that you don't understand the reasons for staying, but that you are there to help when the victim *is* ready to leave.

A common theoretical language is also suggested by social systems theory. For the interviewer this means that criminal justice professionals will improve their ability to communicate by borrowing from other disciplines in order to understand the concepts of human behavior. Common language provides the interviewer with *techniques,* which are the devices whose application enables us to accomplish our purposes and carry out our professional responsibilities. When you read this book, note the many techniques that are included. Many of the methods for conducting interviews borrow ideas from psychology and sociology. These ideas provide insight into human behavior and how you can use that information to become successful interviewers. Don't shy from theory—it gives you more than you may have thought!

CHARACTERISTICS OF PURPOSEFUL INTERVIEWING

Purposeful interviewing refers to the realization that statements are sought for specific reasons (Gosselin, 2002). Purposeful interviewing is not a method, but is a broad approach to the process. Active listening and rapport development are useful in developing a technique for accomplishing the interview goal, regardless of the situation.

Active Listening

Active listening is a skill that makes evident to the person being interviewed that you are attentive to what is being said. It requires the interviewer to mentally relax and draw on his or her self-esteem and confidence. Express a willingness to commiserate and listen by exhibiting patience. It is important not only to listen to what is said, but also to know how it is said. Emotional outbursts and inflections of the voice may give a clue to sensitive areas of the interview. Sudden silence, uncertainty or confusion, or the shifting of conversation to an unrelated subject may indicate that information is being withheld. Nervous bodily reaction or facial reactions may signal that a sensitive area has been reached.

Understand the subject's frame of reference in order to understand what is being told. Listen to the tone, voice inflection, and level of excitement from the subject during the interview. Watch for body language and facial expressions to see if they match what is being said.

The interviewer must remember what he or she hears. Notes should be taken in a manner that does not interrupt the interviewing process. Some witnesses are reluctant to talk if they notice that the officer is taking down every word they say. Brief notes can be made without deterring or distracting witnesses. In some situations a room that has recording equipment can be set up in advance of the interview. Alternatively, a microphone can transmit information to another room where a note taker is making a full report.

Active listening may be demonstrated verbally and through nonverbal attentiveness. Examples of ways to show that you are actively listening include the following:

- **Body language**—nod your head, look interested, smile, vary your eye contact, lean slightly forward
- **Body posture**—face squarely or at a 45-degree angle, lean forward, shift as the subject does, be careful not to shift to show displeasure
- Concentrate and listen carefully
- **Detachment**—be cool and calm without showing emotion
- Do not roll your eyes in response to a statement
- **Gestures**—keep arms open and palms extended
- **Patience**—do not rush the interviewee
- **Positive silence**—silence can indicate acceptance or can be used to signal your control

Rapport Development

Chapter 1 introduced the concept of rapport. Rapport should be considered the first step in any interview. Although it is difficult to describe, it is basically a two-way communication. The concept represents a working relationship between the interviewer and the subject being interviewed. Whatever the individual may be feeling, the interviewer is not responsible for what happened to him or her, but is responsible for interviewer's own reaction. The victim may be feeling pain or confusion, and may directed anger at the interviewer. When interviewing an angry person talk slowly and more softly than normal. Anger is a sign of weakness that indicates a lack of self-control. Don't ever become visibly angry at a victim. Once it has occurred, the ability to negotiate rapport is gone.

If the interviewee is acting superior to the interviewer, maintain an emotional detachment. The successful interviewer should not take the

> **BEEN THERE... DONE THAT! 3-1**
>
> For some reason we tend to think of victims as being nice people and offenders as monsters. When the pattern does not fit it makes it difficult to access the credibility of the victims. The key is active listening—get past the anger and hear what happened. During an interview a woman was yelling at the police and shouting obscenities, and was extremely obnoxious. When I sat her down in a quiet place she explained to me how she had been beaten and raped by two men who had left her without clothes to die in the woods. She had been fortunate to find her way out for help, but thought that the police would not do anything for her because she was a prostitute. After a while she calmed down and gave descriptions of her assailants and recounted that what had happened to her had happened to others on the street. As it turned out I was able to identify five women who had been severely beaten by these two men. Both had extensive violent felony records. They selected prostitutes as their victims because they thought that the women could be intimidated into keeping quiet. The assaults by these men had nothing to do with sex for pay; they were vicious attacks because the perpetrators enjoyed beating and torturing women. They were both arrested, found guilty, and sent back to prison where they belonged.

attitude of the interviewee personally or feel offended. Never apologize for asking questions. Be careful about changing the behavior to one of arrogance. To establish a cooperative relationship, the interviewer should:

1. Display a sincere interest
2. Be patient and tactful
3. Be respectful
4. Control personal feelings
5. Provide reassurance
6. Encourage an untalkative witness by asking appropriate questions

OBJECTIVES OF PURPOSEFUL INTERVIEWING

In the previous chapter, preparation was the first phase in the process of interviewing. Central to preparing for the interview is recognizing why police officers conduct interviews. The primary objectives are as follows (Gosselin, 2002):

- To examine the nature of the offense
- To determine if a crime was actually committed
- For the purpose of identifying the perpetrator

The Nature of the Offense

Earlier it was stated that individuals are all different, yet there are some identifiable similarities. That concept comes into play when generalizing about an approach to interviewing based on the nature of the offense.

Remain calm and tactful with contradicting or antagonistic witnesses. Remember that witnesses who are angry, frightened, or emotionally upset usually perceive only a fraction of what they might observe under normal circumstances. Emotional factors can cause a witness to lie or to become uncooperative or forgetful. Purposeful interviewing means modifying an approach to meet the unique challenges of the crime, resulting in a slightly different interviewing approach in order to elicit complete and truthful information.

Being purposeful in your interviewing also requires attention to the nonverbal communication that tell us something about the validity of the message, its urgency, and whether it is being made humorously, seriously, or sarcastically (Kadushin & Kadushin, 1997). Nonverbal behaviors may communicate what interviewees cannot bring themselves to state openly. Feelings and attitudes of which interviewees are only vaguely aware may be clear to the observant interviewer.

Purposeful interviewing also means that the nature of offense will dictate different questioning approaches. The following examples illustrate how the nature of the crime dictates the questioning.

Arson. It is desirable to interview as many witnesses as possible at the fire scene (Federal Emergency Management Agency, 1988) because some witnesses may be reluctant to talk later, the information is fresher, and suspects have less opportunity to plan possible alibis. Moving through the crowd, the investigators may identify a suspect to interview based on the strong odor of smoke. Whom do you interview? Key interviewing witnesses include firefighters on the scene, property owners, spectators at the fire, victims, neighbors, and business associates. Firefighters are first on the scene and need to be interviewed before others. They can tell what they saw and where the damage on the building was located. Second, interview the patrol officers. Third to be interviewed are the owners/occupants and the witnesses. It is not necessary to establish motive for arson prosecution . . . but juries like to hear it! Questions to answer include the following:

- Who will profit?
- Is this for spite/revenge?
- Is it juvenile fire setting?

Hate Crimes. Showing concern for the victim's safety, note and document all injuries. Only one person should conduct the interview, and any other involved person should remain unobtrusive during the questioning (McLaughlin & Walley, 2001). Be careful not to minimize the crime; display genuine concern for the victim's feelings. Note that it would be difficult for someone not targeted in this way to fully understand the emotional impact it has on the individual. There may be a heightened distrust on the part of the victim toward anyone who resembles the attacker; this obstacle to interviewing is import to anticipate and overcome. Document the financial damages if any and photograph both the victim and the scene. Record spontaneous utterances made by the victim.

FIGURE 3-1 Active listening is the most important interviewing skill you can learn!

Use an open-ended initial question format with follow-up questions. Using closed questions, ask for exact wording of what the suspect said before, during, and after the incident and how often. Ask the victim to describe the suspect with as much detail as possible, including tattoos or clothing.

It is the task of the resourceful police officer to overcome witness reluctance to being involved. Ethnic and racial minorities will likely need to be persuaded to cooperate. Examples of helpful statements include the following:

- It is important to stop this individual (these individuals) from doing this to anyone else in your community.
- There is nothing to stop this from happening to your friends and family; we need your help.
- I know this is difficult for you, but there is something that can done about this.

Partner Violence. There are often strong emotional ties between the victim and the offender in these cases. The victim may even be financially dependent on the assailant. In some cases the perpetrator faces loss of employment if convicted of domestic violence. A victim may therefore be unwilling or unable to provide information that will be used against the partner; hence purposeful interviewing aims to verify and give credibility to the victim without expecting a high level of cooperation. Make sure you get all of the available evidence and victim statements regarding the violence at the scene; do not count on victim cooperation at a later date. Questions that will help to establish the seriousness include the following:

- How often has this happened?
- Have you ever been hospitalized due to these attacks?
- Has he (she) ever threatened to kill you?

Sexual Assault. The initial questioning of the acquaintance sexual assault victim should be limited to issues concerning injury assessment, identification and location of the alleged perpetrator, and collection of physical evidence. In other words, don't ask for information that you don't need to know. It is difficult to discuss with a stranger any sexual experience, even more so when it was an unpleasant experience. Typically the victim will give only partial information when he or she is faced with this uncomfortable situation; in addition, the incompleteness of the statement may be used later to impeach the victim's credibility. The responding officer should be more concerned with reassuring the victim of his or her immediate safety. According to research, victims may be confused and upset after a sexual assault, which requires police reassurance of their immediate safety (National Center for Women and Policing [NCWP], 2001). Statements from the responding officer that would be appropriate include the following:

- You are safe now.
- I don't need to ask a lot of questions right now, but I have to know if there was penetration involved.
- I know that this is a lot to ask, but please do not smoke or have anything to drink until you have been examined by the doctor. (Briefly explain the forensic procedure that will follow.)

Do not ask leading or accusatory questions of the victim or witnesses:

- Did he have a gun?
- Why didn't you fight him off?
- Did you let him do this?

A detailed statement would likely follow after the victim is examined at a medical facility, when appropriate. If the victim directs anger at the police interviewer, it is important to understand that this is misdirected. Patience and compassion are needed to establish the necessary rapport for a more detailed interview at the appropriate time. The hospital examination room should be avoided as a place for that full interview. There are conflicting thoughts on allowing a support person in the room with the victim during the interview (NCWP, 2001). This decision may ultimately depend on the gender of the interviewer and their ability to persuade the victim to give a statement in private. Things that would be helpful to say to express empathy with the victim during the interview include the following:

- How are you feeling?
- Would you feel more comfortable if I called you by your last name?
- Do you have any questions?

As with any interview, establishing rapport is an important first step in obtaining a complete statement. When interviewing the acquaintance sexual assault victim there are comments that would impede efforts to build rapport through a lack of respect for the victim. Examples include the following:

- **DO NOT ASK**—Will you take a polygraph?
- **DO NOT STATE**—It could have been worse.
- **DO NOT COMMENT**—Why were you out so late?

> **BEEN THERE ... DONE THAT! 3-2**
>
> An older gentleman came in with the complaint of his car having been stolen. With great difficulty he explained that he was a professor at a prestigious university with a lot to lose by making the complaint. As it turns out he was being blackmailed by a male prostitute who he had picked up in the city a few nights before. Although he had been a homosexual for years, he was in a marriage of convenience. His reputation in the community was at stake, but he could not bring himself to pay off the demand in order to get his vehicle returned. Without the right environment this information would not have been forthcoming. Time would have been wasted and likely the theft would not have been solved. A successful "sting" resulted in the arrest and prosecution of the blackmailer.

Open-ended questions should be asked to allow for the victim to describe the assault in her or his own words. Clarifying questions to establish specific facts should be asked after the victim has completed the narrative. The interviewer should be specifically aware of victim's body language that indicates embarrassment or discomfort. Reassuring the victim that he or she is doing a good job at explaining as well as acknowledging that the questions are embarrassing will help to normalize the conversation.

White Collar Crimes. The negative treatment that victims of white collar crime receive when they seek help leaves them feeling guilty and ashamed (Burnley et al., 1996). Interviewers must overcome the victim's self-blame for having been duped by the con; assure the victim that the perpetrator is experienced at gaining confidence from individuals. Emphasis needs to be on the psychological needs of these victims in order to gain full cooperation and overcome their unwillingness to admit to their full losses. These victims experience anger and fear, which become emotional barriers to communication that need to be eliminated (Burnley et al., 1996). Allow the victim to vent his or her feelings and be willing to validate them with statements like the following:

- Are you okay?
- I would be angry, too.
- You have every right to feel like that.

Was a Crime Committed?

Research has indicated that during interviews police officers have only a tenuous understanding of the legal points needed to prove the offense under investigation (Williamson, 2004). It is not enough for the interviewer to *think* that a crime has been committed. These legal points that must be proved by the prosecution in order to sustain a conviction are the parts of the crime called its *elements*. The interviewer must *know* what information is needed to prove that a crime has been committed. To determine the appropriate questions that need to be asked, taking the time to become familiar with the specific elements of the crimes that are being investigated is well worth it. This preparation provides the interviewer the opportunity to mentally prepare the questions that need to be asked in order to prove that the crime was committed. The confidence of knowing what you are looking for in the interview will also help you to be at ease. For example, if the investigation involves an elderly person, the age that defines "elderly" becomes an element that must be verified in addition to the crime elements. All states have laws specific to protecting the elderly against abuse; some statutes contain enhanced penalties. Although federal statutes and most state laws define an elderly person as one who has reached age 65, some states specify age 60 instead. The National Center for Victims of Crime (1999) points out that an offender in Nevada who commits a crime against a person older then the age of 60, for example, faces a prison term twice as long as what is usually given for the same offense committed against a younger person. When a violent crime is committed against an elderly person in Louisiana, the law mandates a minimum of 5 years of imprisonment with no opportunity for parole. Know before the interview the age that constitutes "elderly" in your state and the crimes that may have enhanced penalties if the interview concerns a crime against an older person.

Collecting evidence that a crime was committed provides the basis for a successful prosecution. Interviews are an integral part of determining if a crime was committed and, if it was, the type of crime. **Testamentary evidence** is what the witness says in a court of law; typically this form of evidence is collected through interviewing. It is evidence that is required to prove any contested fact. Physical evidence is something that may be seen, heard, touched, smelled, or tasted. Evidence may prove or disprove the involvement of a particular person or cast doubt on whether the crime was even committed.

Arson. The major role of the investigator is to rule out accidental causes of the fire such as heaters, appliances, fuses, or electrical outlets. Interviewing is the most important tool of the arson investigator! The goal is to determine if the fire is incendiary or accidental. **Incendiary** refers to the criminal setting on fire of buildings or other property. This determination is based on the physical evidence at the scene and through interviewing.

Hate Crimes. The FBI defines a **hate crime** as a criminal offense committed against a person or property that is motivated, in whole or in part, by the offender's bias against a race, religion, disability, ethnicity/national origin, or sexual orientation (West & Wiley-Cordone, 1999). An overt criminal act must be attempted, threatened, or completed along with the requisite motivation. Bias, bigotry, or prejudice might be indicated through speech or written words from the perpetrator or inferred from the racial, religious, ethnic, disability, gender, or sexual orientation of the victim. It may be inferred from the presence of one or more bias indicators.

Partner Violence. For a crime to be one of domestic violence there must be a legally recognized domestic relationship between the victim and the perpetrator. Frequently acknowledged categories include married and previously married persons; persons who live together as husband and wife; persons who have a child in common; partners of same-sex relationships; parents and their children or grandchildren; siblings; and extended family members through blood or marriage. Some states expand on traditional meanings of domestic through the recognition of persons who live under the same roof, regardless of affiliation. Substantial dating relationships may also meet the definitional standard. If the perpetrator is within one of the domestic categories in relation to the victim, a special legal category exists. Victimization within a domestic relationship provides additional criminal and civil protections and increased sanctions that are not accessible to persons whose perpetrator is a stranger or not a domestic partner. Siblings, in-laws, and extended family through blood or marriage may also fall under the classification. Your state's definition will likely differ from others. Without a legally recognized relationship, there is no crime of domestic violence, although the act may constitute a different criminal category.

Sexual Assault. Sexual assault means any unwanted, forced sexual contact. This can take many different forms:

- Sexual harassment
- Exposing or flashing
- Forcing a person to pose for sexual pictures
- Forcing a person to look at pornography
- Fondling (unwanted sexual touching)
- Rape

Rape is defined as forced penetration with any object against the will of the victim. Penetration may be by a finger, the male sex organ, or any object. Any penetration, no matter how slight, is sufficient to constitute sexual intercourse. The majority of states legally recognize only female individuals as rape victims, although a few state laws are gender neutral. States that do not legally recognize the crime of rape with respect to male victims offer alternative legal protections. Experts believe that 10% of all rape victims are men.

White Collar. Although there has been some debate as to what qualifies as a white collar crime, the term generally encompasses a variety of nonviolent crimes usually committed in commercial situations for financial gain. Both federal and state legislation define the activities known collectively as *white collar crimes*. According to the Legal Information Institute, the most common white collar offenses include antitrust violations, computer/Internet fraud, credit card fraud, phone/telemarketing fraud, bankruptcy fraud, health care fraud, environmental law violations, insurance fraud, mail fraud, government fraud, tax evasion, financial fraud, securities fraud, insider trading, bribery, kickbacks, counterfeiting, public corruption, money laundering, embezzlement, economic espionage, and trade secret theft (Legal Information Institute, 2004). White collar crime is estimated to cost the United States more than $300 billion annually.

Identifying a Perpetrator

A primary justification for interviewing concerns the identification of the perpetrator and recognition of the victim. Obtaining and accurately recording the physical description of a criminal suspect is a basic requirement of the interview. A good physical description can hasten the apprehension of the criminal offender and assist in obtaining a successful conviction. It is the responsibility of the investigating officer to secure the most accurate and complete description possible from those witnesses who had the best opportunity to observe the suspect or who have personal knowledge of his or her identity.

A victim may not be identified in situations where someone is reluctant to come forward. Whether it is real or imagined, this occurs where the victim lacks confidence in the willingness of the criminal justice system to act on his or her behalf. Prostitutes, drug addicts, migrant workers, and other disenfranchised individuals frequently underreport victimization. Child victims, the elderly, and persons with a disability may not be aware of the criminal nature of an act committed against them. When interviewing, the determination of additional victims may increase the credibility of the prosecutions' case. Don't be afraid to ask, "Has this happened to anyone else that you know of?" The answer may surprise you.

Determining the victim from the perpetrator may be a challenging task. Most literature on domestic violence leads to the conclusion that battering is a male-on-female phenomenon, which occurs exclusively in heterosexual relationships. However, battering occurs with similar frequency and severity in lesbian and gay male relationships as compared to heterosexual relationships (Leventhal & Lundy, 1999). Most experts accept the rate of male victimization to be approximately 15 percent of domestic violence.

Primary Aggressor. The **primary aggressor** in a domestic relationship is the person who is exercising power and control over the other. Identifying the primary aggressor in a domestic relationship is becoming the standard for determining who is at fault when it appears that there is mutual abuse. The standard was developed due to the dilemma faced by the criminal justice system when responding to family violence calls. The courts and the legislature discourage the practice of arresting both parties in situations that appear to be mutually combative. Making a primary-aggressor determination assists the officer in arresting the person who is responsible for the violence.

Neither the gender nor the size of the individual provides enough information to make that primary-aggressor determination. Separating the parties and interviewing them provides the best available option. First, the situation should be examined to find out if violence was used by one person only. Absent evidence of self-defense, it would be a single-arrest situation. If violence was used by both individuals, questions must be asked about prior assaults to find out if one person was acting in self-defense. Without a history of violence the next step would be to see who is the most fearful and who is in control.

BEEN THERE... DONE THAT! 3-3

Just prior to Christmas a call came in at 10 AM from a crying child that daddy was hitting mommy and had pushed her into the Christmas tree. By the time we arrived at the scene the tree was upright and there was no evidence of domestic abuse. The wife was interviewed apart from her husband and children and refused to give any information and denied that she had been hit. There were no marks or bruises evident. The husband also denied any battering. There was no probable cause to make an arrest, even though I was sure that the man had hit his wife. The child who had called said she made up the story. No probable cause meant that no arrest could be made.

I next interviewed the three children and asked if they were ok, conducting an assessment on the level of risk for harm to them if we were to leave them. I asked if there were any guns in the house, and the children told me that there was rifle in their bedroom closet! It was fully loaded and did not have a trigger guard attached. Following up these claims led to evidence that the weapon belonged to the husband. Because the failure to secure a weapon in a locked container or with a safety lock is a felony crime, the guns in the house were confiscated and the husband was arrested.

Healey, Smith, and O'Sullivan (1999) suggested the following guidelines to help in determining the primary aggressor:

1. Question the couple and any witnesses closely before coming to a conclusion and making an arrest. Do not assume that the physically larger partner is always the primary aggressor.
2. Question the partners separately and determine how the visible marks were made and why. Did the victim bite an arm that was holding him or her down, for example?
3. Ask if there has been a recent escalation in the violence and why. Determine if there has been a history of abuse.
4. Do not mistake anger for primary aggressive behavior. An angry victim's conduct is not a justification for arresting him or her.
5. When signs of injury are exhibited by both parties, consider the possibility of self-defense and examine the relative level of injury or force involved. Determine who the initial aggressor was.

Approximately half of the states have laws that require police officers to make a primary-aggressor determination rather than arrest both individuals (Hirschel & Buzawa, 2002).

Risk Assessment. The police officer has an obligation to make an assessment of the situation and form an opinion on the level of risk for harm. This principle applies in a variety of crime situations. If the crime scene is the home of the victim or a place known to the perpetrator, basic security measures could be suggested. Does the perpetrator have a key? Change the locks. Is the house equipped with an alarm? Alarms are fairly inexpensive. Are the doors and windows locked at all times? Does the victim keep the car locked? Does the victim carry a cell phone to call during an emergency? Is a restraining or no-contact order needed to increase the measure of security? These and many other questions related to safety can easily be discussed during an interview. What may seem like common sense to the average cynical police officer may be insightful to someone more trusting. Taking the time to discuss with the victim methods of increasing his or her potential for safety will afford a greater peace of mind for that person and also has the benefit of increasing future cooperation.

Making an Identification

Eyewitness identification is not considered the most reliable form of evidence and will be closely scrutinized by the court. Mistaken identifications are not uncommon. Eyewitness identifications are made under strict legal requirements and must avoid any suggestiveness by the police. A suspect has a right to counsel for a show-up or lineup identification once a formal complaint has been filed or an indictment has been handed down. No show-up or lineup or any other confrontation for identification purposes can occur after formal charging unless the suspect is provided with an attorney or expressly waives his or her right to counsel (*U.S. v. Wade,* 1967).

Composites, photographs, or sketches may be used to help identify persons. Composites are developed from separate photographs or sketches of facial features. Do not show a witness a photo or live lineup prior to developing a composite; it may influence his or her memory of the suspect and cause contamination.

Field Identification

A *show-up* or field identification is a lineup with only one participant that occurs a short time after the commission of a crime. Courts strongly disapprove of the use of one-person show-ups (*Stoval v. Denno,* 1967). The reason for the disapproval is that the show-up method of witness identification is inherently suggestive (Technical Working Group for Eyewitness Evidence, 1999). The Wisconsin Supreme Court recently affirmed that evidence obtained from a show-up would not be admissible except in cases where it was conducted out of necessity (*State v. Dubose,* 2005). Based on a totality-of-circumstances test, the show-up would not be necessary under the *Dubose* standard unless the police lacked probable cause to make an arrest or as a result of other exigent circumstances.

Its use is further limited to circumstances in which a crime has just been committed and a suspect has been apprehended very close in time and place to the offence. Typically the suspect who has fled the scene is brought back to the witness to see if he or she can make identification. Its limited use is to prevent an innocent person from being arrested. The suspect has no right to counsel at a show-up (*Kirby v. Illinois,* 1972).

If this method of identification is used, it requires careful procedural safeguards. When one or more witnesses interviewed at the scene indicate they are able to make an identification of the perpetrator, document that description prior to conducting the field identification show-up. If there is

> **BEEN THERE... DONE THAT! 3-4**
>
> A photo lineup may or may not result in the identification of the perpetrator during an investigation. Care must be taken to make sure that the victim understands that the perpetrator may not be in the photo array and that he or she must look at all photos before commenting out loud about any of the pictures. In one case the victim told me that she thought the number 3 picture was the man who had assaulted her, then went on to say that she was mistaken—he was number 5. This identification was worthless and therefore discarded. It was later learned that none of the men in the photo array had been the attacker.

one or more witnesses, only one at a time should have access to the suspect. If possible, bring the witness to the place that the suspect is being detained. Caution the witness that the perpetrator may not be at the location. Fully document both positive identifications and nonidentification outcomes that occur, the time of the procedure, and its location. The suspect should not be handcuffed or in a jail cell during this form of identification. There is no requirement that the suspect be given *Miranda* warnings because the evidence is not testimonial or communicative.

Lineups

During an interview the witness or victim may indicate a willingness to identify the suspect from a lineup. Careful instructions to the witness prior to the viewing of either a photo or physical lineup are imperative. Explain that the purpose of the procedure is not only to identify the perpetrator, but also to exonerate the innocent (Technical Working Group for Eyewitness Evidence, 1999).

Photo Lineup. The suspect has no right to counsel that affects his or her photo from being used in a photo lineup (*U.S. v. Ash,* 1973). The array should consist of at least eight photos of different people, including only one photo of the suspect. The nonsuspect photos should be consistent for unique features such as scars or tattoos, but do not need to closely resemble each other in all features. The photos should be viewed one photo at a time. If a witness picks out a suspect during the photo array, insist on showing all of the photos. Do not use the same photos in a lineup of a new suspect to the same witness. Document the photo lineup order and the witness responses.

Live Lineup. The suspect has no right to counsel at a lineup prior to formal charges being brought against him or her (*U.S. v. Ash,* 1973). One suspect is included with a minimum of six nonsuspects. General resemblances are all that is needed, with the suspect significant features being similar. Avoid using individuals who are so similar as to make identification difficult. Be sure that the suspect does not stand out due to

FIGURE 3-2
Overcome witness reluctance to give information through patience and common sense statements.

difference by race, ethnicity, age, or height. Document the instructions that were made to the witness and the responses, the time and place of the lineup, and the identities of its participants.

Assessing the Accuracy of a Statement

Always consider the possibility of false reporting. The job of the interviewer is to discover the truth if that is possible; therefore the interviewer should adopt a neutral position to conduct interviews. A full investigation is still necessary even if it is suspected that the person is lying, distorting the facts, or withholding important information. Do not initially accuse the individual of falsely reporting or treat the person as if they were lying. Obtain as much information as possible and follow the leads that are provided. The facts of the case will speak louder than an accusation. It is not necessary to make judgments, and it is unwise to jump to conclusions.

When a claim appears to be exaggerated consider whether the victim who reports having been assaulted has any motivations for exaggeration. Look at the repercussions of the act. Is the victim a juvenile, married, or ashamed? Do not judge the reliability of the statement based solely on a moral evaluation of the person providing the information. Reality is stranger than fiction. To dismiss a complaint based on an initial statement because the individual does not fit the profile of a victim exposes the person to further violation and potentially allows a perpetrator to go free. Instead, take the position of corroborating the victim statement to increase its credibility whenever possible.

A witness may provide information that is correct in some ways and incorrect in others. The entire statement does not have to be ignored if it is discovered that part of the statement is inaccurate. It is not unusual for eyewitness accounts to vary on specifics of the situation. One person may remember a vehicle as red and another report the vehicle as blue. This does not mean that one or the other is lying; just note the inconsistencies for further evaluation. Review the statement for inconsistencies to other statements or known evidence in the case.

There are many reasons why interviewers need to be observant when taking statements from victims, witnesses, and perpetrators. Concerns over the reliability of interviews taken with child victims have caused convictions to be overturned (*State v. Michaels,* 1994). False allegations and witness misidentifications have caused imprisoned men to be freed after many years in prison (Death Penalty Information Center, 2004). Since 1973, 117 people in 25 states have been released from death row based on evidence of their innocence. Finding the truth demands the evaluation of all evidence, including that obtained during an interview.

▲ CONCLUSIONS

This chapter introduced the concept of purposeful interviewing. This is not a method, but a general approach to conducting interviews. This approach brings with it a determination to conduct interviewing with the goal of obtaining as much accurate information as possible. Different crimes may require different interviewing approaches. Consider this information as an invitation to develop your interviewing technique. Be flexible and responsive—the reward will be improved quality in your interviews and the development of new skills. Develop active listening skills and rapport to enhance the communication within the interview.

The implicit idea is that each phase of the interview leaves nothing to chance; you are in control. Looking at the allegation and making the determination of whether a crime was actually committed, taking the sometimes more difficult way to figure out who the perpetrator is, and questioning with a purpose have their rewards. All the information that brings you to your objective is useful for explaining the crime and justifying the response.

■ QUESTIONS FOR REVIEW

Short-Answer Questions

1. What are the three general characteristics that assist in framing the purposeful interview?
2. Why is understanding nonverbal cues received from interviewees important to the interviewer?
3. Why is it so important to interview the first-arriving firefighters in a suspected arson?

4. What are some of the main reasons victims of domestic violence may be reluctant to provide details associated with their assault?
5. What are some of the requirements necessary for a crime to be one of domestic violence?
6. How accurate are eyewitnesses? What are some of the issues affecting eyewitness testimony?
7. What are the main characteristics of purposeful interviewing?

Fill-in Questions

1. Two types of lineups that are often used to identify the suspect are _____ and _____.
2. _____ refers to the realization that statements are sought for specific reasons.
3. _____ may communicate what interviewees cannot bring themselves to state openly.
4. When interviewing the victim of a hate crime there may be a _____ on the part of the victim toward anyone who resembles the attacker. This obstacle to interviewing is important to anticipate and overcome.
5. When interviewing illegal aliens a false name may be given due to the fear of _____.
6. When interviewing the victim of a sexual assault _____ questions should be asked allowing the victim to describe the events in his or her own words.
7. _____ are developed from separate photographs or sketches of facial features.
8. Sudden silence, uncertainty or confusion, or the shifting of conversation to an unrelated subject may indicate that _____.
9. The interviewer should listen to the _____, _____, and _____ from the subject during the interview.

Exercises

1. The New York State Defenders Association has an interesting site that provides information and links on police lineups and identification techniques. Choose one problem that has been linked to police identification techniques and find a proposed method to change it. The Web site is http://www.nysda.org/Hot_Topics/Eyewitness_Evidence/eyewitness_evidence.html
2. Take 10 minutes to have a conversion with someone in the class you do not know and with whom you have never spoken. Ask him or her to explain something that he or she enjoys doing in his or her spare time. Listen intently to the words that he or she uses. What can you tell about where this person comes from based on the way he or she speaks?

REFERENCES

Burnley, J., Edmunds, C., Gaboury, M., & Seymour, A. (1996). *National Victim Assistance Academy textbook*. Washington, DC: Office for Victims of Crime.

Death Penalty Information Center. (2004). Innocence and the death penalty. [Online.] Available: http://deathpenaltyinfo.org/article.php?did=412&scid=6.

Federal Emergency Management Agency. (1988). *Arson prosecution: Issues and strategies* (Report No. FA-78). Washington, DC: U.S. Fire Administration.

Gosselin, D. K. (2002). Victim interviewing in cases of domestic violence: Techniques for police. In L. J. Moriarty (Ed.), *Policing and victims* (pp. 87–107). Upper Saddle River, NJ: Prentice Hall.

Healey, K., Smith, C., & O'Sullivan, C. (1999). *Batterer intervention: Program approaches and criminal justice strategies*. Collingdale, NY: Diane Publishing.

Hirschel, D., & Buzawa, E. (2002). Understanding the context of dual arrest with directions for future research. *Violence Against Women, 8*(12) 1449–1473.

Kadushin, A., & Kadushin, G. (1997). *The social work interview*. New York: Columbia University Press.

Kirby v. Illinois, 406 U.S. 682 (1972).

Legal Information Institute. (2004). White-Collar Crime: An Overview. [Online.] Available: http://www.law.cornell.edu/topics/white_collar.html.

Leventhal, B., & Lundy, S. E. (1999). *Same-sex domestic violence*. Thousand Oaks, CA: Sage Publications.

McLaughlin, K., & Walley, A. (2001). *Responding to hate crimes: A multidisciplinary curriculum for law enforcement and victim assistance professionals* (Report No. NCJ 182290). Newton, MA: National Center for Hate Crime Prevention Education Development Center.

National Center for Victims of Crime. (1999). Elder abuse and the law: [Online.] Available: http://www.nycagainstrape.org/survivors_factsheet_74.html.

National Center for Women and Policing. (2001). *Successfully investigating acquaintance sexual assault: A national training manual for law enforcement*. Beverly Hills, CA: The National Center for Women and Policing.

State v. Dubose, WI 126 (2005).

State v. Michaels, 136 N.J. 299, 311-12, 642 A.2d 1372 (1994).

Stoval v. Denno, 388 U.S. 293 (1967).

Technical Working Group for Eyewitness Evidence. (1999). *Eyewitness evidence: A guide for law enforcement* (Report No. NCJ 178240). Washington, DC: U.S. Department of Justice.

U.S. v. Ash, 413 U.S. 300 (1973).

U.S. v. Wade, 388 U.S. 218 (1967).

West, K., & Wiley-Cordone, J. (1999). *Toward a national voice: Maximizing our effectiveness*. Newton, MA: National Center for Hate Crime Prevention.

Williamson, T. (2004). USA and UK responses to miscarriages of justice. In J. R. Adler (Ed.), *Forensic psychology: Concepts, debates and practices* (pp. 36–57). Devon, UK: Willan Publishing.

Part II

Methods and Techniques

This section includes information on the most common methods and techniques used in criminal justice interviewing. Chapter 4 discusses typical approaches to the criminal justice interview. These may be used with the cooperative or uncooperative victim and witness. The traditional interviewing approach is based on answering the "five W's and How." The approach is simplistic and without cumbersome procedures. Traditional interviewing is useful for determining the level of cooperation that can be expected from a witness, gathering emergency and crisis information, and field operations. The structured interview is a three-step method of interviewing. It adds rapport building, narrative descriptions, and ample interviewing opportunity to the traditional approach and is a valuable tool for interviewers. A third approach in this chapter is inferential interviewing. Inferential interviewing is a deception-detection approach. Promising a high rate of accuracy, it is a question-by-question analysis of each statement for statement coherence, response length, type–token ratio, and verbal hedges. Statement analysis is the next approach covered. It involves a word-by-word examination of the grammar within a statement. The approach looks at the parts of speech, extraneous information, lack of convictions, and balance of the statement in a four-part process. Each one of these methods is adaptable to the situations in which questioning might occur. Finally, the field statement analysis is a shortened version of statement analysis for field application.

Chapter 5 covers forensic hypnosis and cognitive interviewing. These are two major forms of interviewing that use memory-jogging techniques to facilitate recall. Both are recommended as interviewing approaches for cooperative witnesses and victims. The approach used in forensic hypnotic interviewing is different from cognitive interviewing. The techniques of hypnosis are introduced in this chapter with the understanding that proficiency in this method should be obtained through continued study before its use in criminal investigation. Given the complexity of hypnosis and the regulation of its use for investigative purposes, this is just an introduction to the approach. Cognitive interviewing is a memory-jogging approach that can be mastered by even the novice interviewer. It is easily learned and can be adapted to a variety of situations that require information retrieval. The foundation of the cognitive interview is the use of four mnemonics that are the memory-jogging techniques. These should be learned and practiced for use in any interviewing situation.

The behavioral interviewing techniques in Chapter 6 provide valuable tools for investigative interviewing and interrogation. The behavior indicators that are covered include nonverbal posturing, sensatory verbal communication, and eye movement. The techniques provide situations for interviewer interpretation. There are no step-by-step methods in this chapter. The techniques, once learned, are applicable in any interview or interrogation as additional tools when determining truthfulness versus deceit. Kinesics, a nonverbal communication form, was introduced in Chapter 1. Here its practical application is illustrated. Founded in the late 1940s, kinesics is a common approach to behavioral interviewing. A second approach covered in this chapter is neurolinguistic programming (NPL). It is still being developed for interviewing use, and uses facial expression and coding in addition to eye movements to provide interesting insights into learning and communication.

CHAPTER 4
Traditional, Structural, and Inferential Interviewing with Statement Analysis Techniques

Key Terms

Traditional interviewing	Inferential interview
Side-tracker	Verbal leakage
Complainant	Statement analysis
Actus reus	Extraneous information
Mens rea	Lack of conviction

Chapter Objectives

After completing this chapter you should be able to:

- Identify the sources of information
- State the motivations of a side-tracker
- Explain the traditional approach to interviewing
- Define *actus reus*
- Explain the structural approach to interviewing
- Compare and contrast traditional interviewing and structural interviewing
- Describe the characteristics of inferential interviewing
- List the four parts of statement analysis
- Explain the concept of the field statement analysis
- List ways of detecting deceit

Introduction

The chapter starts out by identifying the sources of information that may be encounteral. Included in this section are methods of traditional interviewing, structural interviewing, and statement analysis. **Traditional interviewing** is a straightforward asking of questions to obtain information about a case. The approach is typically referred to as a "just-the-facts" way to get answers to the questions that describe an incident. It is a neutral process during which the interviewer attempts to determine the truth through the statement from the subject (Hand, 2003). Hand (2003) describes this perspective as one in which the interviewee is considered a passive possessor of knowledge and the interviewer objectively protects the facts from influence or contamination. Questions are rarely formulated and no particular technique is involved. The approach has been criticized because the question format is usually closed ended and the manner of questioning is abrupt. Historically it has not encouraged interviewee participation or the free exchange of information, and therefore its use is limited. For these reasons, the traditional approach does not enjoy a good reputation as an effective method of interviewing. Also referred to as the standard interview, its purpose is to limit the information from eyewitnesses to that considered specifically necessary for the investigation being conducted (Kebbell, 1996).

The traditional approach to interviewing has been criticized for its excessive simplicity, abruptness, and lack of direction. Other models, such as cognitive interviewing and the behavioral approaches that will be discussed later in the book, come under fire for extreme complexity, cumbersome techniques, and questions that must be asked in specific and difficult-to-remember order. The structured interviewing approach uses the best of traditional questioning methods while applying principles used in cognitive interviewing. This approach provides direction in the questioning to facilitate cooperation. A new approach, which is included in this chapter, is the inferential interview method. Think of inferential interviewing as structural interviewing with a twist! The technique improves on prior methods by including simple methods to detect deceit in the interview. The final section expands on the idea of deceit detection with an in-depth section on statement analysis.

IDENTIFYING THE SOURCES

Solving a crime depends on the ability of the interviewer to acquire accurate information regarding the details of the event. Information typically comes from multiple sources that must be approached to determine their willingness to provide information. The statements must be evaluated for their reliability and applicability to the case. A traditional approach to interviewing provides an adequate way in which to make these preliminary assessments.

In the early stages of an investigation it is important to find out which individuals may have information about the case versus those who do not. Sometimes a person will want to give information about a case or claim to be a witness when he or she is not connected with the situation at all. Referred to as a **side-tracker,** this is a person who is falsely claiming involvement as a witness or suspect to a crime. The side-tracker may be a person with emotional or mental disturbance, a person who seeks publicity, or a person simply has a grudge against the person about whom he or she wants to provide information. He or she may be the perpetrator, who is purposefully attempting to mislead the investigator. If the motive for the giving of information is not clear, attempt to find out about any relationship the person may have had with the primary individual involved in the investigation. Check all information against the known facts to determine if any of the information is useful before discarding it. A side-tracker can take valuable time away from the focus of an investigation.

The person who reports a crime or accuses another person of an offense is called the **complainant.** The complainant may be the victim, someone who saw the crime occur, or one who has information about the crime being investigated. Sometimes the complainant is the perpetrator who is attempting to divert police attention away from his or her own actions. If preliminary questions reveal that the complainant may be the suspect, then the approach changes from an interview to an interrogation as necessary.

If the source of the information comes from the victim, keep in mind that stress or shock may influence the individual's memory of an incident (Artwohl, 2002). Multiple interviews may be needed to obtain an accurate

FIGURE 4-1 Identify your sources! Is he the complainant, the victim, or a side-tracker? Is he purposefully attempting to mislead the investigator?

victim statement. The victim may be overly cooperative or highly emotional at the time of an initial interview. It is probably not necessary to do an in-depth interview under these conditions. Obtain enough information to provide emergency or medical attention and to identify a suspect if an assault was committed.

Ask questions to determine if the complainant is a witness. What did this person see or hear about the incident? When interviewing, always separate the individuals and interview them one at time and outside of hearing by any other persons. Encourage the person not to discuss the situation with any other witness. A dilemma exists for someone who does not want to tell something that might be hurtful to another. The alternative to not wanting to lie may be to avoid telling the truth or not answering the question directly (DePaulo, Lindsay, Malone, Muhlenbruck, Charlton, & Cooper, 2003).

GUIDELINES FOR THE TRADITIONAL INTERVIEWING APPROACH

Asking the person questions that follow the "five W's and How" guidelines will make the best use of the immediate cooperation being offered. The six guidelines to traditional interviewing involve questions that answer who, what, when, where, why, and how—the five W's and How. A primary purpose of the traditional approach is to gather only the information that is absolutely necessary for the investigation. This approach is used most often in field situations in which time for conducting interviews is scarce. It can be followed up with more directed interviewing as time permits in the future. The vast majority of information that is gained through traditional interviewing is helpful for any investigation. The difference between traditional methods of interviewing and other approaches is the manner in which the questions are asked. In the traditional method is often abrupt and straight to the point. Rather than encouraging narrative responses, this interviewing approach tends to limits answers. There is no particular order of questioning and no suggested steps for conducting the interview.

One reason to use the traditional interview approach is to determine the level of cooperation that can be expected from a witness. A potential witness may be called on the phone to determine if a full interview might be helpful to the investigation. An additional use of the traditional interviewing approach is to obtain emergency response information and general details of the event at the scene of the crime.

People should be approached in a manner that is most likely going to encourage their cooperation. Understand the reasons why a person may or may not want to provide information. Avoid antagonizing the person being interviewed because they are less likely to provide information if they sense conflict or anger. There is no required order for the guidelines to be used during the interview. Instead, think of the five W's and How as a checklist to make sure that as much information has been gathered as possible.

What?

Questions should not be phrased in a way that leads the person being interviewed to give a particular answer, nor should they be accusatory. Individuals seeking to please the interviewer may inadvertently provide information that is false rather than give no information at all. Instruct the person that although you are depending on their cooperation, you understand that they will not have all of the answers.

In obtaining complete information about an incident the interviewer should search for what happened before the incident, what happened during the incident, and what happened after the incident. An initial determination of *What* is made for the following circumstances:

- What offense was committed?
- What happened?
- What weapon was used?
- What was said?
- What did the eyewitness hear or see?
- What happened after the event was over?

Is the situation a complaint of abuse, a fight, a theft, or a case of stolen or damaged property? The initial response of the interviewer will vary greatly based on the general knowledge of what is alleged to have occurred. Is the situation even a violation of the law? Here the interviewer determines the **actus reus,** a term that means the "guilty act"

(Schmalleger, 2004). Based on the description of the event by the victim or witnesses, determine if a crime has been committed and the nature of that offense.

Who?

Find out the names and descriptions of all people involved. If this is a primary response, ask the dispatcher for the name of the complainant when in route to the scene. Determine when possible if the complainant or suspect will likely still be at the scene at the time of arrival and request both be instructed to wait there. If the call originated from a neighbor or witness, obtain names, addresses, and telephone number through dispatch or within the case file. If an anonymous reporter is involved in reporting, attempt to identify that individual through caller ID or through witnesses. Relevant questions to be asked include the following:

- Who is the victim?
- Who is the perpetrator?
- Who are the witnesses?

Are there likely to be a group of individuals to be reckoned with, or is the situation between two persons? This makes a difference on who might be interviewed relative to the case and how the officer will approach persons at the scene. If the dispatcher has the names of persons at the scene, ask for a records check to determine if either party has been involved in prior offenses, has an outstanding warrant against them, or is the subject of a current restraining order. In particular, when the response is to a disturbance, determine if either party has a current firearms license. Find out if there are any children in the home.

Who are the people in relation to each other? Is there a relationship between the victim and the perpetrator? Are they friends or acquaintances? Could they be related through someone? The existence of any relationship opens the possibility of motives to give inaccurate information because of trying to protect someone or having a grudge against someone. Ask people being interviewed about their prior law enforcement contact. Have they been arrested before? Have they been a victim or witness in a previously reported crime? Are they related to a law enforcement person? These questions on the relationship of the individual to those involved can help in establishing rapport and for assessing the credibility of the individual.

When?

Find out if the incident is still ongoing. Is the complaint about recently discovered missing property or is this an old complaint? The response will be different than that to an offense involving a recently discovered theft of property and an allegation of violence. Has the complainant made similar allegations about this person in the past? Is this a situation of reoccurring abuse? Is there an order of protection or restraining order that is in effect? Has this type of offense ever occurred against the victim in the past? Possible questions include the following:

- When did this incident occur?
- When was the event reported?
- When did injuries occur?

Where?

Did the offense occur at the place where the witness or victim is currently? This information may help to determine if the offender is likely to in the vicinity of the crime or not. Of equal importance is whether evidence of the crime may be at a different location than the victim, which would require the preservation of the scene. Consider exploring the following issues:

- Where was the location of the incident?
- Where did the event begin and where did it end?
- Where were the witnesses located in relation to the offense?
- Where is the best place to conduct the interview?

In addition to knowing the place where the event happened, questions should be asked to determine why it happened at that particular place. In a purse-snatching example the event may have taken place on a street with a burnt-out light. This may indicate that the perpetrator was familiar with the area rather than it being a random attack. If the event was in a home, whose home is it? Was the person an invited guest or an intruder? Were there indications of forced entry?

When doing the initial assessment for victim cooperation using the traditional approach it is useful to take into account the place where the interview should be held. If this occurs in the field, care should be taken to keep the interviewee outside of sight and earshot of other individuals.

Why?

Motivation for an event may not be readily observable and could be related to the value structure or relationship of the person to the situation. Attempting to determine why something occurs may involve some value judgments on the part of the interviewer. Be careful to properly phrase information that is a judgment rather than a fact in any report that contains it.

- Why did this occur?

Interviewing should establish the *mens rea* of the case. **Mens rea** refers to the state of mind of the perpetrator, not the victim. *Mens rea* is the guilty-mind requirement or the knowledge of a wrongful purpose (Garner, 2004). This condition is not the same as intent; it is present when a person should have known better, even if he or she did not intend

> **BEEN THERE... DONE THAT! 4-1**
>
> On a warm summer day the body of a missing 15-year-old girl was located in the river. Her hands were tied behind her back with a man's sock. The autopsy confirmed that she had died of drowning, so she was likely bound and thrown into the river while she was still alive. Why did this occur? It was puzzling because she was still dressed, including her underwear. Early in the investigation the motive of sexual assault was dismissed because of her being fully clothed. I noted that she was wearing a sanitary pad at the time of her death.
>
> Two male suspects were later identified and interrogated. They were both under the age of 20 years. When asked how they knew the victim, they responded that she was a friend. She got into their car willingly because she knew them. Together the three of them went to a secluded spot on the river where kids often go for underage drinking. It still did not make sense. Why would they kill their friend?
>
> During the questioning I asked if they had had sex with her, knowing that they had not. Immediately one suspect drew his lips tight as if in anger! They wanted to have sex with her, but she had said "NO." She had before; they didn't understand why she would not do it then. They fought with her to remove her clothing; she struggled and yelled. In anger one man had taken off his socks and tied her hands. Partially pulling down her underwear, they noted that she was having her period. One of the young men had been arrested for rape in a neighboring state but had received a suspended sentence. He became frightened that she would tell someone. He convinced his friend that they had to keep her from telling anyone. To cover up the attempted rape, they threw her into the river, still struggling and screaming. The tragedy still did not make sense to me, but the "why" had been answered.

the consequences. Determining that the individual did not intend the consequences does not mean that he or she is not legally responsible for what happened. There are four levels of *mens rea* (Schmalleger, 2004):

1. **Purposefulness**—The act is intentional and is done for a reason or goal. An example is when a person kills another for monetary gain, such as life insurance or an inheritance.
2. **Knowing**—If a person engages in activity that he or she should know will have dire consequences, then responsibility for that act exists. Walking into a crowded room swinging a baseball bat would be likely to hurt someone. Even if the person did not intend to hurt anyone, it is a likely consequence of his or her actions.
3. **Reckless behavior**—A person may engage in activity that is reckless, that is, increases the risk of harm. Driving at high speeds and driving under the influence of alcohol are examples.
4. **Neglect**—This situation may occur though the failure to do something. When a legal duty to care for a child or an elderly person is established, the failure to provide the care results in criminal culpability if harm results. Criminal neglect is an extreme failure, for example, when a child dies because the parent did not provide food.

> **BEEN THERE... DONE THAT! 4-2**
>
> A mother left her two children alone in the apartment so that she could get some dope. She locked the children in their bedroom when she left because she did not think she would be gone long. The two young boys started to play with matches and their bed caught on fire. They could not get out of the room... they died there. Their death was a tragic accident—their mother did not mean them any harm. Was she responsible? She lacked the *mens rea* because she did not intend that her actions would cause the deaths of her children. She had a duty to care for these children, but a few years earlier the state had repealed its law on criminal neglect. The mother could not be charged with having committed any crime. In part due to this case a new law was passed that defined acts of neglect that would be considered illegal. If this same scenario happens again, the mother would be charged with a crime, but the law is not retroactive.

How?

The how of a crime is concerned with the event and everything leading up to it. How did the perpetrator get access to the victim, to the money stolen, or to the area to cause damage? Once access was gained, what was the manner in which he or she committed the act? What instruments or tools were used in the commission of the act? What evidence would there be to support information that is being provided in the interview?

- How did it happen?
- How was the victim approached?
- How did the perpetrator gain access?
- How often has a similar event occurred?

Of particular importance is the sequence of events of when things happened during the incident. Knowing the exact sequence of events can render the event plausible or not.

Now that each component of the traditional interview method has been outlined, look at Figure 4-2 and see how many of the questions you can answer!

What Is Structural Interviewing?

The **structural interviewing** approach builds on the traditional interview by adding the following components: rapport building, narrative description, and an ample interviewee response opportunity. Many of the positive aspects of the cognitive approach to interviewing are also incorporated into structural interviewing, such as active listening, use of open questions, and appropriate nonverbal behavior (Memon & Higham, 1999). The organization of the structural interview is meant to maximize recall and minimize eyewitness contamination (Colwell, Hiscock, & Memon, 2002).

FIGURE 4-2 Look at the picture as if it were a real situation that you are investigating. Can you answer: Who? What? When? Where? Why? How?

STEPS FOR STRUCTURAL INTERVIEWING

Structural interviewing is carefully planned and followed to maximize the amount of useful information that is gathered. Following these suggested steps may result in an accuracy rate of about 62 percent according to a recent study (Colwell et al., 2002).

Step One: Build Rapport

Establish rapport. Research confirms that rapport may be more important than any particular technique for increasing truthful information (Memon, Wark, Holley, Bull, & Koehnken, 1997). Attempt to build rapport so that the person being interviewed is at ease and is willing to give information. Remember from earlier chapters that the purpose of rapport is to establish a two-way communication between the interviewer and the interviewee. It is a relationship of trust.

Step Two: Encourage Participation

Encourage the individual to participate actively and to report information rather than just respond to the questions that are being asked. Do not volunteer information about the case or the suspect when conducting an interview. Ask open-ended questions frequently and do not interrupt the person who is making a statement. Record the statements accurately and completely. If it is practicable, take notes during the interview. As soon as possible after the interview, write the full statement down using the witness's own words.

To obtain information on an incident, ask open-ended questions followed by closed-ended questions to clarify the first answer (Technical Working Group for Eyewitness Evidence, 1999). Ask nonleading and open questions that allow for a free narrative account. The interviewer should specifically request the free narrative. Ask the subject to describe, in as much detail as possible, everything that he or she remembers about the event. To avoid contaminating the statement, avoid introducing any new information or details about the event. Avoid interrupting the account or asking for clarification of the details at this stage. For example:

1. "Can you tell me about the car?" This opened-ended question gives the person an unlimited range of answers without leading him or her to what you might be expecting to hear.
2. "Can you tell me anything about the color, make, or model of the car?" This is a opened-ended question that is not limited to any particular aspect of the car. It does not imply that the person should remember any particular aspect of the car. It is not leading the witness or suggestive because it does not suggest any particular color, make, or model of vehicle.

Specific probing questions are next used to elaborate on the details that were provided by the interviewee during the free narrative account. Open-ended questions are preferred. The interviewer may incorporate the five W's and How in this step.

Step Three: Review the Statement

In the final step of the structural interview the subject is asked to recount the entire scene or event again for the purpose of bringing new recollections into the account. When it is completed, allow the witness to read this statement and make corrections to it. Do not write a statement as if it were the words of the witness unless it actually is. For example, a

FIGURE 4-3 To detect deceit according the principles of the inferential interview, listen for statement coherence, response rate, type–token ratio, and verbal hedging.

4-year old would not use the word "intercourse"! Be careful not to substitute your words for someone else's without specifying that the statement is a paraphrase of the witness's statement.

INFERENTIAL INTERVIEWING

A promising new approach to interviewing is called the **inferential interview.** This method detects deception by analyzing statement characteristics and making a question-by-question analysis. In a study by Colwell et al. (2002), subjects were given information and tested for their complete and accurate recall, or accuracy, using the inferential interview method. The authors found that statement accuracy was an astounding 82 percent. This comparison study found the accuracy of the structural interview to be 62 percent and that of the cognitive interview to be 68 percent.

Colwell et al. (2002) suggested that through the inferential interviewing method four dependent measures can be used by the interviewer to discover dishonesty in a statement. Deception, they theorized, is associated with less coherence, shorter responses, more verbal hedges, and an increase in the type–token ratio (to be defined later). Standardized instruments for assessing the accuracy of statements through the question-by-question analysis have not been developed. The authors suggested that research is needed to develop checklist formats to improve an interviewer's ability to determine statement deception. The following factors are important aspects of the inferential interviewing method for determining whether a statement is deceptive:

1. Statement coherence
2. Response length
3. Type–token ratio
4. Verbal hedges

Statement Coherence

A statement should make sense by not violating the rules of nature or contradicting itself. This step is an examination for dishonesty that includes the statement as a whole. Does the statement make sense when it is complete? Are there questions that are unanswered that must be asked to determine if it is complete? Did the statement contradict itself? Does the statement contradict the laws of nature?

Response Length

Deception that is highly motivated has been associated with a shorter response length, a slower rate of speech, and more speech errors. These behaviors, collectively known as **verbal leakage,** are the unconscious verbal responses that indicate deception. Follow-up questions that are used to probe suspected deception have been helpful in uncovering purposeful deceit by nonskilled liars (Talwar & Lee, 2002).

> **BEEN THERE... DONE THAT! 4-3**
>
> Sketchy details of a kidnapping and an attempt to commit murder were the reasons why I was called out in the middle of the night. While en route to the scene I thought about the absurdity of this alleged crime. A woman reported that while she was hitchhiking in her rural home town she was picked up and given a ride by a man who she knew. She said that she was strangled to unconsciousness by him and later woke up in the trunk of his car. Furthermore, I was told, when the car stopped and the trunk was opened, she found that they were parked on the side of a bridge with a long drop to the river below. She reported to the police that he was going to throw her in the river but that she pleaded with him and he took her home instead!
>
> The report sounded like a lie, yet I knew that it was important to find out more information. When I interviewed the victim I was looking for more signs of dishonesty. What convinced me that she was telling the truth was that she recounted waking up in the car and described in detail that the driver had stopped at a gas station—she heard the gas going into the tank and smelled it. She described how frightening it had been in the small, dark place without any way to get out. In detail she described the roads as being bumpy or smooth so that she had an idea where they were at the point he opened the trunk. Taken together the entire statement was coherent. It made sense that she could describe sequentially the experience and feelings she had while locked in the trunk.
>
> The next day I called for the forensic specialists to look inside the trunk for evidence of her being there. They found one long blonde hair belonging to her... it verified that she was telling the truth.

Type–Token Ratio

The type–token ratio is the ratio of the number of different unique spoken or written words (types) to the total number of spoken or written words (tokens). For example, if a text is 1,000 words long, it is said to have 1,000 tokens. There may be only, say, 400 different words (types) in the text because many of them may be repeated. The ratio between types and tokens in this example is 400/1,000, or 40 percent. Statement fabrication is associated with higher type–token ratios as compared to truthful statements.

Verbal Hedging

Verbal hedging techniques are used to buy additional time for answering the questions or as a way to avoid commitment to the facts. The number of verbal hedges in the interview is counted to gauge the extent to which these have been used.

1. Methods for avoiding answering and buying time include the following:
    - The unnecessary use of connectors—Uh... Um... and... or.
    - Repetition by the subject of all or part of the interviewer's questions before answering—"Tell you what happened from the beginning?"

2. Ways to avoid committing to the statement include the following:
   - Claiming a lack of memory
   - Offering extraneous information

STATEMENT ANALYSIS

Based on the idea that statements of experience will contain language characteristics that are absent from statements that are the products of imagination, **statement analysis** is the word-by-word examination of the grammar within a statement (Klopf & Tooke, 2003). Statement analysis is a more complex method of detecting deception then the inferential approach. It is used to gauge the credibility and reliability of a statement concerning a crime that has been alleged to occur. It can be used along with any form of interviewing method as an assessment of the information recorded in a statement. Adams (1996) suggested that the technique of statement analysis is twofold: First, determine what is a typical truthful statement; this is referred to as the norm. Second, look for any deviation from this norm because truthful statements are different in both content and quality from fabricated ones. Both written and oral statements can be evaluated using this approach. Although the vast majority of statements are believed to be truthful, both structure and content will vary between persons who are deceptive and those who are not (Memon, Gabbert, & Hope, 2004).

CONDUCTING STATEMENT ANALYSIS

The four basic components of statement analysis are parts of speech; extraneous information, lack of conviction, and statement balance.

Step One: Parts of Speech

Examine the individual parts of speech that are used in the statement, particularly pronouns, nouns, and verbs, and establish the norm for each. If a change from the norm becomes apparent, seek the reason for that difference. Word choices are purposeful, even when they are selected subconsciously. Noun, verb, and adjective choices represent a limited example for applying the principles of statement analysis (Adams, 2004). The following phrase used by Robert, a sexually dangerous pedophile, is illustrative: "My story has never changed; I never hurt the boy, I love him." From years of experience, it is not unusual for an offender to refer to his or her statement as a *story*. When this occurs without prompting, it is noteworthy because the term refers to something that is made up and not real. As Adams (2004) concluded, using this noun to describe what happened may indicate a false statement. The verb *hurt* in this example minimizes the crime of anal rape, which was perpetrated against the young boy. By minimizing the offense the offender is also playing down his role in causing any harm to the child. Using the verb *love* suggests a positive experience rather than the heinous crime that actually occurred. Here the perpetrator uses the phrase *the child* rather than the name. Distancing himself, this offender objectifies the victim.

Understanding grammatical terms is the first step toward statement analysis. The following definitions apply (*Merriam-Webster's Collegiate Dictionary,* 2004):

- **Pronoun.** Words that are used as substitutes for nouns (p. 995).
- **Noun.** Words that serve as the subject of a verb and refer to an entity, quality, state, action, or concept (p. 849).
- **Verb.** The part of speech that expresses existence, action, or occurrence in most languages (p. 1389).
- **Adjective.** A word that modifies a noun to denote a quality of the thing named, indicate its quantity, or extent, or to specify the thing as distinct from something else (p. 16).

Pronouns. Common pronouns are I, me, you, he she, we, they, and it. Truthful people provide statements using the pronoun "I," which is first person singular. Deviating from the use of first person singular during an interview is a signal of possible deception. An overuse of the pronoun "we" indicates a lack of commitment to the statement and unwillingness to take responsibility for something.

> **Example of truthfulness:** I woke up at 7:00 AM, got dressed, and went to school. I met some friends and we went into class. At noontime we all left and drove around.
>
> **Example of a lack of commitment:** We all met at school and went to class. We left when the bell rang for lunch and drove around.

When the statement concerns more than one person and "we" is the best description, then the lack of "we" is cause for concern, particularly if the subject is talking about a spouse. This signifies a distancing between a husband and wife and a lack of the togetherness that is expected between spouses.

> **Example of the norm:** My wife and I went to a local restaurant. We met up with some friends there and had dinner. After dinner we went right home.
>
> **Example of a deviation:** My wife and I went to a local restaurant. My wife and I then met up with some friends and had dinner. After dinner my wife and I went right home.

In allegations of rape and abduction the interviewer should be concerned when the victim uses "we" to refer to himself or herself and the perpetrator. This pronoun suggests togetherness, a deviation from the norm in these reports. The interviewer should ask if the victim knew the perpetrator previously if he or she refers to the attacker in this way. If there is no relationship then there is reason to believe that the statement is false.

> **Example of the norm:** I got into the car and he pointed a gun at me and told me to drive. He was hiding in the front seat under a blanket. I drove north on Rte. 91 until he told me to take exit 12.

> ### BEEN THERE...DONE THAT!   4-4
>
> The phone rang. It was 2 AM. A kidnapping and rape had just been reported. Arriving at the scene, I found it strange that the victim had been driven so far off of the highway when the first report I had received said she had been abducted from another state. How did the perpetrator know to come off the highway at this particular exit and travel 15 minutes to this location, which was secluded? In my interview of the victim she was very calm and matter of fact about her abduction, claiming that there was a man hiding under a horse blanket in the passenger front seat who had risen up to abduct her. This did not seem possible given the size of the area or the close proximity to the driver. There were also verbal clues that indicated that her situation was questionable. She referred to the kidnapper with a "we" statement over and over. When pressed for specifics about the assault, she used equivocating terms with a lack of detail. There were attempts to absolve her of responsibility when she stated that she could not have possibly known that he was hiding under the blanket. Her statement was difficult to understand because she started at the middle of the incident, went to the beginning, and then to the end. It made little sense, and I found myself asking her repeatedly to explain things to me—they lacked any chronological order.
>
> The investigation continued after the initial interview with the victim. Even the identification was so unclear that it was meaningless. Finally I called the police department where she lived and found that the victim was well known to them. She had made a similar kidnapping complaint a year earlier to that department and to a third police department before that. There was no evidence of a kidnapping; it was a false report. The victim was making a plea for help. Appropriate referrals were made.

> **Example of a deviation:** I got into the car and he pointed a gun at me and told me to drive. He was hiding in the front seat under a blanket. We drove north on Rte. 91, and then we took exit 12.

Possessive pronouns such as my, our, your, his, her, and their suggest a relationship between a person or object and the interviewee. Changing the relationship is a deviation from the norm and suggests a distancing from that person or object.

> **Example of the norm:** My grandchild and I were walking in the woods. She needed to go to the bathroom, so I helped her take down her underwear. I did not touch her other than to help her go to the bathroom.
>
> **Example of a deviation.** My grandchild and I were walking in the woods. She needed to go to the bathroom, so the child was helped with taking down the underwear. The child was never touched in a bad way.

Nouns. Because nouns represent persons, places, and things, a change in noun usage may represent a change in the way that the suspect perceives a situation. Interviewers should look for a change in the noun that is being used in the statement. Something has changed in the reality of the suspect when a noun change occurs after frequent usage. It is almost impossible for a perpetrator to admit harming a family member, according to Adams (1996). Thus:

Example of the norm: I loved my mother. I did not mean to hurt my mother, but I stabbed her.

Example of a deviation: I loved my mother. I did not mean to hurt her, the devil was stabbed.

Verbs. When someone uses memory to recall past events it is normal to use the first person, singular past tense. It becomes significant if an individual being interviewed varies the verb tense during the statement because the event occurred in the past. Any change in the tense of the verb should provide a signal to the interviewer that deception may exist.

Example of the norm: I saw the shooting. I was so scared that I ran as fast as I could.

Example of a deviation: I saw the shooting. I am so scared that I run away as fast as I can.

Here the sentence starts in the past tense and moves to the present tense, which indicates a lack of commitment to being the witness; it is suggestive of greater involvement than the interviewee has admitted. Change of tense from the past to the present tense may signal deception. Using the past tense when referring to missing persons is also considered a deviation of the norm.

A statement that contains a verb such as "tried" or "started" represents a weakened assertion of the facts. An individual who states during an interview that something occurred will state that it did occur; he or she will commit to that statement fully. When an individual weakens the statement of the fact it may mean that he or she did not actually do what is claimed. This may be due to a perceived expectation of what the interviewee should have done in those circumstances. An interviewer faced with a weakened assertion of the facts should question further to determine what actually happened. A victim who states that she "tried to say no" may have been inhibited from saying "no" due to force or fear, for example. It may also mean that she realized that she should have said "no" but failed to verbalize it. A weakened assertion of a fact changes the description of what occurred.

Example of the norm: I ran.

Example of a deviation: I tried to run.

Adjectives. Additional information is provided by the use of adjectives. Using the adjectives of "that" and "those" to reference a person or object suggests distancing. Referring to a person though spatial adjectives is a deviation of the norm, particularly when a relationship should exist:

Example of the norm: I did not hurt David.

Example of a deviation: I did not hurt that child.

Step Two: Extraneous Information

Extraneous information refers to irrelevant or unnecessary statements, and should be looked for. It refers to situations in which the interviewee provides information that does not answer the question and or is presented out of order. When a truthful person with nothing to hide is asked, "What happened," he or she will generally provide the events in chronological order. Subjects will avoid revealing information by asking questions in response to interviewers. The extra information is given to avoid talking directly about the event rather than denying the allegation or lying about it outright. Extraneous phrasing associated with deception includes "I believe," "I think," Kind of," and "To the best of my knowledge." Although the subject may actually provide truthful extraneous information, it could be used as an alternative to specific details about the incident. Guilty or involved persons will use this tactic to justify their actions.

Step Three: Lack of Conviction

Lack of conviction refers to words that are used to label or change the meaning of something; these are equivocating terms. Examples of equivocating terms are the phrases "sort of," "kind of," "I guess," "little bit," and "hopefully." When an individual claims not to remember parts of the narrative it is known as repression (Rabon, 1994). The interviewer should always look more closely at a statement in which a person consistently says "I don't recall" or "I don't remember." Other qualifying terms such as "I think" or "I believe" are used to minimize the statements conviction. A victim's use of terms that minimize the event such as "kind of surprised" or "sort of hurt" suggests a deviation from the expected norm. False claims are rarely made as convincingly as truthful ones because liars are unwilling or unable to fully embrace them (DePaulo et al., 2003).

Step Four: Balance of the Statement

A truthful statement will contain three parts: prior to the incident, the incident itself, and the events after the incident. The statement should be examined for balance; if any part is missing, it is most likely false. It is more likely that the statement is true when it contains equal amounts of information in all three parts. A person who is attempting to justify his or her actions will give information that does not answer the questions or will include more than is necessary to explain what happened. An extremely large "before" section compared to the "after" section is an indication of a lack of emotion and may be a false or incomplete accounting of what happened.

Missing time within the statement changes the balance and suggests something has been left out. The interviewer should attempt to determine what was not included and whether the information was not important or was perceived as not being important to the subject.

FIELD STATEMENT ANALYSIS

Application of the statement analysis technique is time consuming and can be tedious if the statement is complex. It is further limited by a lack of understanding and training in the entire approach. Preliminary research has suggested a way to use the statement analysis approach quickly in a field situation. Klopf and Tooke (2003) developed a quick method to evaluate statements called the statement analysis field examination technique (SAFE-T). They tested two components of statement analysis in their study to develop an accuracy measure of statements taken in the field: extraneous information and lack of conviction. These terms were defined earlier in the chapter.

Truthful individuals will state events chronologically and concisely when asked what has occurred. To measure extraneous information, count the statements' total number of lines, identifying which lines contain unnecessary information. Determine the percentage of extraneous information as part of the whole statement. If there are 100 lines in the statement and 10 lines contain irrelevant information, the amount of extraneous information is 10 percent. Klopf and Tooke (2003) suggested that fewer than 25 percent of the statement should consist of extraneous information to be considered accurate.

Lack of conviction is illustrated by the use of equivocating terms; the interviewee is failing to commit to the statement and modifying his or her description of something. When these words are used to quantify or limit the situation described, this represents an attempt to avoid personal accountability. To detect deception, the number of terms that indicate lack of conviction are counted. When the count is between six incidents or more of lack of conviction, there is a concern about the truthfulness of the statement (Klopf & Tooke, 2003). The higher the number of terms indicating a lack of conviction, the higher is the possibility that the statement is not true.

▲ CONCLUSIONS

This chapter covered the primary methods of interviewing used by law enforcement officers. Each approach has its pros and cons. Traditional interviewing is best used in situations in which the intent is to limit the amount of information that is being gathered. As suggested earlier, this approach can be used to make a preliminary assessment of the value of the witness, identifying the individual for future, more in-depth interviewing. It is comprehensive, but it is often used in a haphazard way that diminishes its value.

The structural interview offers a humanistic approach to obtaining information. This approach is more comprehensive and focused than the traditional method. The added value of using a structural interview is that there are no difficult steps to memorize, it is fairly easy to use, and it has a decent response rate. The reason the structural interview is so widely used is its lack of complexity.

New to the arsenal of interviewing techniques is the inferential interview method. Inferential interviewing is an improvement on the structural interview because it contains the same steps and adds additional ways to detect deceit.

The statement analysis approach contains many useful tools to assist the interviewer in looking for clues to deception and indications that further investigation may be needed. The method is complex and may be difficult to use. The modified approach of field statement analysis is an improvement on statement analysis.

QUESTIONS FOR REVIEW

Short-Answer Questions

1. What does traditional interviewing hope to attain?
2. Why is it important to determine the role the complainant may have played in the commission of a crime?
3. Is it important to know why a crime has occurred at a particular location? Explain.
4. Why is learning the proper sequence of events so important to an interviewer?
5. Is it important for the person being interviewed to know the position of the interviewer? If so, why? If not, why not?
6. In a structural interview should the person being interviewed be encouraged to be an active part of the discussion? If so, why? If not, why not?
7. During an inferential interview what inferences may be drawn from the sentence structure of the answers received?
8. What types of interviews can benefit from statement analysis?

Fill-in Questions

1. The structural interviewing approach uses the best of _____ methods while applying principles used in _____.
2. In the early stages of an investigation it is important to find out which individuals _____ about the case versus those who _____.
3. If preliminary questions reveal that the complainant may be the suspect, then the approach changes from a(n) _____ to a(n) _____ as necessary.
4. Questions should not be phrased in a way that _____ the person being interviewed to give a particular answer, nor should they be _____.
5. Interviewing should establish the _____ of the case.
6. Use _____ and _____ when helpful to make sure that you and the person being interviewed have a mutual understanding of the event.
7. A promising new approach to interviewing is evidenced by the _____, a method of detecting deception through statement characteristics and question-by-question analysis.
8. Based on the idea that _____ will contain language characteristics that are absent from statements that are the _____,

statement analysis is a word-by-word examination of the grammar within a statement.
9. When asked, "What happened," a truthful person with nothing to hide will provide the events in _____.
10. When an individual claims not to remember parts of the narrative, this is known as _____.

Exercises

1. Pair off with a classmate for about 10 to 15 minutes. Interview your partner about the last TV show he or she watched. Use the traditional interviewing approach, and only the five W's and How. Verbally or in writing report what you learned about the program.
2. Pair off with a classmate for about 10 to 15 minutes. Using the structural interviewing approach, interview your partner about the last TV show he or she watched. Verbally or in writing report what you learned about the program.

REFERENCES

Adams, S. (1996). Statement analysis: What do suspects' words really reveal? *FBI Law Enforcement Bulletin, 65*(10), 12–20.

Adams, S. (2004). Statement analysis: Beyond the words. *FBI Law Enforcement Bulletin, 73*(4), 22–23.

Artwohl, A. (2002). Perceptual and memory distortion during officer-involved shootings. *FBI Law Enforcement Bulletin, 158*(10), 18–24.

Colwell, K., Hiscock, C. K., & Memon, A. (2002). Interviewing techniques and the assessment of statement credibility. *Applied Cognitive Psychology, 16*(3), 287–300.

DePaulo, B., Lindsay, J., Malone, B., Muhlenbruck, L., Charlton, K., & Cooper, H. (2003). Cues to Deception. *Psychological Bulletin, 129*(1), 74–118.

Garner, B. (2004). *Black's Law Dictionary* (8th ed.). St. Paul, MN: West Publishing Co.

Hand, H. (2003). The mentor's tale: A reflexive account of semi-structured interviews. *Nurse Researcher, 10*(3), 15–28.

Kebbell, M. R. (1996). Enhancing the practicality of the cognitive interview in forensic situations. *Psycoloquy, 7*(16), *Witness Memory* (3). [Online.] Available: http://psycprints.ecs.soton.ac.uk/archive/00000508/.

Klopf, G., & Tooke, A. (2003). Statement analysis field examination technique. *FBI Law Enforcement Bulletin, 72*(4), 6–15.

Memon, A., & Higham, P. A. (1999). A review of the cognitive interview. *Psychology, Crime and the Law*, 5, 177–196.

Memon, A., Gabbert, F., & Hope, L. (2004). The ageing eyewitness. In J. R. Adler (Ed.), *Forensic psychology: Concepts, debates and practice* (pp. 96–112). Devon, UK: Willan Publishing.

Memon, A., Wark, L., Holley, A., Bull, R., & Koehnken, G. (1997). Eyewitness performance in cognitive and structured interviews. *Memory, 5*(5), 639–657.

Merriam-Webster's collegiate dictionary (11th ed.). (2004). Springfield, MA: Merriam-Webster.

Rabon, D. (1994). *Investigative discourse analysis*. Durham, NC: Carolina Academic Press.

Schmalleger, F. (2004). *Criminal Justice*. Upper Saddle River, NJ: Prentice Hall.

Talwar, V., & Lee, K. (2002). Development of lying to conceal a transgression: Children's control of expressive behaviour during verbal deception. *International Journal of Behavioral Development, 26*(5), 436–444.

Technical Working Group for Eyewitness Evidence. (1999). *Eyewitness evidence: A guide for law enforcement* (Report No. NCJ 178240). Washington, DC: U.S. Department of Justice.

CHAPTER 5
Forensic Hypnosis and Cognitive Interviewing

Key Terms

Forensic hypnosis	Hypermnesia
Cognitive interviewing	Memory hardening
Confabulation	Mnemonics
Age regression	Scripts

Chapter Objectives

After completing this chapter, you should be able to:
- Define forensic hypnosis
- Discuss the advantages and disadvantages of forensic hypnosis
- Explain the difference between cognitive interviewing and hypnosis
- Understand how to encourage interviewee participation
- Describe practical techniques for facilitating memory retrieval
- Articulate the sequence of the cognitive interview
- Use the four mnemonic principles
- Explain the limitations of cognitive interviewing
- Incorporate cognitive techniques into most interviewing approaches

Introduction

There are two forms of memory retrieval discussed in this chapter, forensic hypnosis and cognitive interviewing. These approaches to interviewing share the same goal, which is to increase the information that the interviewee can remember. They both use memory-jogging techniques to obtain information but differ in the methods they use to jog the memory. The forensic interviewing approach seeks to promote memory through a process of heightened awareness brought about by the interviewer. The cognitive interviewing approach jogs the memory by a process that is completely controlled by the person being interviewed. Both approaches require an interviewee who is willing to participate. Neither of these approaches is recommended as a tool to use when interrogating an alleged perpetrator. Forensic hypnosis is a controversial approach whose popularity has recently resurfaced. The National Institute of Justice recommends cognitive interviewing for criminal justice use.

Forensic hypnosis is an investigative memory retrieval technique used to enhance recall in legally relevant situations. Hypnosis is a state of increased receptivity to suggestion characterized by an altered state of consciousness. Its use in court testimony has been traced back over 150 years (Webert, 2003).

The **cognitive interviewing** method is a family of memory-jogging and retrieval tools for evaluating survey questions and questionnaires and conducting interviews. The approaches to cognitive interviewing are as diverse as the individuals who apply them. During the last decade, many institutions from around the world have come to rely on cognitive methods. Federal statistical agencies that use this approach include researchers from the U.S. Census Bureau, who commonly evaluate the quality of survey questionnaires (Honey & Mumford, 1982), and the U.S. Bureau of Justice Statistics. Cognitive methods are used to facilitate learning for members of the British Air Force (Royal Air Force, 2001), for dealing with depression (Makoi, 2002), and for police interviewing (Fisher & Geiselman, 1992).

What Is Hypnosis?

Hypnosis is a process during which a person allows himself or herself to become more suggestible; results differ according to individual responses (American Psychotherapy and Medical Hypnosis Association [APMHA], 2000). Individuals do not lose control, and some describe the experience as a heightened awareness (APMHA, 2000). Persons under hypnosis are aware of what is going on; they do not become zombies. There are three common uses of hypnosis in criminal investigation (Newman & Thompson, 2001):

1. To enhance an accused defendant's memory about events occurring around the time of the crime.
2. To help an eyewitness to a crime to provide details about the behavior or physical appearance of the perpetrator.
3. To assist in generating leads for investigators through recall of salient details.

Advocates of hypnosis in criminal investigation cite numerous cases in which police investigators successfully solved crimes using hypnosis as a tool (McConkey & Sheehan, 1995; Niehaus, 1999). The goal of forensic hypnosis is memory enhancement and retrieval for use in a specific civil or criminal case. Strong arguments have been made that forensic hypnosis sessions should be conducted by police officers who are skilled in relevant interviewing techniques and have sophisticated legal knowledge. Others suggest that clinicians are the most appropriate forensic hypnotists. The debate has drawn attention away from the more important issue of the practice of investigative hypnosis by untrained lay hypnotists (McConkey & Sheehan, 1995).

Forensic Hypnosis Interviewing Methods

The public's perception of hypnosis is quite favorable. Recent research shows that a large percentage of people believe overwhelmingly in the positive use of forensic hypnosis (Webert, 2003). In contrast, the legal and medical communities have long taken positions against the accuracy of facts recalled under hypnosis in hotly contested debates regarding its reliability. During the 1970s and 1980s severe attacks were made against the use of forensic hypnosis (Reiser, 1984). In 1985 the American Medical Association recommended that the use of hypnosis be limited to the

> **BEEN THERE... DONE THAT! 5-1**
>
> A child had been abducted and there were no leads to locating the child or identifying the kidnapper. In desperation a hypnotist was called to conduct interviews of the family members. No useful information came from the interviews, but the procedure did cause a lot of discussion among the detectives. In the state of Massachusetts, information obtained after a person has been hypnotized is not acceptable as evidence in court. Sometimes it is worth taking the chance that evidence will not be admissible in court if the process might save a life. The decision is one that should be debated. A number of states do allow hypnotically refreshed memory. What is the status of hypnotic evidence in your state?

investigative processes and its results not be used as evidence in court because the increased memory is not limited to only accurate recollections (Moenssens et al., 1995). Nonetheless, hundreds of cases presented in court do include testimony enhanced through hypnosis. The primary objection to hypnosis is that eyewitnesses may become more susceptible to leading and misleading questions (Fisher & Geiselman, 1992).

Guidelines for the Use of Forensic Hypnosis

According to McConkey and Sheehan (1995), the successful application of forensic hypnosis depends on satisfying the following requirements:

1. The use of forensic hypnosis should be consistent with federal and state legislation.
2. Its use must be consistent with clinical and legal safeguards designed to ensure the well-being of the subject.
3. A clear statement of the rationale for using hypnosis must be made prior to the session.
4. Hypnosis should be used for major crime investigations and only after all standard procedures have been exhausted.

Caution must be exercised in cases involving the hypnosis of a juvenile or any witness whose ability to give informed consent is questionable. A person who has successfully completed appropriate specific training in its methods may conduct the session. If the hypnotist is not a member of a police department, then adequate credentials on the application of legal forensic procedures is necessary. Hall (1999) recommended the following guidelines:

1. The hypno-investigator should not be involved in the direct investigation of the case.
2. Before the hypnosis, a written record should be made that includes a description of the subject matter and the information that was provided.
3. The session should be both videotaped and audiotaped.
4. There should be no lineup or mug shot viewing prior to the session.
5. Hypnosis should be explained to the subject before the session.

The forensic hypnotic approach begins with preparation. There are four phases: the induction phase, the narrative phase, the closure phase, and the recall phase. The preparation and the induction phase of the forensic hypnotic session are described next.

Preparing for the Hypnotic Session

Evidence established prior to the session must be documented to differentiate between pre- and posthypnotic information. The hypnotist should arrange for a quiet room free of distractions. Only the hypnotist and subject are allowed in the room, unless the hypnotist determines that it is necessary to include others. There should be a two-way mirror for session viewing by persons involved in the investigation such as legal representation and police investigators. Ideally, there should be a form of communication from the viewers to the hypnotist, such as via a small ear receiver. All conversations between the hypnotist and the subject should be videotaped prior to, during, and after the session. The documentation includes the place, date, and time of the session. Prior to beginning, the hypnotist makes an independent assessment of the subject's suitability for hypnosis and willingness to proceed.

Induction Phase

During the induction phase, the hypnotist attempts to relax the witness and tests the witness's responsivity to suggestion. The hypnotist instructs the witness using an unrushed and calm voice to sit with a straight back in a comfortable chair without crossing his legs or arms and to place his hands in his lap so that he may remain comfortable during the entire session.

FIGURE 5-1 The first phase of hypnosis is the induction phase. Eye fixation is a common approach.

Induction consists of a general relaxation technique; many formats of induction are available. An approach suggested by Niehaus (1999) begins with an instruction that the subject take three deep breaths and let each one out slowly, closing his or her eyes at the third breath. Slowly, the hypnotist instructs the subject to relax through releasing tension, breathing deeply, and slipping further and further into relaxation. Describing each part of the body to be relaxed encourages the subject to drift further into a relaxed state of hypnosis. The hypnotist may suggest that pleasant surroundings such as a beach or vacation be envisioned to encourage relaxation. Induction into hypnosis can be induced through the following approaches adapted from the Ohio Academy of Hypnosis Basic Forensic Hypnosis manual (Niehaus, 1999):

- **Eye-fixation method.** The subject fixates on some point or object overhead.
- **Chiasson's technique.** The subject puts his or her hands directly in front of his or her face with the fingers pressed together. The subject is told to watch the fingers spread apart as they come closer to his or her face. When the face is being touched the subject is to go deeply into a restful, peaceful state of hypnosis.

Narrative Phase

A major technique used for memory recall in forensic hypnosis is **age regression** (Newman & Thompson, 2001). It is used during the narrative phase, and is the most common technique used in hypnosis. The hypnotist suggests that the subject return to an earlier time. Asking the subject to imagine a calendar going backward, watching television, or walking toward the scene of the crime are among the ways to get the subject to the time of the crime. In step one of the narrative phase, once the person has reached the crime scene, he or she is asked to describe the events he or she sees them. The approach should be not to lead the subject in any way. The hypnotist can only ask the person to describe what he or she experiences through his or her senses. In other words, what the subject sees, hears, smells, or feels through touch regarding the event. "What do you see?" and "What is happening now?" are suggestive phrases that are nonleading.

The calendar procedure is a popular age regression technique. The subject is instructed to imagine a calendar on the wall (Howell, 2003). The person is then instructed to look at the calendar and see that it is the appropriate month, date, and year, which is a particular day of the week. The hypnotist takes the subject backward by each day until the date prior to the event is reached. The subject is asked to state the sequence of events as they are occurring.

During step two of the narrative phase the hypnotist asks specific but nonleading questions. It is important that the subject be told that "I don't know" is an acceptable answer. For example, the subject may be instructed to view the back of the vehicle used in the crime and slowly describe everything that he or she sees. The hypnotist gives the subject the opportunity to make comments on anything he or she wishes prior to closure.

Closure Phase

Hypermnesia is another major technique used in forensic hypnosis (Newman & Thompson, 2001). Through direct suggestion, this technique enhances the memory of the individual after the hypnotic session. The suggestion may be as simple as instructing the subject to remember what was discussed during the hypnosis once he or she awakens. Irrelevant suggestions made by the hypnotist to the subject are canceled at this time. An appropriate deinduction procedure to end the hypnosis session is then used during the closure phase. A simple counting of 1 to 5 or use of a similar technique may be used to close the session.

Recall Phase

The final phase, recall, actually occurs after the hypnotic session has ended and the subject is deinducted. During this phase, the subject is asked to recall all that he or she has remembered about the crime since the memory enhancement. Any questions can be asked of the subject regarding the incident. The subject may also want to make comments or ask questions about the process.

CHALLENGES TO HYPNOTIC MEMORY RETRIEVAL

As with any approach to interviewing, there are challenges to the use of the forensic hypnotic technique. Situations of abuse, particularly child abuse, should be approached with extra caution. There are indications that events are altered, deleted, and created by events that occur during and after the time of encoding, during the period of storage, and during any attempts at retrieval (McConkey & Sheehan, 1995). In other words, the memory of abuse may be influenced by abuse that occurs after the initial event or at any time, including the hypnotic session.

Forensic hypnosis is not recommended for use on a defendant or person suspected of being involved in the crime under investigation. People can and do lie while under hypnosis. Confabulation can occur. The results of a hypnotic session with a suspect are of questionable value.

Few states allow hypnotically refreshed recall as evidence in court. Among these are Texas and Nevada. Hypnotically refreshed recall has been admissible in Texas in both criminal and civil cases since 1988 (Howell, 2003). Texas mandates minimum training standards, testing, and certification of police officers who use investigative hypnosis. In 1997, the Nevada legislature declared that hypnotically refreshed testimony was admissible in both civil and criminal cases (Nevada Revised Statutes, 1997). Nevada specifically named police officers trained in forensic hypnosis as among the persons whose interview may qualify as admissible in court. It is suggested that all information be independently verified when possible and its use limited to witness and victim statements.

The FBI revised its guidelines on the use of hypnosis in 1979, mandating that certain safeguards be in place for hypnotic sessions (Newman & Thompson, 2001). Among these requirements was the recording of hypnotic session. Concern has also been raised regarding police bias along with the noted increase of police officers using hypnosis as a part of the criminal investigation (Newman & Thompson, 2001).

Confabulation

Critics claim that **confabulation** is very common while under hypnosis (Newman & Thompson, 2001). Confabulation is a filling in of the memory gaps to make the event more comprehensible. It may result from the subject's desire to please the hypnotist through the creation of complete and coherent memories.

> A confabulation is a *fantasy* that has unconsciously replaced *fact* in memory. A confabulation may be based partly on fact or be a complete construction of the imagination. It is used to describe the memories of people claiming to have been abducted by aliens, as well as false memories induced by therapists or interviewers, memories that often involve bizarre notions of satanic ritualistic sexual abuse of children (Adams, 2004).

In response, advocates suggest that forensic hypnosis does tend to increase recall with witness who are motivated and cooperative and that the accuracy of information in these cases may be as high as 90% (Reiser, 1984).

Faking

Hypnosis can be faked, and people are capable of lying in hypnosis. Although it is extremely difficult to determine whether an individual is faking during the hypnotic session, McConkey and Sheehan (1995) stated that it does occur. They suggested that no single indicator exists to be sure that the subject is faking, but an accumulation of factors make the possibility probable. Here are some possible indicators of deceit:

1. Frequent occurrences of logical thinking that are unsolicited and unsuggested.
2. Reflection on what the person is saying to the hypnotist.
3. Zealous overplaying of the role of the hypnotized subject.
4. Indications of behavior consistent with expectations communicated outside of hyp- nosis.
5. Behavior atypical of an individual under hypnosis.

Memory Hardening and Suggestibility

Opponents to the use of forensic hypnosis believe that hypnotism is **memory hardening.** The phenomenon gives the subject increased confidence regarding the facts remembered during hypnosis, regardless of whether the supposed facts are true or false (Webert, 2003).

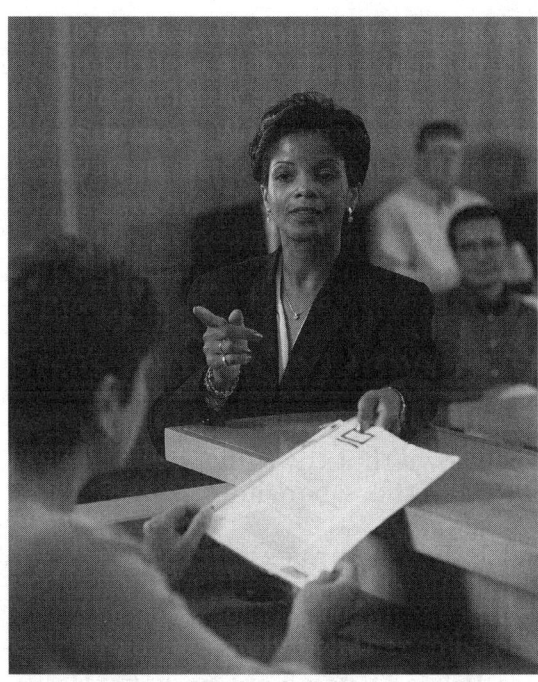

FIGURE 5-2 The admissibility of hypnotically induced evidence is determined by each state.

Posthypnotic suggestion can become permanent if it is repeated many times or over several sessions (Niehaus, 1999). In addition, the effect of hypnosis varies among individuals; some individuals may be hypersensitive to these techniques. Critics argue that a person undergoing hypnosis experiences an increased susceptibility to suggestion and a loss of critical judgment regarding cues planted by the hypnotist (Webert, 2003).

HYPNOSIS EVIDENCE IN COURT

Rock v. Arkansas (1987) is the most significant case concerning the admission of forensic hypnosis evidence. In this case the Supreme Court ruled that the lower courts could not ban the use of evidence retrieved via hypnosis because hypnosis did not fall under the test of per se inadmissibility set by the Court in *Illinois v. Gates (1983)*. The majority of states, however, do not allow posthypnotic memories as evidence in court (Webert, 2003).

Scientific evidence must meet certain tests in order to be admitted by the courts. According to the *Frye* test, the scientific method must have gained general acceptance in the medical and psychological communities as a reliable method in order to be acceptable *(Frye v. United States, 1923)*. The *Frye* rule was first articulated in a criminal case that attempted to introduce evidence from a polygraph test. Forensic hypnosis is used in both medical and legal settings, but is not generally accepted as reliable. Those states that determine scientific reliability based on use of the *Frye* rule generally exclude the use of hypnotic memories. A more recent test of the reliability of scientific evidence is articulated in *Daubert v. Merrell Dow Pharmaceuticals (1993)*. The four-part *Daubert* test, which has become the federal standard concerning the admissibility of scientific evidence, has replaced *Frye* in some states. It asks:

1. Whether the type of evidence can and has been tested by scientific methods.
2. Whether the underlying theory or technique has been subjected to peer review and published in the professional literature.
3. How reliable the results are in terms of potential error rate.
4. Whether there is general acceptance of the technique (the Frye test).

Some courts may allow information gathered prior to the witnesses being subjected to hypnosis if it can be shown that the evidence was indeed provided prior to the hypnosis, whereas others ban its use in criminal proceedings altogether.

Edward Geiselman and Ronald P. Fisher, professors at UCLA and Florida International University, respectively, used cognitive methods to develop a technique for overcoming the challenges that limit the use of hypnosis in criminal investigations (Geiselman & Fisher, 1985). They worked closely with the Los Angeles Police Department and the Metro-Dade Police Department to develop a method to address the specific needs of police interviewing. Their success was evidenced in a *Frye* hearing in California court in 1995 that concluded that the cognitive interviewing method was a reliable investigative tool (Geiselman & Fisher, 1985).

What Is Cognitive Interviewing?

Cognitive Interviewing (CI) is an approach for increasing the amount of information recalled by a witness without increasing the level of confabulation. It is deceptively simple and might not seem to be particularly useful or different. However, the four methods for jogging memory used along with several specific techniques provides a very powerful and effective means of eliciting a complete and accurate picture of the events recalled. The most important thing about cognitive interviewing is that when it is done properly, it works.

Although cognitive interviewing has been compared to hypnosis, its original authors maintain that there are major differences between the two (Geiselman & Fisher, 1985). For example, there is no hypnotic induction in cognitive interviewing. Evidence indicates that although it is a successful memory retrieval tool, it does not heighten an interviewee's confidence in the memories or increase the error rate (Geiselman et al., 1986). There is no evidence to suggest that cognitive interviewing techniques increase the misleading-question effect, and it may even reduce the effect. Although cognitive interviewing involves memory-jogging and retrieval techniques, there is no induction phase, and the interviewee is a full participant in the process.

> **BEEN THERE... DONE THAT! 5-2**
>
> There are a number of approaches to cognitive interviewing. One is a seven-step enhanced method. Another was published by the National Institute of Justice (NIJ) in its manual on eyewitness evidence (U.S. Department of Justice, 1999). The NIJ incorporated many of the principles found in the cognitive approach to interviewing in an update to the traditional approach. For more information on the national recommendations for police interviewing go to their Web site (http://www.ncjrs.org/pdffiles1/nij/178240.pdf). A shorter version is provided in this chapter. Familiarity with the concepts along with the willingness to practice the mnemonics will prepare the student for its use. The concepts are flexible and can be incorporated into a more elaborate interviewing approach or into a more traditional approach.

Studies testing the usefulness of cognitive interviewing have taken place in Germany, Britain, and the United States (Geiselman & Fisher, 1985). Results have indicated that it is an effective approach. With relatively little training, the results from a cognitive interview may increase the gain in information by almost 50 percent compared to interviews without its use (Fisher, Geiselman, & Amador, 1989). In trials in which individuals were reinterviewed after a standard interview, they reported new facts with the cognitive approach.

Both specific and general memory-jogging guidance techniques are combined to form the cognitive interview technique. Because a memory is composed of a collection of several elements, the more elements a memory retrieval aid has in common with the memory of the event, the more effective the aid is. The general idea is that memory is accessible through several access routes, so that information that is not accessible though one retrieval cue may be reached though another. For an interview to be successful, the details of the crime need to be recalled and communicated to the interviewer.

The cognitive interview technique has been adapted for use with children. The version specific to interviewing children is given in Chapter 7 and has been shown to be very effective in such cases (Geiselman, Bornstein, & Saywitz, 1992).

COGNITIVE INTERVIEWING TECHNIQUES

The approach stresses using a secluded, quiet place free of distractions for the interview as well as urging subjects to speak slowly. Cognitive interviewing encourages the witness to do the talking while the interviewer listens. It attempts to avoid some of the mistakes commonly associated with police interviewing such as interrupting the narrative and rushing the account. Witnesses must feel comfortable in taking the time to think and reflect about what happened. They should feel free to say anything, knowing that there is sufficient time to speak and that the interviewer will not make judgments on the statements. Specific questions are for clarification. The interviewer holds these back until the narrative is fully stated. It is common knowledge that cases are solved when someone talks about what happened! Cognitive interviewing is designed to get the interviewee talking. A major challenge is not to interrupt.

Mnemonics

Mnemonics are methods for remembering information that is otherwise difficult to recall. The three basic stages of memory are encoding, storage, and retrieval (Wrightby & Merrill, 2002). Encoding is a process that the brain goes through when something happens. The information received is filtered and stored. Mnemonics are merely ways to find the information. Think of the brain as a filing cabinet. There are many drawers; within the draws are file hangers. Typically, the files are labeled by category or alphabetically, but that depends on who is doing the filing! If you cannot find a file, then it is necessary to think about how you categorized the information. Was the order by the case number, incident type, perpetrator, or victim? Was the date or the location used as a method to file the information? This is similar to the process used for mnemonics.

Recall through mnemonics requires the use of imagination, association, and location. Use of imagination does not suggest fantasy, but imagery. The description of an event will be more realistic and complete if an individual verbalizes how he or she felt or reacted at the time of a crime. The association aspect of cognitive interviewing allows the individual to remember one thought in order to move to another. The interviewer asks, for example, whether there was a familiar smell, shape, or feeling during the incident. The third principle in the attempt to promote recall has to do with the location of the incident. The interviewee pictures the place where the incident occurred in order to describe in detail everything about the place.

Mnemonics are not complicated; they are simply ways to jog the memory in order to find information that is not easily accessible. The foundation of the cognitive interview is the use of the following four mnemonics as memory-jogging techniques (Geiselman & Fisher, 1985):

- ✔ Mentally reconstruct the context of the event.
- ✔ Report every detail, regardless of apparent importance.
- ✔ Recall the events in a variety of orders, moving backward and forward in time.
- ✔ Change perspectives and recall events from different points of view.

These four principles are tools to use within the interview process. Explained to the witness before the interview begins, they allow the witness to approach memory recall and retrieval from several different avenues. The first two methods attempt to increase the overlap of elements between the stored memory and retrieval cues. The goal is to encourage witnesses to construct a new description of the event. The last two methods encourage using many retrieval paths.

> **BEEN THERE...DONE THAT! 5-3**
>
> On a back country road in the middle of the afternoon, a female jogger sprinted effortlessly. It was a warm and sunny summer day. The woman being interviewed said that her mind was blank as she enjoyed her run, until a truck stopped in front of her and a man came toward her. Grabbing her, the man pushed her into the tall corn stalks along the side of the road. She struggled while he lay on top of her and fought until she got free. Once free, she ran like she was in a marathon in the other direction and went into the first house to call the police.
>
> During the interview it was apparent that details were missing that would enhance the case. By use of imagery I asked her to tell me every detail, no matter how small. She changed the order of the attack and reconstructed the context of the event. She was able to describe the smell of the field and the sound of a car going by. He did not rape her; he struggled to get her pants down. His pants were unzipped and part way down his hips when she escaped. From this information I knew that there was at least one other witness who had seen the truck parked on the side of the road. A check with the local police department confirmed that someone had called them with information on that suspicious truck. We now had a plate number and were able to locate the driver. The driver was located and interrogated. His clothing was taken, and evidence of his being in a corn field was clear. His pants and underclothes were taken and sent to the lab. Pre-ejaculatory fluid in his shorts confirmed his sexual intentions. He was convicted of an assault and attempted rape.

Reconstruction Technique

For reconstruction, the investigator assists the witness to recreate the incident scene. Instructing the interviewee to think about the circumstances that surrounded the incident, the investigator suggests that he or she think about the room where the incident occurred, the location of furniture, vehicles, weather, lighting, any nearby people, objects, or smells. The individual interviewed is to think about how he or she felt at the time and his or her reaction to the incident. The purpose of this line of inquiry is to return the witness deeply to the scene of the crime. Visualizing a situation strongly through imagery helps an individual to remember. Reconstruction is accomplished by asking witnesses to relive mentally the events prior to, during, and after the crime.

The interviewer instructs the witness that reconstruction includes talking about the time of day, day, month, and year of the event. In other words, the witness reconstructs the scene according to when it happened. What was the weather? How did he or she know? Was it light or dark? This line of thinking will open up thoughts particularly when multiple events or assaults occurred and they need to be separated into single occurrences that are otherwise blurred over time. Reconstruction also includes talking about the location of the incident in relation to other houses, furniture, equipment, or any other tangible item that can be described.

Reporting-Everything Technique

For the reporting phase, the investigator explains that some people hold back information because they are not quite sure that the information is important. The witness should not edit anything, even things that may not seem important. Providing this permission to recount everything may cause the witness to remember something otherwise forgotten. Throughout the interview the interviewee should be reminded to talk about everything he or she remembers. One should continue to encourage his or her participation.

Changing the Order of Events

This aspect includes an instruction to recall the events in a different order. Typically, a witness is asked to begin at the beginning, which may cause him or her to fill in gaps so that the story sounds logical. Sticking to an expected order may lead to an account that may not be completely accurate. The instruction for this technique may ask that the beginning point be the thing that impressed the witness (frightened him or her, or made him or her aware that something was going on). The witness is asked to try starting from a point that he or she remembers most vividly and either go backward or forward from that point.

Changing the Perspective

In the fourth phase of this process, the witness is instructed to recall the incident from different perspectives or adopt the perspective of others who were present. Depending on the circumstances of the event, the investigator may also instruct the witness to place himself or herself in the role of someone else in the incident and think about what he or she must have seen.

Additional Memory-Jogging Techniques

1. **Appearance.** What type of clothing was the witness or perpetrator wearing at the time of the event? Was there anything unusual about the physical appearance of the individual involved? What was it that seemed unusual? Did the perpetrator remind the witness of anyone, and why? The characteristics that are familiar to an individual may cue him or her to think of someone else. The behavior, speech, or physical appearance may be one of many characteristics that lead the witness to remember the individual in more detail than previously thought. As a description of physical appearance evolves, the investigator should take note of the mention of detail that goes beyond a typical description. Examples include a hat, haircut, condition of the hair or skin, jewelry, or tattoos. Keep in mind that individuals have preferences in underclothing that may not change, for example, the kind of underwear or t-shirt worn.
2. **Conversation.** In what place did conversation occur, if any? What was said and by whom? Was something happening that

prompted the statements? Were there particular words that seemed to be significant? Was there a way that the person spoke that was peculiar?
3. **Names.** If a name was spoken, does the witness remember it? The interviewee should be instructed to think about the number of syllables or letter of that name.
4. **Senses.** Was there a smell associated with the event? What did the person, place, or surroundings smell like?
5. **Speech.** Did anyone involved have a speech impediment or speak with an accent? Was the conversation loud or soft, high-pitched or deliberate?

STEPS OF THE COGNITIVE INTERVIEW METHOD

As basic skills for effective cognitive interviewing; the interviewer is expected to have developed the skills for establishing rapport, listening actively, and avoiding interrupting. Additional competence is required for encouraging intense concentration and the use of imagery. Asking open-ended and compatible questions assists in obtaining detailed descriptions and recreating the original context of the event.

The order of the cognitive interview is important; the steps must take place one after the other to be effective.

Step One: Meet and Greet

In the first step, the interviewer explains to the interviewee that there will be seven steps in the interview process. The first step describes cognitive interviewing and what to expect during the interview. The person is told that full cooperation is expected and that no information or details should be left out, regardless of whether they appear important or not. Most of the interview will consist of the interviewee doing the talking. Instructions will come on how to jog memory along with techniques proven to improve the interview process.

The interviewer asks questions in a standard approach but instructs the interviewee to think aloud, express his or her opinion, and say if he or she has any difficulty in answering questions. In other words, the investigator gives the control of the interview to the person being interviewed. Police officers and other interviewers are used to asking the questions. In this approach, they are listeners and encourage the witness to do the talking.

- Control anxiety and develop rapport with the interviewee. This may be done by helping the subject to feel more comfortable through the development of rapport. Refer to Chapters 1 and 3 to refresh your memory on rapport and its development. Nervousness and anxiety are sometimes evident through laughing, yawning, sweating, shaking, or crying. Be concerned about the subject's comfort and ask about it. Avoid comments that may be judgmental or are confrontational.

- Encourage active participation by outlining what you expect from the interviewee. Explain that you are not going to ask all the questions but are depending on him or her to explain what happened.
- Ask the witness to reveal every detail regardless of whether he or she thinks that the information is important. *Note:* This is one of the mnemonic memory-jogging techniques.
- Give the interviewee permission to say that he or she does not know the answer to a question.

Step Two: Narrative Phases

This step involves three parts: free recall, guided recall of the event, and clarification. First, the interviewee is asked to supply a narrative report of the incident in his or her own words. Active listening requires that the interviewer avoid interrupting or asking for details during this phase. Paying particular attention to the narration, the interviewer notes the perspective of the statement. For example, where does the subject alter the level of description, alter his or her voice to mimic the assailant's speech, or deflect his or her gaze away from the interviewer?

Next comes the part where the interviewer assists the interviewee in recall. Talking about the need for concentration, instructions may include questions such as "How did you feel?", "What did you hear?", and "Tell me what happened." The investigator asks for the witness to think about what happened as perceived through their senses; what did the interviewee see, hear, smell, or touch? The interviewee is reminded to talk about everything he or she remembers, even if it seems unimportant. Reconstruction techniques are employed in this directed segment of the interview. Context reinstatement is used to help the interviewee to go back to the place or context in which the event occurred. This is done by asking open-ended questions designed to stimulate stored memories. The interviewer should not attempt to fill in gaps or interrupt even if questions arise or something needs clarification.

FIGURE 5-3 Aiding in recall through the use of mnemonics is an important part of cognitive interviewing.

At this point in the narrative-gathering process, the interviewer may have a list of questions concerning missing or unclear information. Taking care not to verbally pounce on the interviewee, the interviewer reminds him or her to share all information by reporting everything. Now is the time for extensive note taking and asking of questions. One should avoid closed-ended questions that will limit the response of the interviewee.

Step Three: Extensive Recall through Mnemonics

The interviewee should be encouraged to retrieve more information through memory-enhancing techniques. The interviewer should explain that the strategies for obtaining more information are being used not because the statement was faulty, but that these techniques have been shown to increase memory retrieval. Primary techniques that provide more information include the reconstruction technique, recalling events from a different order, and changing the perspective.

The reconstruction technique involves talking to the interviewee about concentration and asking that he or she think about the sound environment, the rooms, the furniture, the weather, lighting, or people. What was the witness feeling or hearing at the time of the event?

Recalling events from a different order, also called switching the temporal order, is another mnemonic used during this stage. The interviewee is instructed to recall the incident backward. Prompting takes place by asking, "What is the last thing you remember? What before that? What happened before that?"

Changing perspectives is also helpful during this stage of the interview. The purpose is to see the event from the eyes of another, but it should be made clear to the interviewee that he or she must only report facts that were actually witnessed and not to fabricate or guess. Additional memory-jogging techniques that were described earlier in the chapter may helpful at this time.

Step Four: Summary and Closure

This may be the last chance to get information from this individual. Ask if there is anyone that he or she recommends you speak with or anything else you should know. Briefly summarize the information that the interviewee has provided.

Closure occurs by reestablishing the personal connection with the interviewee. Always end on a positive note with appreciation for the time and effort put into the interview. Update the contact information and encourage the interviewee to call with any new information.

CHALLENGES TO MEMORY RETRIEVAL

Everyday memory-encoding problems such as challenging lighting conditions or distance to the event and distractions will negatively affect the way that recall occurs. An individual's emotions and the process of scripting cause interference with memory retrieval. Memories do change over time, and the new memories may or may not reflect the reality more accurately.

Contamination

One of the most common sources of eyewitness error occurs when witnesses' memories become contaminated by information that they acquired since they witnessed the event. Sometimes referred to as misinformation, the source of contamination is typically someone involved in the case who shares his or her bias early on in the investigation.

Leading, misleading, and forced questions can confuse a witness and produce contaminated information. For example, "Did you hear her scream?" implies that someone did scream. The interviewee is now led to believe that someone screamed, misled if that did not occur, and forced to state that they did not miss something. The answer will probably be "Yes, I heard her scream," even if it did not occur. An investigator may not know whether the question he or she is asking IS misleading; open-ended questioning avoids this problem. In the same situation the witness may be asked, "Did you hear anything?" Or "What did you hear?" One should avoid mentioning any new information that has not been previously given.

BEEN THERE . . . DONE THAT! 5-4

Memory can be changed by contamination, high emotion, and scripting. Recall of an event is different than playing back a movie with all of the details of what happened. Memory is more delicate and can be influenced by what a person thinks he or she should have done and by guilt for what he or she may have done. I once interviewed a woman named Stella whose child was in the hospital with apparent shaken-baby syndrome. The baby was not expected to live due to massive injuries to the brain. Stella told me that the baby woke up crying in the middle of the night and woke up her live-in boyfriend. The boyfriend was very angry and yelled at her to do something to stop the crying of the baby. There were two rooms in the apartment, the bedroom where two children slept with their mother and boyfriend and the kitchen. Stella got up from bed and carried the baby into the kitchen. On the way she tripped over a toy that was left on the floor and dropped the baby. It was a horrible accident. At my request Stella drew a picture of the kitchen and indicated where she had tripped and where the baby had landed after the fall.

I served a search warrant on the apartment to collect the toy and document the accident. What I found was surprising. There were no toys at all in the apartment, not one—nothing to trip over. Looking at the drawing that Stella had provided of the place where the baby had landed indicated that it was not where the trip had occurred, but that the baby had landed to the left of where Stella had "tripped." To the right was a stove with a small dent. If the baby had been thrown to the right against the stove, he would have landed to the left and forward of where Stella indicated that he had fallen. Was this faulty memory or a lie? You decide.

Emotion

The accuracy of the memory of an event is challenged by the emotions of the individual recounting it. Witnesses' guilt about what happened or their participation in the event will likely affect their perception. Stress or fear will also influence the memory-encoding process. It has been suggested that individuals process information differently in states of high and low emotional arousal (Artwohl, 2002). In a high-emotion state, an individual may switch from rational thinking to experimental thinking. During life-threatening or highly emotional situations memory is more likely to become fragmented, include past events, become intuitive instead of analytic, and become oriented toward immediate action instead of reflection. A person in this situation may be described as being seized by emotions. Tunnel vision, diminished hearing of loud sounds, temporary paralysis (short-term freezing), and distracting thoughts are among the problems experienced by individuals who experience traumatic events. Cognitive interviewing techniques are helpful in facilitating accurate memory retrieval of the dissociated experiences of a high-stress experience (Artwohl, 2002).

Scripting

Because memory may have gaps due to encoding problems, the brain fills in with scripted memories. **Scripts** are memories of how things are supposed to happen (Wrightby & Merrill, 2002). For example, a driver who hits and kills a young child may recall having slowed the vehicle prior to the impact. That is what is supposed to happen, right? Onlookers who do not have the same perspective may give an account that the driver struck the child at full speed. The use of scripting is not an indication that the individual is lying, but may mean that he or she is filling a memory gap. To avoid interviewee scripting, one should encourage narrative responses without prompting or interrupting. The individual should be allowed to reflect and respond after having been involved in stressful situations.

▲ CONCLUSIONS

Forensic hypnosis remains a controversial evidence-gathering technique. Numerous court cases have provided guidance on its use and standards for admissibility as evidence. Hypnotically refreshed evidence should be used as tool in the investigation and not as the sole source of information. Corroboration is necessary to support the information gathered through hypnosis. The professionalism of those practicing forensic hypnosis has been increased through uniform training standards, testing, and certification. Despite the controversy, hypnosis seems to be making a small comeback in recent years as a positive and reliable information-gathering tool.

Cognitive interviewing is the most respected form of interviewing. Proper use of the memory-jogging techniques along with the overall atmosphere of cooperation has been shown to improve interviewing results. The use of cognitive interviewing increases the information recalled by a witness without increasing confabulation. It has successfully survived court challenge. Cognitive techniques can easily be incorporated into any interviewing method that the investigator chooses to use, and this flexibility increases it potential use. It also works well for interviewing children.

QUESTIONS FOR REVIEW

Short-Answer Questions

1. What are some of the arguments against the use of hypnosis during court testimony?
2. What are three common uses of hypnosis for a criminal investigation?
3. What does the successful application of forensic hypnosis methods depend on, according to McConkey and Sheehan?
4. What is the calendar procedure for age regression?
5. Why is hypnosis not recommended for use on a defendant or person suspected of being involved in the crime under investigation?
6. What is the basis for the federal standard known as the *Daubert* test concerning the admissibility of scientific evidence, which has replaced *Frye* in some states?
7. How do mnemonics jog the memory in order to find information that is not easily accessible?
8. What is the reconstruction technique?
9. What is the correct order of the cognitive interview and why is it important?
10. What is scripting?

Fill-in Questions

1. _____ refers to an investigative memory retrieval technique used to enhance recall in _____ situations.
2. Persons under hypnosis are _____; those in the state of hypnosis do not become zombies.
3. The goal of forensic hypnosis is _____ and retrieval for use in a specific civil or criminal case.
4. During the induction phase, the hypnotist _____ the witness and tests his or her responsivity to _____.
5. The two major techniques used for memory recall in forensic hypnosis are _____ and _____.
6. The final phase, recall, actually occurs _____ and the subject is deinducted.
7. Critics argue that a person undergoing hypnosis experiences a _____ to suggestion and a loss of _____ regarding cues planted by the hypnotist.

8. The _____ refers to the consideration of all relevant information in determining reliability, a test advocated by the Supreme Court in *Illinois v. Gates*.
9. _____ encourages the witness to do the talking while the interviewer listens.
10. One of the most common sources of eyewitness error occurs when the witnesses' memories become _____ by information that they acquired _____ .

Exercises

1. Think about something that happened to you. This incident will be the basis for the practice interview; it can be a positive or negative experience. The interview will be concerned with obtaining information about that experience. Form interview teams of two students each. Practice the cognitive interview steps in these following exercises.

    1. Practice step one of the cognitive method, meet and greet; 5 minute-exercise.
    2. Practice step two of the cognitive method, narrative phases; 20-minute exercise.
    3. Practice step three of the cognitive method, extensive recall through mnemonics; 25-minute exercise.
    4. Practice step four of the cognitive method, summary and closure; 10-minute exercise.

2. To illustrate enhancing recall through mnemonics, pair off for this brief 15-minute exercise. Identify one student as the interviewer and one as the interviewee. Have the interviewer ask the interviewee, "What was the last program you watched on TV?" The interviewer should then use step three of the cognitive interview method, extensive recall through mnemonics. Asking for recall from a different order and changing the perspective, the interviewer should attempt to obtain more information about the particular TV program.

REFERENCES

Adams, S. (2004). Statement analysis: Beyond the words. *FBI Law Enforcement Bulletin, 73*(4), 22–23.

American Psychotherapy and Medical Hypnosis Association. (2000). Definition of the process of hypnosis and trance states. [Online.] Available: http://apmha.com/page8.htm.

Artwohl, A. (2002). Perceptual and memory distortion during officer-involved shootings. *FBI Law Enforcement Bulletin, 158* (10), 18–24.

Daubert v. Merrell Dow Pharmaceuticals, 113 S.Ct 2786 (1993).

Fisher, R. P., & Geiselman, R. E. (1992). *Memory-enhancing techniques for investigative interviewing: The cognitive interview.* Springfield, Il: Charles C Thomas.

Fisher, R. P., Geiselman, R. E., & Amador, M. (1989). *Memory-enhancing techniques for investigative interviewing: The cognitive interview.* Springfield, IL: Charles C Thomas.

Frye v. United States, 23 Fed. 1013 (1923).

Geiselman, R. E., Bornstein, G., & Saywitz, K. (1992). *New approach to interviewing children: A test of its effectiveness* (Report No. NCJ 135011). Washington, DC: National Institute of Justice.

Geiselman, R. E., & Fisher, R. P. (1985). *Interviewing victims and witnesses of crime* (Report No. NCJ 99061). Washington, DC: National Institute of Justice.

Geiselman, R. E., Fisher, R. P., Cohen, G., Holland, H., & Surtes, L. (1986). Eyewitness responses to leading and misleading questions under the cognitive interview. *Journal of Police Science and Administration, 14,* 31–39.

Hall, E. G. (1999). Watch carefully now: Solving crime in the 21st century. *Police, 23*(6), 42–45.

Honey, P., & Mumford, A. (1982). *The learning styles questionnaire.* Maidenhead, England: Peter Honey.

Howell, J. (2003). *Preventing and reducing juvenile delinquency: A comprehensive framework.* Thousand Oaks, CA: Sage Publications.

Illinois v. Gates, 462 U.S. 213 (1983).

Makoi, K. (2002). What are emotions? [Online.] Available: http://www.kimakoi.com/emotions.htm.

McConkey, K. M., & Sheehan, P. W. (1995). *Hypnosis, memory, and behavior in criminal investigation.* New York: Guilford Press.

Moenssens, A., Starrs, J. E., Henderson, C. E., & Inbau, F. E. (1995). *Scientific evidence in civil and criminal cases,* 4th ed. Westbury, NY: Foundation Press.

Nevada Revised Statutes. (1997). Testimony of witness who previously underwent hypnosis to recall subject matter of testimony. Vol. Title 4 *Witness and Evidence,* Chapter 48, Section 039.

Newman, A. W., & Thompson, J. W., Jr. (2001). The rise and fall of forensic hypnosis in criminal investigation. *Journal of the American Academy of Psychiatry and the Law, 29*(1), 75–84.

Niehaus, J. (1999). *Investigative forensic hypnosis.* Boca Raton, FL: CRC Press.

Reiser, M. (1984). Police use of investigative hypnosis: Scientism, ethics, and power games. *American Journal of Forensic Psychology, 2*(3), 115–143.

Rock v. Arkansas, 483 U.S. 44 (1987).

Royal Air Force. (2001). Learning forces. [Online.] Available http://www.learning-forces.org.uk/2-10/learnbetter.htm.

U.S. Department of Justice. (1999). *Eyewitness evidence: A guide for law enforcement* (Report No. NCJ 178240). Washington, DC: U.S. Department of Justice.

Webert, D. R. (2003). Are the courts in a trance? Approaches to the admissibility of hypnotically enhanced witness testimony in light of empirical evidence. *American Criminal Law Review, 40*(3), 1301–1327.

Wrightby, K., & Merrill, K. (2002). The wilderness incident investigative interview: Mitigating memory challenges utilizing the enhanced cognitive interview (ECI) technique. [Online.] Available http://www.outdoored.com/articles/Articl.asp?ArticleID=141.

CHAPTER 6
Behavioral Interviewing and Interrogation Techniques

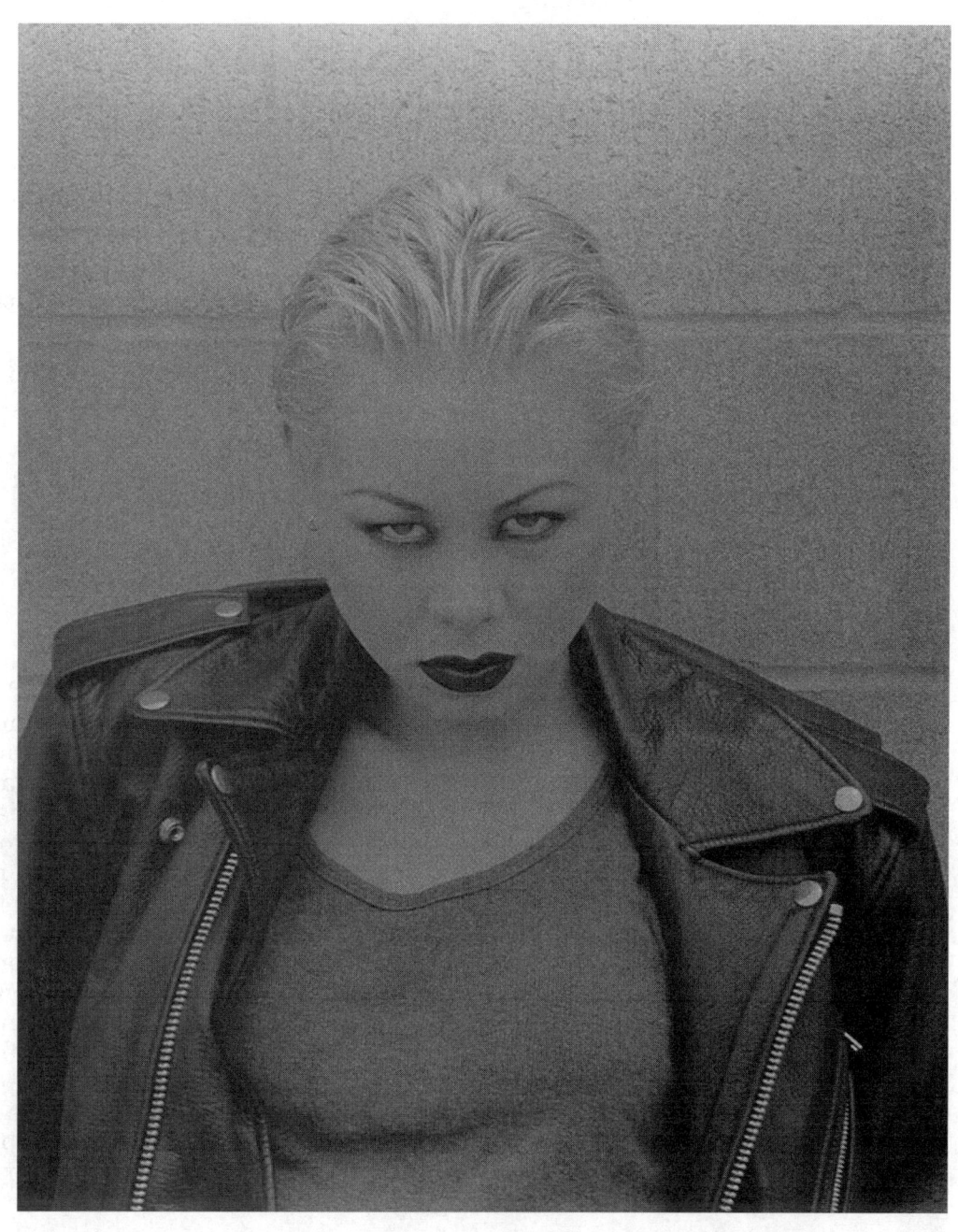

107

Key Terms

Behavioral interviewing	Mirroring
Emblems	Shifting
Neurolinguistic programming	Auditory thinkers
Facial-coding system	Qualifiers
Modeling	Hedging

Chapter Objectives

After completing this chapter you should be able to:

- Define the term *neurolinguistic programming*
- Explain what is meant by the term *facial-coding system*
- Describe the visual person and his or her methods of verbal communication
- Describe the verbal characteristics of an auditory thinker
- Explain kinesthetic verbal processes
- Discuss how eye movements reflect learning processes
- Describe the eye movements that characterize visual reasoning
- Explain the eye movements that can be seen when the auditory learner is recalling or constructing information
- List clues of possible deception

Introduction

Behavioral interviewing and interrogation are based on theories of communication and learning that influence unintended communications that can be observed by the astute interviewer. The techniques described in this chapter can be used for behavioral interviewing or interrogation. The common thread to all of the techniques is the belief that human communication is affected by learning, which in turn affects behavioral indicators that can be observed and interpreted. Behavior indicators such as nonverbal posturing, sensory verbal communication, and eye movement are among the phenomena presented. The techniques involve the recognition of unintended communications, also called neurocommunications, when they may present themselves, and possible interpretations by the interviewer. Rather than a method, behavioral interviewing is an increased awareness derived through the application of numerous techniques that have relevance in any form of interviewing. There is no step-by-step method to use for behavioral interviewing. These tools should be used along with any other form of interviewing and are not a stand-alone method.

Knowledge of learning processes and their application to behavioral responses are useful for persons conducting interviews and interrogations. Acknowledging that individuals will vary in their responses due to differential encoding, this chapter will provide a broader understanding of human interactions.

> Knowledge is only potential power. True personal power is the ability to take action and implement your knowledge. (Hogan, 2002)

Brain development begins in utero; incomplete at the time of birth, it continues to maturity. Experiences during childhood affect intellectual function and some aspects of normal language skills. Due to the influence of experience on the processes of learning, no two people will think exactly alike. Some forms of communication appear to develop independent of experience; these involve the complex nervous system, the brain, and the senses (Bloom, Nelson, & Lazerson, 2001). Sensation, the unconscious reception of information by our sense organs, begins shortly after birth and matures over time (O'Leary, 2002). This occurs through touching, hearing, tasting, seeing, and smelling. By the age of 1 year, most aspects of visual development are complete. Approximately 99 percent of the stimuli to the brain are received unconsciously, with about 80 percent of this taken in by the eyes (Bureau of Alcohol, Tobacco, and Firearms [ATF], 1997). The importance of appealing to the unconscious/subconscious mind cannot be underestimated and is a central tenet of behavioral interviewing. Because we learn though our senses, it is reasonable that we might be persuaded through them also. The remainder of the chapter will refer specifically to these techniques for interviewing and interrogation.

What Is Behavioral Interviewing?

Behavioral interviewing is the application of communication theory and the study of patterns of behavior to guide the interview process. It involves taking cues from the interviewee, whether these involve subconscious behavior responses or verbal patterns. The introduction to kinesics and neurolinguistic programming provides the background and history for these approaches. It important to listen not only to what is said during an interview, but also to how it is said. Emotional outbursts and inflections of the voice may give a clue to sensitive areas of the interview. Sudden silence, uncertainty or confusion, or the shifting of conversation to an unrelated subject may indicate that information is being withheld (Massachusetts Municipal Police Institute, 1981). Nervous bodily reactions or facial characteristics may also signal that a sensitive area has been reached. By noting these things, an interviewer will know what portions of the statement may require further probing or clarification. It is estimated that nonverbal communication often conveys a larger share of social information, approximately 65 percent or more, whereas verbal communication plays a less salient role, 35 percent or less (ATF, 1997).

Kinesics

A "kine" is the smallest observable unit of body movement, and *kinesics* refers to the scientific study of gestures and other body movements (Wainwright, 2003). As introduced in Chapter 1, kinesics is a form of nonverbal communication known as body language (Sandoval & Adams, 2001). Anthropologist Ray Birdswhistell coined the term *kinesics* in the late 1940s. According to this pioneer, up to 65 percent of a message's meaning is communicated through nonverbal cues (Birdwhistell, 1970). Since its inception, the term has been widely used in discussions on nonverbal communications for behavioral interviewing. The premise is that behavioral communication is determined by individual learning styles. The three categories of learners are visual, auditory, and physical (also known as kinesthetic). From the Learning Styles Questionnaire developed by Honey and Mumford (1982), we know that approximately 30 percent of people are visual learners, 30 percent are auditory learners, and 40 percent are physical learners (Royal Air Force, 2001).

Ekman and Friesen (1969) classified kinesics into five categories: emblems, illustrators, affect displays, regulators, and adaptors. Of these categories, emblems are most frequently referred to within the context of interviewing and interrogation. **Emblems** are nonverbal gestures that have a verbal counterpart. By themselves, emblems have little meaning, but they are widely understood within a given culture (Ekman, 2001). Examples of these deliberate and often unconscious slips of body movements include the following:

- Giving a person the "finger" means "fuck you."
- Shrugging indicates "I don't know" or "What difference does it make?"
- A head nod means "Yes."
- A head shake means "No."

Clues that an emblem may be a leakage of information that the individual did not intend includes an incomplete gesture, such as only one shoulder raised, and presenting an emblem out of a normal position, such as two hands slightly tilted outward on a table. Look for a slight nod of "yes" while a person is saying "no." Although every liar does not evidence emblematic slips, when they occur, they are very reliable as to the true sign of a message that the person does not want to reveal (Ekman, 2001).

Neurolinguistic Programming

The term **neurolinguistic programming** (NLP) refers to the interconnectedness of primary forms of human communication: thinking, speaking (verbally and nonverbally), and patterns of behavior. Developed during the 1970s by John Grinder and Richard Bandler, it involves the psychology of how individuals think, communicate, and decipher information. Grinder and Bandler define NLP as *the study of subjective experience* (Dilts, Bandler, & Bandler, 1980).

"Neuro" refers to the brain and the neural network that feeds into the brain. Neurons, or nerve cells, are the working units used by the nervous system to send, receive, and store signals that add up to information. Neurolinguistics includes the idea that behavior originates from the five senses: seeing, hearing, smelling, tasting, and touching. Incorporated into the theory are psychological reactions to ideas and events. The way that we communicate both verbally and nonverbally is referred to as "linguistics." The "programming" part of the term refers to the unique way that human beings manipulate the signals and convert them into useful information. Based on prior experience, the brain directs the programming process into thinking patterns and behaviors that become part of our life experiences and emotions.

CULTURAL AND PERSONAL CONSIDERATIONS

Nonverbal communication is generally considered to be culture constrained. Dahl (n.d.) pointed out that although facial recognition appears to be universal, the way that feelings and emotions are expressed through facial expression is dictated by culture. Interpretations are therefore most accurate within a similar cultural background. Demographic changes and the growth of ethnic minority populations in the United States suggest that behavioral indicators must be used with caution. By 2050, Asians are expected to make up 8.2 percent of the population, African Americans 13 percent, and Hispanics 24 percent (Leigh, 1998).

Nonverbal communications are also affected by gender. Interpretation and use of facial expressions can be different. Men appear to use different nonverbal communication styles when speaking to other men than when speaking to women (Dahl, n.d.). Women may smile more frequently than men. Age differences may also impact communication styles.

Because of variances due to personal characteristics, ethnicity, gender, and age (to name a few), a critical aspect of behavioral interviewing is the establishment of a baseline through conversational speech in order to determine the normal communication modes of the individual. It is important to analyze the responses during conversational speech prior to beginning the interview itself.

FIGURE 6-1 Real emotions are difficult to control. Some individuals may attempt to cover up their emotions through fake facial expressions.

EMOTIONS AND OBSERVABLE BEHAVIORS

Because of the different neural networks involved in emotion and conscious reasoning responses, emotions seem to short-cut the circuits for reasoning. Once believed to be psychologically based, scientific discoveries have shown that emotions are physiologically based. Emotions seem to occur spontaneously and cannot be called forth on command, nor can they be terminated simply by choice (Ekman & Davidson, 1994). Facial expressions, however, may fake emotion or attempt to cover it. Whereas the expression of an emotion can be suppressed, the feeling cannot. Studies suggest that some emotions elicit observable responses. If noted, these emotional behavior states can be observed and evaluated in the context of the situation. Those of potential value to the interviewer include facial expressison and body posture.

Facial Expression

Extensive research conducted by Ekman and associates suggests that emotions include facial activity that may be visible or not, and that certain facial expressions of emotion are universal (Ekman, 1999). Furthermore, facial configurations may relate to specific emotions felt by the individual being interviewed. Facial expressions may include movements to emphasize speech, so the interviewer should note movements that are not typical of the individual. A baseline should be formed by observing conversational speech. A lie catcher should never rely on one clue to deceit; there must be many. It is only liars who know they are lying when they lie who are likely to be caught. The liar who succeeds in deceiving himself or herself into believing that the lie is true is not likely to exhibit signs of deceit. Facial clues should be confirmed by clues from voice, words, or body.

People may attempt to conceal emotion with facial expressions. The smile is the most common cover or mask, noted when there is not a full expression across the face. A smile that indicates pleasure may be concealed by pressing the lips together and pushing the chin muscles up. Some expressions are more reliable than others; examples include the following (Ekman & Rosenberg, 1977):

- Sadness, sorrow, or grief is indicated when the lip corners go down; this expression is reliable and difficult to fake.
- Sadness, grief, or distress is indicated by the wrinkling of center forehead muscles. The inner corners of the eyebrows typically are pulled upward. These facial movements should not be present due to a false sense of distress or sadness.
- Fear, worry, apprehension, or terror is noted when the eyebrows are raised and pulled together. This eyebrow configuration is also common when someone is concentrating.
- One of the best clues for anger is a narrowing of the lips; they are not sucked in or pressed, just thinner and less visible.
- A crooked expression, particularly one more visible on the left side of the face, is one that is faked and not felt.
- Expressions of long duration are likely to be false.

- A contempt smile involves a tightening of the muscle in the lip corners, producing a muscle bulge in and around the corners, often a dimple, and a slight angling up of the lip corners.
- A miserable smile, indicating negative emotion, involves the lower lip pushed by the chin muscle and the corners tightened or down without any evidence of the muscle around the eyes tightening.
- A false smile will not be accompanied by the involvement of the muscles around the eyes.
- A smiling face with the lower eyelids straight across, covering part of the iris of the eye, and with the disappearance of the wrinkles below the eye can indicate an underlying wariness, guardedness, or even anger that is not being expressed.

Some dangers exist for the interviewer who relies solely on expressive characteristics to determine innocence or guilt. These are tools that should be used in conjunction with other interviewing techniques for the optimum results. Failure to recognize that an innocent person may feel guilty about something else or afraid of being disbelieved and may leak emotion is one hazard to be aware of. Most guilty people will not avert their gaze because they know that everyone expects experts to be able to detect deception in this way. Psychopaths and natural liars have an extraordinary ability to inhibit facial signs of their true feelings.

Here are some other indicators of emotional information from the face and eyes that complete a picture of deceit:

- An averted gaze downward may signal sadness; down or away may indicate shame or guilt; and looking away may be due to disgust.
- Blinking increases when people are emotionally aroused; this can be due to excitement, anger, or fear.
- When hearing something they disagree with, a person's may eyelids tend to close longer than a normal blink.
- Pupils dilate when people are emotionally aroused, which may be because of excitement, anger, or fear.
- Face blushing could leak embarrassment or shame.
- The face turning red indicates anger.

Facial Coding. Ekman introduced an aspect of neurocommunication through the coding of facial behavior (Ekman, 1993). The **facial-coding system** (FACS) is a comprehensive, anatomically based method of measuring all visually discernible facial movements. There are five universal expressions controlled by the autonomic nervous system: anger, fear, disgust, sadness, and enjoyment (Ekman & Rosenberg, 1977). According to this theory, the 44 muscles of the face contract in a particular way in response to unconscious stimuli to the brain. Embarrassment is a recent addition to the five original universal expressions. It is identified through gazing down, smiling, turning head or touching face, and then pressing the lips (Ekman, 1993).

Facial-coding research has led to practical applications for interviewing and interrogation. A group working under Terrence Sejnowski has claimed to have discovered ways to distinguish between false facial

> **BEEN THERE... DONE THAT! 6-1**
>
> Susan was a very religious woman whose brother was a Catholic priest. She knew and respected many of the local priests and was very involved with the ministry. Frequently she volunteered at the church and got to know Father Tom. She reported that he had come to her home while her husband was at work and had forced her to have sex against her will.
>
> I interviewed Father Tom, who denied that he had raped his parishioner. He had difficulty looking at me while he answered my questions; during most of the interview his head was down and his eyes were averted. He was fidgety and appeared very nervous. Verbally, he hedged frequently. Continuing the investigation, I learned that Father Tom was promoted within the week and transferred to Rome. Was he guilty? Rome is one of the few places in the world where it is impossible to extradite a suspect.

expressions and genuine emotional ones (Howard Hughes Medical Institute, 2001). Using the facial-coding system developed by Ekman (1993), the team has designed a computer program to recognize facial movements and measure variables such as the degree of skin wrinkling at various points on the face. The CIA is funding research on a similar software program that could result in improved lie detection (Howard Hughes Medical Institute, 2001). Using face recognition software, the researchers have claimed a 91 percent accuracy rate on the recognition and coding of facial expressions. Computer software programs are used by law enforcement for face recognition in London (Erskine & Stewart, 2001). Cameras strategically located throughout the city of London scan thousands of faces and match them against those in the law enforcement database for terrorist identification. The accuracy of recognition is improved through computer software use, which aids investigators to overcome barriers to uncovering deceit.

Body Posture

Behavior indicators include well-known body positions that make a statement about the individual or send signals about the way they think of themselves. Authority stances are among the most common. Someone who stands with hands on hips and feet spread apart is showing defiance or aggression. This is also seen when someone is making a power play. Take on the same stance and you are telling the individual you represent that same power. Then modify your stance; for example, if confronted with someone who has his or her arms crossed, uncross your arms to see if he or she will follow your behavioral lead. If he or she does, you have achieved control over the situation! Truthful people tend to lean forward, indicating they are listening. Deceitful people tend to move away. Kinesic posturing has been long been taught by interviewing experts. The following examples are common suppositions (Naramore, 1988):

Generally Truthful Body Postures
- Open and relaxed posture
- Frontally aligned

- Upright in the chair
- Smooth changes in body positions

Generally Deceptive Body Postures
- Rigid posture
- Head and body slump
- Rapid, abrupt changes of posture
- Slouching in a chair
- Head and body slump (toilet position)

Personal Gestures Indicative of Stress
- Rubbing of hands
- Picking a nose or earlobes
- Hair twirling
- Licking of lips or difficulty swallowing
- Nail biting
- Profuse sweating

Studies have shown that when an individual is introduced to a group, his or her status influences his or her perceived size (Cialdini, 1993). A person introduced as a professor is estimated as being taller than when she is introduced as a student. Without being pretentious, let the individual know what you represent by introducing yourself as a police officer or other official if you are not wearing a uniform. Be confident, but not cocky. Any attempts to mask or downplay your authority serve to reinforce to the person that "This important person is just like me." The majority of individuals have a deep-seated sense of duty to authority (Cialdini, 1993). Further establish your status through your clothing. If you wear a uniform, take care that it fits properly and that it is clean and pressed prior to an interview. For those in civilian clothes, wear professional-looking attire that is well suited to your work. Looking sloppy does little to promote confidence or respect.

Actors are taught that there are two body postures: rising/approaching and sinking/withdrawing. Rising energy is reflected in a lift of the body, ebbing energy in a drooping body. Upward movement is associated with life: a growing plant, a young child, a person of vigor. Downward movement is related to death, sickness, weariness, and discouragement. This fundamental rising/sinking action is usually motivated by our inner feelings and emotions. Excellent posture suggests power, such as the stance taken by a military individual. Exhibiting respect and attention, such a person will stand with heels together and toes pointed out at a slight angle. Male aggression is communicated when the individual stands with feet wide apart. Typically, people who walk rapidly and swing their arms freely tend to be goal oriented. People who habitually walk with their hands in their pockets tend to be critical and secretive. When people feel depressed, they shuffle along with their hands in their pockets and seldom look where they are going, making it difficult for them to be goal oriented. Stooped or bowed shoulders usually mean something negative. One could be afraid, submissive, guilty, or self-conscious. Raised shoulders denote fear or tension. Squared shoulders suggest strength or responsibility.

A major strategy in the NLP method is **modeling**, which refers to learning to reflect individual behavior (Ekman & Friesen, 1969). Also referred to as "pacing" or "matching," it is a form of imitation that indicates to the subject (subconsciously) that you are alike. Used during an interview, modeling suggests harmony and agreement between the interviewee and the subject. When two people adopt similar sitting positions, the nonverbal statement is "We are alike." Numerous possibilities exist with respect to what might be matched with a subject in either posture or gesture. Notice whether the individual presents with stiff-fingered palms and an extended, rigid thumb. This is a control gesture warning people to remain at a distance. It also signals, "I will not give up my position." The interviewer would want to match this gesture to relay the same emotional position.

Modeling is an approach that is also used to establish rapport. Matching posture and gesture must be done in a subtle way that does not appear to mimic the person or it will have the opposite effect. When the person changes body position, wait an appropriate period of time and change yours to match. Don't assume that you must be exactly like the individual to use modeling. Establish yourself as the authority through your status, clothing, and other symbols to achieve a meaningful figure worth modeling to maximize your influence on the subject.

EYE MOVEMENT

Gaining knowledge into the dominant sensory mode of the subject through his or her use of language offers insight, yet sometimes the terms people use are neutral. How do we know the best way to respond? Observing the eyes provides another way to access the information needed to make an appropriate response. Rapport and control can also be established through the unconscious or subconscious movement of the eyes. To determine a person's preferred representational system, look for patterns of movements or clusters within the same modality. For more information on eye movements and NLP, a concise description of the theory is available online in an article by Robert Dilts (1998).

Everyone processes in all three modes and develops a preference or dominant pattern of response. Prior to identifying the eye pattern in response to questioning, a baseline must be established to find out the dominant response for that particular individual. Watching the direction of the subject's eyes in response to visual, auditory, or kinesthetic terms during a rapport-building phase in which nonthreatening, nonobtrusive, and nonoffensive questions are asked establishes the norm for that individual. Eye movements should only be seen as deviations from that norm and should occur in clusters for greater reliability (ATF, 1997). Generally, when the eyes are defocused or staring straight ahead it indicates recalled or remembered images. Hogan (2002) suggested that knowledge and application of eye-accessing cues is a powerful way to enhance all communication processes. Some people's eye movements will appear reversed from the patterns discussed in what follows. This may occur when someone is left-handed; look for consistency when evaluating an individual.

The Visual Right-Handed Person

People communicate that they're in the visual channel by looking up or lifting up their heads. When a person is asked a question containing visually constructed images, the eyes tend to go up and to the person's right if the image is new; if the question brings out a recollection, the eyes go up and to the person's left (Hogan, 2002). Other possible indicators of a visually communicating individual include a hand gesturing up or pointing up or out; an erect standing position with the shoulders more or less straight across; a voice that is usually higher and faster; and less color in the face as the person uses visual process words.

If, during the investigation of arson, for example, you ask the owner/suspect, "When did you last visit your property at Warren Wright Road?" you would expect the owner to have been at the property at some time. The reason for asking is to determine if the last visit could be related to the time of the fire. On answering, a suspect who is visually oriented will typically look up to the left and then look straight ahead. The answer might be, "Well, let's see, I got there about 7:30 PM." The movement to that section of the brain allows the mind to recover visually stored data. Both the eye movements and the verbal response indicate visual orientation to something that has actually occurred. On the other hand, if the owner looks up and to his or her right, one might question why the information was being visually constructed.

It is normal that a victim of a personal crime be asked to provide a description of his or her assailant. If the description is made while the victim's eyes shift up and to the right, the information provided is being constructed versus remembered. The quandary for the interviewer is

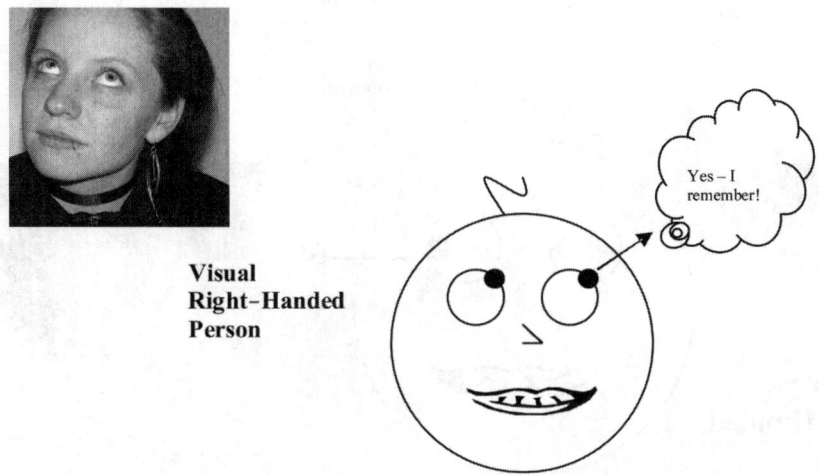

Visual Right-Handed Person

FIGURE 6-2 There is no significance in a single eye movement in response to a question. The interviewer must first determine an individual's preferred way of accessing information.

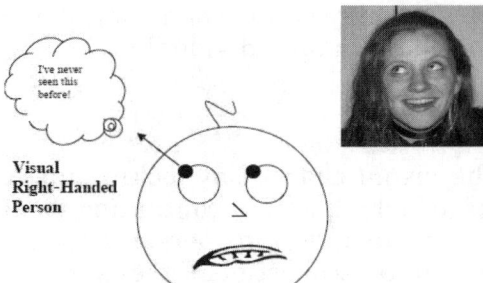

FIGURE 6-3 Once clusters of eye movements have been noted that indicate a visual right-handed person, for example, it is possible to attach significance to those movements.

then to determine why the person would have to construct a piece of information about something that had happened—is it not true? Taken by itself, little importance could be attached to this perceived inappropriate eye-accessing response. Other factors should be taken into consideration to help determine if this information is fabricated. First, has a definite pattern of visual thinking been adequately established through both verbal communication and eye movements?

The Auditory Right-Handed Person

People communicate that they're in the auditory channel by cocking their head as if they were on the telephone. The responses to questions that are constructed for the auditory person tend to elicit eye movements that are level to the right or left of the face. When the person is confused or unaware, the eyes level to the person's right; if a recollection is sparked, the eyes tend to level toward the person's left (Hogan, 2002). You might note the individual pointing to his or her ear; gesturing to the side; drumming fingers or toes; moving the eyes from side to side or down to the person's left; and holding the shoulders back.

FIGURE 6-4 If the interviewer recognizes a person as a right-handed auditory individual, the eye movement to the left, in response to a question, would signify remembering.

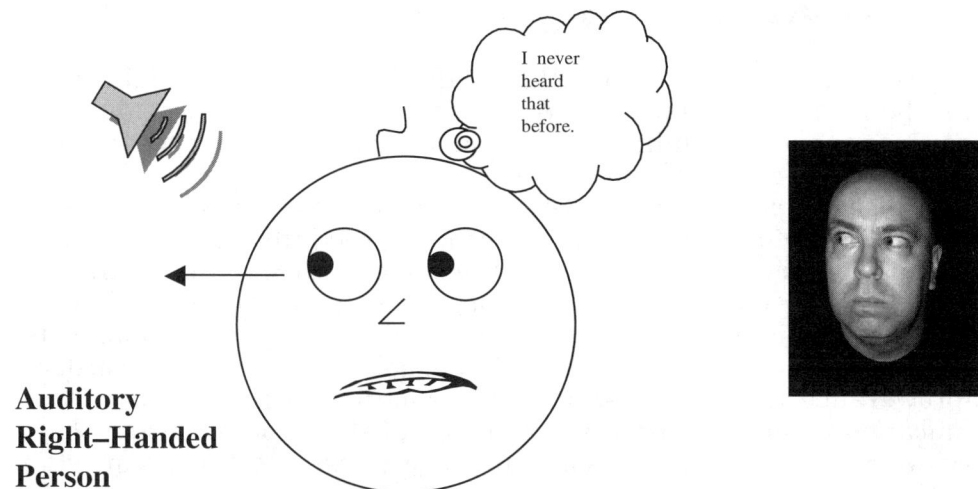

FIGURE 6-5 When the person's eye movements consistently suggest a right-handed auditory individual, the person who is providing factual information might be betrayed through their eye movements to the right.

The Kinesthetic Right-Handed Person

When people access their kinesthetic system, they'll look down to the right or usually have more skin color. They generally have a lower, slower voice tone; gesture down by their middle or stomach; point to their heart or put their hand over their heart; and breathe low and deep in the abdomen. The kinesthetically oriented person will look down to his or her right recollecting past feelings, smells, or tastes or imagining future ones (Hogan, 2002).

Rabon (1992) suggested that additional eye patterns associated with feelings occur when the person looks straight down, closes his or her eyes, or blinks rapidly. The downward gaze is often associated with the "giving up" of a suspect. It signals a change in behavior from being unwilling to being willing; this is the time for the investigator to press for information. Rapid blinking and the closing of eyes signify that the person is feeling an increase in tension.

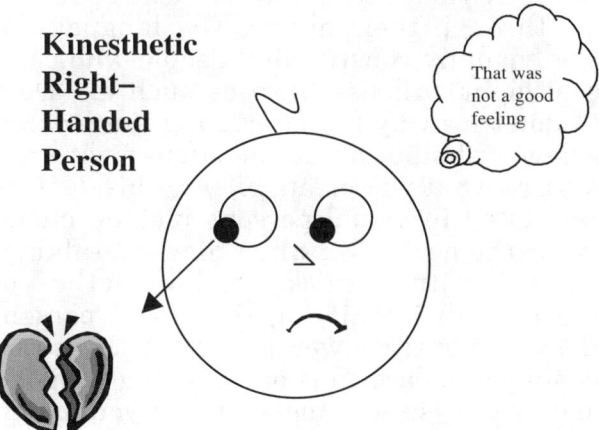

FIGURE 6-6 A kinesthetic right-handed person would be expected to look down to the left when describing something that felt unpleasant, even if the person is describing an incident without emotion.

Sensory Verbal Communication

The learning methods in the NLP model involve visual, auditory, and kinesthetic (tactile) properties. Voice characteristics can provide important clues to the truthfulness of the person speaking. Changes in speech may be notable during the interview.

Generally, people will speak in the same sensory manner by which they learn. To aid in the building of rapport, the interviewer will mirror the same sensory language used by the subject. **Mirroring** occurs when the interviewer uses the same sensory language as the interviewee to establish common ground on which the subject feels comfortable. It is a legitimate way to speak the same language as the subject in order to improve rapport. Another use of the information regarding sensory communication is for the purpose of shifting. **Shifting** occurs when the interviewer uses the same sensory language to ask the subject questions and to move that person into the area under investigation through comfortable and familiar language. This occurs when the interviewer has determined the preferred sense of communication and uses the terms provided by the subject to move to the preferred topic for discussion. Involving the senses in descriptions by victims and witnesses tends to increase their credibility in many cases, particularly for sexual assault complaints, for children, and when interviewing developmentally challenged adults.

In attempting to shift the interview from one sense of relating to another, one incorporates new terms into the questions. For example, consider a victim who states, "It was awful, I can still feel his hands on me." A response calculated to shift the conversation to the visual mode is, "When you felt his hands on you, what did you see? Did he wear any rings? Were there any tattoos on his fingers?" To move the conversation into the auditory type of thought, the interviewer might ask, "When you felt his hands on you, what did you hear? Did he say anything while he was touching you?" Another use of sensory analysis include exploration of other kinesthetic areas such as smell or taste. An example is, "When he was touching you, what did he smell like?"

The vast majority of the population are visually affected by charts, graphs, and pictures. They think in visual terms; when asked a question, a picture of thoughts go through their minds. The language of these learners will therefore be visually constructed. People who communicate through the sense of sight will use phrases such as "Do I have to draw you a *picture*"? I don't *see* why I am here. You are *looking* at the wrong guy!" The interviewer should mimic the subject with appropriate verbal cues such as "I *see* what you mean, *picture* this, *look* at it this way." Common gestures noted in visual persons include movement of the hands and arms near the neck level when they are talking. They become quick and animated, with a quick, shallow method of breathing. These traits should help in identifying the visual person. *Mirroring* is a method used by the interviewer to reflect the same sensory language used by the subject as a means of achieving rapport. For mirroring the visual personality, it is recommended that you match

> ### BEEN THERE . . . DONE THAT! 6-2
>
> Historically, child allegations of sexual abuse are viewed with skepticism. During an interview with a 6-year-old, she told me that he had put IT in her mouth. I asked, "What did IT taste like?" She shuddered and exclaimed, "Ugh, white stuff came out and it tasted like spinach." The spontaneous description accomplished two things: First, it verified a key element of the crime of rape, oral penetration had occurred. Second, the manner in which the child screwed up her face and described the taste of the ejaculation gave strong evidence that this was not a situation of coaching or witnessing sex. The child was describing an experience based on her senses. When the defense attorney saw the videotaped interview a plea bargain was struck that sent the perpetrator to prison.

your speaking rate to his or hers and use the same types of words (Hogan, 2002).

A small portion of persons, notably musicians, singers, and orators, are auditory. People who rely primarily on the sense of hearing will tend to speak moderately and rhythmically. **Auditory thinkers** hear the thoughts as they are being processed and in turn are affected by what they hear. To reach these individuals, the interviewer's language should use similar auditory expressions: "I *hear* what you're saying, *listen* to this, and *tell* me what you mean." When such a person is asked to explain something, the interviewer might notice the person's hands or arms move below the shoulder while pointing to the ear. According to Hogan (2002), the way to persuade an auditory thinker is to moderate your vocal rate and breathe deeply.

A small percentage of people are emotional thinkers, who have a kinesthetic thought process. Facts and charts are not impressive to these people; they may be athletes or have heightened spiritual awareness. Their language will contain "feeling terms," which the interviewer should also use. These include phrases like "I *feel* your pain; I know what you are *going through*, how do you *feel*?" Note whether their gaze is frequently down and their breathing is slow and deep during an interview. Slow down and be particularly calm to communicate with this type of person!

QUALIFIERS, HEDGING, AND MANIPULATORS

Physiological variations that occur during the course of an interview or interrogation may also give clues to the truth of a statement. Examples are changes in speech pattern and the use of qualifiers or hedgers. **Qualifiers** are words that modify or limit the general meaning of a phrase (Rabon, 1992). An example of a qualifier occurs when a witness uses the term "it" to referring to an assailant. This could be an attempt to soften the image, or it might be that there was not an individual, but an imagination at work.

Hedging is a lack of commitment to the statement. For example, "I think" is a hedger, a failure to commit to the description. When a person becomes less fluent and begins to stutter, it may signal deception. When answers become deceptive the use of fillers such as "uh" or "ya know" often increases.

According to research, most people associate lying with "shifty eyes" and fidgeting behavior (Ekman, 2001). Referred to as *manipulators,* these are poor indicators and are unreliable when attempting to detect deceit. These movements may indicate discomfort or relaxation and vary according to the stakes involved. Liars will consciously control these behaviors because of their known interpretations. Lip biting and lip sucking are other manipulative behaviors easily constructed to feign concern or hide other emotions. Instead, look for physiological changes that people cannot easily control. Changes in skin color, voice tone, and breathing rate are examples. An irregular breathing rate is associated with increased anxiety levels. Stress also causes a dry mouth, which may result in repeated clearing of the throat or cracking of the voice. A liar will raise irrelevant issues, such as remarking about a relative who gets him into trouble or that the police are always picking on him.

DETECTING DECEIT

Ekman (2001) said it best, "There is no sign of deceit itself—no gesture, facial expression, or muscle twitch that in and of itself means that a person is lying. There are only clues that the person is poorly prepared and clues of emotions that don't fit the person's line." Knowing that people suspected of being liars are judged by their words, not their behaviors or the display of most emotions, a deceptive person will closely monitor what he or she says.

When attempting to detect deceit the greatest danger is in disbelieving the truth; this occurs when a person trying to catch a liar mistakenly judges a truthful person to be lying. The following considerations are suggested when used the techniques in this chapter:

1. Remember that the absence of a sign of deceit is not evidence of truth.
2. Comparisons must be made between the suspect's usual behavior and that when under suspicion.
3. Consider the possibility that a sign of emotion is not a clue to deceit but a clue to how a truthful person feels about being suspected of lying.
4. Discount the sign of an emotion as a clue to deceit if the suspect's personality makes the suspect likely to have such a feeling even if the he or she were being truthful.
5. Realize that the polygraph only measures the arousal of emotion, not which emotion is felt. Studies indicate that it is better than chance that a person feeling strong emotion at being suspected may actually fail the polygraph although he or she is being truthful. (Ekman, 2001)

The implication of learning about neurocommunication is that the improvement of interviewing skills through behavior awareness increases the detection of deceit. Knowledge of sense behaviors, both verbal and nonverbal, should raise the level of proficiency in accurate statement taking. However, studies have shown that police officers are extremely poor at detecting deceit, no better than the general public in fact. By measuring the ability of law enforcement officers from the CIA, DEA, FBI, and others, attempts were made to determine the extent to which we can identify liars (Ekman, 1996). It was found that these trained professionals fared no better at detecting deceit than mere chance, fifty-fifty. Ekman (1966) forwarded five explanations to account for this situation: we live in circumstances that encourage lying, our parents teach us not to identify lies, we generally prefer not to catch liars, we often want to be misled, and we are too polite to steal information.

The first explanation refers to the increased mobility of our society without an increase in sensitivity to the trouble-makers who roam among us. In today's society the social consequences are not disastrous for lying (or worse); one can change jobs and even spouses, and a damaged reputation does not follow. We have not been prepared by our evolutionary history to be sensitive to the behavioral clues that suggest someone is lying. Second, parents conceal their activities from their children. They have a stake in not educating offspring to detect lies from demeanor in order to protect their own privacy. Therefore, awareness of deceit is not part of the growing-up educational process. Third, Ekman (1996) suggested that we generally prefer not to catch liars because a trusting rather than a suspicious stance enriches life. Trusting people makes life easier, regardless of the cost in not detecting someone who may take advantage of you. Ekman further suggested that those whose lives are at risk if they are not constantly alert to betrayal are more accurate in detecting lies than those who live with peace of mind. The fourth explanation, that we often want to be misled, relies on our stake in not knowing the truth. Consider a philanderer husband; neither husband nor wife may want the infidelity confirmed, particularly as long as resources to care for their children are not being diverted. Last, we are raised to be polite in our personal relationships and interactions. To steal information would be worse than staring at a person while he was picking his nose (Ekman, 1996). The true messages are often not the ones that we care to hear about on a daily basis, so we learn to tune them out.

Ekman (1996) acknowledged that these reasons seem to fall short of explaining why criminal justice professionals do so poorly in identifying liars based on their demeanor. An added factor is that more than three fourths of the people they talk to lie to the police. With such a high base rate of lying, it is difficult to spot a liar because the conditions are not conducive to learning the subtle behavioral clues to that betray deceit. The criminal justice emphasis is therefore diverted to getting the evidence to convict the liar.

A study of the appropriate use of facial movement, voice, and speech analysis netted showed an 80 percent chance of correct classification of who was lying and who was telling the truth in a high-stakes situation (Ekman, 1996).

CONCLUSIONS

Communication is both verbal and nonverbal, influenced by the way that we learn through our senses. Becuase most of the stimuli to the brain occur on an unconscious level, attempts to persuade through the subconscious often occur. Interviewers can gain insight into a person by identifying the person's primary learning mode and using that information to mirror and model. Shifting is a method of playing back to the individual the mode in which he or she feels most comfortable communicating in.

Behavioral interviewing is not an interviewing model but a rich source of techniques that incorporates nonverbal communications awareness. During an interview or interrogation the investigator should be acutely aware of the behavioral indicators that may signify deceit.

QUESTIONS FOR REVIEW

Short-Answer Questions

1. Define neurolinguistic programming and neurocommunication through the facial-coding system. Briefly state their implications for interviewing.
2. What are the three primary learning methods? What is their role in mirroring? How does it differ from modeling?
3. What techniques should you use for each type of sensory learner?
4. What is the significance of facial expressions? What cautions should interviewers take in regard to facial expressions during an interview?
5. What are examples of qualifiers, hedging, emblems, and manipulators?
6. What is the greatest danger when attempting to detect deceit and how can you prevent it?

Fill-in Questions

1. _____ refers to the interconnectedness of primary forms of human communication: thinking, speaking, and patterns of behavior.
2. Persons who use the _____ sensory learning method think in verbal terms. When asked a question, pictures of thoughts go through their minds.
3. A small percentage of the population has a(n) _____ thought process. They are emotional thinkers and their language will contain "feeling" terms.
4. When this type of person is recalling an event his or her eyes will move up and to his or her left: _____.
5. This type of person keeps eyes level to the right or left of the face when responding to questions: _____.
6. _____ look down and to the right or usually have more skin color when responding to questions.

7. Facial clues should be confirmed by clues from the _____, _____, or _____.
8. Narrowing of the lips indicates _____.
9. _____ is indicated when the corners of the lips turn down; this expression is reliable and difficult to fake.
10. It is better to focus on _____ changes instead of _____ ones when trying to detect deceit.

Exercises

1. The class breaks into pairs for this exercise on eye-accessing cues. The instructor reads these questions while one person in each pair answers and the other watches his or her eye movements. Switch roles every other question.

    - **How many windows are in the front of the house where you live permanently (not at school)?** Movement of the eyes up and left represents a visual remembering.
    - **Describe your mother.** Up and left represents a visual remembering.
    - **Which one of your friends has the most annoying voice?** To the side and left represents an auditory recall.
    - **What is the name of your favorite song?** To the side and left represents an auditory recall.
    - **What was the color of your first car?** Up and left indicates a visual remembering.
    - **Imagine what your best friend would look like with purple hair.** Up and right represents a visual construct.

2. Practice mirroring. Pair up with a member of the class for this 10-minute exercise. Sitting across from and facing one another, one of the students to describes what he or she did since getting up that day. During this "interview" the listening partner should match the interviewee's posture and gesture in a subtle way that does not appear to mimic him or her.

REFERENCES

Birdwhistell, R. (1970). *Kinesics and context: Essays on body motion communication*. Philadelphia: University of Pennsylvania Press.

Bloom, F., Nelson, C. A., & Lazerson, A. (2001). *Brain, mind, and behavior*. New York: Worth Publishers.

Bureau of Alcohol, Tobacco, and Firearms. (1997). *Advanced analytical interviewing program*. Washington, DC: Bureau of Alcohol, Tobacco, and Firearms.

Cialdini, R. B. (1993). *Influence: The psychology of persuasion* (2nd ed.). New York: William Morrow and Company.

Dahl, S. (n.d.). Cultural and non-cultural aspects of non verbal communication. [Online.] Available: http://stephan.dahl.at/nonverbal/culture_and_nonverbal.html.

Dilts, R. (1998). Eye movements and NLP. [Online.] Available: http://www.nlpu.com/Articles/artic14.htm.

Dilts, R., Bandler, L. C., & Bandler, R. (1980). *Neuro-linguistic programming.* Capitola, CA: META Publications.

Ekman, P. (1993). Facial expression and emotion. *American Psychologist, 48*(4), 384–817.

Ekman, P. (1996). Why don't we catch liars? *Social Research, 63*(3), 801–817.

Ekman, P. (1999). Facial expressions. In T. Dalgleish & M. Power (Eds.), *Handbook of cognition and emotion* (pp. 301–320). New York: Wiley.

Ekman, P. (2001). *Telling lies: Clues to deceit in the marketplace, politics, and marriage.* New York: W. W. Norton.

Ekman, P., & Davidson, R. J. (1994). *The nature of emotion: Fundamental questions.* New York: Oxford University Press.

Ekman, P., & Friesen, W. (1969). The repertoire of non-verbal behaviour: Categories, origins, usage and codings. *Semiotics, 1,* 49–98.

Ekman, P., & Rosenberg, E. (1977). *What the face reveals.* New York: Oxford Press.

Erskine, J., & Stewart, D. (Directors). (2001). *The human face* [DVD]. London: BBC.

Hogan, K. (2002). *The psychology of persuasion.* Gretna, LA: Pelican Publishing.

Honey, P., & Mumford, A. (1982). *The learning styles questionnaire.* Maidenhead, England: Peter Honey Publications.

Howard Hughes Medical Institute. (2001). Facing the truth. [Online.] Available: http://www.hhmi.org/bulletin/may2001/faces/faces2.html.

Leigh, J. (1998). *Communicating for cultural competence.* Prospect Heights, IL: Waveland Press.

Massachusetts Municipal Police Institute. (1981). Police and procedure: Interviewing witnesses. Unpublished.

Naramore, D. (1988). Psychology of interviewing. NESPAC: Homicide School. Unpublished.

O'Leary, K. D. (2002). Conjoint therapy for partners who engage in physically aggressive behavior: Rationale and research. R. Geffner & A. Rosenbaum (Eds.), *Domestic violence offenders: Current interventions, research, and implications for policies and standards* (pp. 145–164). Binghamton, NY: Haworth Press.

Rabon, D. (1992). *Interviewing and interrogation.* Durham, NC: Carolina Academic Press.

Royal Air Force. (2001). Learning forces. [Online.] Available: http://www.learning-forces.org.uk/2-10/learnbetter.htm.

Sandoval, V., & Adams, S. (2001). Subtle skills for building rapport using neuro-linguistic programming in the interview room. *FBI Law Enforcement Bulletin,* 1–5.

Wainwright, G. (2003). *Teach yourself: Body language.* Chicago: McGraw-Hill.

Part III

Interviewing Special Populations

The next three chapters discuss interviewing and interrogation approaches for special populations. Criminal justice professionals frequently are involved in circumstances that require interviews and interrogations with children, the elderly, and persons with disabilities. This section prepares you for some of the unusual circumstances that you might encounter in situations with these populations.

Chapter 7 covers interviewing children. Different models for child interviewing are provide along with child-adapted versions of cognitive interviewing and forensic interviewing. These can be practiced for increased understanding and proficiency. It is important when interviewing children to take account of developmental considerations according to the child's age. Knowledge of the developmental stages can assist the interviewer to avoid the limitations inherent in child interviews.

As the elderly population increases in America, the criminal justice community must grow to meet the needs of that population. A greater understanding of the complexities of interviewing older persons is addressed in Chapter 8. The types of crimes and approaches to interviews are among the topics discussed. Although physical limitations due to aging can be expected, these can be anticipated by the interviewer. In most cases the limitations can successfully be overcome.

Interviewing persons with disabilities is the topic of Chapter 9. It addresses the legal requirements of the Americans with Disabilities Act as it pertains to criminal justice personnel. Reasonable accommodations must be made for persons having a disability. In addition, the courts are increasingly holding criminal justice professionals accountable for their actions when confronted with persons who have a disability. This responsibility translates into a need for increased awareness on the part of the police and court and corrections personnel. Individuals with mental retardation, mental illness, and personality disorders are overly represented in the jails and prisons in the United States.

CHAPTER 7
Interviewing Children

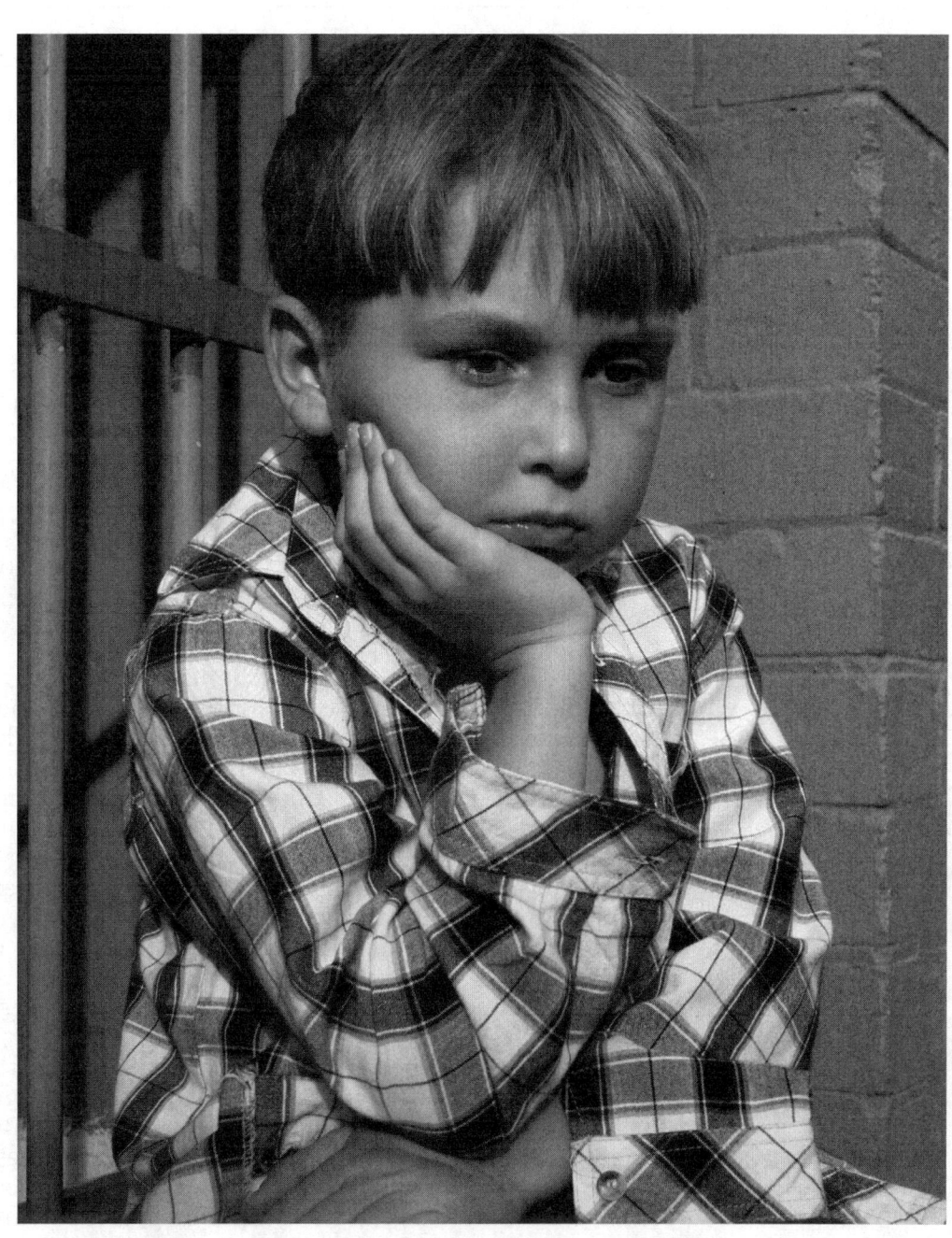

Key Terms

Risk assessment	Forensic interviewing
Child interview model	Comprehension monitoring (CM) preparation method
Parent–child interaction model	Cognitive interviewing method
Multidisciplinary team approach	Secondary abuse
Preliminary considerations checklist	Credibility

Chapter Objectives

After completing this chapter you should be able to:

- Compare and contrast the forensic and cognitive approaches to interviewing
- Explain what is meant by the term *secondary abuse*
- Describe the methods for risk assessment
- Provide information on the tools for interviewing children
- Explain problems associated with child interviewing
- State how the accuracy of a child's statements may affect the criminal justice process
- Describe the multidisciplinary approach
- Explain the CM preparation method
- List the stages of child development and their characteristics

Introduction

Interviewing children can provide unique challenges and opportunities for crime investigators. It is helpful to understand child mental development from the subjective experiences of a child for a variety of reasons. Communicating with children through interviews is highly dependent on their developmental level. As criminal justice professionals we are concerned with the violence perpetrated by children and against children and in the effects of their being witnesses to domestic violence. Child eyewitness testimony is potentially important to decision making in a range of criminal and civil matters (Hayes & Delamonthe, 1997). In addition to the theoretical reasons for exploring methods of effective interviewing is the practical and pressing concern of forensically documenting abuses against children (Saywitz, Goodman, & Lyon, 2002).

Both the identification and recognition of child abuse and the impact of violence are also of consequence to the investigator. Insight into the reactions of the victim may provide a more detailed and accurate portrayal of a harmful situation to the child. The investigator has a unique opportunity to document the full extent of injury, both physical and psychological, if those signs and symptoms present themselves. The likelihood

> **BEEN THERE... DONE THAT! 7-1**
>
> A multidisciplinary task force was established in my county to jointly investigate major crimes committed against children. We came from many different professions. I was the police officer; there was a medical doctor, a prosecuting attorney, a social worker, a clinician, and a victim-witness advocate. After an interview in a particular case the team recommended that I arrest the alleged perpetrator. Even though I also believed that the child had been sexually abused, there was a lack of sufficient probable cause. It was a heated discussion, without compromise. Now what—leave the child unprotected from further abuse? The suggestion was made that we offer the suspect a pretrial diversion. In exchange for him admitting guilt and going to counseling as well as staying away from the victim, we would not prosecute. He agreed. It was a win–win for everyone. Never compromise your reputation by effecting an arrest that lacks probable cause—it will come back to haunt you.

of successful prosecution is enhanced with increased documentation and evidence of harm.

The role of criminal justice investigator differs from and may be in conflict with that of investigators from social service agencies. Criminal investigators have the duty to determine *what* happened rather than an emotional belief that *something* happened (Lanning, 2002). The determination of whether a crime has been committed and the development of admissible evidence are central to the criminal justice perspective. To be effective, interviewers and investigators must be in control of their feelings about abuse and have the ability to react dispassionately.

During the investigation of suspected child abuse the most likely source of information will come from the victim. Second-hand disclosure regarding the abuse of a child should never be considered reliable without corroboration. It is necessary to verify as much of the information as possible. Reliability issues compounded with the suggestibility of children and limited memory development heighten the urgency of finding methods to improve child testimony.

CHILD DEVELOPMENTAL STAGES

The ability of a child witness or victim to accurately report experiences is limited by the child's developmental stage. Because all children do not mature at the same rate, one should be careful about overgeneralization. Poverty, culture, exposure to violence, and a variety of other variables affect cognitive development. The investigator can go into the interview with a rough idea of what might be expected from the interviewee. This knowledge is most helpful before the interview begins. Use it to determine where to conduct the questioning, who should be present, and how to structure the questions.

Age-Related Limitations on Reporting

The child is expected to be preverbal during *infancy,* and direct questioning is unlikely to be productive. Documenting connected terms or crying that indicates an injury or expresses pain is worthwhile for the investigator to include in the report of suspected child abuse. During *early childhood* the ability to verbalize is increased, particularly through play. The best approach for eliciting information from a child under the age of 6 years is within a play therapy framework. *Middle childhood* brings an improvement in the ability to answer questions and to describe events. Exact dates are still a problem, but seasons associated with clothing and events occurring around holidays help to establish the timing of supposed assaults.

Infancy: The First 2 Years. An infant's language consists of utterances, crying, and gestures. A high level of anxiety is reached when immediate needs are not met, such as hunger and relief of pain. The earliest documentation regarding an infant victim refers to the recognition of pain or discomfort. In addition to the medical report of injury, the investigator should note verbal expressions that indicate pain while the child is being examined by a physician in addition to the reports given by the caretaker. Vocabulary is established slowly through single and then connected words. By the time the child is 24 months of age, he or she is likely to be using expressive terms such as "me want," "man bad," and "hit you." Behavioral indicators of abuse are more likely the "language" during infancy.

The investigator should obtain interviews with all caretakers, regardless of their status as a suspect. A parent who says that the infant does not cry excessively or appear in pain may later become a suspect if the child is found to have extensive internal injury, for example. Early documentation of suspected infant abuse is extremely important. Physical examination by a medical professional is required to provide evidence of a crime; a team approach is most beneficial for cases involving an infant victim.

Early Childhood: Ages 2 to 6 Years. These years are collectively referred to as the preschool stage. During early childhood, there is an expectation that the child will verbally communicate, particularly through play. This child will have an active imagination that is grounded in reality; fantasies are about things similar to what the child has experienced, but are not necessarily what happened to them. It is necessary to clarify what the child heard, saw, or felt in order to determine the origin of his or her experiences regarding the topic of the interview. Such children have an inability to concentrate on any one thing for more than a few minutes, although their attention span increases as they grow older. Interviewers need to assess the attention span and structure the interview to accommodate the needs of the child. For example, a child can be encouraged to color between questions.

An intense single experience or a repeatedly rehearsed situation may be retained in a child's long-term memory. Time and space are concepts that the young child has difficulties expressing. The extent of recall is dependent on the level of the child's social interactions. By age 5 years, most children can recall and recount things that occurred in the past (Morison, Moir, & Kwansa, 2000). Extended questioning should not be expected; this does not mean that the interview will be short. The opposite is true; the structure needs to involve purposely provided natural breaks. The interview will require significant time with a great deal of concentration on the part of the interviewer. Only in rare instances should a child of this age be interviewed for longer than 1/2 hour.

As young children mature, they will push their physical limits by running, leaping, and climbing. Unsupervised or neglected children are susceptible to injury caused by falling.

Middle Childhood: Ages 7 to 12 Years. During their middle years a children's mental processes develop at a faster rate than in the earlier stages. Their language is well developed and their understanding of time and space concepts improves. These children can be more specific in explaining when and where they had the experiences that you want to document. Having a strong need for trust, a victimized child at this age may require additional attention and support to compensate for the violation that occurred toward them.

Play remains their primary expression, supplemented with emotion language. This age group should be capable of explaining what they felt as a result of their experiences. During an interview follow-up questions such as, "What did that feel like?", "What did it taste like?", and "How did that make you feel?" are quite appropriate in response to their descriptions. Their cognitive development becomes more sophisticated, including increased reasoning capacity and the ability to distinguish fiction from reality. "How do you know" and "What is he like?" can stimulate expressive responses. Their perception of others may be categorized as "good" or "bad," and they will be able to tell why.

FIELD ASSESSMENT

In cases where a police officer is responding to a complaint of child abuse or neglect, an assessment is made to determine whether criminal action should be investigated. This assessment includes a field interview with the child. The majority of calls will not be acted on independently by the police officer; he or she may act as the first responder who then makes a report to the social services. In making an assessment in the field, the child should be interviewed at the scene, with documentation of the name, address, and age of the child in addition to his or her demeanor. The names and addresses of the caretaker and the family situation are also documented.

After explaining the reason for the visit to the caretaker, the police officers should ask to see the child. If the child is old enough to understand, he or she should be told why the police are there and what they will be doing. Depending on the allegations and/or the child's age, the investigators will need to visually examine the child for signs of obvious trauma. Investigators should document any injuries noted and, if possible, photograph areas of injury or of questionable physical findings.

The child should be interviewed outside the presence of the caregiver. If the child has sustained life-threatening or severe injuries, the first priority is securing emergency medical attention. The U.S. Department of Health and Human Services (Pence & Wilson, 1992) suggests that the following information should be determined from the interview:

- The child's developmental level
- The child's explanation of any injuries
- Who the child perceives as his or her caretakers
- How the child is disciplined
- How other children in the home are disciplined
- How often the victim and/or siblings have been injured in the past
- What type of weapon or implement was used and where it is now
- If the child bled after the assault, where the clothing is now, or any other item that might have been stained
- Who else saw the incident
- Whom the child told of the incident

INITIAL CONSIDERATIONS FOR CHILD INTERVIEWS

As this chapter progresses, differences will emerge regarding interview techniques with children. That is because the purpose and scope of the interview with a child may change at any point during the interview process. A child who is being questioned primarily for having been victimized may also have begun perpetrating. The child may have been victimized by more than one person and through different forms of abuse. Children who have been victimized may also have witnessed other victimizations; they may have information from the perpetrator of others who have been abused. These variables will in turn affect the choice of the person to conduct the questioning.

Step 1: Risk Assessment

Before beginning any investigation that involves interviewing a child, a determination must be made on whether that child is safe. Assessing the present and future risk of harm to a child is more than just an indication about the investigator's level of caring, it is a legal requirement called **risk assessment.** All 50 states and the District of Columbia have legislation that requires certain professionals to report when a child is at risk due to suspected child abuse and neglect. The standard of proof necessary to make this assessment is mere suspicion alone. Some questions that are helpful in making a risk assessment include the following:

1. Is there any reason to believe that this child has been abused, neglected, or witnessed abuse toward a parent or sibling in his or her home?
2. Has the child received a suspicious injury or threat of injury?

3. Has another child in the home been abused or neglected?
4. Are there weapons or ammunition that is accessible to this child? *Note:* Some states make it illegal to have unsecured weapons or ammunition in the home.
5. Does the primary caretaker abuse alcohol or drugs?
6. Is the child depressed or suffering from lack of medical attention?

If the answer to any of the questions above is "yes," then a report of suspected abuse must be filed with the appropriate receiving agency for that state. Child protection services, departments of social services, and police departments are examples of agencies that are designated by law as obligated to receive these reports.

If the child divulges during an interview that abuse has occurred from a caretaker, the interviewer must determine whether the child is likely to be punished for having made the report about a family member or intimate of a parent. This would be a high-risk situation that requires immediate intervention. A local child protection agency should be called regarding this case before the child is released to the caretaker. Police officers in every state have temporary or emergency removal powers for the purposes of protecting children. Removal of the victim to a safe living environment is an option that should be exercised only if a nonoffending parent or guardian is unwilling or unable to protect the child from the suspect.

Step 2: Models for Evaluating Abuse

After conducting the risk assessment and determining that appropriate measures have been taken to assure the safety of the child, the approach to be used for interviewing the child should be determined. This step requires that the model be consistent with the goals of the investigation. The approach to child interviewing may vary widely based on this decision.

The American Professional Society on the Abuse of Children (APSAC) categorizes the approaches to child sexual abuse evaluation into three different models. Although these are specifically suggested for evaluating sexual abuse, they provide a way to conceptualize the way that abuse is determined by external agencies. This framework is helpful for the criminal justice professional in understanding the complexities of child maltreatment allegations from the perspective of clinicians. The recommended approaches are the child interview model, the parent–child interaction model, and the comprehensive evaluation model (Faller, 1996).

The **child interview model** relies most significantly on the interview with the child to determine whether abuse has occurred. The inherent assumption in this model is that children are usually reliable when they give accounts of their sexual abuse and that they rarely make false allegations (Faller, 1996).

The **parent–child interaction model** is theoretically based on expected behaviors between an offending and a nonoffending parent and their children. Mere conversation is used to determine whether the relationship between the parent and child is appropriate. This is a controversial method even among clinicians and should not be used as the basis for criminal complaints.

The third model is the comprehensive evaluation or **multidisciplinary team approach.** Teams may consist of physicians, social workers, psychologists, lawyers, and police officers. Medical exams of the victim and psychological testing may be conducted and considered by the team for abuse evaluation. Interviews with the victim are an important aspect of this approach. Due to the time and expense of the multidisciplinary approach, it may not be appropriate in all allegations of maltreatment. However, abuse against children is a complex problem that requires the coordination of efforts through a multidisciplinary approach to ensure that the needs of the victim are met as well as the criminal justice requirements (Walton, 2003).

The multidisciplinary approach to investigating child abuse requires a substantial knowledge of child development. Current trends lean toward the use of nonpolice persons to conduct these interviews. Lanning (2002) suggested that police officers should become familiar with child development and the interviewing processes from other disciplines in order to remain an active participant in investigative interviewing of children. Lanning cautioned that police officers should not blindly accept the opinions of clinicians and always maintain control over the interview, even if it is conducted by a social worker or other child advocate.

Step 3: Preliminary Considerations

Step 3 consists of using a checklist that will assist the interviewer in determining the type of interview that will be needed. There are four components to the **preliminary considerations checklist:** determine the reason for questioning, determine the purpose of questioning, identify the population, and identify the interviewer.

1. *Determine the reason for questioning*
   - Has the child been victimized? (Requires lengthy interview)
   - Has the child been witness to a crime? (Requires short interview)
   - Is the child suspected of having committed a crime? (Requires interrogation)
2. *Determine the purpose of the questioning*
   - Abuse determination: What is the best model to meet your needs?
   - Risk assessment: Is this child at risk for future victimization?
   - Obtaining evidence: Will the child be able to give verbal or written evidence?
3. *Identify the population*
   - Age: What are the expectations and limitations of this child?
   - Gender: What are the gender-related expectations and limitations of this boy or girl?
   - Special needs: Are special accommodations necessary to conduct the questioning?
   - Cultural background and ethnicity: Can certain outcomes be predicted or avoided?

- Current or recent traumatizing events: What do you know about this person?
4. *Identify the interviewer*
    - Age: Can he or she interact with the target?
    - Gender: Would this make a difference with regard to target response?
    - Ethnicity: Will the interviewer have credibility with the target?
    - Specialization: What sort of special knowledge of interview or interrogation techniques should the interviewer have?
    - Experience of the interviewer: What is the skill level with the target population?
    - Approach: What attitude is required according to the purpose of questioning?
    - Confidence: Is he or she comfortable with the target?

Step 4: Remaining Neutral

It is essential to approach each interview without bias. The purpose of the interview is to determine the truth; this is done based on facts and evidence. The kind of evidence that is sought includes the interview with the child, corroborating physical evidence, and testimonial evidence such as statements taken from persons with knowledge about the case.

To obtain testimony for legal evidence the investigator cannot rely on second-hand information garnered from another agency. Even statements that were taken by another police agency should not be accepted without the present investigator having had an active role in the interview process. This is extremely important in order to protect the victim as well as the rights of the accused. As with any criminal investigation, certain criteria must be satisfied for the matter to be considered a criminal offense. Resist the temptation to run out and make an arrest without reviewing the statement to determine if probable cause has been adequately established through the following information *for every allegation*. Here are some questions to which the interviewer must have answers to proceed with the criminal process:

1. What, if any, crime has occurred?

    All criteria for the commission of the crime must be satisfied. For example, if the allegation is the rape of a child, penetration must have occurred. What is the evidence of penetration? Penetration may be perpetrated by any object into any orifice. Determine the genitalia that were penetrated and the object that was used. It may be a body part or a physical object inserted into the child. Depending on the age of the victim, force may also be an element of the crime. The issue of force may be satisfied by any level of force; depending on the relationship, this might be a "command." Identify what level of force was used, if any. For a young child this is not an issue.

2. Who had committed the crime?

    It may be difficult for a young child to adequately identify the perpetrator. A person cannot be accused of a crime without having positively been identified. If the child only knows the first name of the individual (and this is not unusual), it is necessary to follow up with a question on where he or she knows John or where the abuse occurred. With a younger child the information might be obtained from the guardian. For example, if "John" was responsible, how does the child know him? Where did it happen? If the offense occurred in "John's house," find out whether John is the grandfather, the uncle, or a babysitter. It is not appropriate to suggest that a child has been abused, but once the statement is made that abuse did occur, direct questions for the purposes of clarifying what has already been stated are permissible. Keep asking questions until you are satisfied that the alleged perpetrator's identity is firmly established.

3. Where did the crime occur?

    Expect that the description of the place will be age appropriate. "In the woods," "In the house," and "At school" are examples of what you might hear. Build on what the child says if clarification is needed. If the place of victimization was at day care, find out the times and dates that the child was enrolled in and attended day care. If the abuse occurred at the house of a relative, find out whether the person cared for the child regularly or on a sporadic basis.

4. When did the crime occur?

    Many young victims will not be able to state the exact date that they were victimized. Their concept of time is different than that of adults, and they may have been victimized over a long period of time. To clarify the times of victimization, ask questions to help the child to narrow down within a time frame. For example, ask, "What were you wearing?" The answer may indicate the season. Determine the last time that the alleged perpetrator had access to the child. Children older than the age of 6 years are more likely to be able to accurately define the time period in relation to an important event in their life such as a holiday or birthday; ask, "Was it before your birthday or after?" If you know that the alleged perpetrator had frequent access to the child, ask whether "it" happened the last time they were together.

5. Against whom was the crime perpetrated?

    Clarify with the child whether he or she was the victim or might have seen something happen to someone else. If there is any question in your mind, be direct; ask, "Did this happen to you?"

6. How was the crime perpetrated?

    This part of the questioning can be most difficult for the interviewer. He or she must be comfortable asking for specific clarification on how the crime was perpetrated. It can be helpful for the interviewer to feign misunderstanding; ask the child to help understand what happened. Here are a few examples (depending on the crime being investigated): "You told me that a stick was there; what happened with the stick? Can you show me on the doll (or picture) where the stick was put? Did it touch you outside or did it go inside?

What did that feel like?" When asking questions for clarification interviewer neutrality is important. Do not act surprised, angry, happy, or thankful. It is appropriate to thank the child for clearing up the misunderstanding.

WHAT IS THE FORENSIC APPROACH TO CHILD INTERVIEWING?

The forensic approach to child interviewing is used when primary victimization is suspected. Based on the multidisciplinary model, it involves multiple individuals with different expertise working together to gather information and collect evidence. The approach is legal oriented with an effort toward maintaining the integrity of the case so as to meet possible future court challenges. All interviews and collection of evidence must be conducted by individuals who are trained and familiar with the legal standards of the state where the offense is alleged to have occurred. The interviewer may be a police officer, a child psychologist, a certified forensic interviewer, or any member of the team who is qualified to conduct the questioning of the victim based on the preliminary considerations. Collaboration with mandated reporting agencies means that members of the forensic team are consulted and have full participation in the process.

There is a recent trend toward the use of a certified forensic interviewer who can establish a nonbiased position as neither an advocate for

FIGURE 7-1 When asked to draw a picture of the person who "touched her in a place she didn't like" a 4-year-old girl drew this picture. It was used as evidence of her sexual assault.

the child nor an employee of the court. This method is meant to reduce the number of interviews that may ultimately contaminate the child's testimony through repetitive questioning. It involves a standardized procedure that documents the affect or nonverbal report of the child as well as the verbal account. Often this is accomplished by videotaping the victim during the interview. There is no legal requirement that children be informed that they are being interviewed. The decision on giving this information to the child is a matter of organization policy. The permission of a parent or guardian should be obtained prior to videotaping a child.

Forensic interviewing is a traditional structured format for a child interview that is designed to minimize future court challenges through strict adherence to legal principles. The interview requires planning and precision. A detailed history of abuse or suspected current abuse is obtained prior to the interview. An interview room is specifically designed for the comfort of the designated age group to be interviewed. Direct questioning is necessary to elicit details of an assault, but care is taken not to be suggestive in the form of questioning.

FORENSIC INTERVIEWING TECHNIQUES

Interviewing children takes time and can be a difficult process. The purpose of the interview will determine how complex it will be. Young children are easily distracted and often reluctant to disclose abuse. When they feel attached to the abuser they may fear the consequences, including what the interviewer might do to them as a result. To avoid this problem, the interviewer should not show approval or disapproval at anything the child says. The emotions of the interviewer must be held in check. Signs of disgust, disbelief, or even approval are not appropriate because they may influence the child.

Phase I: Caretaker Instructions

Prior to meeting with the child instructions should be provided to the caretaker. The caretaker should be advised not to answer any questions about the interview from the child. No attempt should be made by the caretaker to gain further information from the child about the event. Warn the caretaker not to discuss case specifics because others may also be involved who have not yet been identified. Explain to the caretaker that a bathroom break needs to be provided for the child just prior to the interview.

If it does not compromise the investigation, attempt to put the caretaker at ease by telling him or her about the process at this stage. Include the fact that you will need to talk to the child alone.

Immediately prior to the interview have the guardian sign a prepared form of release to conduct and document the interview. This is important because the process may result in information that implicates the caretaker or those who the caretaker wants to protect. When an interrogation of a juvenile is the focus, additional legal requirements must be met. See Chapter 13 for issues concerning juvenile interrogation.

Phase II: Evaluation

Using the common preliminary considerations checklist, conduct an evaluation of the upcoming interview. From this exercise the interviewer will know the approximate length and approach that will be needed.

Determine the appropriate place to conduct the interview. For all interviews, the room should be quiet and free of distractions. There should not be any electronic devices in the room that will make noise: no phone, cell phone, beeper, pager, clock, or radio. For a child interview, no chairs are necessary if there are comfortable places to sit on the floor. This puts the interviewer at a more even level with the child and is less threatening. Audio or video recording devices should not be visible to the child because he or she may "ham it up" for a camera. For an interrogation there should be a table for writing and a visible recording device if one is to be used.

Preparation for the interview includes the reading of any statements that may have brought the child to the attention of the police. Any information regarding past or present allegations of abuse should be researched. A background check of the alleged perpetrator should be made prior to the interview with the supposed victim.

Phase III: Preparing the Child

Interviewers are often frustrated by inaccurate and unreliable statements taken from young children. This is, in part, due to developmental limitations on children's ability to communicate when they don't understand the questions. The interviewer is not made aware of the situation because children will merely provide an answer that is false rather than communicate that they don't understand. Current research on this issue suggests a method that can greatly diminish the error rate. The **comprehension monitoring (CM) preparation method** uses a practice session to assist the child to identify information that he or she does not understand and improve the child's ability to tell the interviewer when he or she doesn't understand. Using the CM preparation method, someone other than the interviewer should prepare the child for the interview. The approach may cut erroneous reports in half by improving the communication between the interviewer and the child (Saywitz, Snyder, & Nathanson, 1999).

Children being prepared for the interview should (1) practice identifying instances of noncomprehension, (2) practice responding with verbalizations that indicate their lack of understanding (after being taught by someone using explicit feedback, modeling, and praise), and (3) increase their awareness of the negative consequences of responding to questions

> **BEEN THERE... DONE THAT! 7-2**
>
> Building rapport is a critical component of any interview. When first meeting a child it is important to get to his or her level and say hello. Introduce yourself properly and treat the child with respect. They do know the difference at any age! Although I conducted interviews with children in civilian clothes, I typically introduced myself as a police officer whose job it was to talk to children about things that might be important to them.

not fully understood (e.g., misordering in a restaurant and receiving the wrong food, missing out on a favorite activity). After the preparation phase, the child should be given adequate time for some food, beverage, and, of course, a bathroom break.

Phase IV: Establishing Rapport

The interviewer should meet and greet the child in a relaxed and comfortable manner. Rather than asking for his name, say, "Hi, you must be Bill," and state your first name. Tell the child that you have been expecting him, and then ask the guardian if it is all right for Bill to take a walk with you. This simple act reassures the child that you are someone to whom he is able (given permission) to go with and to talk to. Make this introduction appropriate to the age of the child. If this is a young child, kneel down to the child's level at the beginning of the meeting. The interview should be conducted without the presence of the guardian unless his or her presence is absolutely necessary.

Take whatever time necessary to ensure that the child is relaxed and does not feel threatened. The interview room should afford flexibility for the child to move around, but should not be large enough to allow "escape." Crayons and paper should be available to occupy the child and allow him or her to talk unguarded. Talk about the child's likes such as colors, activities, games, movies—get to know the child. Let the child know a bit about you. This is the time to access the developmental level of the child and his or her ability to communicate. For very young children it might be sufficient to say that you are someone who talks to kids about things on their minds. Older children may want to know more about your role as a police officer, social worker, and so on. This is the stage in which you determine the sexual terminology of the child if the interview concerns sexual abuse. Use appropriate tools to aid in this vocabulary development. You may want to ask questions to determine the child's level of sophistication, such as "Can you write?", "Do you know your alphabet?", "Do you read?" With an interrogation, the child must be told if you are a police officer.

Phase V: Conducting the Interview

At this point, the interviewer is ready to find out what happened. Establish that the child knows the difference between the truth and a lie and that the child is willing to tell you if he or she does not understand questions. Ask "Do you know what a lie is?" Ask for an example. "Do you know what telling the truth is?" Ask for an example. "If I said your name was Bill, is that a lie or the truth?" "If I say that this crayon is red, is that the truth or a lie?" Give the child license by saying that you also will ask when you don't understand something.

Don't use "cop talk." Use language that is appropriate to the child's age and developmental level. Words like incident, occur, penetration, prior, ejaculation, and perpetrator can be confusing to a child. Look for signs that the child does not understand you. Avoid using language that sounds accusatory, such as "Why?" Don't say, "Why did you do that?", "Why did you go to that house?", "Why did he touch you?" Never threaten or try to force a reluctant child to talk. If gentle coaxing is insufficient to overcome the child's unwillingness, stop the interview.

Do not lead the child by offering a possible place for the event or name for the perpetrator. Start the conversation by asking what happened, or "I need for you to tell me what happened to you." Ask simple and direct questions for clarification. Be as open-ended as possible to solicit narratives. Don't ask questions that can foreclose possible additional information by being be answered with a simple "yes" or "no." Determine whether threats were made against the child if he or she told what happened. Close the interview by thanking the child for his or her cooperation. Do not try to exact promises about testifying.

WHAT IS THE COGNITIVE APPROACH TO INTERVIEWING CHILDREN?

The **cognitive interviewing method** is a memory-jogging and retrieval tool that was developed in the hope of improving the completeness and accuracy of eyewitness accounts. Originally designed for adults, it has been modified for interviewing children. Studies have determined that cognitive interviewing increases the amount of correct information elicited from eyewitnesses without increasing the proportion of incorrect information (Geiselman, Bornstein, & Saywitz, 1992). However, it does not prevent the child from reporting false information after having been subjected to a misleading suggestion.

COGNITIVE INTERVIEWING TECHNIQUES

The cognitive approach is useful when interviewing younger children because they tend to give less complete information, although their cognitive ability is not that different from older children (Hayes & Delamonthe, 1997). The method is deceptively simple, but requires practice in order for one to become proficient in it. It stresses using a secluded, quiet place free of distractions along with urging subjects to speak slowly. It is useful for questioning both victims and witnesses. Most of this approach incorporates traditional interviewing techniques, but it includes an improved method of recalling information through memory-jogging techniques rather than direct questioning. This method is only used with a willing participant.

Caretaker Instructions

Prepare the guardian, parent, or caretaker in the same way as for any forensic interview. Request that the person not ask the child about the supposed abuse. Put the caretaker at ease by answering any questions that would not jeopardize the investigation. Obtain the necessary release forms from the guardian, parent, or caretaker to conduct the interview with the child.

Practice Interview

A practice cognitive interview is optional but recommended (Geiselman et al., 1992). If a practice interview is used, the interviewer should be different than the person who conducts the practice session. Giving the child experience with being interviewed serves to clarify the methods that will be used in the actual interview and encourages the child to use recall techniques. The child is introduced to a scenario that will be used to practice for the actual interview through a short video or the introduction of a person who has short conversation with the child and leaves the room. Tell the child that he or she will now practice for the interview that will happen another time with the "detective" or "Mary" or "the social worker." Research indicates that children who were given a practice cognitive interview on an unrelated event prior to the actual cognitive interview gave the most complete reports about the event (Geiselman et al., 1992).

Establishing Rapport: Cognitive Interview Step 1

The new interviewer must establish rapport and prepare the child prior to questioning. Instruct the child that this is the interview he or she has been waiting for to talk about what happened. Rapport development here is the same as with the forensic interviewing approach. Consideration must be given to assuring that the child is relaxed and comfortable prior to the interview. Positive and open-ended questions promote expanded conversation, such as asking the child about his or her favorite TV show.

The interviewer prepares the child for upcoming questions with the following instructions (Geiselman et al., 1992):

1. There may be some questions that you do not know the answers to. That's okay. Nobody can remember everything. If you don't know the answer to a question, then tell me "I don't know," but do not guess or make anything up. It is very important to tell me only what you really remember, only what really happened.
2. If you do not want to answer some of the questions, you don't have to. That's ok. Tell me "I don't want to answer that question."

> **BEEN THERE... DONE THAT! 7-3**
>
> Leading questions are dangerous in interviewing because they may provide misinformation to the person being interviewed. It can happen very subtly that a victim or witness is given misinformation without specifically stating the answer; they come to believe a response is expected. If they don't know the answer, they make one up. Once a victim or witness has misinformation there is a chance that he or she will repeat it with increased emphasis. One day I took a 6-year-old boy through the station as a way to establish rapport. He went over to my desk and was allowed to sit in my chair. We lingered for a few moments, making easy conversation. We then started walking though the office back to the room where the interview was to occur. This child knew exactly why he was there and started talking about being abused before we made it past all of the desks in the office.
>
> My mistake was in not insulating him from distractions that would cause misinformation. Walking past the rows of detectives sitting at their desks, he caught a glimpse of the shiney gold badge worn by the sergeant. At that exact time I asked, "What did he (the man who sexually abused him) look like?" Without hesitation the child pointed to the sergeant with the shiney gold badge and loudly exclaimed, "He looked like HIM!" As I ran the child out of the room I heard something like, "get that _____ kid out of here!" I would not recommend starting an interview while walking by other people.

3. If you do not know what something I ask you means, tell me "I don't know what you mean." Tell me to say it in new words.
4. I may ask you some questions more than one time. Sometimes I forget that I already asked you that question. You don't have to change your answer. Just tell me what you remember the best you can.

Reconstruction and Reporting Everything: Cognitive Interview Step 2

Two mnemonic techniques are used in Step 2. The child is asked to **reconstruct the circumstances** surrounding the incident by being coaxed to give a narrative account of what happened. The interviewer should listen intently and not interrupt. Notes should be taken sparingly; it would best if the interview were being videotaped or audiotaped. Someone listening to the interview but outside of the view of the child can take more complete notes.

In instructing the child to reconstruct the circumstances of the incident, one should include sample directions such as the following: "Picture the time when [the scenario] was happening as if it was happening right now. Tell me what it was like. Tell me out loud. Were there any smells? Was it dark? Was it light? Was there anyone else there? Who? What things were there? How were you feeling?" The description includes not only the appearance of the scene and the people present or nearby, but also the child's thoughts and feelings at the time of the scenario.

The next part is to ask the child to start at the beginning and say from the beginning, to the middle, to the end, everything that he or she remembers, even little parts he or she doesn't think are very important. Ask the child to **report everything** that happened. Do not interrupt while the child is talking. Prompt by asking what happened only when needed. Clarify at this point by asking open-ended question whenever possible. Do not ask more than one question at a time. Speak in a relaxed tone. When clarifying details that the child has provided, use a positive questioning approach.

Praise the child's effort, not the content of the responses. For example, the interviewer should say, "I understand what you are saying" or "You are doing a great job in explaining to me." Do not say, "Thanks for telling me what Uncle Joe did to you."

Changing the Order and Perspective: Cognitive Interview Step 3

The third step in the child version of cognitive interviewing consists in using two additional memory-jogging techniques to enhance the narrative account. Any or all of these techniques may used in the interview depending on the information that is being sought.

- **Change the order.** Ask the child to recall what happened in backward order, from the end to the beginning. Prepare the child for that technique before asking. After each response ask the child, "What happened right before that?"
- **Change the perspective.** Ask the child to recount the incident from a new perspective. This is done by instructing the child to say what he or she would have seen through the eyes of an inanimate object, such as a stuffed animal that was present. Avoid asking the child to recount the story from the perspective of the supposed perpetrator.

Additional memory-jogging techniques may be useful when seeking to clarify specific information that has been provided by the child. Examples include the following:

- **Alphabet search.** In order to help the child to remember names or places, ask the child to go through the alphabet to help recall the information.
- **Speech characteristics.** Probe for speech traits if the offender was not identified. Ask if the voice reminded the child of anyone or was unusual in any way.
- **Conversation.** Ask how the child felt about what was said. Were there any unusual phrases or words used by the perpetrator?

Research suggests that using only two of the cognitive procedures mentioned in this section will have a positive impact on the quality of the interview with a child (Hayes & Delamonthe, 1997). In the most recent version of the cognitive method the two methods incorporated into the child interview are **reconstruct the circumstances** and **report everything.** The approaches of thinking out loud and giving a narrative account add to the completeness of the child's report.

> **BEEN THERE... DONE THAT! 7-4**
>
> Early in a career of interviewing children I learned from trial and error what items should be kept out of the interview room. One particular child grew increasingly anxious as he began to divulge being sexually molested. As I pressed him with follow-up questions about specifics he became avoidant. Everything that could be picked up became a focus for him. Gently I would take the toys away and ask for him to explain things to me. Exasperated, he picked up a bottle of glue and poured it into my hair! That was quickly followed by a toy hurled in my direction. We did talk some more, but afterward, everything sharp and sticky was removed from the room! Don't expect children to enjoy the process any more than you would if you were asked to talk about your negative experiences. Your goal is to make a potentially uncomfortable situation as comfortable as possible though your attitude and kind nature. The articles in the child-interviewing room should be selected carefully. Do not include toys or otherwise distracting items, and leave out the glue.

THE CHILD AS REPORTER

The only people who should be present in the interview room are the child being interviewed and the person designated to conduct the interview. The presence of significant others of the child WILL affect the interview process (Morison et al., 2000). The interviewer cannot know beforehand whether that influence will be positive or negative. Supporting parents or friends may act to encourage the child to divulge, and a disapproving parent (or one the child perceives to be disapproving) will have the opposite effect.

The nature of the relationship between the child and the interviewer is one of the most important components of a successful interview. A child who feels respected and secure will communicate more openly and honestly than one who feels threatened by the process.

Accuracy

A child's account of events may be incomplete. This does not mean that the child isn't telling the truth. Children tend to block out unpleasant events, and the interview may produce information regarding a prior incident intermingled with present events. Before beginning the interviewer should know any history that might exist of prior victimization so that clarifications can be made during the interview. If leading questions are asked, the responses may be distorted. Inaccurate responses also occur if the child does not fully understand the question but does not acknowledge that comprehension is an issue. Interviewers can increase the probability of accurate responses through the use of age-appropriate language and confirming throughout the interview that the child understands.

Children may have difficulty disclosing events that they find embarrassing or humiliating (Morison et al., 2000). Then again, adults have similar problems. This means that the interviewer should be sensitive to the child's self-esteem. Compliance during the process can be increased if the child is a willing participant in the interview. Taking the time to engage cooperation through the rapport-building stage is extremely important. Neutralizing the setting for the interview may help in decreasing shyness.

Memory and Fantasy

Research suggests that a child is being interviewed it is difficult to determine with certainty, on the basis of the child's memory alone, whether the child is recounting something suggested, coached, or actually witnessed (Lindberg et al., 2003). It is possible that the best results for a pristine memory recall can be obtained by learning to keep quiet and allowing the child to take over in the first open free-recall attempt. Although adult memory is not always accurate, we do not question adult recollections to the same extent as we question the memory of children. Always investigate for corroborating evidence in cases of child abuse. To minimize fantasy during a child interview, avoid using terms such as *pretend* or *imagine*.

THE CHILD AS VICTIM

There are numerous considerations when interviewing a child who is suspected of being a victim of abuse. The interview may uncover both direct and indirect forms of abuse. An injury or a pattern of injuries that is nonaccidental characterizes direct child abuse. It is damage to a child for which there is no explanation that is reasonable or fitting to the injuries that the child has sustained. Such abuse may take the form of emotional and psychological maltreatment, physical injury abuse, and sexual abuse. Another form of direct maltreatment is considered passive: the action or inaction of a legally recognized caretaker who fails to fulfill his or her responsibility to a dependent child. These neglectful categories of abuse are becoming more familiar to criminal justice and social service agencies as they struggle to enforce an increasing number of child protection statutes. Examples of passive maltreatment are neglect, which may be physical or emotional; educational neglect; inadequate care in such areas as food, clothing, and shelter; lack of supervision; denial or the lack of medical care; nonsupport of a minor child; and parental kidnapping.

Two categories of **secondary abuse** are covered here: witnessing domestic violence and witnessing the homicide of a parent. Secondary abuse occurs as the consequence of residing in a violent home. Violence toward an intimate partner causes a variety of psychological problems for children and places them at greater risk for delinquency and adult criminality. Research has suggested that children subjected to violence through child victimization and the witnessing of abuse in the home have higher rates of violence as adults (Heyman & Slep, 2002). In homes where a parent is battered, there is approximately a 50 percent chance that children in the home are also being abused. Although we cannot predict which children will become victims of abuse, those who reside in violent homes are at greater risk. When responding to calls of domestic abuse an officer should interview all children residing in the home. This type of interview is generally short. Questions should not be asked within sight of either parent. An initial question is, "Are you ok?" Watching for

> **BEEN THERE ... DONE THAT! 7-5**
>
> The interviewer needs to speak the language of the child. To allow children to get comfortable with anatomical dolls and to supply me with vocabulary to use during the interview, I would point to the eye, the nose, the chest, and so on of the doll. Each time I would ask, "What is this called?" Sometimes it is hard to keep from laughing; no positive or negative response should be given. Be prepared for anything. Wingy, dingy, fred, flop, friend, mine, po, pet, and ping are among the many responses I have heard.

the response, the officer/interviewer will determine if he or she needs to sit down and talk in depth about the situation.

Victims can be found throughout society with no regard to age or gender. This does not mean that all children are victimized, but boys and girls of all ages can be victims. A child is defined as a person under the age of 18 years, except in those states that specify a younger age. Always interview the children in a home when responding to domestic violence.

Tools for Interviewing Children

The use of drawing is very helpful when interviewing any child younger than the age of 12 years and in some cases older children. Paper and crayons are important tools to have available in all interview rooms. Use crayons to build rapport. Ask the child what his or her favorite color is; allow the child to use one crayon that he or she has chosen. This simple act gives some control to the child, acknowledges something of value to him or her, and establishes whether they know colors. Then the rest of the crayons may be put aside so that they do not become a distraction. Do not have glue, scissors, or toys available in the interview room that will provide an opportunity to avoid distressing topics. Drawings may be used to express better what has happened to the child.

In recent research, ninety 4- to 13-year-old victims of sexual abuse were interviewed by police officers who showed the children a human figure drawing and asked questions (Aldridge et al., 2004). The drawing and associated questions brought an average of 86 new forensically relevant details of the event and was particularly helpful with 4- to 7-year-olds. The authors of the study recommend that a gender-neutral drawing be used and that it should be introduced in the later part of the interview to expand recall. When using the pictures, instruct the child to mark a picture using his or her crayon. Instructions should be clear and simple. For example, "Put an X on the place where you were kissed and put a circle on the place where you were touched."

Anatomically correct dolls are a helpful tool for a variety of reasons. First, they help to establish the child's vocabulary so that you can use language that is understood by both of you. Dolls can also be used by the child to demonstrate what occurred. Caution should be exercised in using dolls in interviews with extremely young children, whose reasoning may not be developed enough to realize that one object can also serve as a representation of an another object (Morison et al., 2000).

BOLSTERING CREDIBILITY THROUGH EVIDENCE

Credibility refers to the believability of the witness or victim. It is a major factor that must be established during an interview. To help determine whether a person is credible, the interviewer must consider whether the person can comprehend what is being said. How well is her or his observation of things? Can the person see well enough to describe events as he or she observed them? Does nonverbal behavior indicate possible deception? For states that do not have a predetermined age required to testify, credibility is established as part of the process of determining competency. Gathering physical evidence is a way to enhance the credibility of a child.

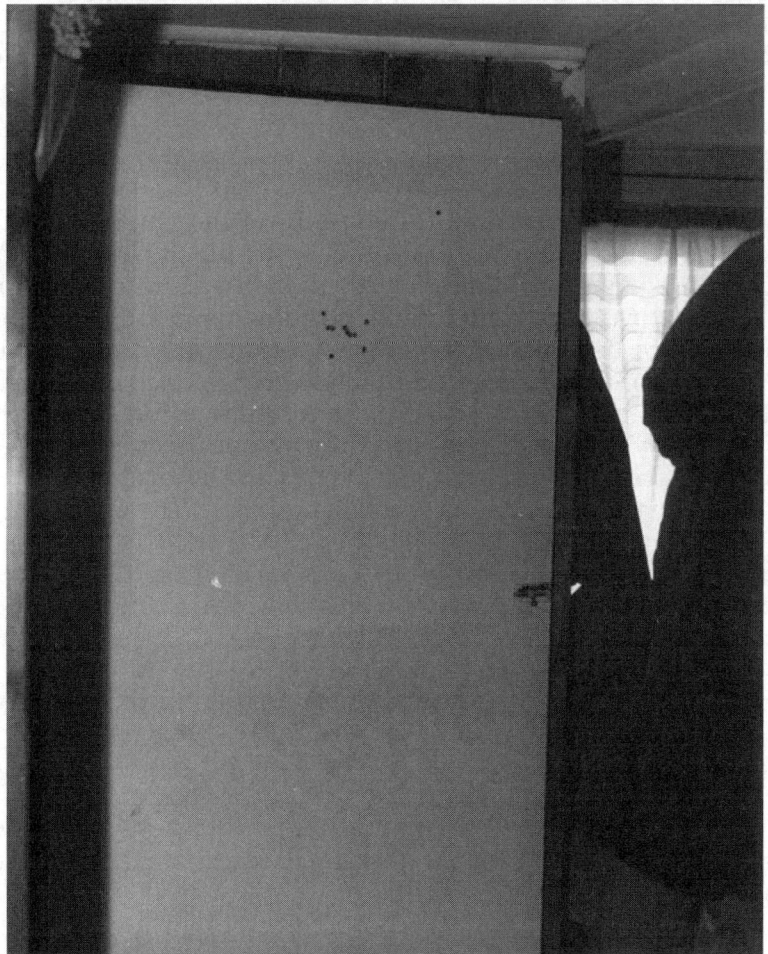

FIGURE 7-2 This is a picture of the door where Tim was made to stand while being shot at. Notice the bullet holes and the place where the Mickey Mouse picture had hung. Read on for the rest of the story!

Interviewing Children 151

FIGURE 7-3 Note the bullet holes on Mickey's face! This was the poster that was found in a search of the home where the assault in Been There . . . Done That! 7-6 occurred. It was hidden under a mattress.

> **BEEN THERE... DONE THAT! 7-6**
>
> Nine-year-old Tim reported that mommy's boyfriend made him stand in front of Mickey Mouse while he shot Mickey. Tim stated that he thought he was *dead* when the bullets went so close to his head. When Virgil put the gun down Tim ran into the bedroom and jumped onto the bed. Virgil came after him and tried to break his head open with the end of the gun, but it hit the wall instead. A search warrant was obtained for Virgil's one-bedroom house. The wall next to the bed evidenced a hole that was consistent with the butt of a rifle. Small ammunitions and a handgun were retrieved in addition to a rifle. As the search continued, a poster of Mickey Mouse was located between the mattresses. There were small holes that perfectly matched the ones found on the hall door. One hole was measured as being 1 inch higher than the height of Tim. The door was seized along with the other evidence. At trial, Tim's mother testified that Tim was a liar and had fabricated the assault. Nothing spoke louder than the poster of Mickey Mouse and the door riddled with bullet holes. The jury gasped when Tim was instructed by the prosecution to stand in front of Mickey Mouse and they saw that the bullet holes aligned with his little body. Virgil was convicted.

There is no substitute for physical evidence to support the child's statement. When interviewing a child, note any object that is involved with the crime that might later be seized with a legally obtained search warrant. Clarify during the interview the exact location and description of any possible evidence. Obtaining physical evidence for use in prosecution is helpful when the victim is an adult. For abuses against children, this is a critical part of the case. Merely presenting the word of a child against the word of an adult makes prosecutions more difficult. Seek a search warrant if the place of the event is exactly known and the alleged perpetrator has positively been identified.

What should the interviewer search to bolster credibility? Anything. If a child describes being physically assaulted with any object, the investigator should seize that object. If the place is anywhere other than the child's residence, it might be photographed inside for comparison with the child's description of the area. When the victim reports sexual molestation the subject of the search includes any area where tissues, towels, magazines, lubricants, or photos are kept by the alleged perpetrator.

If the child is severely injured or has died, the place of death must be searched to determine, if possible, whether the explanations for the injury are consistent with the environment.

DETERMINING COMPETENCY AND RELIABILITY

During the investigation of suspected child abuse the most likely source of information will come from the victim. Standing alone, eyewitness testimony is considered the least reliable form of evidence. Reliability issues compounded with the suggestibility of children and limited memory development heighten the need for methods to improve child testimony. Studies have confirmed that children do have the ability to communicate reliability when questioned properly (Morison et al., 2000).

Competency is a preliminary question of law that a judge must decide before a witness is permitted to testify. There is no federal standard for determining competency. The 1974 federal rules of evidence abolished the competency rule for trial in federal courts. More than one third of the states followed the federal example when it comes to child witnesses and do not require a competency inquiry (Abrams & Ramsey, 2000). We assume that all adults to be competent; 13 states presume that a person older than the age of 10 years is competent to testify. Eighteen states require demonstration that the child understands the nature and obligation of the oath to tell the truth. One aspect of competency determination hinges on whether the child has the capacity to recall events, separate fact from fantasy, and maintain those memories independently without being influenced by others. The second aspect of the determination is that the child has a sense of moral responsibility defined as understanding the duty to speak the truth (Abrams & Ramsey, 2000).

CONCLUSIONS

This chapter began with a description of child development stages. This is an important foundation for conducting interviews with children. Although all children do not develop in exactly the same way, knowledge of child development can assist the interviewer to determine the best individual to conduct the interview. The chapter also provided some insight into the role of the criminal justice investigator in interviewing children. Discussed throughout are the problems specific to obtaining reliable and credible statements from children given their suggestibility and immature cognitive development. Specific techniques, cognitive and forensic, were explained in detail with example questions suggested. The cognitive approach has been shown to provide more accurate information, but it is a lengthier method.

QUESTIONS FOR REVIEW

Short-Answer Questions

1. What are the considerations in the common preliminary checklist?
2. What are the three models for evaluating abuse?
3. In regard to obtaining evidence, what are the answers an interviewer must know in order to proceed with the criminal process?
4. Compare and contrast the forensic and cognitive approaches to interviewing on each dimension.

5. What are some of the concerns that an interviewer should be aware of regarding the child as reporter?
6. What are the types of abuse that can occur to a child?
7. Briefly discuss the developmental stages of childhood.
8. What are the four mnemonics used in the cognitive approach to the child interview?

Fill-in Questions

1. The three approaches recognized by the American Professional Society on the Abuse of children are _____, _____, and _____.
2. A(n) _____ will assess the present and future risk of harm to a child.
3. How many states have legislation that requires certain professionals to report when a child is at risk due to suspected child abuse or neglect?
4. Evidence that is sought through a police investigation of child abuse includes _____, _____, and _____.
5. The _____ is conducted when primary victimization is suspected.
6. The two categories of secondary abuse are _____ and _____.
7. _____ and _____ are helpful tools when interviewing children.
8. During _____ children communicate with utterances, crying, and gestures.
9. _____ age group usually needs to gain your trust and needs more attention and support to compensate for the violation that occurred toward them.

Exercises

Practice your cognitive interviewing techniques. Divide into pairs. One student will be the interviewer and the other will be the interviewee.

1. The interviewer is to find out as much detail as possible about the interviewee's last experience in taking an exam. Instruct the interviewee on the **report everything** approach. Take 5 minutes for this mnemonic exercise.
2. The interviewers are asked to recall what they learned about their partner's last exam. Take 5 minutes for this discussion.
3. Continue with the interview. Instruct the interviewee on using the technique to **reconstruct the circumstances** surrounding his or her exam experience. For example, ask him or her to describe the surroundings, room, furniture, and so on. The interviewer should not interrupt his or her partner once they begin. Take 5 minutes for this mnemonic exercise.
4. Share any new information with the class that came out of this approach. Take 5 minutes for this discussion.

5. Continue with the interview. Ask the interviewee to recall the story in reverse order and then from the perspective of someone else who was there at the time. Take 10 minutes for this mnemonic exercise.
6. Discuss with the class any new information you learned about the exam.

REFERENCES

Abrams, D. E., & Ramsey S. H. (2000). *Children and the law: Doctrine, policy, and practice.* St. Paul, MN: West Group.

Aldridge, J., Lamb, M., Sternberg, K., Orbach, Y., Esplin, P., & Bowler, L. (2004). Using a human figure drawing to elicit information from alleged victims of child sexual abuse. *Journal of Consulting and Clinical Psychology, 72*(2), 304–316.

Faller, K. C. (1996). *Evaluating children suspected of having been sexually abused.* Thousand Oaks, CA: Sage Publications.

Geiselman, R. E., Bornstein, G., & Saywitz, K. (1992). *New approach to interviewing children: A test of its effectiveness* (Report No. NCJ 135011). Washington, DC: National Institute of Justice.

Hayes, B. K., & Delamonthe, K. (1997). Cognitive interviewing procedures and suggestibility in children's recall. *Journal of Applied Psychology, 82*(4), 562–577.

Heyman, R. E., & Slep, A. M. S. (2002). Do child abuse and interparental violence lead to adulthood family violence? *Journal of Marriage and Family, 64*(4), 864–871.

Lanning, K. (2002). Criminal investigation of sexual victimization of children. In J. Myers, L. Berliner, J. Briere, C. T. Hendrix, C. Jenny, & T. Reid (Eds.), *The APSAC handbook on child maltreatment* (2nd ed., pp. 329–348). Thousand Oaks, CA: Sage Publications.

Lindberg, M. A., Chapman, M. T., Samsock, D., Thomas, S. W., & Lindberg, A. W. (2003). Comparisons of three different investigative interview techniques. *Journal of Genetic Psychology, 164*(1), 5–28.

Morison, M., Moir, J., & Kwansa, T. (2000). Interviewing children for the purposes of research in primary care. *Primary Health Care Research and Development, 1,* 113–130.

Pence, D., & Wilson, C. (1992). *The role of law enforcement in the response to child abuse and neglect.* Washington, DC: National Center on Child Abuse and Neglect.

Saywitz, K. J., Goodman, G. S., & Lyon, T. D. (2002). Interviewing children in and out of court. In J. E. Myers, L. Berline, J. Briere, H. Terry, C. Jenny, & T. Reid (Eds.), *The APSAC handbook on child maltreatment* (2nd ed., pp. 349–377). Thousand Oaks, CA: Sage Publications.

Saywitz, K. J., Snyder, L., & Nathanson, R. (1999). Facilitating the communicative competence of the child witness. *Applied Developmental Science, 3*(1), 58–69.

Walton, S. (2003). When violence hits home. *State Legislatures, 29*(6), 31–34.

CHAPTER 8
Interviewing the Elderly

KEY TERMS

Self-neglect	Sexual abuse
Abandonment	Fiduciary abuse
Active neglect	Conversation-observing evaluation
Passive neglect	Source confusion
Physical abuse	Aging-out

CHAPTER OBJECTIVES

After completing this chapter you should be able to:

- Explain the changing demographics of the elderly population
- State the concerns regarding elderly perpetrators
- Define self-neglect
- Explain the difference between active and passive abuse
- Compare and contrast the interviewing techniques involving older persons
- List the categories of crimes targeting the elderly
- Describe the characteristics of the most common perpetrators against the elderly
- Explain the concept of a multidisciplinary approach to elder crime
- List ways of building a case involving an elderly victim

INTRODUCTION

There is a growing awareness among professionals that older Americans are particular targets of illegal activities; crimes are committed with little intervention from traditional sources. These targets are identified by age and graying hair; they are perceived as being vulnerable to offenders including bullies, impaired or overwhelmed caregivers, and greedy individuals. The situation may be the result of how our nation has undervalued the elderly for so many years. Responding to crimes against or committed by the elderly is historically of low priority for the criminal justice community. The offenses are viewed as crimes against individuals rather than in terms of the traditional view of crimes against society. Few perpetrators are prosecuted; even less crime is reported.

These cases present many challenges to the criminal justice community; our responses produce less than stellar results. Listening to the complaints of elder citizens is time consuming and often arduous, and is seldom acknowledged as meaningful police work. Policy makers and researchers are now recognizing the extent of problems that affect the elderly and have only recently identified the role of the criminal justice system in dealing with them. Protecting victims and holding offenders accountable *is* real police work, regardless of the victim's characteristics or relationship to the offender. Unless the criminal justice community views the criminal acts of elder abuse as criminal behavior, the violence will continue (Rohn, 1999).

Responses to elder crime are being modified, but what has changed? Demographics is the largest contributing factor to the shifting policy concerning elder crime. No longer is the United States dominated by the youthful. The number of teenagers in the United States was surpassed by the number of elderly (defined as age older than 65 years) in 1983. Seniors are the fastest-growing segment of the population, which is expected to double by 2030, when 1 in 5 Americans will be age 65 years or older (Centers for Disease Control and Prevention [CDC], 2000). Along with this population explosion comes the shameful problem of crime committed against the elderly. Every year an estimated 2.1 million older Americans are victims of physical, psychological, or other forms of abuse and neglect. These high numbers exist in spite of the fact that majority of older citizens (70 percent) report their health as good or excellent (Bonnie & Wallace, 2002).

Past practices relied almost exclusively on interviewing elderly victims and dealing with their requests for prosecution of the perpetrator. This approach puts the senior in the position of being further threatened and physically abused by the offender. Caregiver stress is often cited as a major cause of elder abuse. This "excuse" has been dismissed in the majority of cases involving domestic abuse of elders (Brandl, 2000). Unreliable memory, infirmity, and even concern with the possible impending death of the victim place extraordinary importance on the victim interview. For these reasons, this chapter is broadened to include a general approach to these crimes in addition to suggestions on interviewing. Legislative changes have amplified the role of the criminal justice community in cases involving crimes against the elderly. Simply put, law enforcement must be concerned about its response to elder abuse because it is the law (OVC, 1993).

CRIMES TARGETING THE ELDERLY

According to the Bureau of Justice Statistics, the elderly in the United States are victimized by crime at rates far below those of younger people (Klaus, 2005). Only personal larceny, such as purse snatching and pickpocketing, occurs against the elderly at approximately the same rate as against other age groups. Although persons aged 65 years and older are not victimized by violent crime as often as younger persons, when they are targeted they are as likely to be seriously injured.

Domestic Violence

Most violence against the elderly is domestic abuse. In 1987, the federal government first described elder abuse, neglect, and exploitation under the Amendments to the Older Americans Act (National Committee for the Prevention of Elder Abuse, 2005). Abuse is categorized into domestic abuse and institutional abuse. Within these broad categories, physical, sexual, and emotional/psychological abuse may occur along with neglect, self-neglect, abandonment, and financial exploitation. It is estimated that for every case of elder abuse, neglect, exploitation, or self-neglect reported to authorities, about five more go unreported (National Center on Elder Abuse, 1998).

FIGURE 8-1 Domestic violence among older Americans mirrors that among younger counterparts. It can occur in any socioeconomic relationship. The only difference is that the woman is statiscally as likely as the man to be the abuser when the couple is married.

Examples of domestic crimes that may be directed at the elderly include the following:

1. **Self-neglect:** The failure to provide for one's own essential needs. This is the most frequent form of elder abuse. This is a noncriminal activity that might result in civil intervention by criminal justice and social services systems on the victim's behalf.
2. **Abandonment:** The desertion of an elderly person by an individual who has assumed responsibility for providing care for him or her or by a person entrusted with his or her physical custody (National Committee for the Prevention of Elder Abuse, 2003).
3. **Active neglect:** The deliberate attempt by a caregiver to inflict injury or emotional stress on an older person; examples include intentional withholding of needed medication or food due to the costs.
4. **Passive neglect:** The unintentional failure to fulfill a caretaking obligation in which no willful desire to inflict physical or emotional distress exists; examples include the denial of adequate food or health services due to ignorance or carelessness on the part of the caretaker.
5. **Physical abuse:** Causing harm to the victim. This can involve a number of activities such as hitting, slapping, and physically restraining the victim.
6. **Sexual abuse:** Forced sexual contact with an individual who has not given consent or who is incapable of giving consent because of physical or mental impairments.

Investigator needs to ask questions that will determine whether the condition of the elderly person is the result of self-neglect or is the consequence of criminal activity due to any of the foregoing categories. Procedures that may be helpful in making this determination include the following:

- Interview neighbors and other witnesses to identify who might have relevant information and how they might be contacted.
- Identify and interview the victim's doctor, conservator, attorney, and social worker and any agencies that provide services to the victim.
- Ask the victim who lives with them or makes visits.
- Look to see whether there are any ligature marks on the wrists or legs or around the neck of the victim that would indicate the use of restraints.
- Check to see whether the elderly person has food available; ask whether someone prepares meals for him or her and determine who does the shopping.
- If the elderly person seems confused, determine with the aid of medical personnel whether the individual is being overmedicated or is suffering from mental impairment.
- If the abuse occurred in a residential care setting, interview the staff to determine who witnessed it.

Fiduciary Abuse

A major category of crime against the elderly is fiduciary abuse. **Fiduciary abuse** is the financial exploitation or economic abuse of elderly; it covers a range of criminal conduct concerning misappropriated property. Two categories of fiduciary abuse are fraud committed by strangers and financial

---

BEEN THERE... DONE THAT! 8-1

In response to a call on stolen property I went to the home of Mr. James, who was 82 years old. He stated that someone had stolen his wallet. He told me that he was in his barn putting blueberries in boxes when he realized the wallet was not in his back pocket. Because he sold blueberries from a street stand, Mr. James claimed any one of the people who bought berries that morning could have been a pickpocket. Before jumping to any conclusions I asked Mr. James to retrace his steps with me. As we moved from the farmstand to the barn I noticed a wallet lying on the ground. He said the wallet was in fact his. After checking its contents he said that nothing was missing. He was very embarrassed, so I assured him that it was no problem, and we shared a few blueberries. Was Mr. James' fear of being victimized by a pickpocket unrealistic? Had we not found the wallet, what would be the next step?

exploitation perpetrated by family members or caregivers. These two categories require different approaches by law enforcement due to the different offender/victim relationship (Johnson, 2003). In some states there is a legal requirement that the elderly person suffer harm due to the financial abuse or that the perpetrator gain from the financial transaction (Johnson, 2003). Indicators of fiduciary abuse include the following:

- Uncharacteristic bank activity.
- Suspicious activity on the person's credit card accounts.
- Frequent or unauthorized use of the person's ATM card.
- The drawing up of an unwitnessed will.

Although the exact numbers are believed to suffer from underreporting, the elderly are victimized by consumer fraud at a rate that exceeds the victimization of those younger than age 50 years (U.S. Department of Health and Human Services, 2000). Telemarketing scams and bogus health care and investment schemes are examples of stranger fraud.

INITIAL CONSIDERATIONS WHEN QUESTIONING THE OLDER PERSON

The priority of the crisis responder is to render first aid and identify the victim. Once the scene is safe, the persons at the scene should be separated and interviewed. The interview should be videotaped whenever possible; an alternative is use of an audio tape. This serves to document the abuse and the condition of the victim at the time of the offense. The videotape serves to preserve the evidence if a prosecution determination is made that does not include the victim testimony. Photographs of injuries and of living conditions should be taken for documentation.

When investigating complaints of crime committed against the elderly the interview process is similar to the approach taken with any other population. An additional initial step helps to determine which interviewing technique is most suitable.

The Pre-Interview

The initial recommended step is a pre-interview to make an assessment. The **conversation-observing evaluation** is an approach to assessing an elderly person through direct observation for the purpose of identifying the limitations of the interviewee and the nature of the offense. The evaluation should not be biased by the opinion of individuals who care for the person or those who have a relationship with that person. Except for a police officer or social service worker observer, no one should be present besides the elderly person and the interviewer. Although a determination must be made of the extent of victim participation that can be expected, the mental or physical status of the abused does not dictate the failure or success of any investigation. Medical and physical evidence in addition to witness statements and expert testimony should be considered in all cases, and particularly those that involve vulnerable victims.

- Begin this phase without preconceived ideas on the ability of the victim to testify or about the nature of the offenses. Health concerns need to be identified but are not the primary consideration in the investigation of crimes against the elderly.
- Speak with the person at the place where he or she is most comfortable. For most elderly persons, this will be the place where they live, although the situation may dictate that this pre-interview take place in a hospital room. The interviewee should be as comfortable as possible.
- Think of this stage as a "friendly visit." Avoid making statements that are judgmental. Have a cup of coffee and talk . . . at the same time remaining alert to behavioral indicators displayed by the victim. This is not the time to delve into specifics of alleged abuse or neglect. A common error made by police officers in other situations that is to be avoided is the failure to develop the situation.
- Put yourself at the same level as the interviewee, asking the victim where he or she wants you to sit. Place yourself face front to the person so that you can observe him or her and where the person can also see your face clearly.
- Refrain from taking notes before asking permission to do so.
- Introduce yourself and state your purpose generally. For example, "My name is Denise Gosselin, I am a police officer. I have been asked to come and talk with you today. Is that okay?"
- Ask the person for his or her full name, even if you already have that information. Refer to the person by her or his title—Miss, Mrs., Mr., Dr., and so on.

At this point it should be obvious whether the interviewee is having difficulty communicating. Evaluate the ability of the person to answer simple questions. Look for signs that she or he is having difficulty hearing or seeing you. Does the person lean forward toward you? Does he or she tend to look at your lips when you speak? If you notice problems, ask the person whether he or she needs an ancillary device such as a hearing aid.

- Encourage the person to talk about himself or herself, and comment in ways that promote discussion. During the conversation the following points should be covered, but the questions are not asked in a traditional interview format:

1. "How are you feeling today?" This question helps to determine what physical conditions and limitations, if any, exist. If the conversation turns to illness, ask whether the person needs medication for the condition. If the answer is yes, ask how often it is needed and whether the person takes it regularly. Does the person take the medication himself or herself, or does someone give it to them to take? Determine whether the interviewee drinks alcoholic beverages on a daily basis, and document the preferred drink.
2. "How old are you?" Encourage the person with positive comments regarding age. Use the information to facilitate conversation about the individual's ability to hear, see, and walk. Determine what forms of aid the individual needs, if any. Although the person's physical condition may seem apparent, the investigator should still talk about the person's strengths and weaknesses.

3. "How long have you lived here?" "Is this your house?" These questions help to determine whether dependency exists with respect to the living arrangements. Listen for indications that *"it used to be my house*, but ...." Determine whether the person is financially dependent on another person.
4. "Do you live here by yourself?" Ask this even if it seems apparent. Clarify whether anyone lives temporarily with the person such as a family member or friend. Look for signs of discomfort when an older person is talking about family or friends that spend time with him or her. How isolated is this person? Are there any social supports?
5. "Do you live with your husband (or wife)?" "How does your spouse treat you?" Be particularly aware of anxiety or discomfort when discussing a spouse. If the individual begins to offer excuses, such as "I am so difficult to take care of" or "He doesn't mean to take it out on me," listen and be patient. Do not attempt to be friendly by adding to or acknowledging the validity of statements regarding behaviors. Attempt to learn as much as possible about the dynamics of the relationship. Remember that both male and female individuals may be abusive to an elder spouse.
6. "Excuse me for prying, but may I ask if you have a retirement pension or receive Social Security?" "Are you doing okay financially?" "Have you made any financial arrangements with someone to take care of you?" Attempt to get a sense of the anxiety level associated with the financial situation of the person. Is there a fear that his or her money will be depleted? What is the source of that fear?
7. "Is there anyone who helps you out with your daily living?" Identify who the individuals are that occupy a caretaking role and the relationship between the person and the caregiver. "Do you pay this person?" "Do they ask for money or gifts?" Does the older person have reasonable expectations on the extent of care that they receive?

During this stage you have been gathering information on the living conditions of the victim and his or her personal relationships. You should be gradually coming to an assessment of the individual, the ability of the person to relate information, and his or her overall ability to communicate. If the victim's skills are within the normal to high range and seemingly accurate information is being related, then using the traditional methods of acquiring the needed information might be the best approach. If the individual appears to be confused or has difficulty remembering events, the cognitive method may be the interviewing choice. When the questioning appears to be difficult due to a mental illness (including Alzheimer's disease) an interdisciplinary team approach might offer the best interviewing alternative. In the event that the person is unable to relate any information that could be considered credible or has died, the investigator must rely on collecting sufficient evidence in the event that prosecution could take place without the victim's testimony.

If evidence of abuse is discovered and the perpetrator is defined as having a domestic relationship to the victim, such as a spouse, former spouse, child, parent, or live-in person, then you should proceed according to your department policy for domestic violence. Mandatory and preferred arrest policies do not have exceptions when the victim is an older person. Financial abuse, physical or sexual abuse, intimidation, and threats are domestic violence offenses when the perpetrator is in a legally recognized domestic relationship. There are no exclusions for police action in cases of domestic violence that are based on age or infirmity. On the contrary, in many jurisdictions if a victim is elderly, the crime is enhanced.

Case Credibility

Case credibility may be enhanced through physical evidence in addition to the testimonial evidence from a victim. Some states allow for evidence to be admitted to court testimony when a victim is unavailable due to death or sickness (Zahner, 1999). Your state law should be researched in the anticipation of cases involving absent elderly victims. Evidence obtained from medical personnel, home-health aides, and advocates is particularly relevant to cases involving elder victimization. In a study of institutional abuse conducted by Pillemer and Moore (1989) approximately one third of the resident physical abuse by staff members was witnessed by other staff members (Loue, 2001).

Medical records are an invaluable tool for the investigation of elder abuse cases (Boutin, 1999). Among other things, medical records contain information on the physical status of the individual, names of physicians, and contact information for family members. Photographs of injuries should be taken at different stages. Bank records and checkbooks provide evidence for building a case of financial abuse. Videotaped interviews with the victim may be introduced into evidence in some circumstances.

The alleged perpetrator should be arrested if probable cause exists to do so and should be interrogated. Avoid premature determinations on the probability of prosecution. Assuming that a crime will not be prosecuted due to victim frailty or desire may result in the insufficient collection of evidence, which will render the case inadequate for prosecution. In serious cases consult with the district attorney and ask what information would be helpful in aiding in the successful prosecution of the case.

CONDUCTING THE INTERVIEW

The steps in interviewing the victim are similar to those with other populations. Preparation for the interview and the establishment of rapport with the interviewee are critical steps in ensuring a cooperative subject.

Step 1: Preparing for the Interview

Prepare for the interview by choosing a quiet location that is free of distractions and noise. Get as much information on the suspect as possible, including prior arrests and commitments. Speak with the victim's neighbors and service providers prior to the interview with the victim to determine their impression of the medical and cognitive status of the interviewee and of the suspect, if one is known.

> **BEEN THERE... DONE THAT! 8-2**
>
> A female resident of a nursing home in her early 80s was refusing to eat. She had instructed the staff that she not was not to be fed intravenously. On investigation it was determined that she was not physically impaired and had no history or indication of mental illness. There was no history of prior abuse. In conversation she stated that her only daughter had abandoned her. The daughter had gone on vacation with her husband. I asked the woman if she was aware of the consequences of not eating; she stated, "Yes." She then asked, "Why is it taking so long [to die]?" I told her that she was not sick and only needed food. The woman told me that she knew what she doing and that she did not want to be fed. This extreme form of manipulation called the "hunger strike" is documented through case examples (Duggal & Lawrence, 2001). In this example the woman was angry at her daughter for having gone away on a vacation.

Step 2: Establishing Rapport

One of the most important ways to establish rapport with an elderly person is through respect. Avoid treating the person as if he or she were a child. Explain your role and what the interviewee might expect during the investigation into the allegations.

Step 3: Conducting the Interview

Begin the interview by using nonleading questions. Avoid asking questions that require a yes or no response. Keep questions short and to the point. Use language that is easily understood but not patronizing. Questions should be open-ended to encourage conversation.

If the interviewee is having difficulty remembering when events took place, it may help to relate them to normal daily activities such as eating or watching television. Allow the victim to relate the crime in his or her own words. Avoid the tendency to make suggestions if the person seems slow in responding; some elderly persons need extra time to collect their thoughts. Encourage the older person to draw pictures to describe abuse or to write down answers if necessary.

Determine whether anyone else was present when the offender arrived. Was anyone witness to the abuse? Ask the older person whether she or he knows the person who did "this." Address any fears that the person have about discussing the incident and reporting it to the police or social service agency. Avoid your natural tendency to react when a victim gives information regarding any crime committed against them. Remain professional and empathetic to any abuse.

Ask the person what they believe the suspect will say about the allegations. The interviewer can anticipate some of the following possible scenarios (Morris, 1999):

- Has the victim been told by the suspect that it was an accident (and apologized), a normal part of aging, or a figment of the confused person's mind? [physical abuse case]

- Has the victim been told by the suspect that what happened is what the elder wanted, that it was an accident, that there was no money for medicine (eyeglasses, food, etc.), or that the suspect was a stressed caregiver? [neglect elder abuse case]
- The defense will center on consent or on an argument that the event never occurred. [sexual abuse]
- Has the victim been told by the suspect that "it was a gift" (and the elder doesn't remember it) or that "it was my inheritance" or "you loaned it to me"? [financial/fiduciary abuse]

Look for all of the above possible defenses when discussing the allegations and the victim's perceptions of what the suspect may have relayed to the victim. Such perceptions may be very revealing.

Step 4: Ending the Interview

Address any objections concerning family members. An elderly person may be reluctant to give permission for charges to be brought against a loved one, particularly if he or she is dependent on that person. Explain that decisions regarding the criminal charging of any person will be left to the district attorney. Advise the person that you are mandated to report suspected abuse or neglect to elder services and that he or she might expect to be contacted by someone who can address his or her needs.

Step 5: Following Up

Subsequent to the interview, referrals to other agencies should be made, if warranted. Examples of referrals include a report to a state-mandated elder abuse hotline or social services. When injury to the elder was noted, a future interview should be scheduled to document the abuse. Documentation of an injury may necessitate photographing it days after the initial response, when bruises and marks are more prominently visible.

EMPOWERING THE ELDERLY VICTIM

Laws specifically protecting vulnerable adults have been enacted across the country. Legislation devised specifically for intervention in cases where in which elderly individuals are unable to protect themselves

---

BEEN THERE... DONE THAT! 8-3

According to a report from the home health aide who visited Mrs. Jane at her home, the 90-year-old woman claimed that she had been sexually abused by her son. Mrs. Jane was complaining about being hurt "down there." She was believed to have dementia. The aide thought that because the victim could not testify in court there was no case. Was she right? What were the options?

against fraud, financial abuse, and personal violence should be used wherever possible. Procedures have evolved for investigating cases involving the elderly that center around the empowerment of this population in order to increase the chances of successful prosecution. When interviewing older victims, respect and deference should always be a consideration. Advocates suggest providing education and enhancing the level of safety awareness and safety planning for the elderly (U.S. Department of Health and Human Services, 2000).

Do not leave the final determination regarding prosecution with the victim. In all cases, victim safety must be the primary consideration, just as it is in all other criminal investigations. Legal provisions and mandated arrest policies that exist for victims of domestic violence must be used regardless of the age of the victim or of the alleged perpetrator. If the victim is overly concerned with prosecution, the reasons should be explored and, if possible, discussed with a multidisciplinary team for a final determination. When the objections of the elderly victim involve fear of isolation or loss of a caretaker, then his or her needs for services must be in place prior to a prosecution.

THE ELDERLY AS WITNESSES

Sexual predators, drug abusers, and thieves may approach an elderly person they view as being vulnerable. Conmen and greedy caretakers target people who are perceived as being needy. Although the likelihood of being afflicted with intellectual deterioration known as dementia or

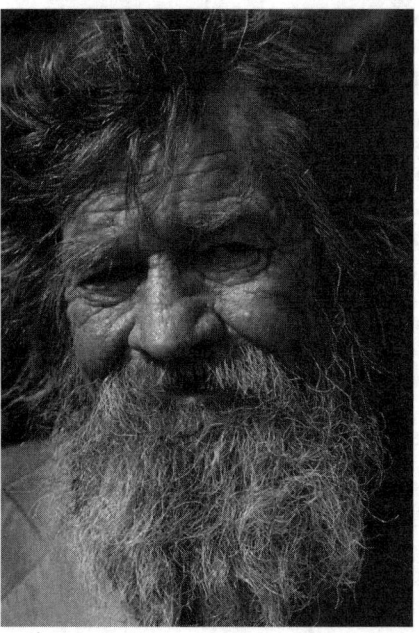

FIGURE 8-2 The majority of the elderly can provide accurate statements about victimization.

senility increases with age, it is not considered part of the normal aging process. The Office for Victims of Crime (OVC, 1993) suggests that it is false to assume that older persons suffer from dementia, which is typically a reversible condition brought on by illness, malnutrition, dehydration, and other physical problems. Only 5 to 7 percent of the population is diagnosed with Alzheimer's disease (OVC, 1993). An interviewer can expect that the majority of elders are capable of giving accurate and reliable information regarding victimization.

Physical Limitations

A factor to consider when interviewing the elderly is the extent of substance abuse within this population. Considered an invisible epidemic, alcohol and prescription drug misuse is thought to affect as many as 17 percent of older adults (Levin & Kruger, 2000). An elderly person may be overly reliant on drugs or alcohol due to changes that come naturally with aging. Remember that the responsibility for victimization or perpetration does not center on substance abuse, it is only a factor to be identified for appropriate referral and intervention.

Compared to men, elderly women who are socially isolated and have hearing impairments are at greater risk of contracting late-onset schizophrenia (Sajatovic, Madhusoodanan, & Buckley, 2000). Characterized by hallucinations and delusions, this mental disease was once thought to only affect individuals with onset prior to age 45 years (Sajatovic, Madhusoodanan, & Buckley, 2000). The disease can be treated successfully; therefore, medical referral is an absolute necessity if this is suspected.

Normal sensatory changes due to aging include visual and hearing loss. Visual acuity may interfere with distane identifications and descriptions of strangers, but is not significant when the perpetrator is known to the individual. Older persons commonly lose the ability to hear high frequencies and experience hypersensitivity to very loud speech. In questioning seniors, the Office for Victims of Crime (1993) suggests keeping in mind that it is easier for an older person to understand a man than a woman because the pitch of men's voices is usually lower than that of women. Persons with hearing loss often compensate by lip reading and viewing facial expressions. The individual may have a hearing aid that is not working properly or is not being worn at the time of the interview. If the interviewee is having difficulties with understanding, ask if he or she has communication devices that can assist.

The following should be considered when interviewing older persons:

- Schedule the interview for midmorning, a time when the victim is most likely to be at her or his best.
- Refer persons for medical screening when substance abuse is suspected.
- Ask the interviewee if he or she is having difficulty in hearing, but do not assume that this is the case.

- Many elderly persons elect not to wear their hearing aid at all times; ask the person whether he or she has a hearing aid when it appears that hearing is an issue.
- Avoid speaking loudly to an elderly person as a way to compensate for a perceived hearing deficiency.
- Position yourself directly in front of the interviewee because he or she may compensate for hearing loss by concentrating on lip movements and facial expressions.
- Establish eye contact with the interviewee prior to speaking.
- Avoid covering your mouth, chewing gum, or smoking during the interview.
- Do not speak too quickly.
- Eliminate background noise as much as possible.
- Use visual aids such as drawings and diagrams when possible.
- Male interviewers may be a preferred option.

Cognitive Limitations

Cognitive impairments vary significantly according to individual conditions. The ability to learn and remember is expected to change as an individual ages. This means older persons may take longer to recall or process information. Memory-jogging techniques may enhance the recall for elderly victims. Questions such as "Were you eating dinner when he came?" and "What were you watching on television when he came?" are examples. Practice patience by allowing the elderly person the time she or he needs to answer a question.

There is a growing amount of contradictory literature looking at the vulnerability of the elderly to source confusion. **Source confusion** is the difficulty in distinguishing what has been personally witnessed from what may have been heard from someone else, or a problem identifying the exact source of the information. The introduction of misinformation has been thought to impair the reliability of statements taken from the elderly and cause source confusion. Researchers have concluded that no clear evidence exists to suggest an age-related vulnerability to misinformation (Memon, Gabert, & Hope, 2004). Each individual being interviewed must be evaluated independently regarding the reliability of the statement, without age bias. These same researchers suggest that the elderly frequently recall fewer correct details of an eyewitness event than younger adults. In addition the elderly are consistently more prone to making false identifications from lineups, and individuals older than 60 years are more likely to raise a "false alarm" to a new face. In other words they are more likely to falsely recognize a face they had not seen previously. In the eyewitness identification setting, the elderly may be more prone to making false choices and providing fewer descriptions of the perpetrator (physical characteristics, clothing, etc.).

Concerns Due to Dependence

A strong reliance on family and friends for assistance may be the reality for senior citizens. In some but not all situations, loneliness, frailty, and medical conditions may cause the elderly person to view the perpetrator as being nonetheless his or her only hope for an improved lifestyle. Because the most common abusers of the elderly are their adult children (National Center on Elder Abuse, 1998), a common risk factor exists when the caretaker is financially dependent on the older person. Dysfunctional family interaction prior to the onset of old age is likely to continue as the members get older unless intervention occurs. Consider the attitude of the elderly person: does he or she have an overly demanding attitude or unrealistic expectations of the caregiver?

When the suspect provides care or services to the older person the exact nature of the care should be determined. An interview with the suspect should document the following circumstances:

- Based on the condition of the person, does it appear that the caregiver has been reluctant to supply him or her with eyeglasses, dental care, medications, or other needed services?
- When bedsores or incontinence exist, is the care being provided sufficient to meet the needs of the person?
- Are the services or care provided under a contract with specified payments?
- How are these payments made?
- Are cash payments provided by the person or requested by the service provider?

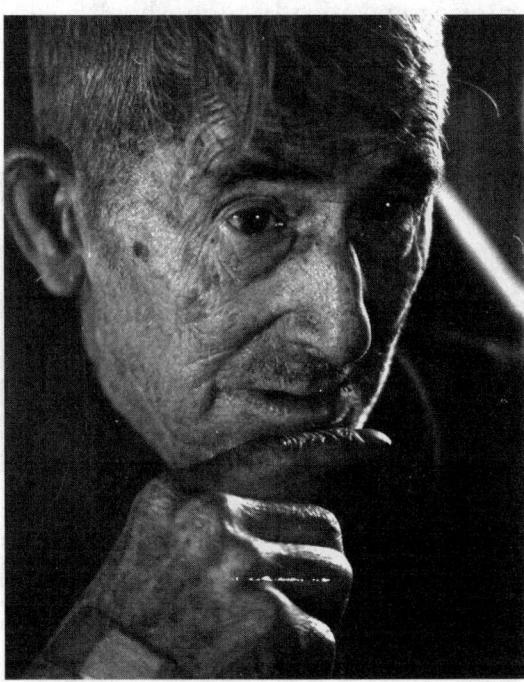

FIGURE 8-3 When abuse of an elderly person is suspected, the police and other professionals are required by law to make a report to the designated authorities.

- Has the suspect accepted personal gifts from the victim? If so, what is the approximate value of those gifts?
- Is the caregiver frustrated or angry due to the responsibilities associated with the providing services to the person?

INTERDISCIPLINARY INTERVIEWING

Increasingly, criminal justice agencies are working with a variety of agencies to identify cases of suspected elder abuse and to gather evidence for prosecution of the perpetrators. The majority of reports concerning elder abuse are made to adult protective services, not the police. The Police Executive Research Forum recommends that investigations should be coordinated with adult protective services personnel or the ombudsman whenever possible to establish cooperative models of intervention (Nerenberg, 1993). Multidisciplinary teams composed of professionals from law enforcement, adult protective services, mental health agencies, the public guardian's office, and public health agencies represent one example. Teams of fiduciary abuse specialists are specially trained to work with bank officials in documenting a paper trail indicative of fiduciary abuse.

Mandatory Elder Abuse Reporting

All 50 states, the District of Columbia, and some U.S. territories require professionals to report suspected abuse or neglect of elders (Teaster, 2003). There is no consistency in the reporting guidelines and definitions. The majority of the states and territories specifically name health care professionals, such as licensed and registered nurses, physicians, and nurse aides, as mandated reporters of elder/adult abuse. Police officers are among those commonly named as mandated reporters of elder abuse.

BEEN THERE . . . DONE THAT! 8-4

The largest investigation that I participated in involved the interviewing of over 100 children suspected to have been sexually abused through a multigenerational sex ring. Working together with the local police department and the department of social services, we identified some of the alleged perpetrators and obtained evidence against them. The sexual crimes against both male and female children were of the worst possible kind you can imagine. Some were crimes of incest, but the men were indiscriminate pedophiles. The oldest person I arrested was a 72-year-old grandfather. Looking extremely frail and pathetic, he was brought before the court after his arrest. The charges were dismissed, and the prosecutor admonished me for bringing in an old man. I arrested him again on charges concerning more children who he had raped. His tools had been hot, sharp objects. The second arrest netted a weekend in jail before an agreement of probation was secured. The man was a monster living among us, just an old one.

CRIME PERPETRATED BY THE ELDERLY

As people get older they commit less crime; this is referred to as **aging-out**. This does not mean that old age renders an individual incapable of committing criminal offenses. In the past, crime committed by seniors was considered insignificant and the perpetrators pathetic rather than criminal. As the elderly population increases in number the criminal justice system should be prepared for the probability of a rise in the amount of domestic abuse crime perpetrated by the elderly. Typically, but not exclusively, this will take the form of abuse against older spouses.

This hidden aspect of criminal activity among the elderly represents a complex social problem. Cloaked under the veil of family secrecy, it is impossible to know the extent of domestic abuse committed by the elderly. The National Center on Elder Abuse reported that an elderly spouse was among those likely to perpetrate domestic violence on his or her elderly partner (Tatara, Kuzmeskus, & Duckhorn, 1997). Although the majority of perpetrators are the adult children of the senior victim(s), approximately one third of abusers are believed to be persons aged 60 years and older (National Center on Elder Abuse, 1998). According to the 2000 Survey of State Adult Protective Services, the majority of identified perpetrators were a spouse or intimate of the elderly victim (Teaster, 2003). The role of the criminal justice system is to investigate, enforce the law, and protect victims, regardless of the perpetrators' age or physical condition or degree of victim participation. Assuming that the victim or the perpetrator is not deserving of intervention would leave nearly to one fourth of the population without criminal justice intervention—a dangerous trend.

▲ CONCLUSIONS

This chapter introduced a pre-interview step entitled the *conversation-observing approach*. This initial phase of interviewing an elderly person is used to assess the individual and learn as much as possible about the conditions under which he or she lives. The phase also provides sufficient information to determine whether a specific interviewing format should be considered in the future. Some elderly persons will present with physical or mental impairments that hinder investigations. Awareness of the signs and symptoms of common afflictions increases the opportunity for successful evidence gathering. Most seniors are capable of providing the information to needed document the criminal event.

Crimes against the elderly, however, may be complicated by the family relationship between the victim and the perpetrator. Law enforcement should be guided by existing legal responsibilities, mandates, department policy, and procedures in handling domestic violence cases. A multidisciplinary team approach is recommended for complicated cases requiring special investigations.

QUESTIONS FOR REVIEW

Short-Answer Questions

1. What is a pre-interview and why is it used?
2. What is the most common form of violence against the elderly?
3. What are the categories of elder abuse?
4. What identifiers should you look for to determine whether elder abuse crimes have been committed?
5. What are the interviewing limitations with this population?
6. Who are the most common abusers of the elderly?
7. What should an interviewer document when interviewing a victim who is dependent on others to take care of him or her?
8. What are the specific legal protections for elderly victims? Find examples in your state code where these exist.

Fill-in Questions and Answers

1. In 2030, _____ in _____ Americans will be age 65 years or older.
2. Every year an estimated _____ older Americans are victims of physical, psychological, or other forms of abuse and neglect.
3. One method to identify limitations of the interviewee and the nature of the offense among the elderly population is through the _____.
4. Elders are more susceptible to _____ than younger adults, defined as difficulty in distinguishing what they witnessed themselves as opposed to what they may have heard from someone else.
5. _____ is the deliberate attempt by a caregiver to inflict injury or emotional stress on an older person.
6. _____ occurs when an older person is tricked, coerced, or unduly influenced to sign away money or property.
7. Considered an invisible epidemic, _____ and _____ misuse is thought to affect 17 percent of older adults.
8. When an elderly victim has difficulty in recalling information during an interview, _____ might be used to help them in this process.
9. The elderly are victimized by consumer fraud at a rate that _____ the victimization of those younger than 50 years.
10. To build a case, evidence from _____, _____ and _____ is particularly relevant.

Exercises

1. Interview a person of age 65 years or older. The person can be a relative, a neighbor, or someone who works on campus. The topic of the interview is whether the person has ever been the victim of a crime. If the subject has never been the victim of a crime, an alternate topic is

whether they have been in a car accident or stopped by the police since turning age 60. Using the steps outlined in this chapter on interviewing the elderly, conduct a pre-interview and then follow each of the steps except for the follow-up. Write a report on the assessment and facts.

2. Explain the role of policing in cases involving the abuse of elders. A good source is available at: http://www.preventelderabuse.org/professionals/law.html.

REFERENCES

Bonnie, R. J., & Wallace, R. B. (2002). *Elder mistreatment: Abuse, neglect, and exploitation in aging America.* Washington, DC: National Academy Press.

Boutin, D. (1999). Medical records as investigative tools in elder abuse cases. *Prosecutor's Brief: The California District Attorneys Association's Quarterly Journal, XXI*(2), 9.

Brandl, B. (2000). Power and control: Understanding domestic abuse in later life. *Generations, 24*(2), 39–45.

Centers for Disease Control and Prevention. (2000). *Profile of the nation's health: CDC fact book 2000/2001.* Washington DC: Centers for Disease Control and Prevention.

Duggal, A., & Lawrence, R. M. (2001). Aspects of food refusal in the elderly: The "hunger strike." *International Journal of Eating Disorders, 30,* 213–216.

Johnson, K. D. (2003). *Financial crimes against the elderly* (Report No. 20 Community Oriented Policing Services). Washington, DC: U.S. Department of Justice.

Klaus, P. (2005). *Crimes against persons age 65 or older, 1993–2002* (Report No. NCJ 206154). Washington, DC: Bureau of Justice Statistics.

Levin, S. M., & Kruger, J. (2000). *Substance abuse among older adults: A guide for treatment providers.* Rockville, MD: U.S. Department of Health and Human Services.

Loue, S. (2001). Elder abuse and neglect in medicine and law: The need for reform. *Journal of Legal Medicine, 22,* 159–209.

Memon, A., Gabert, F., & Hope, L. (2004). The ageing eyewitness. In J. Adler (Ed.), *Forensic psychology: Concepts, debates, and practice* (pp. 96–112). Portland, OR: Willan Publishing.

Morris, D. J. (1999). Interviewing cognitively impaired victims. *Prosecutors Brief: The California District Attorneys Association's Quarterly Journal, XXI*(2), 11–12, 41–45.

National Center on Elder Abuse. (1998). *The National Elder Abuse Incidence Study.* Washington, DC: The Administration for Children and Families.

National Committee for the Prevention of Elder Abuse. (2003). The basics. Available: http://www.elderabusecenter.org/default.cfm?p=basics.cfm.

National Committee for the Prevention of Elder Abuse. (2005). What is elder abuse? Available: http://www.preventelderabuse.org/elderabuse/elderabuse.html.

Nerenberg, L. (1993). *Improving the police response to domestic elder abuse.* Washington, DC: Police Executive Research Forum.

Office for Victims of Crime. (1993). *Improving the police response to domestic elder abuse* (Report No. NCJ 147558). Washington, DC: Office for Victims of Crime.

Pillemer, K., & Moore, D. (1989). Abuse of patients in nursing homes: Findings from a survey of staff. *The Gerontologist, 29,* 314–320.

Rohn, A. L. (1999). A multi-disciplinary approach to elder abuse prosecution. *Prosecutor's Brief: The California District Attorneys Association's Quarterly Journal, XXI*(2), 1–46.

Sajatovic, M., Madhusoodanan, S., & Buckley, P. (2000). Schizophrenia in the elderly: Guidelines for management. *CNS Drugs, 13*(2), 103–115.

Tatara, T., Kuzmeskus, L. M., & Duckhorn, E. (1997). Trends in elder abuse in domestic settings. Available: http://www.elderabusecenter.org/pdf/basics/fact2.pdf.

Teaster, P. (2003). *A response to the abuse of vulnerable adults: The 2000 Survey of State Protective Services.* Washington, DC: National Center on Elder Abuse.

U.S. Department of Health and Human Services. (2000). Our aging population: Promoting empowerment, preventing victimization, and implementing coordinated interventions: A report of proceedings. OJP Issues and Practices Report, Vol. NCJ 186256). Washington, DC: Office of Justice Programs.

Zahner, M. (1999). The absent witness in elder abuse cases. *Prosecutor's Brief: The California District Attorneys Association's Quarterly Journal, XXI*(2), 13–15; 44–45.

CHAPTER 9
Interviewing Persons with Disabilities or Mental Illness

KEY TERMS

Americans with Disabilities Act	Distant field evaluation
Mental retardation	Detailed field evaluation
Mental illness	Appropriate adult
Personality disorder	Facilitated communication

CHAPTER OBJECTIVES

After completing this chapter you should be able to:

- Define how the American with Disabilities Act (ADA) of 1994 applies to criminal justice procedures
- State the appropriate terminology to use in effectively responding to victims with disabilities
- Explain how federals courts interpret the term *arrest* for cases that allege violations of the ADA
- State what effective communication with individuals having disabilities means under the ADA
- Compare and contrast mental retardation with mental illness
- List the steps involved in interviewing persons with disabilities
- Describe how to prepare for the interview of a person with a disability
- Explain the largest impediment to successful interviews of persons with disabilities
- List ways to determine whether a person requires special care

INTRODUCTION

This chapter provides an in-depth discussion of issues that affect the practice of interviewing persons with physical, cognitive, and/or communication impairments. Changes in legal codes governing patient rights that affirmed the right of persons with mental illness to live in the community and deinstitutionalization in the 1960s set the stage for increased criminal justice involvement. Approximately 54 million Americans live with a wide variety of physical, cognitive, and emotional disabilities (Tyiska, 1998). In addition to the increase in the at-large population of developmentally impaired individuals, this community is more vulnerable to victimization.

Impaired adults are at a higher risk for being physically or sexually assaulted, with a rate 4 to 10 times as high as it is for other adults (Sobsey, 1994). Children with disabilities are also victimized more frequently than children without them. A study for the Office on Child Abuse and Neglect found that children with disabilities were 2.1 times more likely to endure criminal physical abuse and 1.8 times more likely to experience sexual abuse than children without disabilities (Crosse, Kaye, & Ratnofsky, 1993). Adding to the newly recognized dilemma of protecting those with disabilities are conflicting studies on the incidence of crime perpetrated by persons with mental illness. Sixteen percent of the adult prison population and 20 percent of those in the juvenile correctional system have a mental illness (Mentally Ill Offender Treatment and Crime Reduction Act, 2004). According to the National Alliance for the Mentally Ill, up to 40 percent of adults who suffer from a serious mental illness will come into contact with the criminal justice system at some point in their lives. Research concludes, however, that only a weak association between mental disorder and violence exists; serious violence is perpetrated by a small fraction of the total number of individuals (Steadman et al., 1998).

One of every 10 police calls nationally involves someone who is mentally ill (Gillespie, 2001). Yet recent studies indicate extremely low levels of reporting victimization by persons with developmental disabilities (Petersilia, 2000). When reporting does occur, few cases are successfully prosecuted. In a scathing article, one newspaper reported that even when evidence exists of a crime against a disabled person, a mere 5 percent of investigated cases end with a conviction (Mishra, 2001). Similar rebukes to the criminal justice response to protecting the disabled have sparked changes, including the development of crisis intervention teams.

The debate regarding the role of the police in dealing with persons having disabilities is intense. Once again, law enforcement is being tasked with policing social problems that often pose often insurmountable challenges. Still, the duty already has been assigned; it is time to meet it head on. This chapter is intended to aid the criminal justice professional to meet the increased needs of communicating with the impaired community.

THE AMERICANS WITH DISABILITIES ACT

Given the increasing likelihood of police encounters with persons who are disabled, training in effective communications with persons in this community has taken on greater significance. The **Americans with Disabilities Act** (ADA) is a legislative mandate to provide equal protections and access of government facilities for persons who have a disability. According to the U.S. Department of Justice, the ADA applies to every aspect of policing, including the following (U.S. Department of Justice, 1996):

- Receiving citizen complaints
- Interrogating and interviewing witnesses
- Arresting, booking, and holding suspects
- Enforcing laws
- Incarceration

Title II of the ADA provides that "no qualified individual with a disability shall, by reason of such disability, be excluded from participation in or be denied the benefits of the services, programs, or activities of a public entity, or be subjected to discrimination by any such entity" (ADA, 1994). This mandate of nondiscrimination extends to all state and government services, regardless of whether or not the person receives federal financial assistance.

Accommodations for Interviewing

The ADA requires that government officials attempt effective communication with individuals having disabilities by providing auxiliary devices (Sigmon & Edmunds, 2002). To facilitate the reporting of victimization for the disabled community, officers need to make arrangements so that individuals with a disability feel comfortable reporting to the police. This accommodation may involve the use of an interpreter or other third party to assist. The department may not charge the individual with a disability for the use of any auxiliary aide. Examples of auxiliary aides and services for those with hearing impairments include: qualified interpreters, note takers, transcript services, videotext displays, closed-caption decoders, and telephones compatible with hearing aids. To assist individuals with visual impairments, qualified readers, taped tests, audio recordings, materials in Braille, and large-print materials may be required. Although public entities are required to provide alternative auxiliary aides if available, they are not required to alter the nature of the service, program, or activity if it would result in an undue financial or administrative burden (Sigmon, & Edmunds, 2002).

Police Liability under the ADA

In light of these changes, communications with persons who may be disabled and are suspected of having committed crimes is a critical skill to develop. Sporadic claims against police departments for failing to train officers on handling persons with disabilities have surfaced in federal court. Under what is referred to as the *wrongful-arrest theory,* courts have been addressing some of the claims arising from Title II of the ADA. The wrongful-arrest situation was addressed in *Jackson v. Town of Sanford* (1994), a case in which the police had arrested a man for drunk driving when in fact he had been sober, his unsteadiness and slurred speech having resulted from a past stroke. In *Lewis v. Truitt* (1997) police were held accountable for beating and arresting a man for resisting law enforcement when in fact he was deaf and could not understand their commands. In their investigation of these claims, the courts have broadly interpreted the term "arrest" to include arrest, pre-arrest investigations, and violent confrontations not technically involving an arrest (*Gohier v. Enright,* 1999). The message is clear; law enforcement is expected to be prepared to handle these difficult cases by recognizing situations where a person has a disability.

Avoiding these situations requires an increased awareness on the part of police. Some suggestions include watching for handicapped license plates on cars that are stopped; using hand signals or yelling to people in a crowd to signal that he or she stop running; speaking clearly; and using breathalyzers to obtain accurate results regarding possible cases of driving under the influence. If while attempting to communicate

BEEN THERE... DONE THAT! 9-1

While on patrol one winter evening I noted a person walking in the breakdown lane coming toward traffic. From a distance I noticed that this woman was not wearing a coat or shoes and that there was snow on the ground. The nonverbal assessment was that she required special care; she did not appear to be aware of her surroundings. Pulling the cruiser over and slowing approaching, I yelled out, "Are you okay?" Oblivious to my presence, she kept walking. Calmly and firmly, I kept talking as I approached her, making a determination as to the level of danger that she posed. A missing or wanted check showed no warrants. I arranged for her to be transported to a local mental health clinic that accepted night admissions, where she was evaluated the following day.

with a motorist it becomes obvious that the person cannot speak, he or she should be offered a pen and piece of paper.

INITIAL CONSIDERATIONS

The first step in interviewing persons with disabilities is self-confrontation. The lack of familiarity with individuals who have a disability may cause you to feel awkward and uncertain on how to proceed. Negative attitudes

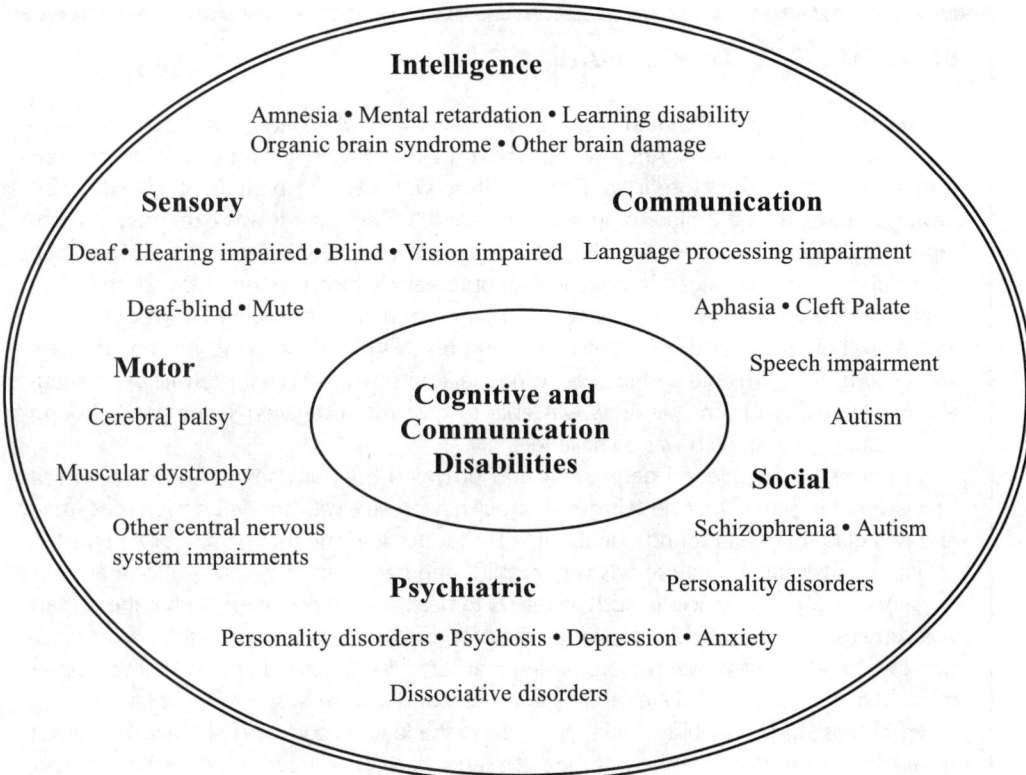

FIGURE 9-1 Forms of disability.

may be the largest impediment to successful interviewing of this population. Speak directly to the individual being interviewed, even if they are accompanied by another person. Their condition should not cause repulsion, sympathy, or admiration.

A common negative attitude exists regarding people whose physical appearance signals to others that they are different. Individuals with a physical or developmental disability are not less of an individual, but do present with different value systems and behavioral expectations. Generally, persons with a developmental disability tend to obey rules and don't want to get anyone in trouble. They may appear overly compliant and initially deny that they have been victimized, or may not realize that what happened to them was victimization. These individuals are not less credible; interviewers must overcome the tendency to treat people with mental retardation as though they were stupid or undeserving of police attention or protection. Don't talk down to them or treat them as children. People with mental retardation are not stupid, although they may learn and comprehend at a slower rate than others.

Taking the time to become familiar with ways to address persons with a disability will also help to put you at ease. Take care not to label a person according his disability; he is "a man with a disability" and not "a disabled man." Although the distinction may seem trivial, to someone

BEEN THERE... DONE THAT! 9-2

Andrew was a 23-year-old man with mental retardation who had been victimized sexually by a 72-year-old man. Andrew did not know that it was not right to have oral sex with another man; therefore it appeared as if he was a willing participant. He was seen having oral sex with the older man and was called "an animal." It was extremely disturbing to Andrew to be called that; he did not understand why someone would say bad things about him. He began to have violent outbreaks, which brought this case to the attention of the authorities. Andrew was formally diagnosed as having Down Syndrome with a level of understanding of between 7 and 8 years old. Prior to the incident, Andrew was known to be amiable and to seek to please adults, which is characteristic of individuals with Down Syndrome. Andrew was able to give me a detailed statement, although understanding his speech was a challenge.

I arrested the alleged perpetrator and provided his warnings per *Miranda*, which he waived. He stated that he felt guilty about having sex with the young retarded man and was glad that I had found out about it. He further told me that he had been arrested 40 years earlier for "unnatural acts with a child" and had spent 1 year in jail for that.

Your goal as an officer in such as case is to determine, if possible, whether the contact was consensual. If it is unclear, ask for an evaluation of the individual from a trained professional who has expertise with persons having that particular disability. In this case, it was determined that the victim lacked the capacity to consent and that the suspect sought him out as a victim because of his disability. Taking this case to the logical conclusion of making an arrest served to teach Andrew that he was the victim and the act was illegal. It stopped that perpetrator, and sent a message to the community that these victimizations would be punished.

who lives with a physical or developmental disability it makes a difference. Prior to any attempt at establishing rapport, the person should be made to feel recognized as an individual, not regarded as an illness. Only ask questions about the disability that pertains to your investigation or to accommodate the individual's needs. Look directly at the person when you speak to him or her, but do not stare at a disfigurement. Treat victims with compassion, dignity, and respect.

IDENTIFYING WHEN SPECIAL CARE IS NECESSARY

Individuals with a mental disorder or physical disability may require special care. Conduct a background check on the individual just as you would with any other individual. A background check may reveal past convictions and information that would provide investigation leads. It might also provide information on the level of potential threat that the person may pose to the interviewer.

Although they usually are able to provide reliable evidence, persons with disabilities may have communication problems that result in misleading statements or inappropriate reactions because of immediate (mis)understanding of the events. The interviewer must watch carefully for signs of disability because the mental or physical impairment may not be immediately obvious.

Defining disability is a difficult task because it is not necessarily an immutable or static condition. A person who has a disability cannot be identified by a single common characteristic. Some persons will be readily identifiable as having impairment due to physical affect, obvious mechanisms needed for assistance, or inappropriate behaviors. Others with less severe impediments or mental illness may not be recognized as requiring special assistance. These individuals present with psychiatric, social, and cognitive disabilities; these represent the most problematic mental illnesses and disorders. Both general categories are protected under the ADA. Individuals with impaired sight or hearing are often assisted in ways that are not immediately noticed.

Disabilities arise from different causes. Some physical disabilities are caused by brain damage, such as cerebral palsy, but do not necessary affect intelligence or the ability to communicate. On the other hand, other individuals with cerebral palsy acquired at birth or through traumatic head injury also have speech production impairments and/or mental illness. Most physical disabilities do not impair communication or cognition, and impairments that affect speech production do not necessarily affect intellectual or cognitive abilities (Baladerian, 1998).

Most persons being interviewed by the police will be apprehensive; be aware if it appears that the apprehension is excessive and/or if an excessive amount of anxiety is evident. A person may require special care if he or she is incoherent and the condition is not solely drug or alcohol induced. Some persons with a disability may not be able to understand or answer questions or will exhibit a mood level that is inconsistent with the situation. Such an individual may have a short attention span, a limited vocabulary, or a speech impediment.

Mental Retardation

Developmental disabilities, sometimes referred to as mental retardation, present different concerns for the interviewer. Persons with **mental retardation** possess significantly less than average age-appropriate ability to process information. Some persons with mental retardation may not be able to understand or answer questions or will exhibit a mood level that is inconsistent with the situation. Persons with mental retardation are usually arrested for less serious crimes such as public offenses, misdemeanors, and minor felony offenses (Davis, 2000). Such as individual may have a short attention span, a limited vocabulary, or a speech impediment. Between 2 and 10 percent of the prison population is believed to be made up of persons having mental retardation (Davis, 2000).

Unusual behavior traits or agitation accompanied by physical activity may also become evident during an interview. Persons with mental retardation may exhibit inappropriate verbal and nonverbal behaviors such as yelling, biting, hugging, and rubbing of genital areas or breasts. The interviewer should set limits by asking the person to stop the behavior or requesting that the person put his or her hands on a desk or table (Baladerian, 1998). The interviewer should take care not to react to unexpected outbursts by laughing or exhibiting anger, but should be firm but gentle and direct the interviewee to more appropriate behaviors if he or she does not comply or acts aggressively.

Attention Deficit-Hyperactivity Disorder

Attention deficit-hyperactivity disorder (ADHD) is a developmental neurological disorder that affects learning and behavior (Barkley, 2000). There are three types of ADHD described in the *Diagnostic and Statistical Manual of Mental Disorders,* 4th edition (DSM-IV) (American Psychiatric Association [APA], 1994): Combined Type, Predominately Inattentive Type, and Hyperactive-Impulsive Type. These terms are often used interchangeably and are referred to as ADD, ADHD, or AD/HD. ADHD is recognized as a disability under federal legislation (ADA, 1994). Compared to persons without ADHD, persons having ADHD have greater problems with law enforcement officials. Research is unclear on whether this is due to greater problems with alcohol and drug abuse rather than the disability itself (Latham et al., 1995). Once thought to afflict only children, this disability is also diagnosed with in adults. Symptoms include hyperactivity, difficulty in deferring gratification or following instructions, greater risk taking, and impulsivity. Coupled with lower self-image and poor self-control, these make individuals with ADHD more likely to come to the attention of law enforcement due to their involvement in automobile accidents, underage drinking, and aggressiveness (Barkley, 2000). Juveniles with ADHD are three times more likely to drive without a valid driver's license. There are no data to suggest that a specific interviewing or interrogation method is necessary for individuals with ADHD, but recognition of the symptoms is helpful in determining the motivation for criminal behavior (Goldstein, 2003). Goldstein (2003) suggests that the following questions be asked during an interrogation to determine whether the disorder contributed to the individual's behavior:

- Do you have difficulty paying attention during conversations, in classes, at work, and so on?
- Do you feel excessively stressed or overwhelmed?
- Do you find that your mind drifts off easily?
- Do you become sidetracked easily, leave tasks unfinished, or disrupt tasks in progress to switch to other matters?
- Do you become frustrated easily?
- Do you forget to complete things that you intended to do?
- Do you have sudden outbursts of intense anger?
- Do you easily misunderstand directions?

Autism

Autism is a developmental disability whose symptoms may become apparent between 15 and 20 months of age (Autism Society of America, 2006). Autism frequently occurs along with other mental impairments, such as mental retardation, seizure disorders, and ADHD (Mayers, 2003). It affects 1 in 166 individuals; there are an estimated 1.5 million Americans with this developmental disorder (Autism Society of America, 2006). It is characterized by impaired social relations and communication deficits that may lead to behavior prohibited by law. This population may become aggressive if interrupted during a preferred activity. Individuals with autism have a high likelihood of victimization (Debbaudt, 1999). During an interrogation there is the possibility of their producing false confessions or providing misleading statements to the police (Debbaudt, 1999). According to the Autism Society of America (2006), persons with autism may exhibit some of the following traits that could affect an interview:

- They may repeat words or phrases in place of normal responsive language.
- They may laugh (and/or cry) for no apparent reason.
- They may have little or no eye contact and appear aloof.
- They may have no real fear of danger.
- They may be unresponsive to verbal cues and act as if they were deaf.

Mental Illness

Mental illness is defined in the DSM-IV as a clinically significant behavioral or psychological syndrome or pattern that occurs in an individual that is associated with present distress (e.g., a painful symptom) or disability (i.e., impairment in one or more important areas of functioning) or with a significant increased risk of suffering death, pain, disability, or an important loss of freedom (APA, 1994). Several studies concluded that only a weak association between mental disorder and violence exists, suggesting that serious violence is perpetrated by a small fraction of the total number of such individuals (Steadman et al., 1998). One study concluded that mentally

Mental Illness	Mental Retardation
• Impacts moods and emotions • Low or high IQ • Occurs at any time • Disability may be noticeable • May be associated with violent outbursts	• Decreased ability to learn • Low IQ • Occurs before age 18 years • Unless severe, disability is not often noticeable • Persons are not violent

FIGURE 9-2 Because there are a disproportionate number of persons in the criminal justice system who are affected with either mental illness or mental retardation it is important to know the difference between them.

disordered inmates were more likely to have been arrested on less serious charges than nondisabled persons, but that they were significantly more likely to have been carrying a weapon and to be perceived as dangerous at the time of the interaction with the police (Engel & Silver, 2000). Severe mental disorders that are highly represented in the prison inmate population include schizophrenia, bipolar disorder, and serious depression (Fellner, 2003). Such individuals may be quick to anger, provocative, and dangerous. Schizophrenia may include disordered thinking or speech, delusions, hallucinations, inappropriate emotions, confusion, and inattention to personal grooming. Bipolar disorder (previously called manic-depressive disorder) is characterized by frequently dramatic mood swings between depression and mania. During manic phases some people may be psychotic and experience delusions or hallucinations. Persons with bipolar disorder in a manic phase can be disruptive, quick to anger, provocative, and dangerous. Serious depression puts people at an increased risk for suicide and self-mutilation.

Persons with mental illness and persons with mental retardation are highly represented in the criminal justice system, but these conditions are not the same.

Personality Disorders

The most common personality disorders among jail and prison inmates are antisocial personality disorder (ASPD) and borderline personality disorder (Fellner, 2003). The DSM-IV defines a **personality disorder** as an enduring pattern of inner experience and behavior that deviates markedly from the expectations of the individual's culture, is pervasive and inflexible, has an onset in adolescence or early adulthood, is stable over time, and leads to distress or impairment (APA, 1994). Persons with antisocial personality disorder, typically men, can be particularly difficult to manage in a correctional setting. They can be manipulative, volatile, disruptive, and likely to engage in aggressive, impulsive acting-out behavior, which can include assaults on others, self-mutilation, and/or suicide attempts. The essential characteristic is a pervasive pattern of disregard for, and violation of, the rights of others (APA, 1994).

FIELD EVALUATION

An important component of policing is astute observation. The purpose of conducting a field evaluation is to determine an appropriate response to the situation. First responders are often expected to make a quick assessment of the environment with limited information. Two methods of evaluation used to make an assessment in the field are categorized based on distance. A **distant field evaluation** is a nonverbal assessment that is conducted from a distance of greater than 3 feet; this is used when a person attracts interest in the field due to one or more of the following conditions:

- The person may be inappropriately dressed for the weather.
- The person is in a place where he or she doesn't belong and personal danger clearly exists.
- The person is stumbling about or appears to be in a confused state.
- The person is engaging in inappropriate actions with peers or people of the opposite sex.
- The individual appears to be gravely disabled either in judgment or because of substance abuse.

A **detailed field evaluation** is an up-close assessment to determine whether the subject is mentally disordered or physically handicapped. Its purpose is to determine whether there are any needs or problems that must be addressed or if a situation of mandated reporting exists. The examination should not be conducted in this manner if there is evidence that the individual is armed or dangerous. The officer's first concern should always be directed toward the safety and protection of persons, both for himself or herself and for others. One should approach the individual in a nonthreatening but controlled manner so as not to agitate or cause distress. Speaking firmly and clearly, one should show concern through actions and words. "Are you okay?" and "Do you need help?" are examples of introductory statements used when assessing the situation in the field.

Ask for identifying information to determine the level of stress and cognitive awareness of the person. If an individual is not aware of his or her name or address, this may be indicative of impairment. Do not assume that a person who fails to answer your questions can hear or understand you. Failure to respond in itself is not indicative of belligerence or criminal behavior. An indication of alcohol use does not necessarily mean that the individual is drunk; you may be dealing with a person who has a disability who also had an alcoholic beverage.

Most persons with a disability present no risk to police. However, unless they are being successfully treated, persons with paranoid schizophrenia pose a documented rate of violence that is several times higher than that of the general population (Mohandie & Duffy, 1999). Individuals with this mental disorder may present with anxiety, anger, aloofness, argumentativeness, and a superior or patronizing manner. To defuse a potentially violent situation takes a show of respect and a calm, nonthreatening approach to communicating. In addition to the

> **BEEN THERE... DONE THAT! 9-3**
>
> At the scene of a homicide the female victim was found to have been stabbed about 150 times. An adult son who lived with her was on the scene and was also stabbed more than 100 times but lived. My partner went to the hospital to interview the survivor. The interview was audiotaped and *Miranda* warnings were issued to the son because he was a suspect in the killing. He appeared to be coherent, and his initial behavior was rational. From time to time during the interview the suspect would start howling accompanied by blood-curdling screaming and sobbing. He told how the "devil" was present in his TV and was transposed to his mother—he could see it through the redness of her eyes (which is why numerous stabbings were to her eyes). He had to rid her of this devil, whom he also thought had gotten into him, which is why he had stabbed himself in every orifice—ears, eyes, and buttocks. The danger was that he believed what he was doing; this goal-directed behavior was organized and premeditated. The goal of the attack was not to kill his mother, but to kill the devil that was in her. Officer safety is an important issue with those who are delusional, suffer from hallucinations, and/or present with grossly disorganized or catatonic behaviors.
>
> This suspect had a long history of severe mental illness and was under a doctor's care. The defense and the prosecution agreed that the he was legally insane and should not be tried for the murder.

methods already discussed, the following guidelines were suggested by Mohandie and Duffy (1999) for dealing with potentially violent mentally ill individuals:

- Assess the risk; does the individual pose a risk, or is it merely threatened?
- Make a noticeable attempt to understand the context of the person's comments.
- Avoid arguing about the person's delusions while attempting to get at reality-based issues.
- Use active listening skills such as paraphrasing, emotion labeling, and "I" messages.
- Allow the person to vent frustration.
- Do not crowd or violate the individual's personal body space.
- Use suggestibility and empathy to attempt a behavioral change.

Interview Considerations

Interviewing a person presenting with a disability involves only a modification of the techniques already discussed throughout this book. Although initially challenging, the interview should be no more difficult than with any other population. As before, the interviewer must maintain control, elicit responses, and clarify statements. How this is accomplished obviously differs depending on the unique characteristics of the individual being questioned. This takes patience and a willingness to communicate through the most effective method.

Victims of crime who have a disability may be targeted for criminal activity due to their real or perceived vulnerability; you may be interviewing someone who has been repeatedly victimized. They are targets for abuse and theft from the caregivers who are assigned to care for them. One study found almost half of the sexual abuse against persons with disabilities was perpetrated by persons who gained access to their victims through disability services (Sobsey, 1994). A cycle of victimization and abuse will make it more difficult to establish rapport and trust from the person being interviewed, another reason to be patient and understanding.

Legal Issues

Prior to the interview with a person who is physically or mentally impaired, the interviewer must have a good understanding of the statutes that are specific to protecting disabled persons. Typically the elements of the crime differ for victimized individuals who have limited cognitive and physical abilities, so it is important to be acquainted with the provisions particular to your jurisdiction before the interview. Numerous distinctions have been made in criminal statutes that provide additional protections for persons with a disability from abandonment, financial exploitation, personal victimization, and neglect. Some examples include the following:

- North Carolina provides that second degree rape (GS14-27.3(a)(2) against a mentally disabled, mentally incapacitated, or physically helpless person requires a lack of consent, but no force need be established.
- The Illinois Criminal Code includes the Home Repair Fraud Act (815ILCS 515/5). Aggravated home repair fraud occurs if the contractor commits a home repair fraud against a person who has a permanent physically disabling condition. Aggravated home repair fraud is a Class 2 felony if the contractor is to be paid more than $1,000 and a Class 4 felony if the amount is less than $1,000. The maximum punishment for a Class 4 felony is a term of imprisonment of not less than 1 year and not more than 3 years.
- According to the Indiana Criminal Code of Battery (IC 35-42-2-1), it is a Class D felony if a person who knowingly or intentionally touches another person in a rude, insolent, or angry manner commits battery that results in bodily injury to a person of any age who is mentally or physically disabled and is committed by a person having the care of the mentally or physically disabled person, whether the care is assumed voluntarily or because of a legal obligation.
- Iowa presents an example in which a crime against a person with a disability may be construed as a "hate crime" (92 Acts, ch 1157, §9). This category includes one or more of the following public offenses when committed against a person or a person's property because of the person's race, color, religion, ancestry, national origin, political

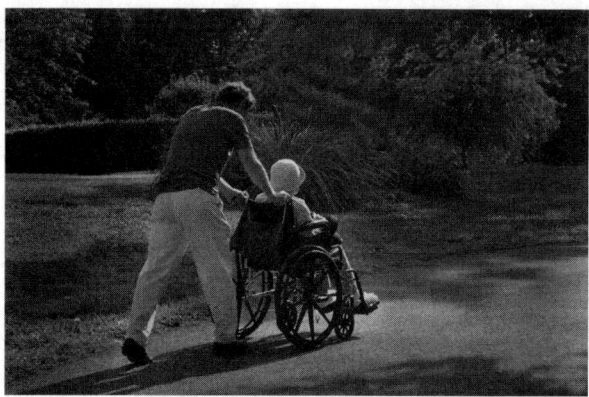

FIGURE 9-3 An "appropriate adult" may be included in the interview to assist in communication with the police.

affiliation, sex, sexual orientation, age, or disability, or the person's association with a person of a certain race, color, religion, ancestry, national origin, political affiliation, sex, sexual orientation, age, or disability:

1. Assault in violation of individual rights under section 708.2C.
2. Violations of individual rights under section 712.9.
3. Criminal mischief in violation of individual rights under section 716.6A.
4. Trespass in violation of individual rights under section 716.8, subsections 3 and 4.

Preparing for the Interview

Prior to the interview, determine a location away from the scene that is comfortable and without distractions. Turn off any cell phone or pager that you carry. The best scenario is a one-on-one interview. In some cases it may be advisable to include an appropriate adult. An **appropriate adult** is someone who is able to provide support to the interviewee and to smooth the progress of communication with the police. He or she should have a good understanding or training in dealing with persons with mental disorders or with the needs of a particular group. He or she should be completely independent of the police and, when possible, the interviewee. As needed, the person should be able to act as an interpreter. It is helpful to have developed a relationship with mental health workers who are willing to be called on in such a case. An alternative is to develop a team approach for interviewing persons who have a disability. It is not the function of an appropriate adult to advise the person being interviewed whether or how to answer any questions or to object to any questions being asked. It is not appropriate for the helping adult to tell the police that he or she disapproves of a particular line of questioning or to lead the witness in any way.

In rare cases, a controversial method called **facilitated communication** can be used as a form of communication. This is designed for people who do not have the physical ability to use sign language or the ability to use keyboards or communication boards on their own. This involves steadying the individual's physical movements to allow the person to make the communication that they desire (Baladerian, 1998). The method uses a keyboard or communication board and the assistance of a trained facilitator. Two separate interviews should be conducted with different facilitators who have not had prior contact with the victim.

Establishing Rapport

Introduce yourself and ask the individual what he or should would like to be called. Referring to someone else by a title and then calling the interviewee by a first name implies a lack of respect, so be consistent. Avoid touching a person with a disability because you do not know whether this would be perceived as an invasion of personal space or remind them of an attacker. An individual who is "touch toxic" may become upset and unable to continue the interview; a person with mental retardation may not feel able to refuse. Take your cue from the interviewee; if he or she puts out a hand for a handshake, respond. Otherwise, keep your hands to yourself. Don't be afraid to maintain your own personal space. Because it is not professional to hug an individual being interviewed, it is appropriate to firmly and gently avoid personal contact of this kind that is initiated by the interviewee. Kindly tell the interviewee that it makes you feel uncomfortable and do not want to hug.

Develop rapport with the interviewee by asking whether he or she requires physical assistance or arrangements to meet his or her needs. Explain the process of the interview; explain that you may need to ask questions more than once to make sure that you understand what is being said. Anticipate an adequate length of time for the interview without the need for excessive time. Arrange for support to be available to the person following the interview, and let the interviewee know that someone will be there for him or her.

For persons with physical disabilities, do not jump up and assume that the person needs or wants help. Keep clear of wheelchairs so that the individual can move around and adopt a comfortable position; the wheelchair is part of the person's space that should not be invaded without specific design. The room should be comfortable without being too large, and absent of children's toys.

Conducting the Interview

Use good listening skills; allow the victim to tell the story at first with as few interruptions as possible. Use open-ended questions and avoid overly complicated or technical phrases. Ask the person if he or she knows why he or she is there to speak with you. It may be helpful to explain that you are someone who speaks with people about difficult subjects, and give

> **BEEN THERE... DONE THAT! 9-4**
>
> I interviewed a woman with retardation about an allegation of rape. She was clear in stating that she had been raped. Instructing her that I needed to understand her terms, I asked that she name the parts of the body. She did this without a problem using a clothed, anatomically correct doll. Next I asked if she would tell me how it happened. The woman immediately picked up the doll and rubbed her face on the chest area. "See," she stated, "he raped me like this." What she showed was not rape, but it was a sexual assault. She did not want this to happen and said she told him to stop, over and over. The man was charged with an indecent assault and battery on a disabled person. The interview had been videotaped, and it was shown in the grand jury; the victim also went into the grand jury and with the use of the doll demonstrated what had happened. The fact that her terms were different did not diminish the crime nor the trauma that resulted from it. The perpetrator was indicted, and he pled guilty to the crime in Superior Court.

them "permission" to talk with you. Give the individual the opportunity to ask questions.

Questions should not be phrased in legal terms; the victim may not know what an "assault" means, for example. The primary goals of interviewing victims are to:

1. Determine whether a crime has been committed
2. Obtain information to help in the identification of the perpetrator
3. Gather evidence for a successful prosecution

The goal of interviewing witnesses is the corroboration of specific events that substantiates criminal activity. With these goals in mind, the purpose of the interview is to acquire the necessary information.

The criminal justice community has already made great strides in interviewing one class of people with cognitive limitations, children. Although care must be taken not to infantilize a person with a disability, we can use the lessons learned from working with children for effective communication. Remember that the person presenting with a disability does not necessarily have limited cognitive abilities along with a physical or neurological limitation. As much as possible, go into the interview without a preconceived notion about the abilities of the interviewee to recount the necessary information.

The cognitive abilities of the individual should be considered when phrasing/asking questions. Be purposeful in your phrasing to avoid miscommunication and misunderstanding. Keep sentences short and to the point. Access the vocabulary of the person being interviewed and attempt consistency in communication. Take extra care not to lead the questioning or to suggest answers. Questions that require a "yes" or "no" response are only helpful for clarification and should be avoided. Encourage the interviewee to express and clarify meanings. All of these considerations must be confined to a relatively short interview period of approximately ½ hour. Persons with a disability may have a short attention span.

Be aware that the vocabulary used by the person being interviewed may have different meanings than you would normally associate with the terms. If the allegation is of sexual abuse, don't just allow the victim to provide the words that he or she uses to describe his or her body parts, but also have him or her show you on an anatomically correct doll or through drawings what that part of the body is. Encourage the individual to use descriptive terms for what he or she experienced. Avoid asking "Why" questions; they are too complicated and can be confusing.

At the end of the interview thank the interviewee for his or her time and patience. Ask any questions on points that you need clarified. Let the victim know that you may need to speak with him or her another time and ask whether that would be all right. Be sure to escort the person outside of the interview room to meet with a counselor or other supportive person.

INTERROGATION CONSIDERATIONS

Persons with disabilities do commit crimes, and accusations must be investigated similar to allegations against any other supposed perpetrator. There are situations in which an officer must interrogate a person suspected of committing a crime where disability is suspected or known. To protect the results of the interrogation, special care must be taken to preserve the integrity of the case. Most important is strict adherence to the preservation of all constitutional rights. Taking short-cuts will likely result in a tainted investigation and a statement that is subject to exclusion or worse. Remembering that the purpose of an interrogation is to find the truth if possible, take pains to make sure that it is the truth that is obtained. Follow any department rules and regulations that may exist relative to interrogating potentially vulnerable persons. Know your state laws relative to the interrogation of juveniles. In all cases, treat the suspect with dignity.

Prior to questioning, make a determination on the level of functioning of the adult suspect. Ask typical questions, such as name, age, and address of the individual. Determine whether the suspect can read; if not, be prepared to read and explain individual rights. Ask questions that are nonleading and straightforward. Avoid questions that require a "yes" or "no" answer. Use language that is simple and easy to understand. Your sentences should be short and to the point.

Follow up any statements suggestive of guilt by asking for details of the event. Answers that typically would be considered "admissions" do not take on the same significance when coming from a person with limited cognitive ability. For example, if a man with mental retardation is asked, "When did you kill Mrs. Smith?" and he replies, "Was it Thursday?," then absent significant evidence that he did in fact commit the homicide, the reply means absolutely nothing. The individual may take your question be about "when" Mrs. Smith was killed and miss the "you" part of the question. Proceed with caution! Justice is not served by arresting the wrong person.

Miranda Rights

There is no requirement that *Miranda* rights be given verbatim or presented to the suspect in written form (*Miranda v. Arizona*, 1966). These practices are police procedures developed to assure compliance and consistency. Officers are therefore given the flexibility of explaining these rights to a suspect in a manner that allows the person to understand. People with mental retardation often do not understand *Miranda* warnings even if they state that they do understand (The Arc, 1996). The interrogator is not a mental health specialist and is not responsible for diagnosing a suspect or determining the actual extent of mental limitations. A balance between the need to protect the public through sound investigation practices and recognizing personal limitations must be made.

Persons with mental retardation may incriminate themselves even if they are innocent in an effort to please the police officer or other interviewer. Persons with retardation are structured throughout their lives to be compliant and submissive. In an interrogation with a suspect who is disabled, do not assume without verification, that he or she understands.

It is not an ADA requirement that statements be audiotaped or videotaped (The Arc, 1996). The practice of recording interrogations is recommended whenever practicable. Preserving a record of the interrogation helps to protect the officer against claims of using excessive interrogation tactics and heavy-handed methods. It also serves to demonstrate that the individual knowingly and voluntarily waived his or her rights.

False Confessions

When interrogating persons who have mental retardation, false confessions should be a major concern for the interrogator. The individual may be confused about who is responsible for the crime and "confess" even though innocent. He or she may be the last to leave the scene of the crime and the first to be caught. He or she may act very upset at being detained and/or try

FIGURE 9-4 Verify that the suspect fully understands the questions that are being asked. Persons with retardation may be overly compliant and submissive in order to please.

to run away. Avoid lengthy interrogations; although they may elicit a "confession," they might miss the goal of interrogation, which is to find the truth.

The Supreme Court expressed in the *Miranda* decision (id. at 24) some of its concerns regarding persons with low IQ and their subsequent false confessions to police. In pointing out that "Interrogation procedures may even give rise to a false confession," the Court provided a conspicuous example: in New York in 1964 an African American man of limited intelligence confessed to two brutal murders and a rape that he had not committed. The Court in its decision relied on a similar case in which the defendant, a 19-year-old heroin addict described as a "near mental defective," was found guilty of the crime he did not commit; his conviction was subsequently overturned (*Townsend v. Sain*, 1963).

Four Maryland cases were highlighted in an article on confessions that later proved to be false (Witt, 2001). Homicide detectives obtained confessions that put the wrong men behind bars while the killers remained free to commit other crimes. Three of the four false confessions were made by individuals with low IQ; a teenager with learning disabilities who said he stabbed a friend; a high school senior who implicated himself in a triple shooting; and an illiterate janitor who shakily signed a statement a detective wrote for him confessing to slaying a co-worker. The four men were detained in the interrogation room from 11 to more than 38 hours. Three of the four insisted that detectives refused to let them speak with a lawyer. In each case, the suspect's alleged statement was virtually the only evidence homicide detectives used to charge him with murder. Without a doubt these officers did not intend to arrest the wrong people. It is very easy to be consumed with finding killers and protecting the public; this is what law enforcement does. Just don't lose sight of the real goal by being overly zealous.

▲ CONCLUSIONS

This chapter introduced you to the challenges of interviewing and interrogating persons with disabilities. Crime against this population is believed to be higher than against the nondisabled community, yet reporting is much lower, and still lower are successful prosecutions. Skillful interviewing and careful lay assessments can increase the likelihood of obtaining sufficient information on which to proceed with cases involving this vulnerable community.

In addition to satisfying the needs of the criminal justice system are the mandates of the Americans with Disabilities Act. Professionals within the field are expected to deal with an increasing number of individuals with developmental, physical, and mental disabilities. If possible, communication with this underserved population is even more important than with others. Generally, such individuals are perceived as easy victims by predators. They need and depend on the criminal justice community to protect them in ways in which some of them are unable to do themselves. The ADA provides the legal impetus to seek justice for this population, but the moral responsibilities exist within every officer.

Dispelling the myths about this population and dealing with personal prejudices is not easy, but definitely can be achieved. It will take time to develop the needed skills for proficiency in interviewing. It will take patience and good judgment. It takes a true professional to give it a try.

QUESTIONS FOR REVIEW

Short-Answer Questions

1. What does Title II of the ADA refer to and how does it affect policing?
2. Because the ADA affects the job of the police officer on so many levels, it is important to understand how the courts define certain actions. According to the federal courts, how is the term "arrest" interpreted under the ADA?
3. What are the two significant issues involved in wrongful arrest, and what techniques can prevent mistakes?
4. Describe some of the challenges that must be overcome for successful interviewing of the disabled and mentally ill populations.
5. What is the difference between a person with a mental illness and a person with mental retardation?
6. What are some of the behavioral traits that may occur in individuals with disabilities?
7. In order to assess a situation, an officer can use a distant field evaluation or a detailed field evaluation. Briefly discuss both.
8. How does the crime rate compare for persons with a disability and the general population?
9. Why would an interviewer use an appropriate adult in an interview with a person who has a disability?
10. During an interview, what concerns should the interviewer have when interviewing a person with a disability?

Fill-in Questions

1. When interrogating persons with mental retardation, _____ _____ should be of great concern.
2. According to *Miranda,* _____ procedures can lead to false confessions among individuals with a low IQ.
3. Impaired adults are at a _____ risk for being physically or sexually assaulted than are other adults.
4. _____ provides that "no qualified individual with a disability shall by reason of such disability, be excluded from participation in or be denied the benefits of the services, programs, or activities of a public entity, or be subjected to discrimination by any such entity."
5. A(n) _____ can be used to help facilitate communication during an interview with a person with a disability.
6. _____ is considered by the federal courts under Title II of the ADA as pre-arrest investigations and violent confrontations not technically involving arrest.

7. The largest impediment to successful interviewing of the disabled or mentally ill population is _____.
8. Persons with mental retardation will have a low IQ, and a person who is mentally ill can have an IQ that is _____.
9. Mental retardation usually occurs _____.
10. Individuals with _____ pose a documented rate of violence that is several times higher than the general population.

Exercises

1. Write an essay on facilitated communication stating the pros and cons of this method. Start your search for information at the Web site of the Facilitated Communication Institute: http://soeweb.syr.edu/thefci/.
2. Break into pairs. In this mock interview let one person assume the persona of a person with a disability. The interviewee should choose and become familiar with one of the major categories of disability—mental retardation, mental illness, and a personality disorder. The interviewer must become familiar with the cautionary approaches to conducting an interview with a person who has a disability. The purpose of the interview is to determine whether the interviewee was sexually assaulted by a neighbor. Take 10 minutes for this exercise. Report your experiences to the class.
3. Reverse roles from Exercise 2. Take 10 minutes for the interview. Report your experiences to the class.
4. Explain the two methods for field evaluation of persons with mental illness and persons with mental retardation and give reasons why the evaluation would be beneficial to potential interviewers. List questions that would be helpful when making a field evaluation of a person suspected of having a disability.
5. Locate "A police officer's guide when in contact with people who have mental retardation" on the Web at www.thearc.org/publications. Write a report on how interrogation with an individual who has mental retardation can affect the criminal justice process.

REFERENCES

American Psychiatric Association. (1994). *Diagnostic and statistical manual of mental disorders* (4th ed.). Washington, DC: American Psychiatric Association.
Americans with Disabilities Act. (1994) 42 U.S.C. §12132.
Autism Society of America. (2006). Defining Autism. [Online.] Available: http://www.autism-society.org/site/PageServer?pagename=WhatisAutism.
Baladerian, N. J. (1998). *Interviewing skills to use with abuse victims who have developmental disabilities.* Washington, DC: National Center on Elder Abuse.
Barkley, R. (2000). *Taking charge of ADHD.* New York: Guilford Press.
Crosse, S. B., Kaye, E., & Ratnofsky, A. C. (1993). *A report on the maltreatment of children with disabilities.* Washington, DC: Office on Child Abuse and Neglect.
Davis, L. A. (2000). People with mental retardation and the criminal justice system. [Online.] Available: http://www.thearc.org/faqs/crimqa.html.

Debbaudt, D. (1999). Avoiding unfortunate situations. [Online.] Available: http://policeandautism.cjb.net/.

Engel, R. S., & Silver, E. (2000). Policing mentally disordered suspects: A reexamination of the criminalization hypothesis. *Criminology, 39*(2), 225–252.

Fellner, J. (2003). *Ill-equipped: U.S. prisons and offenders with mental illness.* New York: Human Rights Watch.

Gillespie, C. (2001). Police training improves safety in dealing with mentally ill. [Online.] Available: http://www.taser.com/documents/akronohiomental.doc.

Gohier v. Enright, 186 F.3rd 1216 (10th Cir.) (1999).

Goldstein, S. (2003). ADHD and implications for the criminal justice system. [Online.] Available: http://www.mental-health-matters.com/articles/article.php?artID=682.

Jackson v. Town of Sanford, 63 U.S.L.W. 2351 (1994).

Latham, P., Goldstein, S., Dickman, E., Latham, P., & Quinn, P. (1995). The criminal justice system and individuals with attention deficit disorder and learning disabilities. [Online.] Available: http://www.add.org/articles/cjaddld.html.

Lewis v. Truitt, 960 F. Supp. 175 (S.D. Ind.) (1997).

Mayers, T. (2003). Persons with autism and criminal justice: Core concepts and leading cases. *Journal of Positive Behavior Interventions, 5*(2), 92–100.

Mentally Ill Offender Treatment and Crime Reduction Act, 2004. 42 USC 3711 Public Law 108-414.

Miranda v. Arizona, 284 U.S. 436 (1966).

Mishra, R. (2001 June). In attacks on disabled, few verdicts despite evidence, law enforcement drops most cases. *The Boston Globe*, p. A1.

Mohandie, K., & Duffy, J. (1999). *Understanding subjects with paranoid schizophrenia.* Washington, DC: Federal Bureau of Investigation.

Petersilia, J. (2000). Invisible victims: Violence against persons with developmental disabilities. *Human Rights, 27*(1), 9–13.

Sigmon, J., & Edmunds, J. (2002). Victimization of individuals with disabilities. In *National victim assistance academy: Foundations in victimology and victims' rights and services* (p. 15). Washington, DC: Office for Victims of Crime.

Sobsey, D. (1994). *Violence and abuse in the lives of people with disabilities.* Baltimore: Paul H. Brookes.

Steadman, H., Mulvey, E., Monahan, J., Robbins, P., Applebaum, P., Grisso, T., Roth, L., & Silver, E. (1998). Violence by people discharged from acute psychiatric inpatient facilities and by others in the same neighborhoods. *Archives of General Psychiatry, 55*, 393–401.

The Arc. (1996). *A police officer's guide when in contact with people who have mental retardation.* Silver Spring, MD: The Arc of the United States.

Townsend v. Sain, 372 U.S. 293 (1963).

Tyiska, C. (1998). *Working with victims of crime with disabilities.* Washington, DC: Office for Victims of Crime, U.S. Department of Justice.

U.S. Department of Justice. (1996). Commonly asked questions about the Americans with Disabilities Act and law enforcement. [Online.] Available: http://www.usdoj.gov/crt/ada/q&a_law.htm.

Witt, A. (2001). False confessions. Available: http://www.washingtonpost.com/wpdyn/metro/md/princegeorges/government/police/confess/.

Part IV

Interrogation

In this section, each chapter presents a different view of the interrogation process. Chapter 10 discusses the legal guidelines for criminal justice interrogations. Although each state may establish procedures and laws that are more restrictive than the federal guidelines, the final authority rests with the U.S. Supreme Court. These rules are categorized under the constitutional provisions that the courts have identified as applicable to the interrogation process. The four-prong test for lawful interrogations is based on the Fourth, Fifth, Sixth, and Fourteenth Amendments. The *Miranda* standard is a major focus governing interrogation practices, and its requirements are clearly outlined. The difference between compelling a suspect to give up protected constitutional protections and compelling a suspect to give a statement after those rights have been legally relinquished is addressed. In addition, the difference between the Sixth Amendment right to counsel and the *Miranda* standard is discussed.

Chapter 11 examines the goal of the interrogation and the methods for reaching that goal. Studies suggest that interrogations should be conducted more frequently than they actually are. This view is bolstered by the fact that when police officers do conduct interrogations, they are very successful. Knowledge of the law can be as important as technique for increasing the number of successful interrogations. Ways to avoid false confessions and techniques for some case-specific criminal interrogations are suggested. Methods for improving interrogations are covered in depth.

Chapter 12 covers techniques for interrogation. The goal of an interrogation is what differentiates it from an interview. The place and timing are critical but do not define the interrogation. Strategies for conducting interrogations in custodial and noncustodial situations are differentiated. Success in interrogation is achieved by using a three-phase approach of preparing, assessing, and getting the confession. Steps for accomplishing each phase are outlined. Assessing the suspect and determining the barriers that inhibit a suspect from making a confession are covered in considerable detail. Numerous confession-eliciting models are outlined; no one method determines how interrogations must take place.

Chapter 13 addresses challenges and legal obligations concerning juvenile interrogations. The criminal justice system treats a juvenile in a different way than an adult. The distinction is important for the criminal justice professional who may be engaged in conducting interrogations. A juvenile is prosecuted under a civil system that closely resembles the adult criminal system. Defining a juvenile can be difficult, and states vary on when a child can be prosecuted as a juvenile or an adult. The situation is further complicated because some state statues mandate that juvenile offenders be tried in adult court if they commit specific serious crimes. Juvenile rights are outlined in this chapter within the context of police responsibility. Specific crimes in which juvenile perpetration is of serious concern are addressed along with suggestions for interrogation in these cases.

CHAPTER 10

The Interrogation Process and the Law

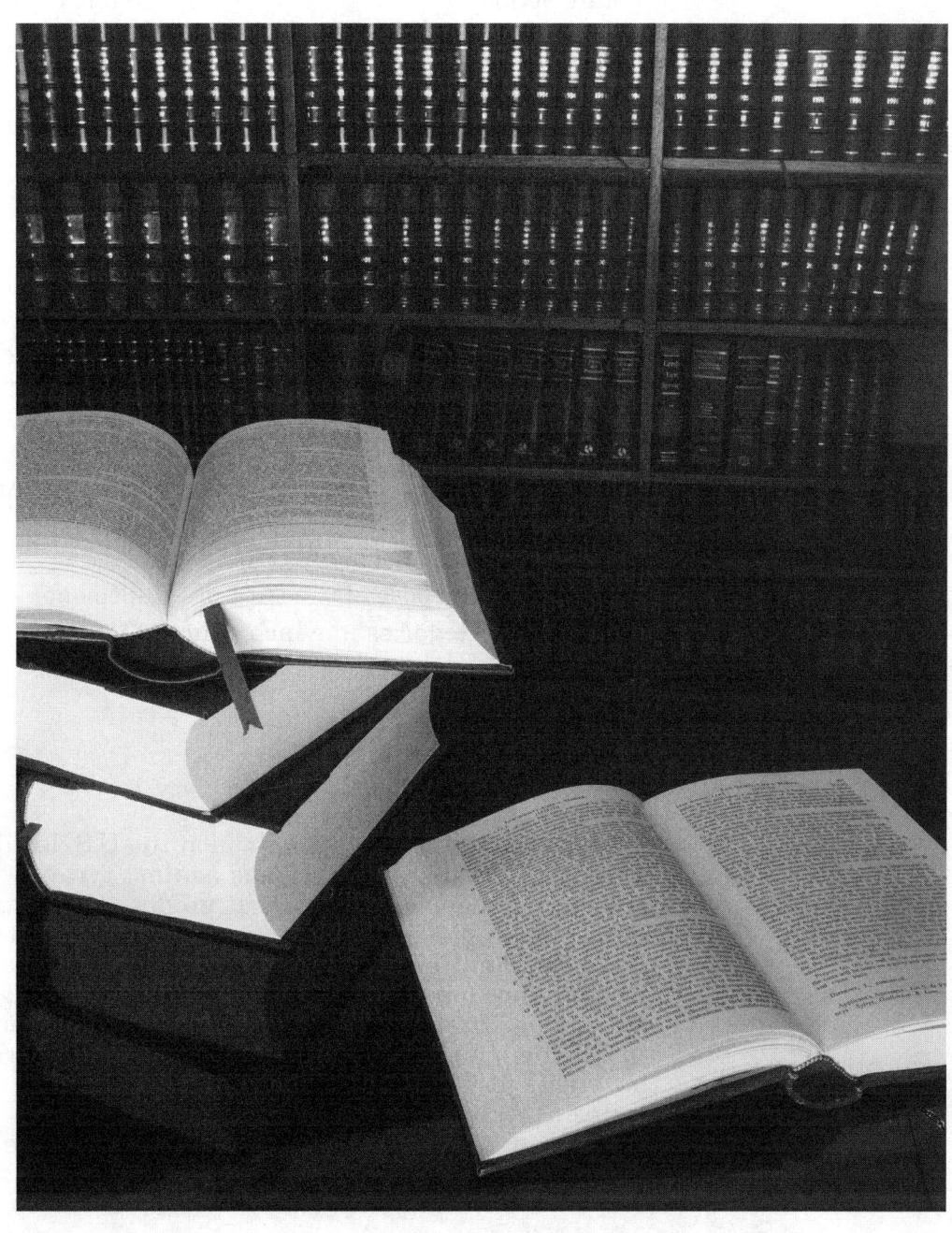

KEY TERMS

Rule of law	Custody
Stare decisis	Exclusionary rule
Totality of the circumstances	Fruit-of-the-poisonous-tree doctrine
Miranda rights	Power to arrest
State action	Probable cause

CHAPTER OBJECTIVES

After completing this chapter, you should be able to:

- Describe the rule of law
- Describe the totality-of-the-circumstances test
- Explain *Miranda* rights
- List numerous forms of coercion that would invalidate a confession, even if the suspect's *Miranda* rights were properly waived
- Compare and contrast the constitutional protections deriving from the Fourth, Fifth, and Sixth Amendments
- Define *probable cause*
- State the protections of the Fourth Amendment and how they apply to interrogation
- Define the exclusionary rule
- State the purpose of the fruit-of-the-poisonous-tree doctrine
- List the categories in which police officers have the power to make arrests

INTRODUCTION

The fundamental principle on which the U.S. legal system rests is that law is created to protect citizens against tyranny and lawlessness and to protect freedom. The law that guides the system comes from many sources, with the Constitution of the United States as the supreme law of the land. The Bill of Rights and other amendments to the Constitution developed further protections to the rights and freedoms of individuals. State constitutions expand and define the protections within their jurisdictions, but no state can deprive the individual of the rights established and guaranteed by the Constitution of the United States.

The **rule of law** holds that those who execute the law must rely on the application of known principles or laws and that those principles must be applied uniformly and fairly to all citizens. This concept is also referred to as the *supremacy of law*. General constitutional principles are the result of judicial decisions determining the rights of individuals. Supreme Court case law makes up the bulk of what is called constitutional law (Garner, 2004). According to the rule of **stare decis,** judges must make decisions that are guided by previous settled decisions. Many of the decisions that govern interrogation practices by the police are interpretations of the U.S. Constitution that have evolved since the 1960s. These contemporary interpretations of the Constitution illustrate that the law is a fluid entity; it relies on settled principles to form the basis for contemporary legal standards. The courts are settling issues that could not have been anticipated by the framers of the Constitution, such as the legality of wiretapping or the taking of DNA samples. Still, the old concepts must be applied in a way that is consistent with what the Constitution demands and in a way that is fair to all. The objective application and enforcement of laws concerning interrogations by government officials and their agents is established in the law itself and interpreted by the rulings of judges.

The four-prong test for the admissibility of a confession is based on the Fourth, Fifth, Sixth, and Fourteenth Amendments. In the past, confessions that were considered voluntary were admissible in court and could be used against a suspect if they fulfilled the Fifth Amendment protections against self-incrimination, regardless of any questions of official legality (*Colombe v. Connecticut,* 1961). Since the Fourteenth Amendment requirement of due process was found to be applicable to state actions, the Fourth Amendment has joined the list of important legal considerations.

Fifth Amendment Considerations

The Fifth Amendment of the U.S. Constitution is discussed first in this chapter because it contains the earliest example of protections applied to the admissibility of confessions. It protects the right of a suspect against compelled testimonial communication and self-incrimination. It states:

> *No person shall be held to answer for a capital, or otherwise infamous crime, unless on a presentment or indictment of a Grand Jury, except in cases arising in the land or naval forces, or in the Militia, when in actual service in time of War or public danger; nor shall any person be subject for the same offence to be twice put in jeopardy of life or limb; nor shall be compelled in any criminal case to be a witness against himself, nor be deprived of life, liberty, or property, without due process of law; nor shall private property be taken for public use, without just compensation.*

The Fifth Amendment requires that no person will be incriminated through compelled testimonial communication. *Compel* means to cause or bring about by force, threats, or overwhelming pressure (Garner, 2004). To be *testimonial,* a "communication must itself, explicitly or implicitly, relate a factual assertion or disclose information" that is the "expression of the contents of an individual's mind" (*Doe v. United States,* 1988). The protection against self-incrimination also permits a person to refuse to testify against himself or herself at a criminal trial in which he or she is a defendant.

The application of the Fifth Amendment to confession has evolved. Under early common law, an admission or confession was allowed to be used in court as evidence of guilt even if it was the product of force or duress. Enforcement officers resorted to torture to extract a confession from the accused during an interrogation rather than conduct an investigation to establish guilt.

Practices of torture as an interrogation method eventually led to the development of rules on the admissibility of confessions in the late eighteenth century. The newer common-law rule excluded coerced confessions from being admitted at trial due to the unreliability of evidence that was the product of torture. During the late 1800s the Court joined the common-law rule to the Fifth Amendment prohibition of compelling an individual to give witness against himself or herself as the standard for judging the admissibility of confessions (*Bram v. United States,* 1897).

The common-law rule was abandoned for the "free and voluntary" rule during the early twentieth century. This rule required that statements must be freely and voluntarily made without duress, fear, or compulsion and with knowledge of the consequences of the confession (*People v. Fox,* 1925). Involuntary confessions were rejected not because of the illegal or deceitful methods used in obtaining them, but because of their unreliability. Torture as a means of extracting confessions was expressly denounced in 1937 (*Brown v. Mississipi,* 1937). Using a *totality-of-the-circumstances* test, the Court in *Brown* concluded that repeated whippings of the suspect produced a coerced statement that could not be used against him in court. A **totality of the circumstances** test is one in which the court focuses on all of the circumstances surrounding a situation rather than any one factor. In 1966 the *Miranda* standard distinguished between the voluntariness of a statement and its validity (*Miranda v. Arizona,* 1966).

THE *MIRANDA* STANDARD

The Court in *Miranda* said that procedural safeguards must be used to secure the privilege against self-incrimination during custodial interrogations. The Court's reasoning was that the practices of custodial interrogation were inherently coercive (*Miranda v. Arizona,* 1966). Whether the *Miranda* requirements are complied with requires an analysis using the Fifth Amendment. Known as the **Miranda rights,** the following procedural safeguards must be stated prior to questioning. The person must be told that:

1. He or she has a right to remain silent
2. Any statement he or she does make may be used as evidence against him or her
3. He or she has a right to the presence of an attorney
4. If he or she cannot afford an attorney, counsel will be provided at government expense

CASE IN POINT 10-1

Case in Point: **Miranda v. Arizona (1966)**

In 1965, the Supreme Court agreed to hear the case of Ernesto *Miranda*, a poor Mexican immigrant who had been arrested after a crime victim identified him in a police lineup. At the same time the Court agreed to hear three similar cases: *Vignera v. New York*, *Westover v. United States*, and *California v. Stewart*. These four cases were combined, and because *Miranda* was the first case listed, the decision came to be known by that name.

Miranda had been charged with rape and kidnapping and interrogated for 2 hours while in police custody. As a result of the interrogation, he had confessed to the crimes with which he was charged. Although his written had statement included an acknowledgment that he was aware of his right against self-incrimination, he had never been informed of his rights under the Fifth Amendment or of his Sixth Amendment right to the assistance of an attorney. He had been sentenced to 20 to 30 years in prison on each count.

Importance

1. The Supreme Court in *Miranda* set specific guidelines for police officers on how they must advise suspects of their constitutional rights and under what circumstances those warnings must be provided.
2. The Supreme Court combined the Sixth Amendment right to an attorney with the Fifth Amendment right against self-incrimination.

When Are the *Miranda* Warnings Required?

Miranda warnings or their equivalent must be given prior to questioning (direct or indirect) that is initiated by an agent of the state if the suspect has been taken into police custody or otherwise deprived of his or her freedom of action by the police in any significant way.

✔ **State Action**

State action is anything done by a government, in particular the intrusion on a person's rights by a government entity (Garner, 2004). It occurs in interrogation practices when communication with a suspect is undertaken by federal or state law enforcement officers or their agents. This includes action taken by federal law enforcement officers such as agents of the Federal Bureau of Investigation, the Central Intelligence Agency, and the Drug Enforcement Agency and Postal Inspectors. State and municipal police officers are governed by these federal standards and may also have additional state laws that restrict their action. It does not cover the actions of private citizens who are not acting under police direction or solicitation.

✔ **Custody**

Custody exists when a suspect is either deprived of his or her freedom in any significant way or is in formal detainment such as an arrest. Custody for *Miranda* purposes is more broadly defined than as the traditional arrest. Custody may be subjective, from the point of view of the person being questioned, due to a coercive environment. Three factors need to be considered in the determination of whether a suspect is in a coercive environment:

1. **Nature of the interview.** Is the interview aggressive or informal?
2. **Atmosphere.** Generally the most coercive site is a police station, yet a police station inquiry is not automatically custodial.
3. **Freedom to leave.** At the time that the incriminating statement was made, was the suspect free to end the interview by leaving the place of the interrogation or by asking the interrogator to leave, as evidenced by whether the interview ended with the defendant's arrest?

✔ **Interrogation**

For a questioning or its functional equivalent by a police officer or his or her agent to be considered an interrogation it must be designed to produce testimonial evidence. The functional equivalent to interrogation includes any words or actions by the police that they should know are reasonably likely to elicit an incriminating response (*Rhode Island v. Innis,* 1980).

When Is a Waiver of *Miranda* Rights Valid?

A defendant may waive *Miranda* rights, provided the waiver is made voluntarily, knowingly, and intelligently. If the suspect waives his or her rights, he or she may refrain from answering questions at any time. The totality-of-the-circumstances test will help the court to determine whether the waiver of rights was valid. This means that all of the factors surrounding the waiver will be considered. Three measures of whether an individual has properly waived his or her right to remain silent are as follows:

- The waiver was made **voluntarily:** The government must prove that the waiver was not the result of coercion or other factors that adversely influenced the defendant's exercise of free will. Torture, threats, promises of leniency, or other inducements may affect the voluntariness of a waiver. If the person is intoxicated to the point that he or she cannot understand his or her constitutional rights, the waiver is not valid.
- The waiver was made **knowingly:** The government must prove that the defendant knew and understood his or her rights. Providing *Miranda* rights to a person who does not speak English, for example, cannot result in a knowing waiver of those rights. If the defendant is suffering from mental disability that renders him or her incapable of understanding his or her constitutional rights, a wavier may not be valid.
- The waiver was made **intelligently:** The government must establish that the defendant intelligently relinquished those rights and

FIGURE 10-1 *Miranda* rights must be waived voluntarily, knowingly, and intelligently for the waiver to be considered valid.

understood that he or she was agreeing to answer questions. This requires that the suspect be able to understand the consequences of not invoking the *Miranda* rights. This requirement does not suggest that the suspect is intelligent or have any particular IQ to make an intelligent waiver of his or her rights.

Voluntary Statements. Statements that are initiated by the defendant are not barred by the *Miranda* decision whether or not the person is in custody. The Court stated that "There is no requirement that police stop a person who enters a police station and states that he wishes to confess to a crime, or a person who calls the police to offer a confession or any other statement that he desires to make." Volunteered statements of any kind are not barred by the Fifth Amendment, and their admissibility is not affected by *Miranda*. If a defendant engages in conversation with a police officer and subsequently makes an incriminating statement, he or she does not need to be warned of his or her rights because there was no interrogation.

If a suspect invokes the right to silence and does not provide a statement to the police, he or she has the right to reinitiate a conversation. The waiver of *Miranda* rights may still be valid if it is clear that it was the suspect who reinitiated the conversation without inducement by the police.

Public Safety Exception. The Supreme Court did not intend for *Miranda* warnings to govern all police interactions with the members of the public. In fact, the vast majority of police and citizen communications do not fall under *Miranda*'s protective umbrella. In situations in which there is an immediate or impending danger to the public safety, called the public safety exception, the police may arrest a suspect without informing him or her of his or her constitutional rights and ask questions to elicit information in order to remove the threat to the public

> **BEEN THERE... DONE THAT! 10-1**
>
> This case involved a man accused of having burned a covered bridge. The case was investigated and a warrant was issued for his arrest. He fled the area, which is when I became involved. I located the perpetrator in Louisiana; he was arrested on the Massachusetts warrant. Arrangements were made for his rendition.
>
> He was picked up at the Louisiana jail, and a sergeant and I transported him back to Massachusetts. While he was in a holding cell at the airport I sat outside as his guard, reading a book. I lit up a cigarette, and the suspect asked for one. I gave him the cigarette without responding and continued to read my book. About half an hour later the same thing happened. He asked for a cigarette and I gave it to him. Saying nothing, I went back to reading my book. This time the man settled back in contentment and started to talk to get my attention. He said, "You know ma'am, I am not such a bad guy—now my brother-in-law, he is a bad guy! He cheats on his taxes and steals tools from the place he works. All I did was burn down an old bridge!"
>
> I looked over to the sergeant, who was sitting across the room. He said, "Trooper, give that man another cigarette." While the man was in custody there was no interrogation. His statement of admission was used in evidence against him in court.

(*New York v. Quarles,* 1984). Officers must then provide *Miranda* warnings once the threat is over.

Requiring a person in custody to stand or walk in a police lineup, to speak prescribed words, to model particular clothing, or to give samples of handwriting, fingerprints, or blood does not fall under self-incrimination within the meaning of the Fifth Amendment (*Schmerber v. California,* 1966). These do not fall under the Fifth Amendment because they are not testimonial in nature.

Right to Counsel under *Miranda*

The *Miranda* standard includes the right to have an attorney present during a custodial interrogation as part of its required procedural process. A suspect is entitled to the assistance of counsel during custodial interrogation even though the Constitution does not provide for such assistance (*Davis v. U.S.,* 2004). *Miranda* went further than previous case analysis of this right by requiring in cases of custodial interrogation that the suspect expressly be told of this right to an attorney and that he or she may voluntarily waive that right under the same standards as govern compelled testimony.

In *Edwards v. Arizona* (1981) the Court reiterated and clarified the concerns specified in the *Miranda* decision with respect to a suspect's right to counsel. The Court held that the waiver of an attorney during custodial interrogation must not only be voluntary, but knowing and intelligent as well. The bright-line *Edwards* rule clearly requires that once a suspect has invoked the right to an attorney per *Miranda*, all questioning must stop. It cannot be reinitiated by the police at any time in the future unless counsel has been made available to the suspect or the suspect initiates further conversation. The request for an attorney must be clearly stated, however, and not be ambiguous. In *Davis v. U.S.* (2004) the Court held that a statement by the suspect, "Maybe I should talk to a lawyer," was not a request for counsel under the requirements of *Miranda*.

If an attorney is made available at the request of the suspect and subsequently leaves, police may not resume interrogation when the attorney is no longer present (*Minnick v. Mississippi,* 1990). The police may not simply avoid the suspect's request for an attorney by changing the direction of questioning to a nonrelated offense (*Arizona v. Roberson,* 1988).

- **Bright Line:** If a suspect in custody and subjected to interrogation requests an attorney, ALL QUESTIONING MUST CEASE IMMEDIATELY!

SIXTH AMENDMENT CONSIDERATIONS

The Sixth Amendment to the U.S. Constitution protects the rights of persons accused in criminal prosecution. The remedy for violation of a suspect's Sixth Amendment right to counsel is that any evidence obtained through such a violation cannot be used in court. The Sixth Amendment to the U.S. Constitution states:

> *In all criminal prosecutions, the accused shall enjoy the right to a speedy and public trial, by an impartial jury of the State and district wherein the crime shall have been committed, which district shall have been previously ascertained by law, and to be informed of the nature and cause of the accusation; to be confronted with the witnesses against him; to have compulsory process for obtaining witnesses in his favor, and to have the Assistance of Counsel for his defense.*

The right to counsel under the Sixth Amendment prohibits law enforcement officers from deliberately eliciting incriminating information from a defendant in the absence of counsel after a formal (criminal) charge against the defendant has been filed (*Massiah v. U.S.,* 1964). The formal charge refers to the preliminary step in prosecution through a formal accusation of a named suspect (Garner, 2004). Examples of formal charging include an indictment by a grand jury and an arraignment.

The Sixth Amendment and the due process clause of the Fourteenth Amendment prohibit law enforcement officers from deliberately eliciting incriminating information from a defendant in the absence of counsel after a formal charge against the defendant has been filed, regardless of whether or not the defendant is in custody (*Rhode Island v. Innis,* 1980). This means that questioning cannot occur by a police officer in any location at any time, regardless of whether or not the person is in custody. The suspect cannot be questioned about the crime for which he or she was formally charged even if the police officer inadvertently has contact with the suspect. Examples of inadvertent contact are the police officer seeing the suspect on the street or arresting the suspect for an unrelated crime. However, the right to counsel under the Sixth Amendment is offense specific. It holds only for the crimes for which the suspect was formally charged; the suspect can be interrogated about unrelated crimes.

Once formal process has been initiated against a suspect, his or her Sixth Amendment right to counsel can be violated by less obvious forms of interrogation, such as bugging, eavesdropping, or contact by an informant (*Massiah v. U.S.*, 1964). No form of interrogation of the suspect is permitted, regardless of whether or not the suspect is aware of being questioned by an agent of the government.

FOURTEENTH AMENDMENT CONSIDERATIONS

The Fourteenth Amendment of the U.S. Constitution affirms the rights, privileges, and immunities of citizenship, including due process and equal protection. The Supreme Court has interpreted the Amendment as restricting the states from denying any citizen the rights that are guaranteed under the U.S. Constitution. Through the Fourteenth Amendment all constitutional rules apply equally to federal and state police action. Section 1, which contains the due process clause and equal protection provision, specifically restrict police action. Throughout this chapter the application of the Fourteenth Amendment to police interrogation procedures will be made evident.

> *Section 1. All persons born or naturalized in the United States and subject to the jurisdiction thereof, are citizens of the United States and of the State wherein they reside. No State shall make or enforce any law which shall abridge the privileges or immunities of citizens of the United States; nor shall any State deprive any person of life, liberty, or property, without due process of law; nor deny to any person within its jurisdiction the equal protection of the laws.*

The Exclusionary Rule

The **exclusionary rule** is a remedy to possible abuse by government officials of the restrictions set by the Constitution. It requires that evidence obtained by police in violation of the Fourteenth Amendment's due process clause, the Sixth Amendment's right to counsel provision, the Fifth Amendment's privilege against self-incrimination, or the Fourth Amendment's protection from illegal search and seizure be excluded from use in a trial against a defendant.

In *Weeks v. U.S.* (1914) the Court first stated that evidence secured through illegal search and seizure and in violation of the Fourth Amendment should be barred from use in federal prosecutions. It was not until

> **CASE IN POINT 10-2**
>
> *Case in Point: Mapp v. Ohio (1961)*
>
> Three Cleveland police officers went to the apartment of Miss Dollree Mapp looking for a person suspected in a bombing. Miss Mapp refused to allow them in without a search warrant. Three hours later, and after four more officers arrived, the police forcibly gained entry. Miss Mapp demanded to see the search warrant. A paper claimed to be a warrant was held up by one of the officers. She grabbed the "warrant" and stuffed it down her blouse. There was a struggle in which the officers recovered the piece of paper. They handcuffed her because she had resisted their official rescue of the paper. She was then forcibly taken upstairs to the second floor, where officers searched her bedroom, a child's bedroom, the living room, the kitchen, and a dinette. In the basement of the building a trunk was found, which was also searched. The obscene materials for possession of which she was ultimately convicted were discovered in the course of that search.
>
> At the trial no search warrant was produced by the prosecution, nor was the failure to produce one explained or accounted for. The State said that even if the search were made without authority, it was not prevented from using the unconstitutionally seized evidence at trial, citing *Wolf v. Colorado* (1949), in which the Court had held "that in a prosecution in a State court for a State crime the Fourteenth Amendment does not forbid the admission of evidence obtained by an unreasonable search and seizure (pg. 33)." The Supreme Court concluded that the Fourth Amendment DOES apply to the states, and evidence obtained in an unreasonable search could not be used against the suspect.
>
> **Importance**
>
> 1. *Mapp* was the first case in which the Supreme Court applied the exclusionary rule to the states.
> 2. This case is an example of the application of the exclusionary rule in a Fourth Amendment context.

1961 that the rule was made applicable to the states through the Fourteenth Amendment's due process clause (*Mapp v. Ohio*, 1961). There are several alternatives to invoking the exclusionary rule, such as undertaking criminal prosecutions against officers who violate a suspect's rights, but these are extremely rare. Internal department discipline and prosecutions for civil rights violations in federal courts are other available remedies. Practical considerations render these options fairly ineffective. As a result, the Court has emphasized the exclusionary rule as the most effective way to deter police misconduct.

Exclusion of evidence that is indirectly obtained when a person's rights are violated may also occur under the rule. Sometimes called derivative or secondary evidence, this is evidence resulting from an illegal search or illegal interrogation. The **fruit-of-the-poisonous-tree doctrine** holds that an illegal search or interrogation taints the evidence obtained as well as facts discovered by the processes initiated by the unlawful procedure and that that evidence must be suppressed (*Wong Sun v. U.S.,* 1963).

The due process clause of the Fourteenth Amendment protects against the admission into evidence of involuntary confessions. For example, a suspect may make a valid waiver of *Miranda* rights, but his or her statement may be in violation of the Fourteenth Amendment because of the police used coercive tactics to obtain it. Statements that are the product of coercion, either physical or psychological, cannot be used as evidence, not because of their unlikely truth, but because the methods used to extract them offend the underlying principle in the enforcement of criminal law: that ours is accusatorial and not an inquisitorial system (*Rogers v. Richmond,* 1961). Confessions are an important component in law enforcement, and any statement given freely and voluntarily without any compelling influences is admissible in evidence (*Rhode Island v. Innis,* 1980). A statement is inadmissible in court if the accused was coerced into making it. A statement is compelled if it is:

1. The product of either physical or psychological coercion
2. Extracted by any sort of threat or violence
3. The product of direct or implied promises
4. Made as the result of the exertion of any improper influence.

When Is a Confession Considered to Have Been Coerced? A statement may not be used in court if it was made in an environment that is so coercive as to support the conclusion that it was not freely and voluntarily given (*Colorado v. Connelly,* 1986). Typically, all of the factors surrounding the incident, or the totality of the circumstances, will determine whether physical or psychological pressures unduly influenced the accused to make a statement.

- Generally a promise of leniency will nullify a confession; certain kinds of promises are acceptable, however.
- In *United States v. Guerrero* (1988) the U.S. Court of Appeals ruled that "it is well settled that police may use small deceptions while interrogating witnesses."
- In *United States v. Mendoza-Cecelia* (1992) the U.S. Court of Appeals ruled that "Isolated incidents of deception . . . are normally insufficient to preclude free choice," and acknowledged "that police may use some psychological tactics in interrogating a suspect."
- Threats to arrest members of a suspect's family may cause a confession to be considered involuntary (*Rogers, v. Richmond,* 1961).

The following factors are among those that the court will look at in determining if an interrogation process was coercive:

Age of the Suspect. The circumstances surrounding statements from juveniles are more carefully scrutinized because they are more susceptible than adults to coercive forces or intimidation. Courts demand that police officers use caution when questioning juveniles to make sure that they do not confess out of fear. The questioning by several officers at the same time or the absence of a parent may be coercive if the juvenile is young.

Experience of the Suspect. A child's or adult's history of contact with the police and the criminal justice system may be a significant factor is determining whether his or her statements were voluntary. A person with a history of criminal activity and familiarity with police practice is less likely to feel threatened to the point of being coerced into speaking.

Intelligence or Mental Illness. Someone with a low IQ or mental illness may be overly suggestible and subject to intimidation. Persons having mental illness or low intelligence need to be questioned in the same noncoercive atmosphere as a juvenile. Extra care must be taken to assure that the person understands the situation in addition to his or her rights per *Miranda*. A lower educational level of the suspect should alert the police officer to the possibility that there is a greater susceptibility to coercion.

Alcohol or Drug Intoxication. Although intoxication alone is not enough to negate an otherwise voluntary act, the fact that a statement is given while a suspect is under the influence of alcohol or drugs is relevant to an evaluation of its voluntariness. If a suspect is unduly susceptible to the coercive forces of police questioning due to intoxication, this may impact the voluntariness of any statement he or she gives.

Physical Condition of the Suspect. An injured or ill suspect or someone who has had little sleep prior to interrogation may be more susceptible to coercive forces.

Length of the Interrogation. The federal courts have stated a preference that a person under arrest be brought to court for arraignment "without unnecessary delay" for a confession to be admissible (*McNabb v. U.S.*, 1943). This requirement, aimed at addressing incommunicado interrogation and coerced confessions, is known as the McNabb-Mallory doctrine. The Court has never imposed the rule on the states, nor has it set a specific time after which a confession is invalid. Congress set a 6-hour period for interrogation following arrest before the suspect must be presented to court (Omnibus Crime Control and Safe Streets Act, 1968). Some states have adopted the rule voluntarily. Under the "Rosario rule," Massachusetts requires that a defendant who has been arrested be brought before a court if it is then in session, and if it is not, at its next session (*Commonwealth v. Rosario*, 1996).

The exclusionary rule has been controversial and criticized since it was established. Numerous decisions have narrowed its application, most notably the "good faith exception." In 1984 the Court held that evidence secured by police officers who rely on a warrant should not be excluded even if the warrant is later found to be defective (*United States v. Leon*, 1984).

Fourth Amendment Considerations

The Fourth Amendment of the U.S. Constitution protects against unreasonable searches and seizures. It states:

The right of the people to be secure in their persons, houses, papers, and effects, against unreasonable searches and seizures, shall not be violated, and no warrants shall issue, but upon probable cause, supported by oath or affirmation, and particularly describing the place to be searched, and the persons or things to be seized.

Since the application of the exclusionary rule to the states, a confession, statement, or admission that is made by a person who is illegally in custody may be excluded as evidence obtained as a result of an unlawful seizure. The application of the Fourth Amendment as a protection against arbitrary arrests has become established law (*Steagald v. U.S.*, 1981). Under the Fourth Amendment a "seizure" does not necessarily mean a formal arrest in order to bring the warrant requirement to bear. An objective justification must validate all seizures of a person, including those that only involve a brief detention.

To protect statements and physical evidence that may be acquired from a suspect, attention must be given to the legality of the detention or arrest prior to the interrogation. Under the Fourth Amendment, a seizure is made reasonable by the application for a warrant that is based on probable cause. Probable cause itself may be sufficient to justify detention or arrest in some situations.

The criminal justice process typically begins when a person is placed under arrest. An arrest occurs when a person is taken into police custody and deprived of his or her liberty by legal authority and is no longer free to leave. An arrest may occur when a police officer states that someone is under arrest. The suspect does not have to be placed in handcuffs or restraints, nor do the words need to be stated for an arrest to have been made. When a person submits to the authority of the police either voluntarily or involuntarily, he or she is under arrest. Police have the **power to arrest** in the following circumstances:

- **When the police officer sees someone commit a crime.** For example, if a police officer is patrolling and sees a man hit another man outside of a bar. The police officer may stop the cruiser and arrest the man for having committed an assault and battery against the other.
- **When an arrest warrant has been issued.** The arrest warrant contains information on the crime, the identity of the person to be arrested, a location where the person might be found, and the command that the police officer make that arrest.
- **When a police officer has a reasonable belief, based on facts and circumstances, that a person has committed or is about to commit a crime.** This is an arrest based on probable cause without a warrant. For example, if a police officer receives a radio call that a store has just been robbed along with the description of the suspect and the officer sees a person matching that description running away from the area, he or she can make an arrest.

CASE IN POINT 10-3

Case in Point: Carroll v. U.S. (1925)

Federal prohibition agents developed information that the Carroll brothers were regularly transporting whiskey from Detroit to Grand Rapids, Michigan, a distance of 152 miles. The boys outran the law once, and they could not be caught in the act, although they had once agreed to sell three cases of whiskey to an undercover agent. On December 15, 1921, agents saw their Fleet Oldsmobile Roadster and gave chase. The vehicle was stopped, and the agents did not see any contraband in the car. Without consent or a warrant, one agent concluded that the upholstery was harder than normal and cut open the leather seat. The agents removed 69 quarts of illegal gin and whiskey that had been hidden. George Carroll handed the agent several 10 dollar bills and told him to take the liquor and give them one more chance. The defense later said that the bribe offer was a misunderstanding.

Importance

1. The Supreme Court held that a warrantless search of an automobile stopped by police officers who had probable cause to believe the vehicle contained contraband was not unreasonable under the Fourth Amendment. This became known as the "automobile exception," by which the warrant requirement of the Fourth Amendment did not apply to searches of an automobile.
2. The Supreme Court defined probable cause as existing where the facts and circumstances within the officers' knowledge and of which they had reasonably trustworthy information are sufficient in themselves to warrant a person of reasonable caution in the belief that an offense has been or is being committed.

Probable Cause

The court has acknowledged that an exact definition of **probable cause** is difficult because it depends on the totality of the circumstances (*Brinegar v. U.S.*, 1949). The courts determine whether probable cause to arrest a person existed by looking at the events leading up to the arrest or detention. However, probable cause means more than mere suspicion (*Carroll v. U.S.*, 1925).

The court will look at the totality of the circumstances to determine whether the police officer had probable cause to make an arrest. Information that was obtained unlawfully, such as statements from an illegal interrogation, cannot be used to establish probable cause for an arrest. An arrest is valid if the police officer had probable cause to make the arrest at that time, even if the person turns out to be innocent. In order to detain or pick up and take a suspect to the police station for interrogation, police must have probable cause to make an arrest or a warrant (*Kaupp v. Texas*, 2003). A violation of the Fourth and Fourteenth Amendments cannot be remedied by *Miranda* warnings alone (*Taylor v. Alabama*, 1982). Without probable cause for an arrest, a suspect can be requested) to come for questioning with a full understanding that this is voluntary.

> **CASE IN POINT 10-4**
>
> Robert Kaupp was a 17-year-old man suspected of murder. The case turned on the Fourth Amendment rule that a confession "obtained by exploitation of an illegal arrest" may not be used against a criminal defendant (*Brown v. Illinois,* 1975). After a 14-year-old girl disappeared in January 1999, the Harris County Sheriff's Department learned she that had had a sexual relationship with her 19-year-old half-brother, who had been in the company of Robert Kaupp on the day of the girl's disappearance. On January 26, deputy sheriffs questioned the brother and Kaupp at headquarters; Kaupp was cooperative and was permitted to leave, but the brother failed a polygraph examination (his third such failure). Eventually he confessed that he had fatally stabbed his half-sister and placed her body in a drainage ditch. He implicated Kaupp in the crime. Detectives immediately tried but failed to obtain a warrant to question Kaupp due to a lack of probable cause.
>
> The police came to his home at 3:00 AM and told him they had to talk. He responded, "okay." Kaupp was handcuffed and brought to the police station in his underwear and without shoes. Although he was given his rights per *Miranda* prior to an interrogation, the Supreme Court held that the initial detainment was paramount to an arrest without probable cause, causing the confession to be suppressed. His response of "okay" was determined by the Court to be nothing more than submission to lawful authority in a situation in which he had no choice but to go with the police officers.
>
> The seizure of a person within the meaning of the Fourth and Fourteenth Amendments occurs when, "taking into account all of the circumstances surrounding the encounter, the police conduct would 'have communicated to a reasonable person that he was not at liberty to ignore the police presence and go about his business'" (*Florida v. Bostick,* 1991, (quoting *Michigan v. Chesternut,* 1988).

Probable cause may be based on personal observations of the officer and through information that is provided from another source:

- **Personal observations.** If the police officer is legally at the location where he or she observes a criminal act, no further probable cause is needed to make an arrest. This means that the officer cannot make a trespass against the person and use the information to furnish probable cause. For example, a police officer may not go onto someone's property and look through the window to gain information to be used as probable cause.

    A suspect's confession or admission that is obtained legally may be used to establish probable cause.
- **Information provided by others.** Police officers may use information that is provided by victims, witnesses, other police officers, and informants to establish probable cause to make an arrest. The reliability of the information must be determined prior to its use. When other police officers provide information, it is generally considered reliable and may be used as the basis for probable cause to

The Interrogation Process and the Law

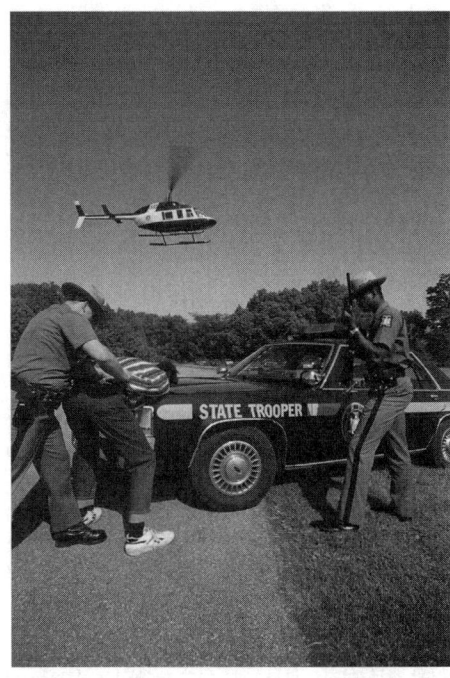

FIGURE 10-2 A valid arrest protects future statements that may be made by the suspect.

arrest. For a full discussion on determining the reliability of information from other sources, refer to Chapter 1.

- **Prior criminal record, furtive conduct, evasive answers, or the nature of the area.**

Although these cannot stand alone in establishing probable cause, they are factors that may be considered in determining whether probable cause exists. For example, prior criminal conduct and furtive conduct are factors when the arresting officer has information that a suspect has committed similar crimes in the past to the one that is under investigation and the defendant attempts to flee when approached by the police officer. During questioning, a police officer may draw reasonable inferences from the suspect's answers and demeanor.

Entry into a Dwelling Unique challenges to the police officer exist for entry into a dwelling in order to make an arrest. The Fourth Amendment sometimes forbids an entry into a dwelling to effect an arrest without a warrant, regardless of exigent circumstances or how likely it is that evidence may be lost or destroyed. Examples where entry is prohibited include entry into a home without a warrant in pursuit of a drunk driver, an underage driver, to pursue fleeing misdemeanants, or to enforce traffic violations. Generally the courts frown on entering a home without a warrant to arrest a minor or a person on a misdemeanor charge, even when evidence might be destroyed or exigent circumstances exist. Entering the home to prevent injury may be considered exigent circumstances. The following factors may contribute to a finding of exigent circumstances (*Commonwealth v. Forde,* 1975):

- The crime was violent and the suspect is believed to be armed and dangerous
- There is probable cause to believe that a felony has been committed and that the suspect is in the dwelling
- There is a likelihood that the suspect will escape if not immediately apprehended
- There is a reasonable basis for believing that the delay necessitated by seeking a warrant would subject the officers or others to physical harm

Probable cause is always a necessary component to making an arrest in a person's home. To arrest a suspect in his or her home in the absence of consent or exigent circumstances, an arrest warrant or search warrant is sufficient, depending on the circumstances.

To arrest a person believed to be in the dwelling of a third party in the absence of exigent circumstances, both an arrest warrant and a search warrant must be obtained (*Steagald v. U.S.,* 1981). If the owner of the home gives the police officer consent to enter the dwelling, than only the arrest warrant is required.

Entry into a third party's house to affect an arrest without a search warrant may be legal under exigent circumstances, including hot pursuit. Hot pursuit is perhaps the best-known example of an exigent circumstance that might justify entry into a dwelling to make an arrest without a warrant. Although police officers may justify entry into a dwelling for the purposes of making an arrest, if exigent circumstances can be foreseen and the officers have time to obtain a warrant, then one should be obtained. A "warm pursuit," such as following distinctive footprints in the snow or following an evidence trail, may be acceptable if the crime is exceptionally serious (*People v. Morrow,* 1982).

Conclusions

This chapter outlined some of the legal restrictions on questioning suspects. The primary source limiting police action and providing rights to the accused is the Constitution. The Court's interpretation of the Constitution has resulted in numerous procedural rules and requirements that define the rights of citizens against actions by government agents, such as police officers or individuals working at their request. It does not protect the rights of citizens from actions taken by other citizens. Because the Constitution is the supreme law of the land, the individual state governments cannot infringe on these rights.

The Fourth, Fifth, and Sixth Amendments of the Constitution provide different protections, although they sometimes appear to overlap. The right to an attorney under the Fifth Amendment *Miranda* rule applies to consultation prior to the interrogation stage and is concerned with police custody of the person. This is different than the Sixth Amendment right, which applies at the time of any formal court proceeding. The Fourteenth Amendment comes into play for all of these requirements when the consideration is one of due process or fundamental fairness.

QUESTIONS FOR REVIEW

Short-Answer Questions

1. What rights of the accused does the Fifth Amendment protect?
2. What rights of the accused does the Sixth Amendment protect?
3. Is the exclusionary rule written in the U.S. Constitution? If not, how did it come to be?
4. Describe the circumstances leading to *Mapp v. Ohio*. What significance does this case have regarding the exclusionary rule?
5. Give an example of circumstances in which the good faith doctrine would apply.
6. Explain a police officer's "right of arrest." Who can be arrested? Where, when, and why?
7. What are exigent circumstances? When do they allow seizures normally outside the parameters of the Fourth Amendment?
8. *Miranda* warnings must be issued when custody and interrogation occur simultaneously. For purposes of the *Miranda* ruling, what constitutes custody? What constitutes interrogation?
9. Discuss the differences in the right to counsel under the Fifth Amendment and the right to counsel under the Sixth Amendment.
10. What rights of the accused does the Fifth Amendment protect? The Sixth Amendment?

Fill-in Questions

1. The _____ provides that those who execute the law must rely on the application of known principles or laws, and those principles must be applied _____ to all citizens.
2. _____, _____, and _____ protect citizens from actions of government officials and their agents and not from other citizens.
3. The exclusionary rule is a remedy that was _____ to limit the power and authority of government officials and to assist in the enforcement of the _____.
4. The court has acknowledged that an exact definition of _____ is difficult to express because it depends on the _____.
5. Police officers may be justified in making a(n) _____ of a person based on probable cause that he or she has committed a felony, a misdemeanor that amounts to a breach of the peace in the presence

of the officer, or in circumstances in which the power to do so is specifically given to police officers _____.

6. The Fifth Amendment of the Constitution contains many protections; of concern in the area of interrogation is that it protects the right against _____ and _____.

7. A defendant may waive *Miranda* rights, provided the waiver is made _____, _____ and _____.

8. The circumstances surrounding the statements from _____ are more carefully scrutinized because they are more susceptible than adults to _____ or _____.

9. The _____ under the Sixth Amendment and the _____ of the Fourteenth Amendment prohibit law enforcement officers from deliberately eliciting incriminating information from a defendant in the absence of counsel after a formal charge against the defendant has been filed, regardless of whether or not the defendant is in custody.

10. The right to an attorney under the Fifth Amendment *Miranda* rule attaches the right to consultation _____ and is concerned with _____ _____ of the person.

Exercises

1. **You be the judge!** Using the cases in this chapter, write the opinion for the court relative to the admissibility of the following confession. Cite your cases and explain your reasoning as if this were a real case.

   John and Jimmy Jones were suspected of a robbery in a liquor store on Fifth Avenue during which the owner was shot and killed. They were brought into the police station for questioning and placed in separate rooms. Officer Smith sat in the room with John and said nothing to him. After 15 minutes Officer Fitzpatrick opened the door to the interrogation room and said to Officer Smith, "Jimmy told me everything," which was actually a lie, and then left. Officer Smith turned to Jimmy and said, "We don't need anything from you now. Talk to me if you want because we got the goods on you. Sounds like your brother put the whole thing on you." John gave a full confession. A motion to suppress was brought in court by his attorney.

2. **You be the judge!** Using the cases in this chapter, write the opinion for the court relative to the admissibility of the following confession. Cite your cases and explain your reasoning as if this were a real case.

   Cheryl Esposito was arrested for the murder of her boyfriend, Jeffrey Tang. Officer Book advised of her rights per *Miranda*, which she waived. During the interrogation Cheryl would not tell who had disposed of the body or why Jeffrey had been killed. Officer Book told her that Cheryl's son was seen leaving the house on the night of the murder (a lie) and that he would be arrested for the murder if Cheryl did not talk. Cheryl gave a full confession implicating her new lover, Bruce.

REFERENCES

Arizona v. Roberson, 486 U.S. 675 (1988).
Bram v. United States, 168 U.S. 532 (1897).
Brinegar v. U.S., 338 U.S. 160 (1949).
Brown v. Illinois, 422 U.S. 590, 603 (1975).
Brown v. Mississipi, 297 U.S. 278 (1937).
Carroll v. U.S., 267 U.S. 132 (1925).
Colombe v. Connecticut, 367 U.S. 568 (1961).
Colorado v. Connelly, 479 U.S. 157 (1986).
Commonwealth v. Forde, 367 Mass. 798 (1975).
Commonwealth v. Rosario, 422 Mass. 48 (1996).
Davis v. U.S., 114 S.Ct. 2350 (2004).
Doe v. United States, 487 U.S. 201 (1988).
Edwards v. Arizona, 451 U.S. 477 (1981).
Florida v. Bostick, 501 U.S. 429, 437 (1991).
Garner, B. (2004). *Black's law dictionary* (8th ed.). St. Paul, MN: West Publishing.
Kaupp v. Texas, 538 U.S. 626 (2003).
Mapp v. Ohio, 367 U.S. 643 (1961).
Massiah v. U.S., 377 U.S. 201 (1964).
McNabb v. U.S., 318 U.S. 332 (1943).
Michigan v. Chesternut, 486 U.S. 567, 569 (1988).
Minnick v. Mississippi, 498 U.S. 146 (1990).
Miranda v. Arizona, 384 U.S. 436 (1966).
New York v. Quarles, 467 U.S. 649 (1984).
Omnibus Crime Control and Safe Streets Act (1968). 82 Stat. 210, 18 U.S.C. Sec. 3501(c).
People v. Fox, 319 Ill. 606 (1925).
People v. Morrow, 104 Ill. App. 3d 995 (1982).
Rhode Island v. Innis, 446 U.S. 291 (1980).
Rogers v. Richmond, 365 U.S. 534 (1961).
Schmerber v. California, 384 U.S. 757 (1966).
Steagald v. U.S., 451 U.S. 204 (1981).
Taylor v. Alabama, 457 U.S. 587 (1982).
United States v. Guerrero, 847 F.2d 1363 (1988).
United States v. Leon, 468 U.S. 897 (1984).
United States v. Mendoza-Cecelia, 963 F.2d 1467 (1992).
Weeks v. U.S., 232 U.S. 383 (1914).
Wolf v. Colorado, 338 U.S. 25 (1949).
Wong Sun v. U.S., 371 U.S. 471 (1963).

CHAPTER 11

Confessions

Key Terms

Interrogation	Miscarriage of justice
Question-first technique	Excited utterance
Suspect paranoia	Subtle compulsion
False confession	Frisk

Chapter Objectives

After completing this chapter, you should be able to:

- Describe the question-first technique and why it is unlawful
- Define *interrogation* according to the Supreme Court
- State the three conditions that must be met for a confession to be considered legally valid
- Describe the qualities of an interrogator
- State why suspects might confess to the police
- Describe the three types of police officer as described by R. C. Schaefer
- List the categories of interview that are not considered interrogation
- Describe the three categories of false confessions
- Explain the problems in interrogation and how to overcome them
- List reasons why miscarriages of justice occur

Introduction

The focus of this chapter is on police and military interrogation and myths associated with the practice. There are two distinct perspectives concerning interrogations. One view is that false confessions constitute a major problem, despite *Miranda* reforms intended to curtail coercive police interrogation practices. The other view is that interrogation has become a lost art since *Miranda*. Fewer interrogations are attempted, crimes remain unsolved, and the innocent are left vulnerable.

A balancing act exists between providing protections to the guilty and jeopardizing the safety of the innocent. The police have become compliant with the *Miranda* rules. Studies on the efficacy of interrogation suggest that interrogations leading to confessions are common and that police officers are good at it. This is a logical but misleading conclusion because the majority of these studies do not take into account those cases in which the police do not attempt to elicit confessions.

This chapter provides some case-specific practices for assessing guilt as part of an interrogation.

WHAT IS AN INTERROGATION?

An interrogation is a process conducted by law enforcement officers and military personnel. Laws on interrogation do not protect citizens from a process initiated by nongovernment civilians. As stated in Chapter 1, the U. S. Supreme Court has defined an **interrogation** as a questioning initiated by law enforcement officers after a person has been taken into custody or otherwise deprived of his or her freedom of action in any significant way (*Miranda v. Arizona,* 1966). Interest in interrogation practices is widespread, and because practices that government officials use during interrogations are scrutinized by the public, it is useful to study current controversies surrounding the process.

Since *Miranda,* the Court has revisited that opinion to prevent a too narrow interpretation of the case and to address the "interrogation environment." Concern has centered on police practices that would subjugate the individual to the will of the examiner (*Rhode Island v. Innis,* 1980). It is clear therefore that the special procedural safeguards outlined in *Miranda* are required not only when a suspect is taken into custody, but also when a suspect in custody is subjected to interrogation. Interrogation, as conceptualized in *Miranda,* must reflect a measure of compulsion above and beyond that inherent in custody itself (*Rhode Island v. Innis,* 1980). The *Miranda* safeguards come into play whenever a person in custody is subjected to either explicit questioning or its functional equivalent. That is, the term "interrogation" under *Miranda* refers not only to explicit questioning, but also to any words or actions on the part of the police (other than those normally attendant to arrest and custody) that the police should know are reasonably likely to elicit an incriminating response from the suspect.

For an interrogation to be conducted lawfully, the following three conditions must be met:

1. The opportunity to interrogate a suspect must be lawfully obtained
2. There must be an absence of force, threat of force, or promise of leniency
3. There must be compliance with requirements for warnings of constitutional rights to a custodial suspect

Compliance with the warnings per *Miranda* must be taken seriously. A recent Supreme Court decision strongly denounced the **question-first techniques** sometimes used by police to avoid the requirements of providing *Miranda* warnings. The *question-first* technique is a deliberate attempt by a police officer to avoid providing a suspect with his or her rights per *Miranda*. It occurs when the suspect is interrogated first, a short period of time is allowed to elapse, and then the warnings are given and the suspect re-interrogated. The second interrogation is made to document the previous confession made without legal warnings.

> **CASE IN POINT 11-1**
>
> *Case in Point: Missouri v. Seibert (2004)*
>
> Patrice Seibert's 12-year-old son, Jonathan, had cerebral palsy, and when he died in his sleep, she feared charges of neglect because of bedsores on his body. In her presence, two of her teenage sons and two of their friends devised a plan to conceal the facts surrounding Jonathan's death by setting fire to the family's mobile home, in which they planned to leave Donald Rector, a mentally ill teenager living with the family, to avoid any appearance that Jonathan had been unattended. Seibert's son, Darian, and a friend set the fire, and Donald died.
>
> When a police officer questioned Seibert about Rector's death, the officer intentionally did not read Seibert her *Miranda* rights, hoping to get a confession. During the interrogation, Seibert admitted that she knew that Rector was supposed to die in the fire. After this admission, Seibert was given a 20-minute break from the interrogation; when it resumed, the officer advised Seibert of her *Miranda* rights, which she waived. Seibert then repeated statements she had made prior to receiving a *Miranda* warning. Patrice Seibert was convicted of second-degree murder and sentenced to life in prison for her role in the death of Donald Rector. This midstream reading of warnings after interrogation and unwarned confession did not effectively comply with *Miranda's* constitutional requirement. The U.S. Supreme Court held that this interrogation technique rendered both confessions inadmissible.
>
> **Importance**
>
> 1. In *Seibert* the Court said that the police cannot purposefully avoid providing warnings per *Miranda* to get a confession. In some cases, questioning of a suspect may be the equivalent of custody for the purposes of *Miranda* warnings. Obtaining a confession without the warnings and then giving the warnings a short time later is not acceptable.

SINCE *MIRANDA*

Miranda has led to professionalization of interrogation practices and contributed to the declining use of coercion in police practices (Leo, 1966a). Early studies on the impact of the *Miranda* warnings were mixed: A Yale study concluded that the warnings were largely ignored by police and wholly ineffective; some studies concluded that its application did not decrease the percentage of felony complaints; others claimed a large decrease in felony cases that reached the grand jury following *Miranda*. Leo (1996a) summed up the literature on *Miranda* up to 1996 with five important findings:

1. After an initial adjustment period, police began to comply regularly with the letter of the *Miranda* requirements
2. Suspects frequently waived their constitutional rights and chose to speak to detectives
3. Once the waiver was obtained, police interrogation techniques did not change as a result of *Miranda*

4. Suspects continued to provide detectives with confessions and incriminating statements, although in some instances at a lower rate than prior to *Miranda*
5. The clearance and conviction rate did not appear to be significantly affected by *Miranda*, although in some cases it too had dropped

The evidence suggests that fewer police officers have attempted to interrogate since *Miranda*. Early impact studies indicated that from 1966 to 1969, detectives chose to interrogate fewer suspects (Leo, 1996a). Confessions lost due to procedural handcuffing is a major concern (Cassell, 1999), and clearance rates in some cities dropped significantly post *Miranda* (Leo, 1996a). In almost half of felony cases there may be no attempt by police officers to gain a confession or gather intelligence information (Colaprete, 2002), although police officers are very successful at interrogation when they attempt it (Thomas, 2004).

Whether police officers follow up with an interrogation or not, they do comply with the mandate to provide warnings to suspects. A recent study found that the police recite *Miranda* warnings to suspects most of the time, with a compliance rate of 95 percent (Thomas, 2004). In only 6 percent of cases did defendants complain that they did not receive their rights.

Who Is Likely to Conduct Interrogations?

As stated earlier, research indicates that police officers are typically successful when they attempt to interrogate a suspect. The problem is that police officers do not attempt an interrogation in almost half of felony

---

BEEN THERE . . . DONE THAT!   11-1

Rarely will a confession be challenged in court if the *Miranda* warnings were given. Determining whether the warnings were given properly is an objective test. Compliance without the use of tricks to overcome a suspect's reluctance to waive his or her rights is sufficient to meet the challenge. If anything, police officers are overly compliant with giving these warnings. The Court in *Miranda* only required that the suspect be provided the warnings once, whereas in many cases a suspect receives them multiple times.

The second aspect of determining whether a person gave a voluntary statement occurs after the waiving of rights. Based on the actions of the police officer during the confession, this test is subjective and depends on many factors. In one case in which an attorney challenged the admissibility of a confession that I had obtained, he based it on my statement "I am here to help you," which I repeated a few times during the confession. Do not take this kind of challenge personally. It is in an alleged perpetrator's best interests to have a confession suppressed, and a defense attorney is only doing his or her job by trying to do this. In this case the confession was so damning that the suspect faced heavy prison time if it was allowed. The challenge was not successful, however.

It is not what you say, but how you say it that matters in these situations. If I had that one to do over, I would have suggested that I was there "To help you help yourself." Think before you speak.

cases. What can explain the large disparity between those highly successful interrogations and the failure to try? No empirical studies have examined the characteristics of a successful interrogator.

A few studies have examined the impact of the police officer's gender during an interview. Policing continues to be a profession dominated by white men. Black men make up a mere 11.8 percent of the nation's policing workforce (Schmalleger, 2004), and women hold approximately 12.7 percent of sworn policing positions in the United States (National Center For Women and Policing, 2002). Research indicates that the biases and perceptions of the interviewee have a greater impact than the gender of the interviewer (Gelinas, 2005). Neither the race nor the gender of the officer has been found to have an impact on the outcome of police–citizen encounters (The Committee on Law and Justice, 2004).

Few experts on interrogation address the issue of the interrogator's characteristics. The ability to use persuasive tactics is often mentioned, particularly dealing with a suspect who is unwilling to provide a statement (Rabon, 1992). The police interrogator must possess a high degree of emotional control and feel comfortable using persuasive tactics that may be morally offensive to some (Inbau et al., 2001).

Others have sought to understand why interrogations are avoided. Some officers fear the tedious task of memorizing an endless set of rules needed to conduct lawful interrogations (Rutledge, 1994). Another suggestion is that few agencies place sufficient emphasis on the development of the needed skills (Hess, 1997). The use of "Gestapo tactics" and rigid methods is one reason interrogations fail (Yeschke, 2003). Ego can be a undermining influence that causes narrow-mindedness on the part of the interrogator (Holmes, 2002).

More to the point, the skills required for successful interrogation require knowledge in the areas of human behavior, psychology, persuasive communication, and the law (Buckley & Jayne, 2005). Officers who are most confident in conducting interrogations possess the skills and knowledge to follow through with the difficult task of interrogating. It takes knowledge and skill to conduct a lawful interrogation.

FIGURE 11-1 The more confident the police officer is about his or her legal knowledge, the more likely they are to routinely conduct interrogations.

Individuals who are most confident in their knowledge of the law are more willing to conduct interrogations. The educated police officer follows up his or her knowledge of the law with information that is beneficial for successfully completing the task. This is not because legalistic officers are predisposed to enforce the law at any cost, but because educated police officers have greater initiative, a wiser use of discretion, enhanced communications with the public, more effective job performance, fewer citizen complaints, and a heightened sensitivity to racial and ethnic issues (Carter, Sapp, & Stephens, 1989). Higher education was significantly correlated with better performance of police cadets (Aamodt & Flink, 2001).

Experts have long categorized police officers and their professional performance according to their legal expertise. In his seminal research on police typology, R. C. Schaefer suggested that there are three types of police officers based on their knowledge of the legal applicability of *Miranda*: law enforcers, servicers, and law enforcers/servicers (Schaefer, 1971).

- **Law enforcers** score highest in their knowledge of the legal applicability of *Miranda*. These officers feel that their role is one of crime control and are most aware of the procedural guarantees that should be extended.
- **Servicers** perceive their role in the criminal justice system as primarily aiding the public in any way possible. These officers score lowest in their knowledge of the legal applicability of *Miranda*.
- **Law enforcers/servicers** are somewhat familiar with the law, and they will interrogate suspects when department policy requires and in specific cases in which they feel comfortable.

Who Is Likely to Waive Rights per *Miranda*?

Initially four of five suspects given rights per *Miranda* waive them and submit to questioning; some change their mind. Ultimately one fourth of all suspects interrogated invoke one or more rights and refuse to talk (Leo & White, 1999). Police officers know from experience that former felons routinely refuse to waive their rights per *Miranda*. These individuals are more seasoned criminals who have been exposed to the criminal justice system. Leo (1996a) confirmed what police officers take for granted: although 78% of suspects waive their rights per *Miranda*, compared to a suspect with no prior record, a suspect with a prior felony record is four times as likely to invoke his or her *Miranda* rights. A person with a misdemeanor record is three times more likely to refuse to talk with police (Leo, 1996a).

The figures are much lower in a study conducted in the Rochester, New York, Police Department that identified the rates of voluntary confessions, attempts to gain voluntary confessions, and missed opportunities (no attempt to gain confessions) (Colaprete, 2002). Voluntary confessions are obtained in about 37 percent of all felony arrests, whereas no attempt was made to gain a confession or gather intelligence information in 46.22 percent of felony cases.

In a study attempting to replicate the interrogation process, the authors found that 58 percent of all suspects waive their rights, corroborating the tendency of suspects in the police station (Kassin & Gudjonsson, 2004). Thomas (2004) found that suspects waived *Miranda* 68 percent of the time. More than 10 times as many suspects waive *Miranda* as elect not to answer questions. In cases in which a confession was elicited, between 42 and 70 percent of suspects waived their rights per *Miranda* and gave statements or confessions (Colaprete, 2002; Kassin & Gudjonsson, 2004).

Why Do People Waive Their Rights?

One reason that people waive their rights is that police use effective techniques designed to obtain waivers (Kassin & Norwick, 2004). Because obtaining a truthful confession from a perpetrator is the goal, the emphasis is on obtaining a voluntary waiver. Establishing rapport with the suspect, offering sympathy and an ally, and minimizing the process as a mere formality are some of the successful approaches that police use when offering a suspect his or her rights per *Miranda* (Leo, 1996b).

A second reason for why persons waive their rights per *Miranda* is simply that people come into the interrogation room with different personalities and experiences (Kassin & Norwick, 2004). As noted earlier, suspects with prior felony records are least likely to waive their rights per *Miranda* and provide a confession to interrogators. Suspects with prior records are at greater risk in the criminal justice system because of heightened penalties for second and subsequent offenders as well as mandatory sentencing for those convicted of multiple felonies.

BEEN THERE . . . DONE THAT! 11-2

There are two things that an interrogator can do to give validity to the voluntariness of a confession. First, when the statement is being typed, make an obvious error on it, something that the perpetrator will notice. Examples are the name of his or her mother or child or time of day. Second, allow the suspect to express his or her feelings in his or her own handwriting.

This is done simply by asking the perpetrator to read the statement after it has been typed and to make corrections. If he or she does not read it carefully and misses the error, call his or her attention to it and ask whether the information is correct. Once it is noticed, ask the suspect to make the correction and initial the change. This demonstrates to others who are trying to determine whether the confession was forced that you DID give the suspect the opportunity to read it and object to anything that is contained in it. Next, ask how the suspect feels, and suggest that they write that at the bottom of the page. Most people will simply write, "I'm sorry" or "I didn't mean to do it." Others may write more. It is the only opportunity that the interrogator has to document the feelings of the perpetrator *at the time of the interrogation*, which may be disputed at a later time. I believe that doing this is why none of the confessions that I took were ever suppressed in court. It is difficult to maintain that one was forced when the evidence says otherwise.

Why Do Suspects Confess?

A suspect may confess because of suspect paranoia (Tousignant, 1991). **Suspect paranoia** is the motivation for a suspect to provide a statement because he or she thinks the police may have information that implicates him or her. Because the suspect is not sure of exactly what information investigators have, he or she may also attempt to give false information to lead investigators in another direction. The first thought is to escape detection and therefore to find out what the police officers know.

Kassin and Gudjonsson (2004) offered a number of explanations from the psychological perspective. People may confess to overcome feelings of guilt and remorse, as well as out of fear of retaliation or losing love. A suspect may become entangled in the decision on whether to speak or invoke the rights to silence and to have an attorney, and make those decisions based on their perceived probability of the long and short-term consequences.

The reasons why suspects confess to crimes are varied and often a combination of factors including the characteristics, of the case, the behavior of the police, and the personality and experiences of the suspect (Gudjonsson, 2003). To overcome the obstacles to obtaining confessions, consider the things that make it difficult for people to confess. Gudjonsson (2003) suggested five major inhibiting factors:

1. Fear of legal sanctions. This includes the fear of punishment and the consequences of having a criminal record.
2. Concern about reputation. The higher a person's standing in the community, the more likely it is that that person will perceive that he or she has something to lose. This may be true for relatively minor crimes.
3. Not wanting to admit the truth to oneself. An offender may push the memory out of conscious awareness to protect his or her psychological well-being and self-esteem.
4. Not wanting one's family and friends to know about the crime. Fear of being rejected by family and friends may inhibit the willingness to confess.
5. Fear of retaliation. An unwillingness to implicate others due to the fear of retaliation may be stronger than the fear of sanctions if one is convicted.

Does a Waiver Affect the Case?

There was no significant statistical difference between those who waived their rights and those who did not in either subsequent charging or severity of punishment (Leo, 1996a). The only difference was that those who waived their *Miranda* rights were twice as likely to have their case resolved through plea bargaining. The fact that these cases are more likely to be disposed of through plea bargaining provides benefits to the victims of the crime, who are not called on to testify, in addition to saving time and money on trials that can be avoided. Plea bargaining can actually mean many different things. In some instances, a defendant may plead guilty only if the charges are reduced. In other cases, the defendant may plead guilty only if there is an agreement on a lenient sentence. If a plea is negotiated, there will be something in it for all the parties:

- Promotes administrative efficiency in the courts
- Saves tax dollars
- Ensures prompt correctional measures
- Promotes rehabilitation
- Reduces humiliation and misery to defendants
- Can result in lesser punishment

False Confessions

False confessions occur in rare circumstances. Hundreds of people usually come forward to confess to the crime whenever a celebrity, a public official, or a well-known person in the public eye is victimized. They cannot all be the perpetrator. Most, if not all, of the confessions must be false. For example, more than 200 people confessed to kidnapping the Lindbergh baby in 1932 and hundreds of people confessed to the 1947 Black Dahlia murder in Los Angeles.

A false confession is a written or oral statement acknowledging guilt made by a person who did not commit the crime.

Although there is no concrete estimate of the number of persons who have provided a **false confession,** it has been found that in cases of proven false confession, a common factor is a lengthy interrogation of the suspect, on average 16.3 hours. Psychologists categorize false confessions into three groups (Kassin, 2005):

1. **Voluntary False Confessions.** People may voluntarily give a false confession due to a pathological desire for notoriety, a conscious or unconscious need to relieve guilt over prior wrongdoings, an inability to distinguish fact from fantasy, or a desire to aid and protect the real criminal. Individuals offer voluntary false confessions without any external pressure from the police. These people simply turn themselves in to the authorities, claiming they have committed a crime.
2. **Compliant False Confessions.** Some suspects will confess falsely to escape an aversive situation, avoid an explicit or implied threat, or gain a promised or implied reward. Examples of this exist in cases of physical or psychological torture. Coerced-compliant false confessions may result from the pressures during the interrogation process. Because such a suspect perceives immediate gains that outweigh the long-term consequences, this person will confess despite knowing that he or she did not commit the crime.
3. **Internalized False Confessions.** Some suspects are susceptible to believing during interrogation that they committed the crime, even though they did not. Persons who are particularly vulnerable are

those who are young, tired, confused, suggestible, and exposed to false information.

The concern is part of a larger problem, miscarriages of justice. A **miscarriage of justice** occurs when a person is wrongfully convicted of a crime. It can result from nondisclosure of evidence by police or prosecution, fabrication of evidence, erroneous eyewitness testimony, overestimation of the evidential value of expert testimony, unreliable confessions due to police pressure or psychological instability, ineffective counsel, and misdirection by a judge during trial. Erroneous eyewitness testimony is the greatest cause of wrongful convictions in the U.S. criminal justice system (Warden, 2001). In known cases of wrongful conviction, approximately half were from eyewitness misidentification and were uncovered when the actual criminal confessed (Cassell, 1999).

Improving Interrogations

Interrogation techniques are considered coercive by critics who claim they result in false confessions. The criminal justice system is evaluating how to improve procedures to minimize miscarriages of justice. To avoid the problems and pitfalls associated with interrogation techniques, some challenges for police officers and ways to overcome them are as follows (Napier & Adams, 2002):

☺ Follow the Facts   ☹ Misread the Suspect's Behavior

Critics denounce police procedures that involve observing the behavior of suspects as a way of selecting someone for more intensive interrogation tactics. Excessive focus on an individual because of a hunch or because he or she avoids eye contact narrows the investigator's vision. Overcome this by following the facts of the case, investigating all possible leads, and interviewing all suspects, particularly in a major case.

The best use of reading a suspect's behavior is for the establishment of rapport. After that point behavioral indicators should be carefully interpreted within the entire context of the interrogation and not as specific indicators of guilt. This is particularly true when interrogating persons with mental illness, retardation, or personality disorders.

☺ Know the Suspect   ☹ Overlook Personal Vulnerabilities

Some individuals are particularly susceptible to police interrogation techniques that may lead to a false confession. Examples are youthfulness, low or borderline IQ, mental handicap, psychological inadequacy, recent bereavement, language barrier, alcohol or other drug withdrawal, illiteracy, fatigue, or inexperience with the criminal justice system. Overcome this by doing a thorough background investigation on potentially questionable suspects prior to the interrogation. Place the vulnerability in context at the beginning of the interrogation to get an understanding of whether the suspect understands. Document all efforts to show that a fair interrogation was conducted.

☺ Preserve the Evidence ☹ Contaminate Confessions

Police officers may inadvertently contaminate confessions by relying on questions that contain crime scene data. Use of crime scene photos may amplify this flaw and educate the suspect about the crime. Avoid contaminating any admissions by asking the suspect to describe and explain instead. Use open-ended questions and encourage narrative responses from the suspect.

☺ Use Psychology Instead of Coercion ☹ Promise Benefits

It is considered coercive to tell the suspect that remaining silent will lead to greater penalties but confessing will result in a reward. Do not offer the death penalty versus life imprisonment or threaten harm by prosecution of a relative. These are as unacceptable as personal threats against the suspect. Instead, rely on psychological tools of minimization, rationalization, and projection. Allow the suspect to maintain his or her personal dignity and self-worth.

WHAT IS NOT AN INTERROGATION?

As stated in *Rhode Island v. Innis* (1980), police words or actions "normally attendant to arrest and custody" do not constitute interrogation. Volunteered statements of any kind, including excited utterances, made to police are not barred by the Fifth Amendment privilege against self-incrimination and are admissible in evidence. An **excited utterance** is a statement made spontaneously by someone while under the stress of excitement caused by an event or condition. It is an exception to the hearsay rule.

Subtle Compulsion

Subtle compulsion is a minimal amount of duress that drives someone to do or say something. It does not amount to an interrogation unless it can also be shown that a suspect's incriminating response is the product of words or actions on the part of police that the police should have known were reasonably likely to elicit an incriminating response (*Rhode Island v. Innis*, 1980). Take, for example, a man arrested in the vicinity of a school for handicapped children as a suspect in crimes committed by a man with a shotgun. After being informed of his *Miranda* rights and telling the police that he understands his rights and wants to speak with a lawyer, he is placed in a police car with officers. He is not "interrogated," in honor of his right to remain silent until he can consult with a lawyer. During the course of the ride in the police car by the most direct route to its destination, the car passes by what the suspect knows to be the site of a concealed weapon. The suspect, on noticing for the first time that the concealed weapon is located near a school for handicapped children, blurts out to the officers that he will show them where the concealed weapon is located. This is subtle compulsion that does not constitute an interrogation.

Traffic Stop

The roadside questioning of a motorist detained pursuant to a routine traffic stop does not constitute "custodial interrogation" for the purposes of the *Miranda* rule (*Rhode Island v. Innis*, 1980). Although an ordinary traffic stop curtails the "freedom of action" of the detained motorist and imposes some pressures on the detainee to answer questions, such pressures do not sufficiently impair the detainee's exercise of his or her privilege against self-incrimination to require that he be warned of his constitutional rights. A traffic stop is usually brief, and the motorist expects that, although he or she may be given a citation, in the end he or she most likely will be allowed to continue on the way. Moreover, a typical traffic stop is conducted in public, and the atmosphere surrounding it is substantially less "police dominated" than that surrounding the kinds of interrogation at issue in *Miranda* and subsequent cases in which *Miranda* has been applied.

However, if a motorist who has been detained pursuant to a traffic stop thereafter is subjected to treatment that renders him or her "in custody" for practical purposes, he or she is entitled to the protections prescribed by *Miranda*. A policeman's unspoken plan has no bearing on the question of whether a suspect was "in custody" at a particular time; the only relevant inquiry is how a reasonable person in the suspect's position would have understood the situation.

Sobriety Testing

An individual suspected of driving under the influence may be compelled to submit to sobriety tests of a nontestimonial nature, including physical tests and a breath analysis, in a driving while intoxicated investigation without implicating the right against self-incrimination (*United States v. Hubbell*, 2000). The privilege against self-incrimination protects an accused person from being forced to give evidence of a "testimonial or communicative nature," but not from being compelled to produce "real or physical evidence" (*Pennsylvania v. Muniz*, 1990).

A Stop and Frisk

A police officer may stop a person to question him or her if the officer has a reasonable suspicion that the person is engaged in criminal activity. For self-protection, the officer can at the same time carry out a limited pat-down search for weapons, which is called a **frisk.** This is not a custody situation nor is this considered a search. No *Miranda* rights are required.

In two cases decided in the 2000 term, the U.S. Supreme Court interpreted the "stop and frisk" rule. In one case, the Court ruled that running away from the police is enough of a reason for the police to stop and frisk the defendant (*Illinois v. Wardlow, 2000*). In another case, the Court ruled that an anonymous tip that a suspect might be armed was insufficient justification for the police to conduct a stop and frisk, absent other facts demonstrating the reliability of the tip (*Florida v. J.L., 2000*).

Although a frisk may not turn up a weapon, it may turn up a suspicious package of a type that the officer knows is commonly used to carry illegal drugs or some other illegal substance. This suspicion may turn into

FIGURE 11-2 There a number of citizen-police contacts that do not require that the *Miranda* warnings be given.

sufficient cause for a more intensive search of the person's clothing. A frisk often leads to a search. If a search produces an illegal substance, it may result in arrests, which then require *Miranda* warnings prior to interrogation.

INTERROGATION TACTICS

Police officers may not use any tactic that will coerce an individual to give up his or her rights that are guaranteed by the U.S. Constitution. After a person has voluntarily waived his or her rights, police have some latitude in how to conduct the interrogation.

In most cases, officers conducting an interrogation use three successful psychological strategies for leading a suspect to voluntarily waive his or her *Miranda* rights: conditioning, deemphasizing, and persuasion (Leo, 1996a):

- **Conditioning** is done with the goal of setting up the interrogation in such a way that the suspect responds favorably to questions. One approach is to walk to the jail to meet the suspect, politely introduce oneself to the suspect, and apologize for handcuffing him or her. Inquire about the suspect's physical condition and walk him or her out of the jail to the interrogation room. At the interrogation room provide the suspect with coffee and possibly a newspaper, politely asking whether anything else is needed. Leave the suspect in the room for 15 to 20 minutes, a strategy for enhancing the suspect's desire to talk. Ask routine booking questions politely when you return. When reading the *Miranda* rights to the suspect, nods your head up and down to suggest agreement.
- **Deemphasizing** refers to the strategy of minimizing the potential importance of reading the *Miranda* rights to the suspect, such as by blending the rights into the conversation in a way that makes them seem casual and little more than a procedure that must be followed so that the suspect can speak. Another method of deemphasizing calls attention to the warnings and implicitly suggests that they are unimportant. Another is to joke about the well-known rights, which the subject probably has heard on television many times.
- **Persuasion** is an explicit attempt to convince the suspect to waive his or her rights per *Miranda* in a way that is subtle and noncoercive. For example, tell the suspect that there are two sides to every story and that the suspect's side can only be told if he or she waives the right to silence, adding that the victim's allegations will become the official version of the event unless the suspect speaks.

Some procedures to use in the interrogation include the following (Holmes, 2002):

1. Question chronologically to enhance recall
2. Determine the person's state of mind or the catalyst of the event
3. Ask questions to differentiate between memory recall and fantasy
4. Ask verification questions
5. Evaluate what you have—even if that is only the alibi
6. Ask questions to determine post-act behavior

CASE-SPECIFIC METHODS OF INTERROGATION

The approach to an interrogation will differ based on the offense that was committed as well as the personality of the interrogator. Generally, perpetrators respond with admissions to a humane interrogation approach. Humane does not mean friendly or oversolicitous. A suspect's perceptions are extremely important; in particular, a suspect's perceptions on the strength of the evidence will affect his or her willingness to confess (Kassin & Gudjosson, 2004). With this in mind, use all available evidence collection methods that are specific to the crime being investigated to increase the perception of a strong case.

Have questions ready regarding the things that you want to know; don't just listen passively. Ask for details and explanations of whatever the suspect admits. Be genuinely interested in what the suspect is saying. Credibility that a suspect is telling you the truth will be gained from his or her answers concerning what he or she smelled, tasted, saw, or heard. Ask why a particular victim was chosen; the perpetrator is rarely indiscriminate. Even a person who chooses randomly will provide that as their method of choosing. Why did the suspect steal from *that* car? Assault *that* person? Break into *that* particular house? Kill *that* person? What happened before the event?

In a seminal study on police interviewing, universal problems were identified that have relevance for interrogations (Fisher, Geiselman, & Raymond, 1987). Interrogators should be aware of the following:

- Do not excessively interrupt a suspect's description. This will cause the suspect to experience a considerable loss in concentration.
- When a suspect describes a recollection of the crime, your follow-up questions should be appropriate. For example, unless it is relevant, do not interrupt the suspect to ask about weight, height, age, and so on.

Alleged sexual offenders and child molesters are among the suspects who may be challenging to the investigator; be prepared to ask the difficult questions. It can be appalling or disgusting to hear details about sexual crimes against children or the elderly. Admissions may cause the investigator to feel anger toward the suspect. Never show emotion or react if the details become disturbing. Any show of emotions from the investigator must be purposeful and self-driven. Examples of case-specific approaches follow.

Child Pornography Cases

Interrogators must respond with compassion and understanding during the interrogation of a child pornography case (Bowling & Resch, 2005). A two-step interrogation process is useful:

Step 1 Make a direct accusation statement that is convincing in its delivery to the suspect; interrupt and dismiss denials.

Step 2 Avoid using judgmental terms, and use interrogation themes. Theme development offers the suspect a logical reason why he or she committed the crime by excusing the behavior.

- **Rationalize the Crime.** Example: "I understand your situation; you love kids so much; you never meant to hurt anyone."
- **Project Blame Onto Others.** Example: "The problem is that parents don't spend enough time with their children."
- **Minimize the Offense.** Example: "We're not talking about hurting children here. We're only talking about a few photographs."

BEEN THERE . . . DONE THAT!   11-3

When Janet was 2 years old she began to have many medical problems including severe urinary tract infections and high fevers. Although the child was taken each time to see a doctor, no reason was found for the urinary tract infections, so she was treated for 6 months on antibiotics. Coincidentally, a new babysitter was found for her after a year and a half with the old one. Within a short time the new babysitter noticed that Janet, now 4 years old, was rubbing herself on a stuffed animal as if masturbating. When asked about it, the child said, "Hank rugs me." Her mother, Susan, reported that soon after she learnt of this, Janet told her that she and Hank had a secret. The secret was that Hank used to put his "sickoo" on her "gina." Hank was identified as the husband of the woman who had been babysitting Janet during the time that the urinary tract infections were occurring. The infections had stopped after the child had been sent to a different home for babysitting.

I conducted an interview with Janet. She told me her secret with Hank and drew a picture of him for me. She pointed out on a picture what the 'sickoo" and "gina" meant so that I was sure what she was saying. The stick figure of Hank was basically a face with a penis.

Knowing that a trial with a 4-year-old victim would be extremely difficult, I attempted to obtain a confession from Hank. Something clearly had happened to the child, but was it rape or indecent assault and battery? During the interview with Hank, he did admit to fondling Janet over her underwear but denied any penetration. To explain why she drew him naked, Hank said that she had seen him coming out of the shower one day. I was sure that he minimized his assaults on her. There is no doubt that Hank was thinking the whole time that his wife and four kids were going hear about what he had been doing with this little girl. A 4-year-old against a 35-year-old was not good odds, so I sought to strengthen the confession to make sure that there would not be a fight in court. At the end of the statement, he wrote that he was really sorry for bringing such hardship on the mother and child and understood why they would be angry. He asked for forgiveness. He thanked me for bringing it forward so that he could get help.

In an investigation by the department of social services, Hank told the investigator that he had never touched the child in a sexual way. He said that he was told by me that if he didn't make a statement he'd be arrested and pulled out of his house in handcuffs. When pressed on that claim, he withdrew it and said that "Denise was quite nice during the interview." Funny how things can get turned around when faced with punishment. He further minimized the touching that he had done, saying that he was just kidding around with the child and had accidentally touched her on the inner thigh.

I went with evidence and the perpetrator pled guilty.

Child Sexual Assault

In a comparison of violent offenders, rapists, and child molesters, the internal need to confess was greatest among child molesters (Kassin & Gudjonsson, 2004). They are more likely to respond to a sensitive approach to overcome their inhibition to confess; most of them will talk to the police. One of the greatest challenges for police officers interrogating a suspect for child sexual assault is in controlling their own emotions. Any expression of anger, disgust, or distain toward the suspect will result in his or her refusal to continue constructively in the interrogation. In many cases the statement from the perpetrator is the strongest evidence available.

1. Give the suspect permission to talk. Start by explaining the investigation. Tell the suspect that you realize that he or she is in a difficult position and are willing to give him or her the opportunity to talk and give his or her side of the story. The interview may be difficult. Assure the suspect that you want to hear the reasons for what happened.
2. Don't share any embarrassing secrets to establish rapport. The suspect who realizes that you are manipulating him or her will become resentful and you will lose any credibility that you have established.
3. Be prepared to listen. During the interview with the suspect, the investigator should (Pence & Wilson, 1992):

- Display an attitude of confidence in the subject's guilt.
- Point out some, but by no means all, of the circumstantial evidence indicative of the subject's guilt.
- Sympathize with the subject by telling him or her that anyone else might have done the same thing under similar circumstances.
- Reduce the subject's guilt feelings by minimizing the seriousness of the offense. It is also helpful to tell the subject that the interrogator has heard many people tell about sexual activities far worse than any the subject can relate. The conduct itself should be discussed as though it were actually normal.
- Suggest a less revolting and more acceptable motivation or reason for the offense than that which is known or presumed. An offender should always be offered an opportunity to save face by letting him or her base the initial admission of guilt on a motivation or reason for the act. To secure the initial admission of guilt, the interrogator should suggest such possible reasons, motives, or excuses. The important point is to have the subject place himself or herself at the scene or to connect himself or herself with the event in some way. Following a partial admission, the interrogator can then point out that the circumstantial evidence negates certain explanations. The inconsistency between the subject's original denial of the crime and his or her present admission will deprive him or her of a possible defense.
- Remember, the main objective of the interview in many instances is to have the subject place himself or herself at the scene or in contact with the victim.
- Display understanding and sympathy because it may help to get the subject to tell the truth. Urge the subject to tell the truth for

the sake of his or her conscience, mental relief, or moral well-being as well as for the sake of everybody concerned, and also because it is the only decent, honorable thing to do.
- Seek an admission of lying about some incidental aspect of the occurrence. Once a subject has been caught in a lie about some incidental detail, he or she loses a great deal of ground. As the subject tries to convince the interrogator that he or she is telling the truth, the subject can always be politely reminded that he or she was not telling the truth just a short while ago.
- Ask the subject a question regarding some detail of the offense rather than seek a general admission of guilt; getting an admission on seemingly insignificant details will sometimes lead the accused into a confession.

Offenders will not come right out and state that they sexually assaulted the victim. There may be claims of temptation, accidental touching, or an innocent bathing incident. Let the subject talk. Document the incriminating statements and ask for clarification where needed.

Hate Crimes

The National Center for Hate Crime Prevention suggests that some suspects may assume that officers share their biased opinions . Armed with this knowledge, interrogators can encourage suspects to talk about their feelings toward a particular minority group. Without using hate language, the officer should ask the suspect to express his or her bias motivations. The Model Hate Crime Protocol suggests that the following specific questions be asked during an interrogation:

1. How would you like it if someone like the victim moved next door?
2. How do you feel about this victim?
3. What did this person say or do to make you mad?
4. How did the victim provoke you?

I'm sorry whats been happening, I don't know I do what I do but I know I need help bad. I'm scared for me and mostly my family.
I'm sorry if I hurt any body, I didn't mean any harm.

Mark A.

FIGURE 11-3 The perpetrator should always be given the opportunity to read and make corrections to their statement. Ask the person if they have anything else to say. The majority will appologize. Have them put it in their own writing at the bottom of the confession.

5. How do you feel about this person or group?
6. Was this your idea?
7. Has the victim's group hurt you or your friends?

Homicide

If the suspect of the homicide is in custody, the first decision that must be made is whether the subject should be interrogated at the scene of the crime or at the police department. The decision requires flexibility based on the background information available to the investigator. If the suspect is talkative or wants to tell the story at the scene, do not delay. Advise the suspect of his or her *Miranda* rights and let him or her talk. Some important observations that should be noted include the following:

- Does the suspect speak rationally or irrationally?
- Is the response to questioning intelligent or confused?
- Is there any evidence of intoxication, or does the suspect appear to be under the influence of any drugs?
- Does the suspect give any reasons for his or her actions?

Transporting the suspect is a critical point in the investigation. If the suspect's attitude hardens against the victim or the police, this could result in an unwillingness to cooperate with the investigating officer. It can also be the period when the suspect develops remorse for the crime. It is imperative that the transporting officers do nothing that would cause the suspect to resist subsequent investigative efforts. The following are recommended during the transportation of a homicide suspect (Naramore, 1988):

1. If the suspect becomes talkative, officers should listen, remember, and later make notes of statements. It is not the duty of the transporting officers to provide *Miranda* rights or attempt to elicit information from the suspect.
2. Do not discuss the case with the suspect.
3. Do not engage the suspect in friendly conversation.
4. Do not use gestures or language that could be interpreted as hostile by the suspect.
5. Do not insult or berate the suspect.

Questions concerning a homicide are generally organized around four phases of the murder: the pre-crime phase, the murder event, the disposal of the body, and the post-crime phase. In addition to obtaining information about the crime, questions in these categories establish the suspect's motive and opportunity to have committed the act.

Pre-Crime Phase. Determine whether the alleged murderer had a conscious or unconscious intent for the act. Murderers with conscious intent are able to describe what triggered the murder. Those without conscious motive typically do not remember why they killed, but are able to describe their feelings prior to the murder. Ask what the offender did the day prior to the murder and his or her thoughts and feelings prior to encountering the victim.

The Murder Event. Questions should concentrate on important aspects of the crime, such as how the suspect gained access to the victim. Conversation and behavior involving the victim, transporting the victim from one location to another, and specifics on methods of torture before or after the victim's death are central to the interrogation. If there is any indication of sexual contact, the interrogator should focus on what was done prior to and after the victim's death.

Disposal of the Body. Determine through questioning what was done with the body, how the offender left the scene, and whether anything was taken from the body. The interrogator should explore the thoughts and feelings of the murderer during this phase.

Post-Crime Phase. The behaviors that occur after the murder are extremely important to the interrogator. What did the offender do right after the murder? Did he or she wash, go out with friends, go to sleep, or eat? Did he or she return to the crime scene or attend the funeral? Include questions about the recovery of the body. Did the offender assist police in the recovery?

When a suspect denies guilt of a homicide, it may help to use a third-party strategy. This involves asking why someone (else) would have committed that crime. This technique may uncover the motive of the homicide and facilitate further discussion surrounding the incident.

Sexual Assault Cases

Sex offenders generally tend to confess more frequently than other suspects because of a strong internal need to confess, despite their feelings of shame (Kassin & Gudjonsson, 2004). Offer the suspect a viable alternative by suggesting that the victim may have said that he or she was older than he or she really was, or ask whether the victim wanted to do it or did the suspect make the victim do it.

When the identification of the alleged offender is made within a reasonable period of time, the collection of evidence from the suspect's body and clothing contributes to a successful interrogation and aids in solving the cases. Evidence such as pubic and head hair samples, body fluids (dried and wet), and articles of clothing can be used as comparative or reference samples with hair, fibers, and fluids found on the victim. Photographing scratches or bruises on the alleged perpetrator may be indicative of victim resistance in addition to notifying the suspect of your knowledge. Proper collection, conducted under all legal requirements, aids in the establishment of status for the interrogator. In addition, it provides possible physical evidence. Accurately record any alibi statements or utterances made by the suspect prior to the actual interrogation during the process of collection.

Evidence of sexual assault may be collected from the body of the suspect without a warrant if the suspect has been arrested and probable cause exists for the seizure of the suspect's clothing and documenting of injuries as a search incident to arrest due to exigent circumstances. A standard "rape kit" may be used to gather evidence from the suspect and maintain the chain of custody, whereas some states use a suspect-specific evidence kit (Gaensslen & Lee, 2001).

TRUTH AND CONSEQUENCES

Many people have erroneous ideas on what a police officer can or cannot legally do. In examining the following statements, consider them in terms of their consequences. Here are some of the most common examples:

1. What really happens if the police fail to read a suspect his or her rights or use coercion to extract information from a suspect? Many people believe that if they are arrested and not "read their rights," they can escape punishment. Not true. But if the police fail to read a suspect his or her rights, they can't use anything the suspect says as evidence against him or her at trial. The prosecution may use the statements to impeach the defendant if he or she decides to take the stand in court. The individual may still be tried if sufficient evidence exists that is not related to the illegally gained evidence. All other evidence not gained in connection with the statement may be used.
2. Police officers interrogate suspects in most felony arrests. Wrong. Officers do not even attempt interrogations in almost half of all felony arrests (Colaprete, 2002). Why? The variables are experience, motivation, training, and, most important, the randomness of case assignment. Heavy caseload and time are other important facts that influence whether an interrogation takes place.
3. Does an undercover police officer have to admit who they are if a person asks? Many people believe that if they ask someone whether he or she is an undercover police officer and the person denies being a police officer, they are safe to sell or share drugs with that person. Not true. Police officers are not required to reveal their undercover identity. There is no entrapment because the officer is not forcing someone to buy or use drugs. The person has shown a willingness to buy or sell drugs—the courts call it predisposition.
4. If you haven't been arrested and a police officer wants to question you about a crime, you must answer the questions. Refusing to answer a police officer's questions is not a crime. Of course, people often voluntarily assist the police by supplying information that might help the police make an arrest. A police officer generally cannot arrest a person simply for failure to respond to questions. This means that unless a police officer has "probable cause" to make an arrest or a "reasonable suspicion" to conduct a stop and frisk, a person approached by the police officer has the legal right to walk away. The fact that there may be a legal right to walk away doesn't mean that this is a wise move, however, because there is no way to know what information the officer is using as a basis for his or her actions. In fact, the officer may have information that gives him or her valid legal basis to make an arrest or to conduct a stop and frisk, even if the individual is, in truth, innocent of any wrongdoing. Although there may be grounds for arrest, no one can be arrested purely because he or she declined to speak to a police officer.
5. There is no law against lying to the police. Wrong. It is a felony offense punishable by 5-years' imprisonment to lie to a federal police officer (U.S. Code, Title 18, Part I, Chapter 47, Sec. 1001). Remember Martha Stewart. Some, but not all, states have similar laws.

CONCLUSIONS

Confessions were the primary focus of this chapter. The question, "Why would a guilty person confess?" can be just as difficult to answer as, "Why would an innocent person confess?" The purpose of laws restricting interrogation practices is to protect the suspect, whether that individual is innocent or guilty. There are no shortcuts or magic words to induce a confession. It takes hard work and self-control, and even then obtaining a confession is not assured. The confession is only part of the investigation process and should never by itself be the basis for a prosecution.

It is not surprising that suspects with prior criminal records are the most hesitant to waive their rights and provide statements. They are the most hardened against the system and typically have a lot more to lose. It is interesting to note that the police are very good at obtaining voluntary confessions but that attempts at interrogation are relatively few. Enhanced professionalism translates into reduced possibility of false confessions; use of the appropriate techniques is the hallmark of good interrogation.

QUESTIONS FOR REVIEW

Short-Answer Questions

1. Explain the early impact of *Miranda* warnings on police interrogation.
2. Explain the three types of police officer depicted in Schaefer's studies.
3. Discuss plea bargaining. What are the potential benefits for the suspect? What are the potential benefits for the state?
4. What are the three major categories of false confessions? Explain each.
5. Subtle compulsion, traffic stops, sobriety testing, and use of stop and frisk are not considered interrogation. Why not?
6. In most cases, officers conducting interrogations use three successful psychological strategies to predispose a suspect to voluntarily waive his or her *Miranda* rights. What are they? What do police officers hope to achieve in each instance?
7. Outline the proper approach for interrogating suspects in cases of child pornography. How does this differ from other interrogation styles?
8. Outline the proper approach for interrogating suspects in cases of child sexual assault. How does this work toward securing admissions from a suspect?
9. Explain the Model Hate Crime Protocol used to interrogate individuals suspected of committing hate crimes.
10. Why is the timely identification of the offender especially important in sexual assault cases? How does this affect the gathering of evidence?

Fill-in Questions

1. There exists a balancing act concerning interrogations, which involves providing _____ to the guilty without jeopardizing the _____ of the innocent.

2. The *Miranda* safeguards come into play whenever a person in custody is subjected to either explicit questioning or its _____ _____.

3. The police interrogator must possess a high degree of emotional _____ and feel comfortable using persuasive tactics that may be morally offensive to some.

4. There is no significant statistical difference between persons who waive their rights per *Miranda* and those who do not, in either subsequent _____ or _____.

5. In cases of proven false confessions a common factor is a(n) _____ _____ of the suspect.

6. Police officers may inadvertently _____ confessions by relying on questions that contain crime scene data.

7. The approach of the interrogator differs slightly based on the _____ as well as the personality of the interrogator.

8. Child molesters are more likely to respond to a(n) _____ approach used to overcome their inhibition to confess; most of them will talk to the police.

9. Sex offenders generally tend to _____ more than other suspects because of a strong internal need to confess, despite their feelings of shame.

10. Evidence of sexual assault may be collected from the body of the suspect without a warrant if the suspect has been arrested and probable cause exists for the seizure of the suspect's clothing and documenting of injuries as a search _____ due to exigent circumstances.

Exercises

1. **What's my lie?**

   In this exercise a panel of three people is assigned to leave the room. Outside of the room something about one of the individuals is selected as the "story" (for example, "I went white water rafting through the Grand Canyon"). The details of the story are shared with the other two panelists. The panel returns to the room and each person states the story. They are then "interrogated" by the class. Which two are lying? How can you tell?

2. **What's my lie?**

   The class breaks into pairs. One person is the interrogator and the other is the suspect. The suspect comes up with a story of something he or she did. (For example, "This morning I made a great cappuccino!") The interrogator needs to determine whether the person is telling a lie.

REFERENCES

Aamodt, M., & Flink, W. (2001). Relationship between education level and cadet performance in a police academy. *Applied HRM Research, 6*(1), 75–76.

Bowling, R., & Resch, D. (2005). Child pornography cases: Obtaining confessions with an effective interview strategy. *FBI Law Enforcement Bulletin, 74*, 1–7.

Buckley, D., & Jayne, B. (2005). *Electronic recording of interrogations*. Chicago: John E. Reid.

Carter, D., Sapp, A., & Stephens, D. (1989). *The state of police education: Policy direction for the twenty-first century*. Washington, DC: Police Executive Research Forum.

Cassell, P. G. (1999). The guilty and the 'innocent': An examination of alleged cases of wrongful conviction from false confessions. *Harvard Journal of Law and Public Policy*, 22, 523–597. Available: http://www.prodeathpenalty.com/guilt.htm.

Colaprete, F. A. (2002). Managing change in the investigative process: A process-centered approach to professional development and change management. *Police Chief*, 69(10), 121–126.

Fisher, R., Geiselman, E., & Raymond, D. (1987). Critical analysis of police interview techniques. *Journal of Police Science and Administration,* 15(3), 177–185.

Florida v. J.L., 529 U.S. 266 (2000).

Gaensslen, R. E., & Lee, H. C. (2001). *Sexual assault evidence: National assessment and guidebook* (2nd ed.). West Haven, CT: University of New Haven.

Gelinas, A. (2005). *Effects of interviewer gender on interviewee response*. Unpublished report, Western New England College, Springfield, MA.

Gudjonsson, G. H. (2003). *The psychology of interrogations and confessions: A handbook*. Hoboken, NJ: Wiley.

Hess, J. (1997). *Interviewing and interrogation for law enforcement*. Cincinnati, OH: Anderson Publishing.

Holmes, W. (2002). *Criminal interrogation: A modern format for interrogating criminal suspects based on the intellectual approach*. Springfield, IL: LTD.

Illinois v. Wardlow, 528 U.S. 119 (2000).

Inbau, F. E., Reid, J. E., Buckley, J. P., & Jayne, B. C. (2001). *Criminal interrogation and confessions* (4th ed.). Gaithersburg, MD: Aspen Publishers.

Kassin, S. M. (2005). True crimes, false confessions. *Scientific American Mind*, 16(2), 24–32.

Kassin, S. M., & Gudjonsson, G. H. (2004). The psychology of confessions: A review of the literature and issues. *Psychological Science in the Public Interest*, 5, 67. Available: http://www.psychologicalscience.org/pdf/pspi/pspi5_2.pdf.

Kassin, S., & Norwick, R. (2004). Why people waive their *Miranda* rights: The power of innocence. *Law and Human Behavior,* 28(2), 211–221.

Leo, R. A. (1996a). The impact of *Miranda* revisited. *Journal of Criminal Law and Criminology*, 86, 621. Available: http://www.lexisnexis.com/universe.

Leo, R. A. (1996b). Inside the interrogation room. *Journal of Criminal Law and Criminology,* 86, 266–303. Available: http://www.lexisnexis.com//universe.

Leo, R. A., & White. W. S. (1999). Adapting to *Miranda:* Modern interrogators' strategies for dealing with the obstacles posed. *Minnesota Law Review,* 84, 397–472.

Miranda v. Arizona, 384 U.S. 436 (1966).

Missouri v. Seibert, 542 U.S. 600 (2004).

Napier, M., & Adams, S. (2002). Criminal confessions: Overcoming the challenges. *FBI Law Enforcement Bulletin,* 71(11), 9–15.

Naramore, D. (1988). *Psychology of interviewing,* Unpublished, NESPAC: Homicide School.

National Center for Women and Policing. (2002). The status of women in policing: 2001. [Online.] Available: http://www.womenandpolicing.org/PDF/2002_Status_Report.pdf.

Office for Victims of Crime. (2004). Responding to hate crime: A multidisciplinary curriculum for law enforcement and victim assistance professionals. [Online.] Available: http://www.ojp.usdoj.gov/ovc/publications/infores/responding/welcome.html

Pence, D., & Wilson, C. (1992). *The role of law enforcement in the response to child abuse and neglect.* Washington, DC: National Center on Child Abuse and Neglect.

Pennsylvania v. Muniz, 496 U.S. 582 (1990).

Rabon, D. (1992). *Interviewing and interrogation.* Durham, NC: Carolina Academic Press.

Rhode Island v. Innis, 446 U.S. 291 (1980).

Rutledge, D. (1994). *Criminal interrogation: Law and tactics* (3rd ed.). Placerville, CA: Copperhouse Publishing.

Schaefer, R. C. (1971). Patrolman perspectives on *Miranda. Law and the Social Order, 81*, 81–101.

Schmalleger, F. (2004). *Criminal justice.* Upper Saddle River, NJ: Prentice Hall.

The Committee on Law and Justice. (2004). Fairness and effectiveness in policing: The evidence. [Online.] Available: http://www.nap.edu/books/0309084334/html.

Thomas III, G. C. (2004). Stories about *Miranda. Michigan Law Review, 102*, 1959–2001.

Tousignant, D. (1991). Why suspects confess. [Online.] http://www.crimeandclues.com/91ar002.htm.

United States v. Hubbell, 530 U.S. 27 (2000).

Warden, R. (2001). How mistaken and perjured eyewitness testimony put 46 innocent Americans on death row. [Online.] Available: http://www.law.northwestern.edu/depts/clinic/wrongful/Causes/eyewitnessstudy01.htm.

Yeschke, C. (2003). *The art of investigative interviewing* (2nd ed.). Boston: Butterworth-Heinemann.

CHAPTER 12
Techniques for Interrogation

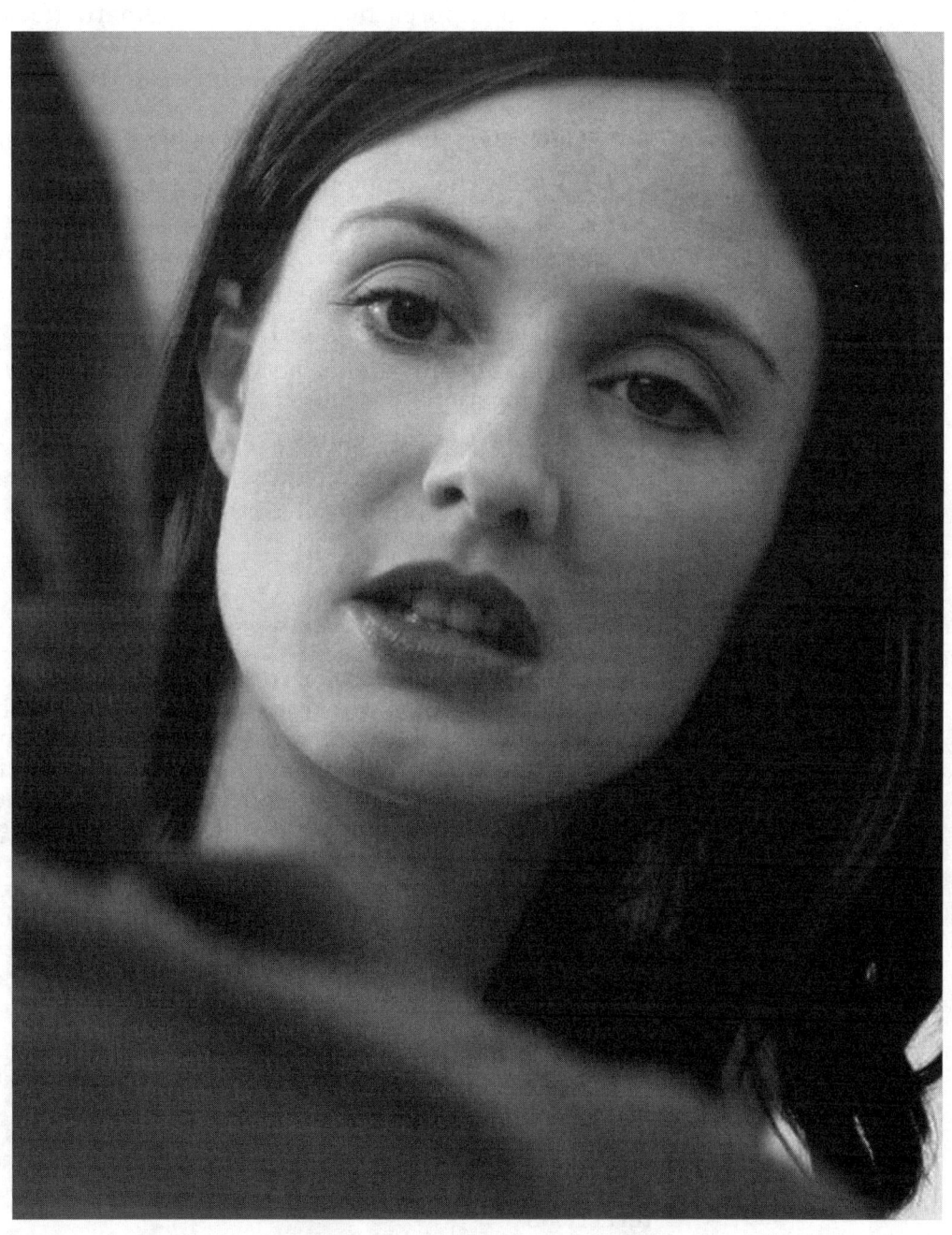

Key Terms

Complementary principle	Noncustodial interrogation
Confession	Custodial interrogation
Admission	*Modus operandi*
Inculpatory evidence	Guilt-ridden offender
Slam-dunk approach	Apathetic offender

Chapter Objectives

After completing this chapter, you should be able to:

- Describe the complementary principle
- Explain the difference between a confession and an admission
- Explain why an interrogation is only one part of an investigation
- Describe the slam-dunk approach to interrogation
- Explain the term *modus operandi*
- Explain the difference between a noncustodial and a custodial interrogation
- Describe the three phases of an interrogation
- List the top 10 interrogation tactics used by police
- Develop outcome-based tactics for interrogation

Introduction

Many of the techniques for interrogation described in this chapter rely on an attempt by the interrogator to understand the behavior of the suspect and his or her resistance to the interrogation process. The interactions between the interrogator and the suspect are critical themes throughout. Understanding the interpersonal relations between the interrogator and the suspect provides a good starting point for using interrogation techniques. A useful approach to understanding interpersonal relations is based on the **complementary principle** of interpersonal psychology, according to which individual behaviors derive from a predictable set of reactions in response to certain actions. The principle involves two major assumptions: first, that interpersonal behaviors, invite reciprocal behaviors, and second, that over time these lead to a repetitive pattern of relating (Gurtman, 2001).

What does this mean to the potential interrogator? First, the complementary principle suggests that the interpersonal style of one individual can influence the reaction of another and bring about an expected set of responses. Potentially, an astute interrogator can persuade a suspect through knowledge of the expected pairings that occur during human interactions.

Second, the primary interactions between humans are friendliness and dominance (Sadler & Woody, 2003). The interrogator can determine which relationship pairing will work best with a particular suspect. When a relationship or connection develops, the suspect will respond to the interrogator in way that is similar. This pairing is seen when rapport is established between the interviewer and interviewee. A connection between two people brings about corresponding levels of friendliness. This connection may be achieved if the suspect feels that the interrogator understands him or her treats him or her with respect. A friendly relationship encourages a friendly response; a cooperative relationship is likely to have a corresponding cooperative effect.

Pairings of expected behaviors to specific responses are somewhat predictable when the suspect grants status to the interrogator. Status may be achieved when the suspect respects the interrogator due to his or her status as a police officer or acknowledges inwardly that the interrogator has sufficient evidence to prove the suspect's guilt. When granting of status occurs, what results is an opposite or negative complementary response. A negative complementary response is dominant to submissive behavior. For example, the suspect may take the role of being submissive in response to a dominant interrogator. The suspect may become cooperative to overcome a distrustful interrogator. Another possibility is that the suspect becomes friendly to the hostile interrogator in an effort to please him or her.

The interrogator should determine if the approach to the interrogation is best made by establishing a status role or connecting through a rapport relationship. An overriding consideration is that once the interrogator has taken on a hostile role with the suspect, it is impossible to go back and later develop rapport.

PURPOSE OF THE INTERROGATION

The interrogation is an important part of a criminal investigation. The Supreme Court has recognized that a suspect's confession may be the most damaging evidence that can be admitted (*Bruton v. U.S.*, 1968). The primary purpose of the interrogation is to obtain a statement from the suspect that acknowledges or indicates the guilt of that person. The best statement is one that provides the interrogator with the truth. If the suspect will not give the truth, then a secondary purpose is to document the lies. Success is achieved with either a confession or an admission:

- A **confession** is a statement in which a person admits to his or her role in committing a crime in a way that excludes the possibility that the crime was committed by someone else.
- An **admission** is any statement that that ties the suspect to the crime, the victim, or the place of the offense, which may be used to infer guilt.

Both confessions and admissions are known as **inculpatory evidence**. Inculpatory evidence tends to show a person's involvement in a crime (Garner, 2004). They are generally treated in the same way with regard to constitutional analysis. This means that the methods used to obtain a statement are judged under the same constitutional standards that were outlined in Chapter 10. A confession or an admission can be valuable for use against a suspect. In criminal cases the prosecution must prove the case beyond a reasonable doubt, and juries may have difficulty in reaching guilty verdicts when a case is based on circumstantial evidence or on witness testimony that has been impeached by defense counsel. A properly admitted confession or admission from the defendant can secure a conviction in these cases.

Although the interrogation is an important part of an investigation, it should not be considered as the primary method of gathering evidence. As stated earlier, interviews of the victim and other witnesses are critical to obtaining evidence. A medical examination when warranted and properly executed search warrants are other methods of gathering critical information. Conducting a background check on a suspect is another valuable aspect of the investigative process.

The process becomes compromised when the investigator puts all of his or her energy into obtaining a confession rather than collecting evidence. This single-mindedness may mean that evidence exonerating the suspect is overlooked or that extreme measures are taken to obtain the confession. Neither is an acceptable alternative to a full and fair investigation. Another reason to be concerned about a strong reliance on interrogations is that in the absence of corroborating evidence, the case is lost if the confession is not admitted (for any number of reasons). A third reason to avoid strong reliance on interrogations is the common view that a confession alone is not enough to prove a person guilty (*Commonwealth v. Forde*, 1984).

It is against the self-interest of a suspect to admit guilt, yet this is the purpose of the interrogation. To obtain a confession the interrogator must obtain the cooperation of the suspect. Cooperation may be based on either aspect of the complementary principle, through granting of status or through making a connection. Either way, this is no easy task. Some people will confess to relieve guilt, some due to the interrogator's persuasion, and others because of the belief that they have been trapped.

The interrogation should take place when the guilt of the suspect is fairly certain. It should not be an attempt to gather information. That is achieved through the interview.

INTERROGATION APPROACH

There are conflicting opinions about the best way to conduct an interrogation, which is a complicated process. Gordon and Fleisher (2002) suggested that the assertion of force plus the weight of evidence should result in a confession. They suggested that the interrogator must forcefully claim that the suspect is guilty and not allow him or her to deny it. This **slam-dunk approach** is too simplistic and should not be used until the interrogator has made an assessment of whether the suspect is cooperative, mentally ill, or emotional. If an interrogator begins the process by being argumentative and angry, it may cause some perpetrators to fear making statements and not talk at all. This approach does not take into account the offense type, which may necessitate a different initial approach. For example, a person who illegally dumped trash should not be interrogated in the same manner as one suspected of murder. Neither does this approach recognize that offenders themselves are different. For example, interrogating a 60-year-old man accused of strangling his wife does not require the same approach as that to a 21-year old gang member who allegedly shot a rival or a 25-year-old woman charged with suffocating her child. All of these crimes are murder, yet they require different approaches during interrogation. The slam-dunk style is not a useful way to begin an interrogation.

Awareness of the differences among offenders is incorporated into the Reid technique (Inbau, et al. 2001), which classifies offenders as emotional or nonemotional (pp. 209–210). Offenders differ considerably based on the level of guilt they experience, and so the interrogator must change tactics to be successful in moving a suspect to confess. The Reid technique is a highly structured, nine-step interrogation approach that is excellent for the advanced practitioner of interrogation. Those who do not take the time to thoroughly understand the method will end up with a false sense of security. It is more than just a matter of follow the steps and the interrogation will be complete. Unless the interrogator is thoroughly familiar with all of the steps and can recite them in order, explain the reasons for each step, AND follow each step in order, he or she may find it difficult to justify the approach when testifying in court.

A somewhat different interrogation approach involves assessing the suspect, strategizing the relationship between the suspect and interrogator, and documenting the proof obtained through the confession (Rutledge, 1994). An assessment is a process of finding the subject's strengths and

BEEN THERE...DONE THAT! 12-1

In this case, three children told their mother that their grandfather had been touching them. The interviews with these children were particularly difficult. The allegation was indecent touching, a situation in which little physical evidence could be expected. I decided to speak with the alleged perpetrator in his home rather than at the police station. This proved to be the best move I could have made. There was no custody, and no *Miranda* rights were necessary to speak with the suspect. He confirmed that he had been the only person with access to each of the children in the incidents that they had described to me as being sexual. He also tried to convince me that these incidents were not sexual, and gave some reasons why the children might be saying that he had touched them. In all cases he had admitted to taking down their underpants. These admissions were not a confession, but they were the information on which the jury based their belief of the children's explanation over his for what had happened. He was found guilty and spent 10 years in jail for the assaults. Why was this an interrogation rather than an interview?

weaknesses to help to convince him or her to provide a confession. Guilt, remorse, and entitlement are examples of emotions that the interrogator can exploit. If the perpetrator is a man who severely beat his girlfriend, for example, the suggestion from the interrogator that she "deserved it" is an example of entitlement that might be used by the suspect to justify his crime. If a similar identity is perceived, then the suspect imagines a relationship with the interrogator and trusts him or her enough to talk. The relationship with the suspect is an important consideration. Because it is in a person's best interest not to give information against himself or herself, he or she will most likely waive his or her rights if there is the perception that it IS in his or her best interest to talk. If the suspect believes that the interrogator can be convinced of his or her innocence, then he or she is also likely to talk. Understating the position and rank of the interrogator is better than demanding respect due to status. Offenders are generally more interested in themselves than with the police officer, so don't bother trying to impress them to obtain a confession.

Another approach to interrogation requires a person to focus on the purpose of the interrogation rather than the place. Typically the interrogation is pictured as a room designed for that purpose in a police station. The goal of an interrogation is to obtain a statement from the suspect that he or she is guilty of a crime. An admission will provide information that may suggest guilt. Most examples of interrogation involve major crimes such as homicide or rape. The importance of confessions and admissions should not be overlooked as part of the investigatory process for all crimes, even minor ones. It is limiting to think of statements taken in the interrogation room as an interrogation and all other encounters as interviews. If one puts the picture of the interrogation room aside for a moment, the possibilities become endless. An interrogation may take place at the home of the suspect, at some neutral setting, or at the police station. The alleged offender can be called on the phone and asked questions that are designed to elicit incriminating information. An interrogation can be conducted whether the suspect is in custody or not.

One major advantage to conducting a noncustodial interrogation is that it typically introduces a strong element of surprise. Getting the suspect to talk is a critical element in obtaining a confession. Remember that an interrogation is not an option after the individual has been arraigned in court or asks to speak to an attorney, regardless of whether the suspect is in custody. Both noncustodial and custodial interrogation situations are described in the next section.

Noncustodial Interrogation Situation

Prior to an interrogation, the approach has to be chosen based on whether the questioning will be in a custodial or noncustodial context. A **noncustodial interrogation** situation is one in which the suspect is not in police custody or under arrest. The suspect must be fully aware that he or she is free to leave at any time. This awareness may be based in part on the location of the interrogation, the attitude of the interrogator, and lack of follow-up arrest of the suspect at that time. As shown in Chapter 10, *Miranda* warnings are not required when the suspect is not

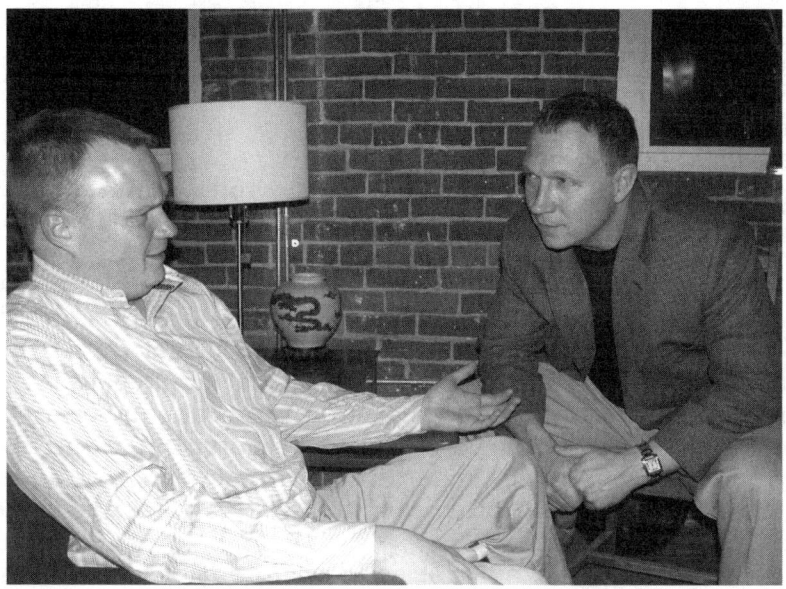

FIGURE 12-1 An interrogation is not defined by where it is taking place, but by why it is being conducted.

in custody. If the situation changes to a custodial one during the interrogation, however, they must be provided. The decision not to arrest the suspect unless it is absolutely necessary must be made in advance.

A noncustodial interrogation is not as threatening to the suspect. In some cases the suspect may feel freer to talk, thereby incriminating himself or herself through admissions. A noncustodial interrogation is less formal, allowing the interrogator to understate his or her position as well as giving the impression that statements are less damning to the suspect.

Conduct a noncustodial interrogation by introducing yourself to the suspect as a police officer investigating the crime. If the suspect is willing to go to the station or office to talk, ask if he or she would like to follow in his or her car or have a friend accompany him or her in the cruiser. This reinforces that notion the suspect is voluntarily involving himself or herself in the process. If the suspect invites you into his or her home to talk, accept any offer for coffee or tea. When the interrogation is ended, thank the suspect for cooperating and suggest that you may want to talk to him or her again in the future.

Custodial Interrogation Situation

In a **custodial interrogation** the suspect is under arrest or is not free to leave because arrest is impending. The *Miranda* warnings are necessary prior to questioning a suspect in custody. The offender must understand his or her rights and voluntarily waive them. For a full discussion of the *Miranda* warnings see Chapter 10. A knowing waiver of rights is compromised if the individual has a mental disability, cannot read or write, or is under the influence of alcohol or drugs. It is the responsibility of the investigator to assess the ability of the suspect to understand his or her rights and make a voluntary waiver. An individual must not be coerced or forced to give up his or her rights. The spirit as well as the letter of the law must be adhered to.

Once an individual has made a knowing and voluntary waiver of his or her *Miranda* rights, it is not necessary to repeat them over and over until the person wonders why he or she ever agreed to speak in the first place. Department policy dictates whether the individual must waive his or her rights in writing. *Miranda* does not require this. Neither does *Miranda* require that an individual be given his or her rights verbatim.

If the individual asks for an attorney, the interrogation must stop. The request for an attorney does not require an unequivocal mention of an attorney or a question asked of the interrogator about the need for an attorney. The interrogator is under no requirement to give advice to the suspect. However, it is good practice to follow up even a vague mention of an attorney.

The waiver of rights against self-incrimination can be revoked by the suspect at any time. Even when the person agrees to speak with the interrogator, the right to stop speaking can be excercised at the discretion of the suspect. The right against self-incrimination belongs to the suspect. No one can take it from him or her, nor can one insist on it for another. For example, an attorney may ask to speak with his or her client and the suspect must be informed that an attorney is available. If the suspect wants to continue to talk with the police without that attorney, the right is his or hers. Do not interpret this as a providing a way to deny individual rights. Tell the suspect that he or she has the right to continue speaking with authorities and let him or her make the decision.

Confession-Eliciting Models

There are numerous techniques for eliciting confessions. Each method slants the approach to interrogation from a different perspective. Gudjonsson (2003) suggested that custodial interrogation approaches fall into five theoretical confession-producing models: the Reid model, the decision-making model, the psychoanalytic model, the interaction process model, and the cognitive–behavioral model (Gudjonsson, 2003). Review these confession-eliciting models and look for them later in the chapter. They are incorporated into the phases of the interrogation:

1. The *Reid model* relies on decreasing the suspect's perception of the consequences of confession. The interrogator uses rationalization to help the offender to avoid full responsibility and projection to distort the account of what really happened. At the same time, the suspect's internal anxiety associated with his or her deception is increased by the interrogator, making a confession more likely. Manipulating the suspect's anxiety is achieved by exaggerating normal feelings of guilt and shame.

2. The *decision-making model* uses a hedonistic calculation by the perpetrator of the options available and the consequences of choosing each one. In this pain versus pleasure analysis the suspect will choose to confess or not based on the factors that pressure the him or her in different directions. The pressures include social, psychological, and environmental considerations that make confession the better choice. The interrogator facilitates the process by reinforcing the pressures to confess.
3. The *psychoanalytic model* rests on the assumption that there is a psychological need to confess based on guilt and the desire for self-punishment. Highly controversial, this approach relies heavily on Freudian concepts. Only after confessing will the suspect begin to release the pressure of guilt. According to this model, the two driving forces are the fear of losing love and fear of retaliation. The anxiety that the suspect endures due to guilt is exploited to elicit the confession.
4. The *interaction process model* views the interrogation as a three-prong process; the characteristics of the offender and his or her offense, the strength of the evidence, and the interrogator's technique. The model stresses the interplay of these influences during the interrogation process. To achieve a confession, the interrogator considers the background characteristics of the suspect, such as age and gender in addition to the type of offense that was committed. The strength of the evidence and the technique used by the interrogator are the additional consideration. The success of the interrogation depends on whether the interrogator correctly accessed the suspect and responded with appropriate methods to overcome the suspect's resistance to providing a confession.
5. According to Gudjonsson's (2003) *cognitive–behavioral model,* suspects are motivated to confess by the social, emotional, and cognitive pressures of isolation, police pressure, personal distress, and the belief that the police know that he or she did it. Additional factors that influence the likelihood of a confession are situational, such as the presence of an attorney or familiarity with police procedures.

INTERROGATION PHASE I: PREPARING

Regardless of the type of interrogation, the approach requires formal and systematic preparation and planning. It is intentionally accusatory, with the interrogator dominating a great deal of the conversation. As stated earlier, the suspect can be interrogated while in custody or not; it depends on the type of case and goals of the interrogation. The systematic nature of the interrogation is important throughout the process. Success is enhanced when the interrogator is well rested and confident about the case. It takes tremendous energy to conduct an interrogation. The interrogator must be one step ahead of the suspect in every way, from anticipating excuses to confronting denials. The interrogation may be as short as 1 hour or may take several hours. As you will see, the preparation for an interrogation begins in the same manner as the interview. The interrogator who starts the interrogation must be prepared to follow through to the end.

The five steps in this preparation phase are (1) know the case, (2) determine the prior record, (3) view the scene, (4) establish the timing, and (5) determine who will do the interrogating.

Step One: Know the Case

The interrogator should be thoroughly familiar with the case. Statements of victims should be reviewed, particularly if the interrogator did not interview victims or witnesses. If the investigation involves a major felony, there may be more than one person involved in the investigation. The interrogator should speak with each investigator, in a group meeting if possible. It is not unusual for facts of the case to be known to one investigator and unknown to others. Take the time to contact the individuals who have been involved with the case or similar cases that may be linked.

Prior to conducting an interrogation, review the statutes concerning the crimes that may have already been charged and those that may be considered in the future. Be familiar with the elements of each law that must be satisfied to obtain a court conviction. During the interrogation it is imperative that evidence concerning the violation of the specific elements be addressed. For example, if the charge is "rape," then the proof of penetration by an object must be established. A lesser crime would be an attempted rape or sexual assault. Did the suspect undress himself or unzip the fly on his pants? This alone could be used to substantiate the intent to rape. As another example, the crime of "breaking and entering with the intent to commit a felony" requires proof of both the "break" and the "intent."

Reviewing the offense to determine an interrogation approach includes having an understanding of the case that includes the numerous ways in which the suspect could be charged. Knowing your legal options provides leverage that can be used throughout the interrogation. Reviewing the case goes beyond merely knowing the category of crime that the suspect is thought to have committed. For example, what are the ways in which the perpetrator has been identified? Examples could include the suspect's voice inflections or the types of words that were used during the crime. It could include an identifying mark on the suspect or even the way the suspect smells. Information on the specific words or gestures used by the alleged perpetrator provides tools that the interrogator will be able to use. Ideally the interrogator should be the investigator in the case who has interviewed the victims and witnesses.

Step Two: Determine the Prior Record

A background check should be done on each individual prior to an interrogation. Determine whether the suspect has been prosecuted and found guilty for crimes in the past. A suspect may be concerned if he or she has a violent felony record from past convictions. In jurisdictions with three strikes or mandatory sentencing laws, the suspect may have an additional fear that will impact the interrogation. Under three strikes and mandatory sentencing a felon will face long periods of mandated imprisonment for a third conviction.

Check to see whether there are any outstanding warrants that may be used to hold the suspect in custody if necessary. It is also of value to find out whether the suspect has any suspended sentences.

Step Three: View the Scene

Conducting a search for evidence is as important as conducting the interrogation. Viewing the scene may produce indisputable facts that could be brought into the interrogation. Faced with physical evidence that points to his or her guilt, the alleged perpetrator may be less likely to deny the charges.

To determine whether the suspect is linked to other, similar crimes, it is necessary to find out how the individual committed the crime. Referred to as the *modus operandi* or methods of operation, these are the usual things that the suspect does during the commission of a particular crime. In a house break-in, for example, what type of neighborhood did the suspect invade? Was entry gained at the front door or the back door? Was a tool used or glass broken? Was there a significant difference in the

---

BEEN THERE... DONE THAT! 12-2

An officer from the Vermont Sheriff's Office contacted the Massachusetts State Police. He had arrested a man who was passing phony drug prescriptions. A search of the subject revealed evidence of scrips being passed in Northampton, Massachusetts. I was assigned the investigation and learned that the suspect, Mr. T, had gone on a 4-day spree during which he obtained narcotics fraudulently. His *modus operandi* was to phone a pharmacy and order a prescription for a Schedule II narcotic while his wife waited inside the pharmacy to see whether the police were called. In this case, Mrs. T would then come outside and warn her husband if the police were called so that they could flee. Mr. T had also gone to a local doctor complaining of pain, requesting Dilaudid (a Schedule II narcotic). At the time of his arrest he had numerous labels from prescriptions for codeine issued by a pharmacy in Massachusetts. He had used the prescribing doctor's name for the phony scrips.

Subsequently I recovered nine prescriptions for Mr. T that had been filled for Schedule II and III narcotics. These supposedly had been phoned in by a "doctor" but were found to be fraudulent. Mr. T and his wife had also stolen scrip pads from legitimate doctors and had written fraudulent prescriptions. The doctors were interviewed and gave statements that they had not issued the medication prescriptions. Mr. T had used at least two aliases in the scheme. An arrest warrant was issued.

type of item stolen, such as jewelry, electronics, or guns and ammunition? These particulars can later be compared to crimes of a similar nature to determine whether the suspect could have been involved in other house break-ins.

Step Four: Establish the Timing

Generally the suspect should be confronted as soon as is practical, ideally before he or she learns about the investigation. This provides an opportunity to lock the suspect into a story or alibi. The less time that he or she has to make up an alibi or justify the offense, the better. In cases in which evidence may be found on the body of the individual, speed is of the essence. Whatever timing is chosen, it is the prerogative of the interrogator to determine the best opportunity. The officer must then assess whether it is safe to proceed.

Although speed and surprise are general principles for an interrogation, there are times when purposeful delay is the best approach. Situations that may cause delay to the interrogation include the following:

- Passage of time since the crime
- Existence of multiple victims
- Previous relationship between the alleged offender and the officer
- Need to execute a search warrant

The passage of time makes it more difficult to solve a crime. Leads dry up and evidence can be difficult to generate. The investigation that

FIGURE 12-2 An interrogation room should be free of distractions.

> **BEEN THERE . . . DONE THAT! 12-3**
>
> This investigation started with a phone call from the Department of Social Services. The social worker told me that she had investigated the death of an infant a few days earlier. She had originally thought that the child had died from fractures due to brittle bone disease (osteogenesis imperfecta), a genetic disorder that is characterized by bones that break easily for no apparent reason. The disorder is present at birth but the individual may not show symptoms for years. In this case, the child had been diagnosed with the disease at the time of birth and had suffered fractures prior to her death.
>
> The social worker was having second thoughts about the cause of death because a second child of the same parent had just been taken to the hospital with severe injuries that were indicative of abuse. It was unknown at that time whether the second child was going to live. When the social worker gave me the name of the child's mother I immediately know who it was. The family was known to be very violent. I had arrested her brother a year prior for homicide. There was no evidence that the mother had killed her sick baby, but I had a sinking feeling that that was exactly what had happened.
>
> I went to her apartment and introduced myself, and explained that I was investigating what had happened to her two children. The mother allowed me in to the apartment to look at the room while she described what had happened. Her explanation of the situation did not fit the scene. For example, she said that she had picked up the sick baby, who was crying and had awakened her sleeping boyfriend. She brought the child into the kitchen and had tripped on a toy that was on the floor. The child fell. At my request she drew a picture of the place she had "tripped" and where the baby had fallen. I took pictures of the apartment. But there were no toys. Not one. It was a two-room, one-bedroom apartment. The two children slept in the same room with the mother and her boyfriend. The child did not fall straight down (as falling objects tend to do), but came to rest at the opposite side of the kitchen. From the position of the objects in the kitchen, it appeared as though the child had been forcibly thrown against the side of the stove and had landed far to the left of it.
>
> After reviewing the case, I made the decision to interrogate the mother during a non-custodial interrogation. I asked if she was willing for me to write down her statement at my office and and whether there was anyone she would like to accompany her. She asked if I could pick up her mother on the way. I did. Her mom stayed outside of the room during the actual statement. The foregoing facts were incorporated into the statement, along with the fact that her boyfriend was very angry when the baby started crying. She in turn became angry at the children and had "probably thrown" them both. The second child did not die but would be brain damaged for the rest of his life. This was no accident. This was not an interview; persuasion was needed to extract the statement. The goal was to have her admit to causing the death and injury to her children. She did admit it and signed the confession before I brought her and her mother home. She was later indicted and pled guilty.

continues after the case is cold requires an approach that is slow and steady. Talk to suspects; take the time to review the files.

The possibility that there were multiple victims can generate a sense of urgency in solving the case. It is an impulse that is best held back. When multiple victims are linked to a single possible suspect, the investigator has the additional responsibility of learning the details of each case. Failure to take the time can result in overlooking details. There may be only be one opportunity to conduct an interrogation, so be careful not to go too fast and miss the opportunity to be thorough.

A previous relationship or newly cultivated relationship with the alleged offender can be used to the benefit of the investigation process. If the suspect is accustomed to seeing the officer and some respect has been established, a major barrier against disclosing has been broken down prior to the interrogation. It can be a sense of relief for the suspect when the time comes for the case to be discussed. It is possible to have the suspect anticipate the day of the interrogation.

Step Five: Determine Who Will Do the Interrogating

Many officers have conducted one-on-one interrogations. The primary consideration is whether the suspect might be a threat to the safety of the officer. The seriousness of the case is not necessarily the determining factor; the decision to delay an interrogation should be based on whether the officer will be outnumbered and whether the suspect is mentally ill, is a member of the opposite gender, or has a violent history. It is dangerous and unnecessary to assume that the size or strength of the interrogator determines the place or timing. The bottom line is that the interrogator needs to have complete control over the questioning and should not be forced into conducting the interrogation in a time or place that is not desired.

Ideally two persons should be in the room with the suspect during the interrogation, but one should do the majority of the questioning. There are several reasons for this arrangement. The primary reason is for officer safety. Second, having two persons in the room allows for flexibility in the interrogation. If the suspect is not responding to the primary questioning officer, the officers can switch roles. It is not uncommon for a suspect to express anger toward one of the officers without reason; having an alternative person available makes it possible to continue the questioning. It is the responsibility of the interrogator to determine when his or her effectiveness is fading and to be willing to step back and allow another person to continue the interrogation. Another reason for a second interrogator is that he or she can take detailed notes, freeing the primary interrogator from that responsibility. The note-taker should be seated behind the suspect and slightly to one side, within sight of the primary interrogator but outside the line of vision of the suspect. This is done so as not to distract the suspect during the interrogation. An alternative arrangement has the second interrogator monitor the interrogation from behind a two-way mirror.

When preparing for an interrogation, the most important aspect of the case is the preservation of the constitutional protections of the accused. Know the federal and state mandates before attempting to conduct an interrogation. For this reason, typically a seasoned investigator is the best choice to conducting the interrogation. Denial of the suspect's rights does nothing but jeopardize the case. Evidence may later be excluded from the trial if an improper interrogation takes place. A confession is only worthwhile if it is obtained correctly. Confession admissibility is guided by the Fourth, Fifth, Sixth, and Fourteenth Amendments of the Constitution, case law, federal law, and state law. It must be established that a suspect's incriminating response was not the result of words or actions on the part of the police that violated these provisions.

The place chosen for the interrogation should be quiet and free of distractions. There should be no telephone, radio, clock, or other electronic devices. The officers in the room should turn off their pagers and cell phones. Ideally the room should have a two-way mirror for observation.

Suspects may be interrogated in their home or any other place where privacy can be assured. The location should encourage suspects to release their burden of guilt in an atmosphere that is private and safe. An absence of judgment from the interrogator adds to the feeling that the suspect has nothing to fear about opening up.

INTERROGATION PHASE II: DEVELOPING OUTCOME-BASED TACTICS

Prior to beginning the interrogation the investigator should develop outcome-based tactics to persuade the suspect to cooperate. These are persuasive arguments that are designed to overcome the resistance of a suspect to confessing. Approaches that are valuable in conducting successful interrogations include minimizing the crime, blaming the victim, decreasing the shamefulness of the crime, increasing guilt, and appealing to the suspect's hope for a better outcome. The experienced interrogator will develop many additional approaches. The characteristics of the suspect such as age, level of education, and marital status complicate the interrogation process. The suspect's employment, community status, and lifestyle also impact the approach used for persuasion.

To get to a confession the interrogator must consider the many reasons the suspect might not want to confess and which persuasive arguments can overcome that resistance. The suspect's fears may cause resistance to the interrogation and inhibit the suspect from admitting guilt. Identifying these fears is an important part of developing persuasive arguments. The following 10 interrogation tactics (Leo, 1996) address suspect fears and suggest methods for interrogation. The fears highlighted here can be exploited using different tactics. These are just some examples for illustrative purposes.

Tactic #1. Appealing to the Suspect's Self-Interest

The most frequent interrogation tactic involves an appeal to the suspect's self-interest, which can also be stated as an appeal to the hope for a better outcome to the case. A common impulse is to suggest that the suspect would be "better off" if he or she confessed. Care must be taken because a promise of leniency violates the suspect's right to due process and may cause legal challenges to any resulting confession. There are other ways to appeal to the self-interest of the suspect. For example, suggest that the suspect will "feel better" if he or she talks about the act. Encourage the suspect to "get it off his chest" or "tell his version of what happened." When you ask someone to do something and they perceive you as a person who has his or her best interests in mind and/or would like you to have his or her best interests in mind, he or she is strongly motivated to cooperate.

When a person is emotionally involved and has a stake in the outcome of the situation, logical reasoning is not enough to persuade him or her to provide a statement. The interrogator may have the suspect face the reality of the situation by asking, "What would I have tell you in order to convince you that talking to me is in your best interest?"

- **Fear of Retaliation.** The suspect's fear for his or her safety or the safety of a family member can be difficult to overcome. This fear is particularly relevant in drug cases and in cases with gang involvement.

Consider telling the suspect that you are concerned with his or her safety because of his or her associations. Ask what you can do to help. Empathize with the suspect's dilemma. Be firm in stating that the suspect has more to fear from the gang or drug dealer than from the police. Explain that not giving a statement will not make him or her safer; his or her presence at the station is already known by the people they fear. The best option is to cooperate with the police.

Tactic #2. Confronting the Suspect with Evidence of Guilt

Another very common approach to persuading a suspect is to confront him or her with evidence of guilt. This may involve telling the suspect about physical evidence that demonstrates that he or she committed the crime. Recognize that the may be trying to turn the focus of the investigation in another direction for fear that they will be discovered as the guilty person. This can cause him or her act as if they are helping the police.

- **Paranoia.** Suspects may fear that the police are looking in their direction as a suspect and may volunteer information that is designed to send the investigation in another direction so that the police will not focus on them. They don't know how much information the police have, so they take the role of a compliant witness who may be helpful to the police. A suspect may identify a fictitious perpetrator or give evidence that would appear to exonerate him or her.

Use any evidence that has been obtained that could indicate the person's guilt. For example, point out a failed polygraph test as providing evidence that the person is guilty. If the person passed the polygraph test, explain that giving the test is not an exact science, which is why it is not allowed as evidence in many states. Suggest that even guilty individuals can pass the polygraph.

Use the relationship that the individual had with the victim in cases of personal violence, house breaks-ins, or even arson. Provide reasons why the individual would want to "get back" at the victim for some perceived wrong. Use the suspect's knowledge of the geographic area as an indication that the suspect had access to the place where the crime was committed. Consider the access that the suspect had to property or money at his or her place of employment for crimes committed at work.

Tactic #3. Undermining the Suspect's Confidence in His or Her Denials

If the suspect does not think that you have sufficient evidence to make an arrest, he or she may be reluctant to provide that information during an interrogation. This can work in the favor of the interrogator. The suspect may agree to talk to convince the interrogator that he or she is innocent. Another approach is to simply not allow denials. Stop the individual from denying his or her guilt and assert firmly that there is sufficient evidence that he or she is lying. Present your firm belief of his or her guilt.

- **Fear of Arrest.** The fear of being arrested is equally high for people who have had little contact with the police as for those who have been arrested before. Suspects who have had prior arrests may fear the laws that mandate jail for multiple arrests. Those with no previous contact with the police fear the consequences of arrest.

  There are two options for overcoming a suspect's fear of arrest. The first is to decide that you will not arrest that individual when the interrogation is over. Based on this decision tell the suspect, "You will not be arrested TODAY; I will consider everything you have to say and make that determination at another time." Add, "This is your chance to tell me everything you want to say; it will be your only chance to do this." Having taken this position, you must follow through and not make the arrest at that time.
  The second option for overcoming the resistance to arrest is to state that the person is already under arrest; nothing is going to chance that (when in fact they have already been arrested). Or, "Regardless of what you say, the facts of the case speak for themselves; you only have the option of cooperating at this point."

Tactic #4. Identifying Contradictions in the Suspect's Alibi or Story

The term "because" has been identified as a powerful persuasive word (Hogan, 2002). Use it liberally during an interrogation to make your point. Tell the suspect that he or she committed the crime BECAUSE. For example, "You did the robbery because you wanted the money, plain and simple." Or, "Your alibi does not make sense because there was plenty of time for you to have committed the burglary before . . . or after . . . ." Or, "Because I think you did not mean to keep that money, I want you to tell me what really happened." Consider in financial crimes that the person might be concerned with returning the money or property or making restitution. Identifying contradictions in a suspect's story is one of the most successful interrogation tactics for obtaining a confession (Leo, 1996).

- **Fear of Financial Repercussions.** The officer should act in a manner that is nonjudgmental. The perpetrator may have committed the crime because it seemed like the only alternative at the time. Afterward the fear sets in and the suspect may be torn on what to do about it.

Faced with evidence that the suspect stole money or property, consider that there may be reasons that the suspect justified the theft at the time but may now feel remorseful. Attempt to engage the suspect about why he or she committed the crime. "Were you late in paying your bills?" Or, "Do have a drug or alcohol problem?" Or, "Do you feel underpaid and undervalued by your employer?" Minimize the crime and offer justifications that would encourage the suspect to talk about his or her reasons for committing the act.

Tactic #5. Asking Specific "Behavioral Analysis" Interview Questions

The suspect may make an emotional or a rational choice to confess to having committed a crime. Determine whether your suspect is a guilt-ridden offender or an apathetic offender so you can tailor an emotional argument or a rational argument. A **guilt-ridden offender** experiences a higher level of remorse, is sensitive about the effects of the offense, and is concerned about what others think of him or her. An **apathetic offender** does not experience remorse, considers himself or herself justified in having committed the crime, and is most concerned with avoiding punishment.

Offenders with a guilty conscience react to the words of the interrogator and may appear to have a more relaxed body posture and an unwillingness to look the interrogator in the eyes (Inbau et al., 2001). This offender may show signs of nervousness such as sweating or frequent licking of lips and wiping of eyebrows. A guilt-ridden offender may stutter and verbally trip over his or her words during conversation.

The apathetic offender appears not to care about his or her situation as the suspect of a crime. This offender may lack remorse due to a mental illness such as antisocial personality disorder. The offender will look the interrogator in the eye with defiance and deny participation in the crime.

Refer to Chapter 6 for additional behavioral techniques for determining the types of questions to ask and some expected responses by a guilty person. Use behavioral indicators of guilt as a means of confronting the suspect. Point out that he or she may be able to hide his or her emotions, but not his or her facial expressions. Look at the person's body posture and determine whether they are generally truthful or evasive. Use this information as a part of the argument to overcome resistance to providing a statement.

Tactic #6. Appealing to the Importance of Cooperating

- **Loss of Job.** If the individual has status in the community or a well-paying job, he or she may fear losing that employment as a result of being arrested. Fear that admitting guilt will have financial repercussions is a real concern.

  During the assessment, questions on employment status are common. Use this information to ask questions like, "What do you think will happen to your job because of this?" This allows the interrogator to firmly but kindly state that yes, you are guilty and there are repercussions. Have the suspect face this issue to overcome denial. Suggest that the suspect can start over when this is behind him or her. If the suspect expresses concern about his or her family, be compassionate and minimize the repercussions.

Tactic #7. Offering Moral Justifications and Face-Saving Excuses

Minimize the crime and never refer to it by its legal term. Encourage the suspect to express guilt, remorse, or anger toward the victim. In sensitive or potentially embarrassing cases tell the suspect that you will not contact the press and give out details of his or her acts. The media may report the crime, but the information will not come from your discussion. Consider the fears that may contribute to resistance in such cases to better use this tactic.

- **Shame.** The suspect's fear may be related to the category of crime that he or she is accused of committing. The suspect may fear that if the particulars of the crime are divulged he or she will lose respect, shock family or friends, or suffer embarrassment. It is likely that the victim was known to the perpetrator; guilt is likely intense.

  Use empathy to counteract the suspect's shame. Ask why the suspect did what he or she did. Abusers of children often speak about their love for the child and how the relationship benefited the child. If the suspect knew the victim, don't circumvent that relationship, put it right out into the open. Ask whether there had been an argument or something that caused him or her to commit the crime. Offering moral justifications or excuses to the suspect is one of the most successful tactics for obtaining a confession (Leo, 1996).

Tactic #8. Confronting the Suspect with False Evidence of Guilt

There are a variety of situations in which confronting the suspect with false evidence of guilt makes sense. This is particularly true when there is more than one person involved in the crime. The suspects should be interrogated separately. Information provided by one suspect can be embellished and presented as fact to another suspect. Stating that a suspect was weak can substantiate that he or she provided information. Suggest that the suspect you are now interrogating was named as the ringleader, the one who pulled the trigger, or the person who planned the crime.

- **Fear of Blame.** A suspect who played a minor part in a crime will fear being blamed for it and being punished disproportionately to the role he or she had. The thought that someone else will get away with the crime and they will be imprisoned will seem unfair to the suspect.

Exploit this fear by pointing out that the suspect will take all of the blame unless he or she provides information on who actually planned and executed the act. Suggest, "You don't seem like the type of person that would kill an old lady, steal from the blind, break into the liquor store [whatever the crime was]."

Tactic #9. Praising or Flattering the Suspect

Some persons exhibit signs of insecurity and self-doubt, whereas others appear to thrive on attention and praise. Look for indications that the suspect is insecure. Considerations include whether the crime committed was without apparent cause. This might suggest that the perpetrator committed the crime because it made him or her feel good. Did the suspect appear to take pleasure in the crime based on evidence that was left behind? Is there any indication that the suspect took an article of clothing, jewelry, or other keepsake from the crime scene?

- **Fear of Insignificance.** A suspect may feel powerless and insecure about his or her identity. Exerting power over a person or situation compensates for that fear of insignificance.

Exploiting a person's fear of insignificance requires acknowledgment from the interrogator of a "job well done." Praise and supportive statements convey a positive judgment to the suspect. This can be accomplished without supporting the act itself, but by stating the obvious about what the suspect did. For example, "You did a pretty good job at cleaning up the scene." Or, "You have been successful at avoiding being caught for a long time." Or, "I noticed that you covered up the victim. That was very considerate." Generally people will respond to praise. Flattery or praise is one of the most successful tactics in obtaining a confession (Leo, 1996).

Tactic #10. Appealing to the Detective's Expertise and Authority

This tactic refers to a display of overconfidence by the interrogator to emphasize his or her the ability as an investigator. It is meant to overcome resistance through an appeal to status. This entails statements to the suspect that downplay his or her ability to "get away" with committing the crime. It can be used with a suspect who appears overly confident. The tactic allows the interrogator to take charge of an interrogation by suggesting that he or she is much smarter than the suspect. Break down the confidence of the suspect through negative statements on the crime, how it was accomplished, and what will result because of it.

Remember that these tactics are goal oriented. They are considered prior to the interrogation and planned to meet its goals. Failure to consider a plan is like appearing a play without having rehearsed your lines.

INTERROGATION PHASE III: GETTING THE CONFESSION

Don't be overly solicitous or friendly; establish yourself as a professional. Always minimize the crime when speaking to the suspect. Do not use legal terminology or police jargon. Speak with the person firmly but with respect. While maintaining control over the interrogation, don't verbally back the suspect into a corner. If the suspect feels that there is no way out, he or she will stop talking, so give the suspect an out from the very beginning. Instead of focusing on the crime, start with what motivated the suspect to commit the crime. Don't invite a denial, ask for an explanation.

Step One: Make the Claim

Suspects should feel that the interrogator will listen. To begin the interrogation, an accusation must be made by the interrogator. There are a number of ways to do this. It is my experience that honesty works best. The interrogator's sincerity will be apparent to all but the hardest of criminals. Use his or her first name and do not shout. Never express anger; it indicates weakness. At all times the interrogator must be in complete control of her or his emotions and reactions.

> *There is one thing that an innocent man has in common with a guilty man: they will both deny having committed the crime.*

When the moment arrives that the claim is to be made, the interrogator should be sitting in close proximity to the suspect. There should be no tables or furniture between them. Lean toward the suspect slightly and firmly tell him or her that you know that he or she is guilty. Say that there is no doubt in your mind, based on the investigation, that he or she did it. An innocent person is more likely to have a quick and strong denial along with anger at having been accused. He or she may jump right out of the chair and begin yelling. A guilty person is also likely to deny the claim but will be slower or protest more weakly.

Step Two: Lock It In

Once the claim has been made, there can be no further discussion on innocence. Having already considered the outcome-based tactics that can be used, this is the time for you to use persuasion. Tell the suspect that he or she needs to move on, understand why the events happened, or tell their version of the story. Present an excuse for the suspect, minimize his or her culpability in the crime, or suggest that he or she was tormented and that there was no other choice. No one likes to be caught with his or her hand in the cookie jar. People do not like being confronted with something they did wrong. Allow the person to express the good intentions; suggest that you understand that he or she did not mean to hurt the person, meant to return the money, or whatever fits the events. This will allow the suspect to maintain face.

The more a person denies something, the more he or she begins to believe in his or her innocence. Prevent this from happening by interrupting the suspect. Encourage the person to continue in a way that is going to move forward and allow him or her to figure out what to do next. Tell the suspect that the situation is not going to go away, and that he or she has an opportunity to have his or her side of the story included when it does come out. Allow the suspect to maintain his or her dignity.

There will be times when the interrogator senses anger or disrespect from the alleged perpetrator that is difficult to overcome. It is perfectly acceptable to recognize that the likelihood of your obtaining a confession is low. If there is another individual who can continue the interrogation with better chances at being successful, step back and allow that individual to take over.

BEEN THERE...DONE THAT! 12-4

Jane Doe was 23 years old. She told me during an interview that she had left her home around 6:30 AM to go jogging. She was wearing a pair of running shorts, a shirt, and sneakers with socks. As she began running, she noticed a commercial truck with faded red letters on the side and back parked by the side of the road. It later drove past her. As she continued running down the country road, a man came running toward her. He was screaming "ARAHAHH." He tackled her to the ground, and she fell into a cornfield. She hit him in the groin and stomach. He got on top of her and forced her onto her back. She asked what he was doing and he replied, "I don't know." He grabbed her on the left side of her shirt and touched her left breast. She told me that she was very much in fear and kept trying to hit him. She thought that her life was in danger and she kept swearing and hitting him. Finally she was able to roll him off of her, and she ran to a house nearby.

She described the assailant as having a high voice for a man. He was a white man in his 20s and was wearing a bright red shirt (pullover type) with a round neck and tight black biker pants that came to his mid thigh. He had blonde, curly hair (not tight curls) with bangs that half covered his ears.

With what crimes (if any) would you charge this suspect? What is your assessment of him? What approach would you use to interrogate him? See the exercise at the end of this chapter.

Techniques for Interrogation 271

FIGURE 12-3 Practice your skills! This is the suspect for the exercise at the end of this chapter. Refer back to this photo as needed.

FIGURE 12-4 At the time of his arrest, your suspect was operating this truck.

▲ CONCLUSIONS

By using the complementary principle, an interrogator can influence a suspect's responses. Persuading the suspect can occur through the primary interactions of friendliness and dominance. This sets the stage for the interrogator to take charge of the interrogation. An interrogation is different than an interview because it presupposes the guilt of the person being questioned. Therefore, the purpose of an interrogation is to obtain a confession or an admission. Obtaining either is a successful conclusion to the interrogation process. The same legal standards that were explained in Chapter 10 governing the admissibility of a confession pertain to an admission.

The chapter covered different interrogation approaches and confession-eliciting models. This should impress on you that there is no one way to conduct an interrogation. The process is complicated. Three phases were suggested as an outline of the interrogation process. The first phase is a preparation that should look very familiar. The first three steps are the same as the preparation for an interview. Because the guilt of the suspect should be fairly certain at the time the interrogation takes place, additional preparation involves its timing and the choice of interrogator. Phase II is an important step in persuading the suspect to confess. The interrogator should go into the process after having already considered the possible tactics to use to overcome resistance to providing a confession. Central to the development of outcome-based tactics is understanding of the suspect's fears. Suggestions were made on how to exploit these fears, but by no means is this an exhaustive list of possibilities.

■ QUESTIONS FOR REVIEW

Short-Answer Questions

1. Explain what the complementary principle can mean to the potential interrogator.
2. Explain the difference between a confession and an admission.
3. In what three ways can the interrogation process become compromised if an investigator puts all of his or her energy into obtaining a confession rather than collecting evidence.
4. Discuss the concept of having two people conduct an interrogation. Why should one person do most of the interrogating? What should the other person focus on?
5. Explain how noncustodial and custodial interrogations differ with regard to *Miranda* warnings.
6. State two reasons why an interrogator should know the case thoroughly prior to conducting an interrogation.
7. What is the value of conducting a background check on the suspect prior to the interrogation?
8. What can be gained from the interrogator viewing the scene of the crime prior to the interrogation?
9. What are some of the factors that might influence the timing of the interrogation?

10. List three suspect fears that can cause resistance to interrogation.
11. Explain at least three of the frequently used interrogation tactics.

Fill-in Questions

1. According to _____, humans interact within the two frameworks of dominance and friendliness.
2. The primary purpose of the interrogation is to _____ from the suspect that acknowledges or indicates the guilt of that person.
3. A(n) _____ is a statement of guilty conduct containing only facts from which guilt may be inferred.
4. The interrogation should take place when _____.
5. An interrogation is not an option after the individual _____ on the crimes under investigation or asks to speak to an attorney.
6. It is necessary to _____ and plan for an interrogation.
7. The interrogation is intentionally _____.
8. Develop _____ tactics prior to conducting an interrogation.
9. One thing that an innocent man has in common with a guilty man is that they will both _____.

Exercises

1. Noncustodial versus custodial interrogation:
   - List the differences between a noncustodial and a custodial interrogation with regard to *Miranda* warnings.
   - Describe three noncustodial situations. Are *Miranda* warnings required for these situations? Why or why not.
   - Describe three custodial situations. Are *Miranda* warnings required in these situations? Why or why not?

   The victim statement for the following exercises is given in Been There... Done That! 12-4. Refer to Figures 12-4 and 12-5 as the evidence for this exercise.

2. Complete each step of interrogation phase I, preparing. Describe in writing what you do for each step and justify any decisions that you make. For step three go to the law library or online and find the statute that defines all of the possible crimes for your state regarding this case. Write down the information on all of the possible crimes. The following site is a place to look for the criminal code in your jurisdiction: http://straylight.law.cornell.edu/topics/state_statutes2.html#criminal_code
3. Complete interrogation phase II, developing outcome-based tactics. Consider the obstacles that may be present in this case scenario. How might they be overcome? What tactics would be beneficial for persuading the suspect to provide a confession? What fears might the suspect have about what he did?
4. Without actually questioning anyone, determine the approach you would take to making the claim of guilt and locking the suspect in on it. Explain your reasoning.

REFERENCES

Bruton v. U.S., 391 US 123, 139 (1968).

Commonwealth v. Forde, 392 Mass. 453 (1984).

Garner, B. (2004). *Black's law dictionary* (8th ed.). St. Paul, MN: West Publishing.

Gordon, N. J., & Fleisher, W. L. (2002). *Effective interviewing and interrogation techniques*. San Diego, CA: Academic Press.

Gudjonsson, G. H. (2003). *The psychology of interrogations and confessions: A handbook*. Hoboken, NJ: Wiley.

Gurtman, M. B. (2001). Interpersonal complementarity: Integrating interpersonal measurement with interpersonal models. *Journal of Counseling Psychology, 48*(1), 97–110.

Hogan, K. (2002). *The psychology of persuasion*. Gretna, LA: Pelican Publishing.

Inbau, F. E., Reid, J. E., Buckley, J. P., & Jayne, B. C. (2001). *Criminal interrogation and confessions* (4th ed.). Gaithersburg, MD: Aspen Publishers.

Leo, R. A. (1996). Inside the interrogation room. *Journal of Criminal Law and Criminology, 86,* 266–303. Available: http://www.lexisnexis.com//universe.

Rutledge, D. (1994). *Criminal interrogation: Law and tactics* (3rd ed.). Placerville, CA: Copperhouse Publishing.

Sadler, P., & Woody, E. (2003). Is who you are who you're talking to? Interpersonal style and complementarity in mixed-sex interactions. *Journal of Personality and Social Psychology, 84*(1), 80–96.

CHAPTER 13
Juvenile Rights and Police Responsibilities

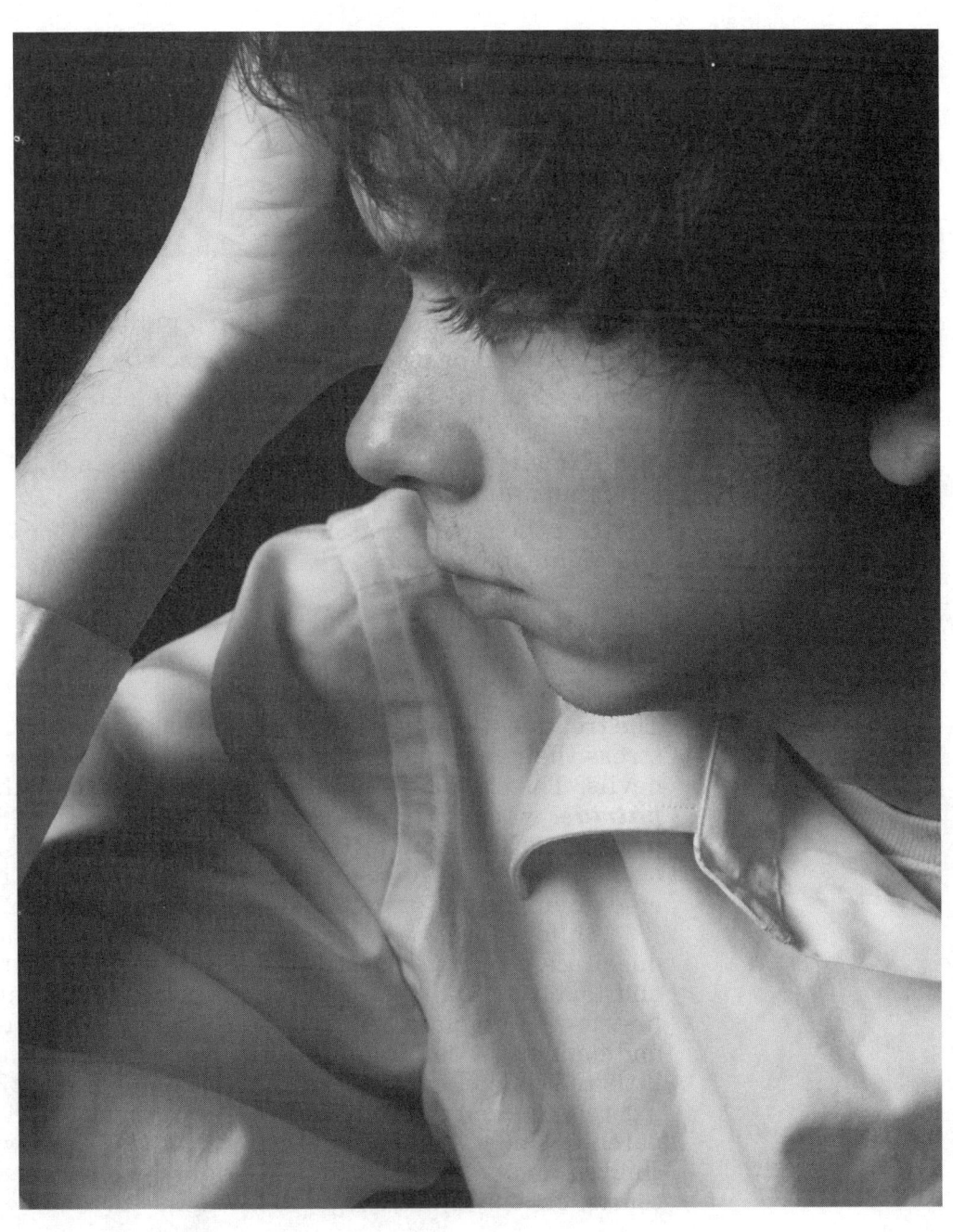

Key Terms

Parens patriae	Juvenile delinquency
Juvenile	Temporary custody
Infancy rule	Fireplay
Status offense	Firesetting

Chapter Objectives

After completing this chapter, you should be able to:

- Describe the difference between the status offense and juvenile delinquency
- Define the term *juvenile*
- State the significance of *In Re Gault*
- Explain the constitutional rights that apply to juveniles
- Explain the infancy rule
- Compare and contrast *firesetting* and *fireplay*
- List the categories of juvenile encounter that do not involve custody
- Describe the method for interviewing an alleged juvenile sexual offender
- Explain the circumstances under which a child may be taken into temporary custody
- List the factors that need to be considered for a juvenile waiver of rights to be valid

Introduction

The treatment of juveniles by society has varied over time. Some cultures stress their innocence, whereas others view children as potential little devils. The English feudal system established the notion of **parens patriae,** which is the power of the State to act in behalf of a child and provide care and protection equivalent to that of a parent, sometimes over the objection of the parent. In other contexts children were considered an important part of economic life as sources of labor.

Children were treated as adults in criminal matters but lacked the due process rights enjoyed by adults. They were sentenced in adult courts and taken to adult jails. It was not until 1889 that Illinois enacted the first law to regulate the treatment and control of dependent, neglected, and delinquent children. Children could be picked up by the police with little reason, held and questioned for long periods of time without notifying their parents, and placed in institutions with no recourse by their parents. Under the notion of *parens patriae* the power of the State over children is absolute and juvenile rights are provided at the whim of the courts. Juveniles are not adults, and as such do not automatically have constitutional protection. The rights that are applicable to juveniles have been expressly granted by the courts and through legislative action.

WHAT IS A JUVENILE?

A *juvenile* defined under federal law as a person who has not attained his or her eighteenth birthday (U.S. Code 18 U.S.C. §5031, 1994). A person older than 18 years but less than 21 years is also accorded juvenile treatment if the act of juvenile delinquency occurred prior to his or her eighteenth birthday. All states specify by statute the maximum age for an individual to be considered a juvenile, typically 17 or 18 years. Some states specify a younger age. In Georgia, for example, a minor is a juvenile until age 16 years (The National Center for Juvenile Justice, 2004), whereas in Connecticut, New York, and North Carolina a juvenile is a person of age 15 years and younger (Sickmund, 2003).

The distinction between juvenile and adult is becoming more important for the police interrogator as states move toward trying juveniles as adults for major crimes. This imposes a responsibility on the interrogator to ensure greater personal protections equivalent to those afforded to adults in addition to special considerations afforded to a minor.

Age of Criminal Responsibility

Children under the age of 7 years are generally presumed to be without the ability to form criminal intent under common law. Referred to as the

FIGURE 13-1 At what age can we hold children criminally responsible for their actions? The age of responsibility varies from state to state.

infancy rule, this is the minimum age at which a child may be charged with a criminal act. Many states have statutes that specify the age of criminal responsibility. The age varies from state to state, and in some cases there is no minimum age. Massachusetts, for example, relies on the common law rule of age 7 years to determine juvenile court jurisdiction, the Colorado delinquency age is 10 years, and Arizona specifies no lower age (The National Center for Juvenile Justice, 2004).

JUVENILE OFFENDING

The vast majority of juvenile offenders enter the juvenile justice system through law enforcement agencies. Approximately 7 of 10 arrested juveniles are referred to juvenile court (Sickmund, 2003). There are two different categories of wrongdoing that apply to juveniles, the status offense and the delinquent offense.

A **status offense** is an act that would not be a crime if it was committed by an adult; it is illegal only because the child is underage. Examples include truancy, running away, and curfew violations. Some states treat status offenders differently than delinquents. In other states, classification as a status offender has relatively little effect on the child's treatment. Many states view these behaviors as indicators that the child is in need of services, in which case the matter is handled though social service agencies. Many states retain juvenile court jurisdiction for status offenses or abuse, neglect, or dependency through age 20 years (Sickmund, 2003).

Juvenile delinquency is the violation of a law of the United States committed by a person prior to his or her eighteenth birthday that would have been a crime if it had been committed by an adult (U.S. Code 18 U.S.C. §5031, 1994. The age for a minor to be adjudicated under the jurisdiction of the juvenile court varies from state to state depending on its definition of a juvenile. The juvenile court's authority may extend to as late as age 24 years as in California, Montana, Oregon, and Wisconsin,

---

BEEN THERE . . . DONE THAT!   13-1

Like other typical 7-year-old boys, Michael and Stephen frequently took turns spending the night at each other's house. The boys, I learned, performed anal and oral sex on each other. This had occurred on at least a dozen occasions. I interviewed them to determine who had been victimized by whom.

It was Michael who had initiated the sex; he had been doing it with his stepbrother, Jerry, every night for about a year. Jerry was 16 years old and had come to live with Michael and his parents. They shared a room with bunk beds, and Jerry would come down from his bunk bed at night to have sex with Michael. Jerry was a special education student who had both physical and learning disabilities.

Who is the perpetrator here? Is there more than one? Is the perpetrator a juvenile or an adult?

although most states end jurisdiction in delinquency cases at age 21 years (Sickmund, 2003). Age and offense together provide another way of determining juvenile delinquency. Some state statutes exclude types of juvenile offenders from juvenile court jurisdiction, mandating that the case be tried in criminal court.

Juvenile Delinquency

The juvenile arrest rate grew substantially during the late 1980s and peaked in 1994. Decreasing steadily since its peak, by 2002 the arrest rate of persons under the age of 18 years was nearly half of its 1994 level (Snyder, 2004). Although this is encouraging, juvenile crime remains a significant problem, with an estimated 2.3 million arrests in 2002. According to the Federal Bureau of Investigation, juveniles accounted for 17 percent of all arrests and 15 percent of all violent crime arrests in 2002. Female offenders represent an increasing proportion of juvenile arrests. Approximately 85 percent of delinquency cases referred to juvenile court in the United States originate from police officers.

DUE PROCESS AND THE JUVENILE

In 1966 the Supreme Court responded to the problem of nonstandardized procedures and a general lack of juvenile protection in one of its first decisions concerning juvenile rights. Although the *Kent* decision was confined solely to the issue of waiver proceedings in juvenile courts, its expression of disenchantment with juvenile justice has had a wide effect on the entire juvenile justice system (*Kent v. United States,* 1966).

The most important case in the history of juvenile justice is the *Gault* decision, an attack on the *parens patriae* doctrine (*In re Gault,* 1967). This case is almost solely responsible for changing the juvenile system into an adversarial process, bringing it closer to the adult system. The Supreme Court stated that due process and the Fourteenth Amendment of the U.S. Constitution apply to juveniles when the juvenile faces possible commitment.

Initiated in 1971, the Juvenile Justice Standards Project developed a set of standards for juvenile justice after the *Gault* decision (Flicker, 2005). Rejecting the conventional medical model based on a need for treatment as the reason for the court's involvement, it adopted a due process model governed by equity and fairness. Several principles were developed, including a greater accountability of the juvenile justice system and clearly stated and enforced rights and responsibilities of the appropriate agencies. According to Flicker (2005), 10 basic principles emerged, known as the Institute of Judicial Administration-American Bar Association (IJA-ABA) Juvenile Justice Standards:

1. Sanctions should be proportionate to the seriousness of the offense
2. Sentences should be fixed by the court and there should be no indeterminate sentencing by correctional authorities

> **CASE IN POINT 13-1**
>
> *Case in Point: In re Gault (1967)*
>
> The case of *In re Gault* involved 15-year-old Gerald Gault and his friend, who made lewd telephone calls to a neighbor. After a complaint by that neighbor, Gault was arrested and detained by the police. His parents, worried that their son was not at home, were never notified of his arrest and only found out later through a friend of his. The complainant, Mrs. Cook, never testified about the phone calls. No one was sworn in, and the trial was not recorded. After proceedings before a juvenile court judge, Gault was committed to the State Industrial School for 6 years, until he reached the age of 21. An adult charged with the same crime would have received a maximum of a 50 dollar fine and 2 months in jail.
>
> The Supreme Court decided that the proceedings for juveniles had to comply with the requirements of the Fourteenth Amendment, including adequate notice of charges, notification of both the parents and the child of the juvenile's right to counsel, opportunity for confrontation and cross-examination at the hearings, and adequate safeguards against self-incrimination. The Court found that the procedures used in this case met none of these requirements.
>
> **Importance**
>
> 1. *In re Gault* is the most significant case in juvenile justice history. The Court established that juveniles do have certain due process rights. This changed the adjudication procedure into an adversarial process and opened the door for juveniles to be treated more formally and increasingly more like adults within the criminal justice system.

3. The least restrictive alternative should be required at every stage of the proceedings
4. Status offenses should be removed from juvenile court jurisdiction
5. Limitations should be imposed on interventions prior to adjudication
6. Open court proceedings should replace closed sessions
7. The juvenile should have part in the decision-making process
8. The parental role in the process should be defined
9. There should be a right to counsel at all crucial stages and an unwaivable right to counsel for juveniles
10. Strict criteria should be established for waiving juvenile court jurisdiction to regulate the transfer of juveniles to adult court

This due process approach dominates the juvenile justice system. Rather than consistency, however, we now have a different juvenile justice system in every state in the nation. The juvenile system increasingly resembles the adult system, but no uniform approach has been adopted. Generally, the due process model favors accountability and punishment, with much less focus on juvenile rehabilitation.

The legal trend is toward the punishment of juveniles as adults for felony crimes; the extent varies from state to state. All states specify circumstances in which juveniles may be prosecuted as adults. To prosecute a juvenile in adult court the vast majority of states authorize juvenile court judges to waive jurisdiction, and prosecutors in 15 states have that authority (Griffin, 2004). In at least 29 states, juveniles who commit specific major crimes must be tried in adult court if they are of a minimum statutory age (Griffin, 2004). Greater access to juvenile records means that subsequent adult sentencing may be enhanced under three-strikes laws or pursuant to sentencing guidelines in both the federal and state criminal justice systems (Shepherd, 1997).

At the same time, there is an increasing concern over the vulnerability of juveniles. Studies indicate that juveniles are among those particularly susceptible to police interrogation techniques that may lead to false confessions (Napier & Adams, 2002). Examples of at-risk persons include the young, people with low or borderline IQ, a mental handicap, psychological inadequacy, illiteracy, or fatigue or who lack experience with the criminal justice system. The questioning approach for juveniles requires both attention to due process issues and the recognition that they require special protections because of their age.

QUESTIONING A JUVENILE NOT IN CUSTODY

Juveniles can be approached informally and asked questions without a parent present or *Miranda* warnings (*Miranda v. Arizona,* 1966). It should not be overlooked that every police encounter is not adversarial or accusatory. In the investigation of crime, it is legitimate to seek witnesses of any age. It should be standard procedure that when a police officer responds to a home, particularly for domestic disputes, each child in the home be interviewed separately at the scene. The reason is to assess the safety of the child and to obtain information on the crime under investigation.

Juveniles may also be questioned in relation to a complaint. There is a great amount of police discretion on how a matter will be resolved. Approximately one fourth of juveniles arrested are handled within the police department and then released (Sickmund, 2003). To settle the complaint, a police officer will likely speak to the juvenile in an encounter. Two general types of police encounters are common in complaints concerning juveniles (Cicourel, 2005):

- **Field examination.** Police officers may be called to the scene or may encounter a situation that appears to be suspicious.
- **Station investigation.** Police officers may conduct an investigation into a crime that may involve a juvenile offender.

In the field examination, there are usually people around who can provide information about what happened. Examples include situations in which a juvenile is accused of stealing, a fight broke out, or a school called to report a student who did not attend. The police officer asks people what happened, including the juvenile who was involved, and the matter quickly may be resolved if it is a minor violation or a status offense. Possible resolutions include calling a parent or guardian

> **BEEN THERE... DONE THAT! 13-2**
>
> A homicide occurred in an otherwise quiet neighborhood. A 15-year-old girl was bludgeoned to death in the woods on her way to school. There was no apparent sexual offense, although her skirt had been raised up to her waist.
>
> The investigation pointed toward a 15-year-old boy who had recently fallen for the girl but had been rebuked. At the home of the boy, his mother admitted the police into the house. She gave permission for a search of her son's bedroom. In most situations, a parent can give consent for a search of his or her home and the space that is occupied by a minor in it. Only when the child has a heightened expectation of privacy due to his or her age, the fact that he of she pays rent, or the presence of a lock on the door that does not allow access by other family members do the parents lose their standing to consent to a search. These conditions vary from state to state. A sneaker was found that appeared to have a blood stain, and it was confiscated.
>
> At the time the law specified that a child in this state could not be tried as an adult unless it could be shown that he or she was not "amenable to treatment." In other words, the prosecution had to show that the minor had been in treatment prior to the offense and could not be rehabilitated. This juvenile had never been arrested before, not even for shoplifting. He was tried as a juvenile and found to be delinquent. At age 18 years he would be released.

to pick up the child along with a warning or a school sanction. If the event is serious or the juvenile is a repeat offender, then a juvenile probation officer might also be contacted. A summons to juvenile court is requested by the police officer or school official if court involvement is warranted.

A station investigation occurs if the offense is serious or the juvenile does not give information about his or her involvement and does not help in the resolution of the complaint. The juvenile may be detained for a short period of time until the matter is resolved or a legal guardian is available to come to the station to pick him or her up. The station investigation allows the officer the opportunity to get background information on the juvenile and collect evidence if warranted. The officer should have experience in dealing with juvenile offenders and be aware of the possible dispositions available in that jurisdiction.

Interrogation Methods

The location for questioning the juvenile should be private and free of distraction. Avoid interviewing the juvenile in a public place where he or she can be seen, which would make him or her more liable to be embarrassed or angered. A juvenile interviewed on the street is mindful that someone may be watching, which may cause the child to be overly cautious of what he or she says. Give the juvenile some privacy; even stepping

CASE IN POINT 13-2

Case in Point: Yarborough v. Alvarado (2004).

Michael Alvarado was 17 years old when he was questioned by police about his involvement in a crime. His parents brought him to the station and waited in the lobby during the interview. He was interviewed by one officer for 2 hours; he was not given a warning under *Miranda* nor was he arrested. During the interview, Alvarado confessed involvement in an attempted carjacking and the death of the vehicle's owner. He was twice asked if he needed a break, and when the interview was over his parents drove him home. Based in part on these statements, Alvarado was convicted of second-degree murder and attempted robbery. After conviction his case was appealed, which resulted in a reversal of the conviction. The Ninth Circuit held that the state court erred in failing to account for Alvarado's youth and inexperience when evaluating whether a reasonable person in his position would have felt free to leave the interview.

The Supreme Court disagreed. Justice Kennedy delivered the majority opinion in a 5 to 4 decision that reversed the Ninth Circuit. The majority found that the state criminal court that convicted Alvarado had reached a reasonable conclusion that the minor was not in custody for *Miranda* purposes when he was interviewed. The Court cited a number of factors that indicated that Alvarado was not in custody at the time he was questioned, including the fact that he went to the station voluntarily, was never told he could not leave, was not threatened by authorities, was told that the interview would be brief, and was allowed to return home afterward. According to the Court, *Miranda* can be distinguished from other cases that require special consideration of age for juvenile offenders.

The majority also stressed the importance of a clear rule for police to apply. Allowing different standards for juveniles makes it more difficult for police to determine when *Miranda* warnings are necessary.

Importance

1. This case answered an important question: When deciding whether a suspect is "in custody" and therefore entitled to *Miranda* warnings, must a police officer consider the suspect's age and previous history with law enforcement? The Supreme Court ruled no. The *Miranda* test is an objective rule with objective criteria that the police officer must consider when determining custody. Age and other subjective individual characteristics do not need to be considered in that determination.

---

inside a store or around a corner may be of benefit. A sign that this is a problem is evident when the juvenile keeps looking around rather than focusing on the police officer.

Interrogating the juvenile at his or her home should be avoided if the he or she is suspected of wrongdoing. It is not unusual for a juvenile to be fearful of how a parent will react to bad behavior or criminal involvement. Avoid contacting the juvenile at school and only remove the child from school as a last resort. Be sure that the parents are notified if the child is removed from school. Involving the school tends to stigmatize the juvenile, regardless of the outcome of an interview.

The officer conducting the questioning should have a general understanding of the developmental stages of children. More important, the police officer should feel comfortable with children, and be willing to speak on whatever level is necessary to put the child at ease. Be mindful that an interrogation without custody means NO custody. The suspect must be fully aware that he or she is free to go and is not under arrest. The atmosphere should not be adversarial or lead the suspect to believe that he or she is not free to stop the questioning. Factors that affect the issue of custody include the following:

- Early-morning or late-evening demands to report to the police station
- An interrogation in which the juvenile is not appropriately clothed or is denied food or water
- The absence of any offer to take a break
- Promises to let the suspect go only if a confession is provided

If possible, a parent or guardian should be contacted and requested to bring the juvenile to the place of questioning. The situation should not be discussed on the telephone, necessitating a personal interview with the child and parent or guardian. Providing the juvenile his or her rights per *Miranda* occurs under the same conditions as with adults; custody and interrogation remain the controlling factors. There are no special interrogation rules or requirements for juveniles that differ from those for adults (*Yarborough, Warden v. Alvarado,* 2004).

To obtain a complete and accurate report from the juvenile, avoid alienating him or her. Do not lose your temper, and avoid a tough-guy attitude. Coercive practices may push an innocent but frightened or emotionally troubled child to confess.

QUESTIONING A JUVENILE IN CUSTODY

When the purpose of the interview is to elicit information that may incriminate the juvenile in criminal activity and the juvenile might be considered to be in custody, he or she must be provided his or her rights per *Miranda*. If a juvenile has been arrested on probable cause, the parent or guardian must be contacted along with any other person required by statute. The questioning of juvenile suspects raises legal issues that could have a bearing on the admissibility of any confession made by the juvenile in custody. In addition to federal doctrine, each state has standards for a juvenile waiver to be considered valid. A legal determination of voluntariness does not depend on youthfulness alone, but is a factor.

There is a national movement toward the requirement of recording confessions for both adult and juvenile offenders. In New Jersey, for example, the recording by videotape or audiotape of a suspect's final statement is required for juveniles facing adult charges (Caher, 2004). All interrogations of juvenile offenders must be documented in writing or through recording.

Temporary Custody and Juveniles

A police officer may take a child into protective or **temporary custody**, typically for 48 hours, without a warrant if there is an emergency or if the officer has reason to believe that leaving the child in the present situation would subject the child to further abuse or harm (Hess & Drowns, 2004). Temporary custody without hearing is allowed under state welfare regulations and codes. Child maltreatment, abandonment, the child's inability to protect himself or herself, and parental refusal of needed medical care are reasons police might take a juvenile into custody that would not be considered an arrest.

In many cases concerning delinquency the police make an initial determination to detain the juvenile following an arrest. A detention hearing is conducted within 24 or 48 hours as specified by state statute. Unlike the adult criminal justice system, in the juvenile system, release on bail is uncommon if it is permitted at all. Release of the juvenile is determined based on whether the minor is a flight risk or a danger to self or others.

Fourth Amendment Considerations

The Fourth Amendment to the Constitution protects citizens from unreasonable search and seizure. The exclusionary rule that prohibits the use in court of any evidence seized illegally was applied to the states in 1961 (*Mapp v. Ohio*, 1961). These same protections against unreasonable search and seizure as well as the remedy of exclusion apply to police action involving juveniles.

The landmark Supreme Court cases that focused on unreasonable search and seizure issues regarding juveniles referred to disputes on the actions of school officials but expressly included police conduct. For example, in *New Jersey v. T.L.O.* (1985) the Court stated as follows:

> The Fourth Amendment's prohibition on unreasonable searches and seizures applies to searches conducted by public school officials and is not limited to searches carried out by law enforcement officers. Nor are school officials exempt from the Amendment's dictates by virtue of the special nature of their authority over school children. In carrying out searches and other functions pursuant to disciplinary policies mandated by state statutes, school officials act as representatives of the State, not merely as surrogates for the parents of students, and they cannot claim the parents' immunity from the Fourth Amendment's strictures.

The language in state courts has made the specific application of Fourth Amendment protections to juvenile cases a bit clearer. In New Jersey, a Superior Court held as follows in *State v. Lowry* (1967):

> Is it not more outrageous for the police to treat children more harshly than adult offenders, especially when such is violative of due process and fair treatment? Can a court countenance a system, where, as

here, an adult may suppress evidence with the usual effect of having the charges dropped for lack of proof, and on the other hand, a juvenile can be institutionalized for "rehabilitative" purposes because the Fourth Amendment right is unavailable to him?

FIFTH AMENDMENT CONSIDERATIONS

A juvenile suspected of committing a crime has a privilege against self-incrimination (*In re Gault,* 1967). A juvenile may waive his or her Fifth Amendment rights and consent to interrogation (*Fare v. Michael C.,* 1979). The relinquishment of a right is voluntary when it is the product of a free and deliberate choice rather than intimidation, coercion, or deception (*Moran v. Burbine,* 1986). A determination on whether the juvenile's waiver is voluntary and knowing needs to be resolved based on the totality of the circumstances surrounding the interrogation.

The court must determine not only that the statements were not coerced or suggested, but also that they were not the products of ignorance of these rights or of fantasy, fright, or despair. A juvenile's waiver of *Miranda* rights will always be suspect if given without the advice of a parent or adult guardian. The presence of a parent or guardian is not required for a voluntary waiver under the federal standard, although it is a factor to be considered. Some states do require that a waiver be made by an interested adult for the juvenile waiver to be valid. Among the factors to be considered are the following:

- The juvenile's age
- His or her experience with the criminal justice system
- His or her level of education
- His or her background
- His or her level of intelligence
- Whether he or she has the capacity to understand the warning
- The nature of the juvenile's Fifth Amendment rights
- The consequences of waiving those rights

THE RIGHT TO COUNSEL

The difference between the Fifth and Sixth Amendment rights to counsel deserves emphasis. The Fifth Amendment right applies during all custodial interrogations. The Sixth Amendment right is not triggered by custody but by the initiation of adversary judicial proceedings. These begin when a formal charge is filed (*Rhode Island v. Innis,* 1980).

The landmark case *In re Gault* (1967) firmly established the right to counsel for juveniles during custodial interrogation. That right does not refer to a probation officer, parent, or other interested adult. A waiver of the assistance of counsel in a majority of states is required by both the juvenile and a parent when the suspect under interrogation is younger than age 14 years. States may require consultation with an adult for a waiver of counsel to be valid. Other states require the "opportunity" for consultation with an adult after age 14 years, and whether that consultation actually occurs is immaterial. Several states prohibit or limit waiver of counsel by juveniles; those that permit it require proof that the juvenile understands the meaning and consequences of a waiver or that the waiver was granted only after a juvenile consulted with parents or guardians.

The Sixth Amendment protects the right to the assistance of a defense counsel (*Gideon v. Wainwright*, 1963), and applies only "at or after the initiation of adversary judicial criminal proceedings" (*Kirby v. Illinois*, 1972). Once adversary proceedings have begun, a defendant may not be interrogated in the absence of counsel nor be induced into making incriminating statements unless he or she initiates further interrogation and freely waives the Fifth and Sixth Amendment rights. After the Sixth Amendment right to counsel applies and is invoked, any statements obtained from the accused during subsequent *police-initiated* custodial questioning regarding the charge (even if the accused purports to waive his or her rights) are inadmissible. Police officers are not prohibited from interrogating a juvenile about uncharged crimes following his or her valid waiver under *Miranda* of his right to counsel just because he or she previously appeared with an attorney at a judicial proceeding on an unrelated offense.

The right to effective assistance of counsel has been acknowledged to apply to juveniles (*Stickland v. Washington*, 1984). Some but not all states require appointment of counsel at all stages of the juvenile proceedings (Jones, 2004).

JUVENILE CONFESSION ADMISSIBILITY

In addition to voluntariness, the courts also have considered the statutory requirement of prompt presentment in connection with the admissibility of confessions. State codes provide similar requirements to the following federal provision (Title 18 U.S.C. §5033):

> The juvenile shall be taken before a magistrate forthwith. In no event shall the juvenile be detained for longer than a reasonable period of time before being brought before a magistrate.

Similar to the McNabb-Mallory rule for adults, some courts have held confessions obtained during a delay in presenting the juvenile before the court to be inadmissible. Factors used in deciding when the federal provision has been violated include a focus on the "forthwith" language, and some courts rely on the phrase, "a reasonable period of time."

What is considered a reasonable time in which to bring a juvenile before the court for arraignment after an arrest? The Second Circuit held that a delay between a 10:15 AM arrest and a 3:00 PM presentment was reasonable under the circumstances (*U.S. v. Smith*, 1978). The Ninth Circuit held that a valid waiver of *Miranda* rights also constitutes a waiver of prompt presentment rights (*U.S. v. Indian Boy X*, 1978). Because of the different approaches to this issue, it is essential to consult the law in your jurisdiction and the requirements under your state law.

> **BEEN THERE... DONE THAT! 13-3**
>
> Fifteen-year-old Alice vanished from her home one afternoon. No one knew what happened to her until her body washed up on the bank of the river a week later with something tied around her neck. A canvas of the neighborhood brought no information until two 12-year-old boys claimed that they knew what had happened. I was called in to interview the boys before their statements could be contaminated.
>
> Each boy claimed that he had seen Alice get into a really "hot car" with two boys. She was not forced into the car, but got into the front seat between the driver and the passenger. They had seen the boys around, but neither boy knew who they were. The boys did not really look at the two boys in the car and could not describe them in any detail. What they did notice was the car. Armed with my drawing equipment, I asked each boy to draw me a picture of the car and explain to me why it was so hot. What came out of that was a very specific car with custom dual tailpipes. From their description we found the car and identified the driver.
>
> The driver of the car was a 17-year-old and his passenger was a 16-year-old. They confessed to me and two other interrogators that they had taken their friend Alice for a ride. At the riverbank, they demanded sex. She said no. Angry, the 17-year-old took off his sock and tied it around her neck. She was kicking and scratching as they took her by the arms and legs and threw her into the river alive. They told me that they were her friends.

SPECIFIC CRIME CATEGORIES

The majority of victims of violence committed by juveniles are juveniles (McCurley & Snyder, 2004), and almost half of the victims of nonfatal violent crimes are juvenile acquaintances of the offender.

Juvenile Firesetting

Arson is the crime most frequently committed by juveniles. If the child is untreated, the probability that he or she will set another fire is greater than 80 percent (Liscio, 1999). The problem of juvenile arson is staggering. Approximately half of all arrests for arson involve a juvenile (Snyder, 2004). Fires set by juveniles claim the lives of approximately 300 people and destroy more than $300 million worth of property each year (Putnam & Kirkpatrick, 2005). A distinction is made between fireplay and firesetting, behaviors with different degrees of damage and intent. **Fireplay** results from curiosity about and fascination with fire, and is most common among children and adolescents; the damage caused is not maliciously inspired. Expressive fireplay suggests unresolved trauma or psychopathology. For example, a young victim of sexual abuse may intentionally set her bed on fire as an expressive means of controlling a situation in which she feels powerless. **Firesetting** is willful action with a higher level of intent to use fire as a weapon and an instrument of power; it is intended to achieve a goal.

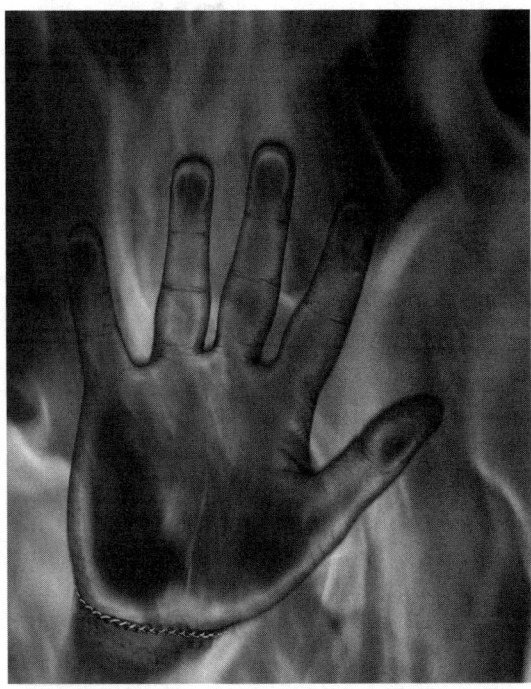

FIGURE 13-2 Arson is the crime most frequently committed by juveniles.

An effective interview of the suspected juvenile may make the difference between an unsolved fire and one with the cause clearly established and the offender arrested (Zipper & Wilcox, 2005). There is give and take between the juvenile and the investigator in which the suspect tests to find out whether the real cause has been determined. The interrogator must go into the interview fully prepared with information from early witness interviews. Similar to other interview techniques, the investigator must first introduce himself or herself and describe the purpose for the interview. Rapport is then established, during which time an analysis of the suspect's living conditions can be determined. Allow the juvenile to give a complete narrative without interruption, using the information to determine follow-up questions. Closure occurs with a statement that there may be a need for a future interview.

Questions to consider during an interrogation of the juvenile firesetter include the following:

- What did you use to start this fire?
- Where did you get these lighters or matches?
- What did you set on fire?
- What did you do after you used the lighter or matches to get the fire started?
- How many others were involved? Who were they?
- How did you feel after you started the fire?
- Has anything happened lately that really bothers you?
- What have you set on fire in the past?

Sexual Offending

Sexual offenses committed by juveniles represent a serious problem. Indications are that one half of adult sexual offenders began their sexually abusive behavior as a juvenile. Almost one third of arrests for sex offenses involve youths under the age of 18 years (Righthand & Welch, 2001). Studies indicate that male perpetrators are the most frequent sexual offenders; however the rate of female sex offenders is believed to be highly underreported (Barnett, Miller-Perrin, & Perrin, 1997). Preadolescent children as young as 3 and 4 years old have been identified as being sexually aggressive, although the common age of onset appears to be between ages 6 and 9 years (Righthand & Welch, 2001). Early intervention is the most successful approach to rehabilitation for sexual offenders; the criminal justice system plays an important role.

Polygraph tests may be an appropriate method for facilitating the more complete disclosure of sexually abusive behavior by juveniles (Righthand & Welch, 2001). Juvenile sexual offenders are often victims as well, and structuring the interview or interrogation requires extreme sensitivity to that possibility. The process of getting ready for the interview is similar whether the juvenile is a victim or a known sexual abuse offender. Preparation includes the following:

- Obtain background information on the offense.
- Obtain a thorough background on the juvenile being questioned. For example, determine whether the child has ever been arrested or accused of a similar offense.
- Determine the living arrangements of the juvenile. Where and with whom does he or she live? Who is the legal or custodial guardian?
- Determine the age and grade level of the juvenile. Does he or she have a learning disability or a low functioning level?
- If the child is suspected of committing a sexual offense, is he or she a known victim?

If any of these preparation questions cannot be answered prior to the interview, the child should be asked about them directly. In some states the interview of the juvenile will be conducted by social service workers as part of the criminal investigation and sometimes prior to police involvement. Sit with the parent or guardian and explain the juvenile's *Miranda* rights and ask for a waiver of these rights. It is not advisable to interview or interrogate a juvenile suspected of a sexual offense in the presence of a parent or guardian. If a voluntary waiver is obtained, then ask the adult to allow the questioning to proceed in private, if the juvenile is willing. Explain that it is difficult to speak about these issues and that they would benefit from the privacy. The six stages to interviewing a suspected juvenile sexual offender are as follows.

Step 1. Introduction. Explain to the juvenile who you are and why you are speaking with him or her. Establish credibility by telling the child that you frequently talk with people about things that have happened with children and families.

Step 2. **Rapport building.** This is an important step in the juvenile interrogation as well as an interview. Provide the juvenile with reasons that he or she should speak with you. Include the statement that the purpose of the interview is to learn the truth.

Step 3. **Background.** Explore information about the juvenile including family composition, criminal history, and employment history. During this phase you can obtain information about the functioning level of the juvenile. Determine his or her general educational level, linguistic comprehension, understanding of the process, and possible mental health issues. Verify the relationship of the victim to the offender and the circumstances under which access to the victim gained. Obtain an understanding of the typical eye contact and body language behavior of the juvenile when discussing general topics.

Step 4. **Allegation.** Explain the allegation in very general terms. Do not use legal language or speak above the juvenile's level of understanding.

Step 5. **Questioning.** Ask the juvenile to explain the criminal acts that are under investigation. Move from general questions about specific topics to abuse-focused questions. Note the changes in body language and eye contact that may occur in response to specific questions or areas of inquiry. Note consistencies and inconsistencies with what is already known about the allegation.

Explore the rationalization for the behavior. A juvenile may have difficulty providing reasons for committing a sexual offense, so do not ask, "Why did you . . . ?" Reasons for committing a sexual offense may be as simple as that it was done to them or that it felt good. Do not make judgments about the child. Explore who offended against him or her in a similar way. Always ask who else they touched in a similar way because multiple offending is common.

For each event, ask where and when the act took place. Determine whether there was anyone else present. Ask for specific details about each event. If the juvenile says that he or she had sex, for example, ask what that means. Juveniles use language for sexual acts and sexual parts that may not mean the same thing to an adult, and so clarification is necessary. An additional reason to ask for specific details is to determine that the juvenile really committed the act under investigation.

Answer questions that the juvenile may have as honestly and completely as possible.

Step 6. **Closure.** End the interrogation as you would an interview. Assure the juvenile that you appreciate his or her honesty even though the subject is difficult to talk about. Leave it open that you may want to speak with him or her again. Provide the supporting parent or guardian with information without going into details of sexual behaviors. Take the time to answer questions for the parent or guardian.

Police officers have an additional legal responsibility in cases of sexual abuse, even when the perpetrator is a juvenile. In all states and Washington, D.C., a report must be filed with the appropriate social services agency on suspected child victims of abuse or neglect. Mandated reporters provide the names and address of all victims discovered through a sexual abuse investigation.

CONCLUSIONS

There are variations from state to state on the age that qualifies a person as being under the jurisdiction of the juvenile court in addition to differences on how juvenile offenders are handled by the system. The consistent baseline is provided by the rights that have been afforded to juveniles by the Supreme Court. No state can infringe on these rights. The basic Fourth, Fifth, Sixth, and Fourteenth Amendment rights as outlined in this chapter are applicable, and probable cause remains the standard of proof. The interrogator must know his or her state's requirements on the conditions under which a juvenile can knowingly and voluntarily waive those rights. The suspect's age and the nature of the crime may be factors, in addition to the presence or opportunity for the juvenile to consult with a parent or other interested adult.

QUESTIONS FOR REVIEW

Short-Answer Questions

1. Compare the absolute rights afforded an adult versus those afforded a juvenile. Why is there a difference?
2. Explain the difference between status offenses and delinquency.
3. Explain the effect the *Kent* decision had on juvenile procedural law.
4. Explain the effect *In re Gault*, 1967 had on the doctrine of *parens patriae*.
5. When is a juvenile considered to be in custody with regard to questioning? What should happen when this point is reached?
6. Under what conditions may police officers take juveniles into temporary custody? How long can the juvenile be held under these conditions?
7. Explain the rights to counsel under the Fifth and Sixth Amendments. What are the differences?
8. Discuss the scope of juvenile firesetting/arson. How does it compare to other forms of juvenile delinquency?
9. List the steps taken to interview a suspected juvenile sex offender. What role should social services agencies play?

10. How does the baseline of juvenile rights outlined by Supreme Court decisions help to mitigate the vast differences in juvenile law from state to state?

Fill-in Questions

1. _____ _____ is the power of the State to act in behalf of a child and provide care and protection equivalent to that of a parent.
2. The distinction between _____ and is becoming more important for the police interrogator as states move toward trying juveniles in court as adults for major crimes.
3. Children younger than the age of 7 years are presumed to be without the ability to form _____ _____ under common law.
4. Initiated in 1971, the _____ developed a set of standards for juvenile justice after the *Gault* decision.
5. Greater access to juvenile records mean that subsequent adult sentencing may be _____ under three-strikes laws or pursuant to sentencing guidelines in both the federal and state criminal justice systems.
6. The _____ investigation allows the officer the opportunity to get background information on the juvenile and collect evidence if warranted.
7. A voluntary relinquishment of a right occurs when the relinquishment is the product of a free and deliberate choice rather than _____, _____, or _____.
8. Almost half of the victims of nonfatal violent crimes are juvenile _____ of the offender.
9. Indications are that one half of adult _____ began their sexually abusive behavior as juveniles.
10. The law requires that _____ _____ make a report to the specified agency of the names and addresses of all victims discovered through an abuse investigation.

Exercises

Decide whether each of the following persons is a juvenile, and answer the questions after each case or hypothetical. Go to http://www.ncjj.org/stateprofiles/ to research juvenile law and procedure in your home state.

1. Angela is 15 years old. She and her 18-year-old brother, Daniel, go to the shopping mall together. Daniel convinces Angela to shoplift a part he needs to repair his car; she puts it in her vest. They are both caught.

   a. Can Angela be tried in juvenile court? Why or why not?
   b. Can Daniel be tried in juvenile court? Why or why not?

2. Richard and his friend Jill are both 17 years old. They are caught driving a car that they took without permission. Richard turns 18 one week after his arraignment. Jill is found guilty at her adjudicatory

hearing (trial) and, based on her prior adjudications, the court orders that she spend 20 weeks in confinement. After Jill has spent 8 weeks in confinement, she turns 18.

a. Can Richard's adjudicatory hearing (trial) take place in juvenile court?
b. Will Jill be transferred from the facility operated by the Department of Social and Health Services at the time she turns 18?

REFERENCES

Barnett, O. W., Miller-Perrin, C. L., & Perrin, R. D. (1997). *Family violence across the lifespan: An introduction.* Thousand Oaks, CA: Sage Publications.

Caher, J. (2004). NJ Attorney General to expand policy of taping suspects' confessions. *The Legal Intelligencer, 231* (121), 4.

Cicourel, A. V. (2005). Process and structure in juvenile justice. In D. L. Parry (Ed.), *Essential readings in juvenile justice* (pp. 136–140). Upper Saddle River, NJ: Prentice Hall.

Fare v. Michael C., 442 U.S. 707, 725 (1979).

Flicker, B. (2005). Introduction to the IJA-ABA juvenile justice standards. In D. Parry (Ed.), *Essential readings in juvenile justice* (pp. 120–124). Upper Saddle River, NJ: Prentice Hall.

Gideon v. Wainwright, 372 U.S. 355 (1963).

Griffin, P. (2004). National overviews. *Juvenile Justice Profiles.* [Online.] Available: http://www.ncjj.org/stateprofiles.

Hess, K., & Drowns, R. (2004). *Juvenile justice* (4th ed.). Belmont, CA: Wadsworth/Thompson Learning.

In re Gault, 387 U.S. 1 (1967).

Jones, J. B. (2004). *Access to counsel* (Report No. NCJ 204063). Washington, DC: Office of Juvenile Justice and Delinquency Prevention.

Kent v. United States, 383 U.S. 541 (1966).

Kirby v. Illinois, 406 U.S. 682 (1972).

Liscio, D. (1999). Juvenile fire-setters. *Firehouse, 1999,* 42–46.

Mapp v. Ohio, 367 U.S. 643 (1961).

McCurley, C., & Snyder, H. (2004). *Victims of violent juvenile crime* (Report No. NCJ 201628). Washington, DC: Office of Juvenile Justice and Delinquency Prevention.

Miranda v. Arizona, 384 U.S. 436 (1966).

Moran v. Burbine, 475 U.S. 412 (1986).

Napier, M., & Adams, S. (2002). Criminal confessions: Overcoming the challenges. *FBI Law Enforcement Bulletin, 71* (11), 9–15.

New Jersey v. T.L.O, 469 U.S. 325 (1985).

Putnam, C., & Kirkpatrick, J. (2005). *Juvenile firesetting: A research overview* (Report No. NCJ 207606). Washington, DC: Office of Juvenile Justice and Delinquency Prevention.

Rhode Island v. Innis, 446 U.S. 291 (1980).

Righthand, S., & Welch, C. (2001). *Juveniles who have sexually offended* (Report No. NCJ 184739). Washington, DC: Office of Juvenile Justice and Delinquency Prevention.

Shepherd, R., Jr. (1997). Rebirth of the infancy defense. *Juvenile Justice Articles*. [Online.] Available: http://www.abanet.org/crimjust/juvjus/12-2shep.html.

Sickmund, M. (2003). *Juveniles in court* (Report No. NCJ 195420). Washington, DC: Office of Juvenile Justice and Delinquency Prevention.

Snyder, H. (2004). *Juvenile arrests 2002* (Report No. NCJ 204608). Washington, DC: Office of Juvenile Justice and Delinquency Prevention.

State v. Lowry, 230 A.2d 907 (1967).

Stickland v. Washington, 466 U.S. 668 (1984).

The National Center for Juvenile Justice. (2004). State juvenile justice profiles. [Online.] Available: http://www.ncjj.org/stateprofiles/.

U.S. Code 18 U.S.C. §5031 (1994).

U.S. v. Indian Boy X, 656 F.2d 585, 9th Cir. (1978).

U.S. v. Smith, 574 F.2d 707, 2d Cir. (1978).

Yarborough, Warden v. Alvarado, 539 U.S. 986 (2004).

Zipper, P., & Wilcox, D. (2005). Juvenile arson: The importance of early intervention. *FBI Law Enforcement Bulletin, 74* (4), 1–9.

Index

Note: Page numbers in italics indicate figures.

A

Abuse, *139*
   child, 135–136
   child interview model and, 135
   children with disabilities and, 178–179
   of the elderly, 159–161, *171*
   fiduciary, 161–162
   mandatory reporting, 172–173
   models for evaluating, 135–136
   multidisciplinary team approach, 136, 139
   parent-child interaction model, 135–136
   secondary, 148
Active listening, 43–44, *47*
Actus reus, 67–68
Adams, S., 19, 76, 78
Admissions, 251
Alibis, 265–266
American Medical Association, 87
American Professional Society on the Abuse of Children (APSAC), 135
Americans with Disabilities Act, 32, 179–181, 195
   interrogation and, 194
   interviewing and, 179–180
   police liability under the, 180–181
   Title II, 179–180
Arson, 46, 50, 288–289, *289*
Attention deficit-hyperactivity disorder (ADHD), 184–185
Autism, 185
Autism Society of America, 185

B

Bandler, Richard, 110
Behavioral interviewing, 104, 109
   of auditory thinkers, 121
   cultural and personal considerations, 111
   definition of, 109
   emblems, 110
   emotions and, 112–116
   eye movement, 116–119
   facial expression, *111,* 112–113
   gender and, 111
   hedging, 121–122
   kinesics and, 109–110
   manipulators, 122
   mirroring, 120
   modeling, 116
   neurolinguistic programming (NLP), 110–111, 116, 120–121
   observable behaviors, 112–116
   posture, 114–116
   qualifiers, 121–122
   sensory verbal communication and, 120–121
   shifting, 120
Berlo, D. K., 4–5, *5*
   SMCR (source, message, channels, and receiver) model, 4–5, 19
Birdwhistell, Ray, 110
Body language. *See also* Nonverbal communication

C

Case interviewing, 8
Child pornography, 238–239
Child sexual assault, 240–241
Children. *See also* Juveniles
Cognitive interviewing (CI), 8, 29, 86–87, 104
   caretaker instructions and, 144
   changing event order, 98, 146
   changing perspective, 98, 146
   of children, 143–146
   definition of, 94–95
   establishing rapport in, 144–145
   extensive recall, 101
   meet and greet, 99–100
   mnemonics, 96, 101
   narrative phases, 100–101
   practice interview, 144
   reconstruction technique, 97, 145–146
   report-everything technique, 98, 146
   steps for, 99–101
   summary and closure, 101
   techniques, 95–99, 143–146

Colwell, K., 74
Communication, 4–5, 16–17
   emotions and, 19
   facilitated, 190–191
   factors affecting, 5
   nonverbal, 4, 17–18, 46, 110, 111
      (*See also* Behavioral interviewing; Kinesics)
   paralanguage, 19
   proxemics, 18–19
   sensory verbal, 120–121
Complainants, 65, 66
Complementary principle of interpersonal psychology, 250–251, 272
Comprehensive questioning, 42
Confessions, 224–248, 251–252. *See also* under *Miranda* rights
   admissibility of, 287
   coercion and, 212
   cognitive-behavioral model, 257
   decision-making model, 257
   definition of, 12
   eliciting, 256–257
   false, 194–195, 232–233
   interaction process model, 257
   juvenile rights and, 287
   locking it in, 269–270
   making the claim, 269
   McNabb-Mallory rule, 287
   obtaining, 269–270
   psychoanalytic model, 257
   reasons for, 231
   Reid model, 256
   voluntary, 229
Constitution (U.S.). *See also* Legal issues; *specific Amendments*
Contamination, 29–30, *30*
Continuation, 43
Court cases
   California v. Stewart (1966), 205
   Carroll v. United States (1925), 214
   Daubert v. Merrell Dow Pharmaceuticals (1993), 94
   Davis v. United States (2004), 209
   Edwards v. Arizona (1981), 208–209
   Frye v. United States (1923), 93–94
   Jackson v. Town of Sanford (1994), 180
   Kent v. United States (1966), 279
   Lewis v. Truitt (1997), 180
   Mapp v. Ohio (1961), 211
   Miranda v. Arizona (1966), 205. (*See also Miranda* rights)
   Missouri v. Seibert (2004), 226
   New Jersey v. T.L.O., 285
   In re Gault, 279, 280, 286
   Rhode Island v. Innis (1980), 234
   Rock v. Arkansas (1987), 93
   State v. Dubose (2005), 54
   State v. Lowry (1967), 285
   United States v. Guerrero (1988), 212
   United States v. Mendoza-Cecelia (1992), 212
   Vignera v. New York (1966), 205
   Weeks v. United States (1914), 210–211
   Westover v. United States (1966), 205
   Wolf v. Colorado, 211
   Yarborough v. Alvarado (2004), 283
Crime scenes
   viewing, 28, 259–260
   warrants and, 28
Crimes. *See also* Abuse; *specific types of crimes*
   arson, 46
   child pornography, 238–239
   child sexual assault, 240–241
   elements of, 49–50
   hate crimes, 46–47, 50, 241
   homicide, 242–243
   incendiary (*See also* Arson)
   partner violence, 47
   against persons with disabilities, 195
   against persons with mental illness, 195
   sexual assault, 47–49, 240–241
   targeting the elderly, 159–162, 173–174
   white collar crimes, 49

D

Dahl, S., 111
deception, 74, 122–123
Diagnostic and Statistical Manual of Mental Disorders, 184, 185
Dilts, Robert, 116
Disabilities, persons with
   abuse and, 178–179
   Americans with Disabilities Act, 32, 179–181, 195
   appropriate adult and, 190
   attention deficit-hyperactivity disorder (ADHD), 184–185
   attitudes toward, 181–182
   autism, 185
   auxiliary aides, 180

crimes against, 195
establishing rapport with, 191
facilitated communication and, 190–191
false confessions and, 194–195
field evaluations and, 187–188
forms of, *181*
interrogation considerations, 193–195
interview considerations, 188–190
interview preparation and, 190–191
interviewing persons with, 181–183, 185–198, *190,* 191–193
legal issues and, 189–190
mental retardation, 183–184, *186, 194*
Miranda and, 193–194
special care needs for, 183–186
victimization and, 189
wrongful-arrest theory and, 180
Dispatchers, 26
Domestic violence, 47, 50–51
the elderly and, 159–161, *160*
Dubose, 54

E

Ekman, P., 17, 110, 112, 113–114, 122–123
Elderly
2000 Survey of State Adult Protective Services, 173
abandonment of, 159, 160
abuse of, *171,* 172–173
active neglect of, 159, 160
aging out, 173
case credibility and, 165
cognitive limitations and, 170
conversation-observation evaluation, 162, 173
crimes targeting, 159–162, 173–174
dependence and, 171–172
domestic violence and, 159–161, *160*
empowering, 167–168
establishing rapport with, 166–167
fiduciary abuse of, 161–162
interdisciplinary interviewing of, 172
interviewing, 158–176
memory-jogging and, 170
Older Americans Act, 159
passive neglect of, 159, 160
as perpetrators, 173
physical abuse of, 159, 160
physical limitations and, 169–170
pre-interview of, 162–165

self-neglect of, 159, 160
sexual abuse of, 159, 160
source confusion and, 170
as victims, 167–168, *168*
as witnesses, 167–168
Emblems, 110
Emotions, 19
Evidence
children and, 150, 152
false, 267–268
inculpatory, 251–252
testamentary, 50
Excited utterances, 234
Eye movements, 116–119
of auditory right-handed persons, 118, *118*
of kinesthetic right-handed persons, *119,* 119
of visual right-handed persons, *117,* 117–118, *118*

F

Facial-coding system (FACS), 113–114
Facial expressions, 112–114
Federal Bureau of Investigation (FBI), 50, 92
Field evaluations
of children, 133–134
detailed, 187
distant, 187
Field identification, 54–55
Fifth Amendment, 234
juvenile rights and, 286, 287
First responders, 26
Fisher, Ronald P., 94
Flicker, B., 279
Forensic hypnosis, 86, 88–94, 103
age regression, 90
challenges to, 91–93
Chiasson's technique, 90
closure phase, 91
confabulation, 92
Daubert test, 94
as evidence, 93–94
eye-fixation method, 90
faking, 92
Frye test, 93–94
guidelines for use of, 88–89
hypermnesia, 91
Illinois v. Gates (1983), 93
induction phase, 89–90
interviewing methods of, 88–91

Forensic hypnosis—*continued*
   memory hardening, 92–93
   narrative phase, 90
   preparation for, 89
   recall phase, 91
   suggestibility, 93
Forensic interviewing, 139–143
   caretaker instructions, 140–141
   comprehension monitoring (CM), 141
   conducting the interview, 142–143
   establishing rapport, 142
   evaluation, 141
   preparing the child, 141–142
   techniques, 140–143
Fourteenth Amendment, 209, 210–213
   coerced confessions and, 212
   due process clause, 209, 211, 212
   exclusionary rule, 210–212, 213
   fruit-of-the-poisonous-tree doctrine, 211–212
   intelligence and, 213
   intoxication and, 213
   length of interrogation, 213
   mental illness and, 213
   suspect's age and, 212–213
   suspect's physical condition and, 213
Fourth Amendment, 214–218
   entry into a dwelling, 217–218
   juvenile rights and, 285–286
   power to arrest, 214
   probable cause, 215–218
Friesen, W., 110

G

Geiselman, Edward, 94
Gender
   interrogation and, 228
   space and, 18
Grinder, John, 110
Gudjonsson, G. H., 231, 256, 257

H

Hall, E. G., 88
Hall, Edward, 18
Hand, H., 64
Hate crimes, 46–47, 50, 241
Healey, K., 53
Hedging, 121–122
Hogan, K., 18, 116, 121
Homicide, 242–243

Honey, P., 110
Hypnosis
   definition of, 87
   forensic, 86, 88–94

I

Identification
   Dubose and, 54
   eyewitness, 54–55
   field, 54–55
   lineups, 55–56
   Miranda and, 55
   show-up, 54–55
inculpatory evidence, 251–252
inferential interviewing, 65, *73*
   response length and, 74
   statement coherence and, 74
   type–token ratio, 74, 75
   verbal hedging, 75–76
   verbal leakage, 74
Institute of Judicial Administration-American Bar Association (IJA-ABA), 279–280
Interrogation, 4–21, *255*, *260*. *See also* Questioning
   admissions, 251
   alibis and, 265–266
   of apathetic offenders, 266
   appeal to expertise/authority, 268–269
   approaches to, 252–254
   behavioral, 104–126 (*See also* Behavioral interviewing)
   "behavioral analysis" questions, 266
   case-specific methods of, 238–243
   in child pornography cases, 238–239
   in child sexual assault, 240–241
   communication and, 4–5
   compared to interviewing, 11
   complementary principle of interpersonal psychology, 250–251, 272
   confessions and, 12–13, 224–248, 251–252, 256–257, 269–270
   controversy over, 11–12
   cooperation and, 267
   custodial, 255–256, 284
   definition of, 225, 234
   eliciting, 10
   evidence of guilt and, 264–265
   excited utterances, 234
   false evidence and, 267–268
   Fifth Amendment and, 203–204, 234
   flattery and, 268

Fourteenth Amendment and, 209, 210–213
Fourth Amendment and, 214–218
gender and, 228
of guilt-ridden offenders, 266
hate crimes and, 241
historical legal background, 11–12
homicide, 242–243
identifying contradictions, 265–266
improving, 233–234
inculpatory evidence and, 251–252
interrogators, 227–229, 262–263
juveniles and, 282–284
legal issues and, 11, 195
length of, 213
Miranda rights and, 204–209, 224–227, 237, 254–256, 284
nature of, 10–11
noncustodial, 254–255, 281–282
persuading, 10
place of, 263
praise and, 268
preparation for, 257–263
prior criminal records and, 257–258
protecting the suspect's rights, 262–263
public safety exception and, 207–208
purpose of, 12–13, 251–252
question-first techniques, 225
race and, 228
Reid technique, 253
right to counsel, 208–209
rule of law and, 202–203
self-interest and, 263–264
sexual assault cases and, 240–241
shame and, 267
Sixth Amendment and, 209–210
skills required for successful, 228
slam-dunk approach, 252–253
sobriety testing and, 235–236
stare decis and, 203
stop and frisk and, 236–237
subtle compulsion, 235
suspect paranoia, 265
techniques, 237, 250–274
timing of, 260–262
totality-of-the-circumstances test, 204
traffic stops and, 235
undermining denials, 265
viewing the crime scene before, 259–260
voluntary statements and, 207
Interrogators, 227–229, 262–263

Interviewers
chairs of, 32, *33*
knowledge of, 15–16
number of, 33
personal qualities of, 13–16
professionalism of, 16
willingness to develop rapport, 15
Interviewing, 4–21. *See also* Interrogation; Questioning
Americans with Disabilities Act and, 179–180
approaches to, 64–84
behavioral, 104
caring, 24–25
case, 8
case review and, 26–27
children (*See also* Juveniles)
cognitive, 8, 86–87, 143–146
developing rapport, 15
elderly, 158–176
environmental factors in, 33
establishing psychological content, 30–33
false confessions and, 194–195
forensic, 139–143
inferential, 65, *73*, 74–76
interview process, 24–40
kinesics, 8
knowledge and, 15–16
leading questions, 29
Miranda rights and (*See also Miranda* rights)
nature of, 5–6
number of interviewers, 33
objectives of, 45–56
on-the-scene, 30, 31–32
order of interviews, 33–34
persons with disabilities, 178–198, *190*
persons with mental illness, 178–179, 185–198
place of, 31–33
in the police station or office, 32–33
postmodernism, 24, 25
power and, 25
preparation for, 25–26
proxemics and, 32, *33*
purposeful, 42–59
questioning, 33–38
self-development, 24, 25
social systems approach, 24, 42–43
special populations, 31, 32
statement analysis techniques, 65
structured, 65, 71–74
suspects, 10

Interviewing—*continued*
   timing of, 31
   tools for, 149
   traditional techniques, 8, 64–65, 66–71
   types of questions, 34–37
   victims, 6–7
   witnesses, 7–10
Investigation, 72

J

Juvenile Justice Standards Project, 279
Juveniles, *150, 151,* 276–295, *277*
   accuracy of, 147–148
   adult punishment and, 280–281
   age of criminal responsibility, 277–288
   age-related limitations on reporting, 132–133
   child interview model, 135
   cognitive interviewing (CI) of, 143–146
   competency of, 152–153
   confessions and, 287
   credibility of, 150, 152
   crimes committed by, 288–292
   custodial questioning of, 284
   definition of, 277
   developmental stages of, 131–132
   due process and, 279–281, 279–281
   establishing rapport with, 142, 144–145
   evaluating abuse of, 135–136
   fantasy and, 148
   felony crimes and, 280–281
   field assessment of, 133–134, 281
   Fifth Amendment and, 286, 287
   firesetting/fireplay, 288–289, *289*
   forensic approach to interviewing, 139–143
   Fourth Amendment and, 285–286
   infancy rule, 278
   initial considerations for interviews, 134–139
   Institute of Judicial Administration-American Bar Association (IJA-ABA), 279–280
   interrogations and, 282–284
   interviewing, 130–155 (*See also* Forensic interviewing)
   juvenile delinquency, 278–279
   Juvenile Justice Standards Project, 279
   maintaining neutrality, 137–139
   memory and, 148
   Miranda rights and, 281–282, 283, 286
   multidisciplinary team approach, 136, 139
   noncustodial questioning of, 281–282
   offenses by, 278–279
   parens patriae, 276
   parent-child interaction model, 135–136
   preliminary considerations checklist, 136–137
   reliability of, 152–153
   as reporters, 147–148, 150, 152–153
   right to counsel, 286–287
   rights of, 276–295
   risk assessment and, 134–135
   secondary abuse and, 148
   sexual offenses by, 290–292
   Sixth Amendment and, 286–287
   station investigations of, 281–282
   status offenses, 278
   temporary custody and, 285
   tools for interviewing, 149
   tried as adults, 280–281
   as victims, 148–149

K

Kassin, S. M., 231
Kinesics, 8, 17–18, 109–110
Klopf, G., 81
Knowledgeability, 15–16

L

Lanning, K., 136
Law enforcers, 229
Leading questions, 29
Learning Styles Questionnaire, 110
Legal Information Institute, 51
Legal issues. *See also* Court cases
   custody, 205–206
   excited utterances, 234
   Fifth Amendment, 203–204, 234, 286, 287
   Fourteenth Amendment, 209, 210–213
   Fourth Amendment, 214–218, 285–286
   interrogation and, 262–263
   juvenile rights, 276–289
   Miranda rights, 204–209, 237
   persons with disabilities and, 189–190, 193–194
   public safety exception and, 207–208
   right to counsel, 208–209, 286–287
   rule of law, 202–203
   Sixth Amendment, 209–210, 286–287
   sobriety testing, 235–236
   stare decis, 203
   state action, 205
   stop and frisk, 236

subtle compulsion, 235
totality-of-the-circumstances test, 204
voluntary statements and, 207
Leo, R. A., 226, 229
Lineups, 55–56

M

Manipulators, 122
McConkey, K. M., 88–89
McNabb-Mallory rule, 287
Memory-jogging, 86–87, 94, 96, 98–99.
   See also Cognitive interviewing (CI)
Memory retrieval, 86–106. *See also* Cognitive interviewing (CI); Forensic hypnosis; Memory-jogging
   challenges to, 101–103
   contamination and, 102
   emotion and, 103
   scripts, 103
Mens rea, 69–70
Mental illness, persons with, 185–186
   compared with mental retardation, *186*
   conducting the interview, 191–193
   crimes against, 195
   establishing rapport with, 191
   false confessions and, 194–195
   field evaluations and, 187–188
   interrogation considerations, 193–195
   interview considerations, 188–191
   interviewing, 178–179, 185–198
   legal issues and, 189–190
   Miranda and, 193–194
   personality disorders, 186
   as victims, 195
Mental retardation, 183–184, *186, 194*
Miranda rights, 194, 204–209
   atmosphere, 206
   bright line, 209
   confessions and, 224, 224–227
   custodial interrogations and, 255–256
   custody, 205–206
   freedom to leave, 206
   interrogations and, 237, 284
   juvenile rights and, 281–282, 283, 286
   nature of the interview and, 206
   noncustodial interrogations and, 254–255
   persons with disabilities and, 193–194
   persons with mental illness and, 193–194
   police and, 229
   probable cause and, 215
   public safety exception and, 207–208
   right to counsel under, 208–209
   state action, 205
   stop and frisk and, 236
   traffic stops and, 235
   voluntary statements and, 207
   waiver of, 206–208, *207,* 229–230, 231–232, 255–256
Miscarriage of justice, 233
Misinformation, 28–29, *30*
   cognitive interviewing (CI) and, 29
   contamination, 29–30
   external sources, 29
   internal sources, 28
Moore, D., 165
Morphostasis, 43
Mumford, A., 110

N

National Alliance for the Mentally Ill, 179
National Center for Hate Crime Prevention, 241
National Center for Victims of Crime, 50
National Center of Elder Abuse, 173
National Institute of Justice, 86
Neurolinguistic programming (NLP), 110–111, 116, 120–121, 123
Niehaus, J., 90
Nonverbal communication, 4, 17–18, 46, 110, 111. *See also* Behavioral interviewing; Kinesics

O

Offense, nature of, 45–49. *See also* Crimes
Office for Victims of Crime, The, 169
Ohio Academy of Hypnosis Basic Forensic Hypnosis manual, 90
Older Americans Act, 159
O'Sullivan, C., 53

P

Paralanguage, 19
Partner violence. *See also* Domestic violence
Perpetrators
   description of, 52
   elderly as, 173
   identifying, 52–54, 54–56
   primary aggressors, 52–53
   risk assessment and, 53–54

Personality disorders, 186
Pillemer, K., 165
Plea bargaining, 231–232
Police, *228*, 229
    law enforcers, 229
    servicers, 229
Posture, 114–116
Presumptive prosecution policy, 6
    evidence-based, 6, 7
    no-drop approach, 6–7
Primary aggressors, 52–53
Probable cause, 215–218
Proxemics, 18–19, 32, *33*
Psychological content, establishment of, 30–33
Purposeful interviewing, 42–59
    active listening, 43–44
    characteristics of, 43–45
    determining the nature of the offense, 45–49
    determining whether a crime was committed, 49–51
    emotions and, 46
    identifying a perpetrator, 52–54
    nonverbal communication and, 4, 46
    objectives of, 45–56
    rapport development and, 44–45

Q

Qualifiers, 121–122
Questioning, 33–38. *See also* Interrogation
    approaches, 37–38
    "behavioral analysis" questions, 266
    closed-ended questions, 36
    comprehensive, 42
    confrontation questions, 37
    control questions, 37
    direct or forced-choice questions, 36
    follow-up questions, 36
    formal approach, 38
    informal approach, 38
    leading questions, 37
    oblique approach, 37–38
    open-ended questions, 34–36
    reinforcing behavior, 35
    types of, 34–37

R

Rabon, D., 119
Race, 228
Rapport, developing, 15, 44–45, 72
Risk assessment, 53–54

S

Sandoval, V., 19
Schaefer, R. C., 229
Sejnowksi, Terrence, 113–114
Senior citizens. *See also* Elderly
Servicers, 229
Sexual assault, 47–49, 51, 240–241, 243
Sheehan, P. W., 88–89
Show-up, 54–55
Side-trackers, 65
Sixth Amendment, 209–210, 286–287
SMCR (source, message, channels, and receiver) model, 4–5, *5*
Smith, C., 53
Sobriety testing, 235
Social systems approach, 24, 42–43
Sources
    complainants, 65, 66
    identification, 65–66
    identifying, *66*
    side-trackers, 65
    victims, 65–66
Space. *See also* Proxemics
Statement analysis, 65, 76–81
    balance of the statement, 80
    conducting, 76–79
    extraneous information, 79–80
    field statement analysis, 80–81
    lack of conviction, 80, 81
    parts of speech, 76–79
    statement analysis field examination technique (SAFE-T), 81
Statement analysis techniques, 65
Statements
    accuracy of, 56–57
    admissions, 251
    excited utterances, 234
    reviewing, 73–74
    voluntary, 207
Stop and frisk, 236–237
Structured interviewing, 65, 71–74
Subtle compulsion, 235
Suspects, *271*
    alibis of, 265–266
    apathetic offenders, 266
    background checks on, *27*, 27–28

confessions by, 231
fear of blame and, 268
fear of insignificance, 268
fear of job loss and, 267
flattery of, 268
guilt-ridden offenders, 266
interviewing, 10
praise of, 268
prior criminal records, 27–28
shame and, 267
suspect paranoia, 231, 265

T

Testamentary evidence, 50
Tooke, A., 81
Traditional interviewing, 64–65
    guidelines for, 66–71
Traffic stops, 235

U

U.S. Bureau of Justice Statistics, 87
U.S. Census Bureau, 87
U.S. Constitution. *See also* Legal issues; *specific Amendments*
U.S. Department of Health and Human Services, 134

V

Victims
    children as, 148–149, 150, 152
    credibility of, 150, 152
    with disabilities, 189
    the elderly as, 167–168, *168*
    interviewing, 6–7
    persons with disabilities as, 189
    as sources, 65–66
    stresses of, 7

W

Warrants, 28
White collar crimes, 49, 51
Witnesses
    accuracy of, 8, 56–57
    anonymous, 8
    characteristics of, 9
    children as, 130–153
    cognitive interviewing (CI) and, 8
    competency of, 152–153
    credibility of, 150, 152
    elderly as, 168–169
    interviewing, 7–10
    reliability of, 152–153
    reluctance of, 8, *56*
    stresses of, 9
Wrongful-arrest theory, 180

Y

Yeschke, C., 32